Janet L. Mullings, PhD
James W. Marquart, PhD
Deborah J. Hartley, MS

The Victimization of Children: Emerging Issues

The Victimization of Children: Emerging Issues has been co-published simultaneously as *Journal of Aggression, Maltreatment & Trauma*, Volume 8, Numbers 1/2 (#15/16) and 3 (#17) 2003.

*Pre-publication
REVIEWS,
COMMENTARIES,
EVALUATIONS . . .*

"**A** FASCINATING, ILLUMIN-
ATING, and often troubling
collection of research on child victimization, abuse, and neglect. This
book, edited by highly regarded
criminal justice scholars who run a
national victimization research institute, is timely, thought-provoking,
and an important contribution to the
literature. NO OTHER BOOK ON
THE MARKET TODAY PROVIDES
SUCH AN AUTHORITATIVE OVER-
VIEW of the complex issues involved
in child victimization. The individual
chapters are well researched, written, and
presented. I HIGHLY RECOMMEND
THIS BOOK."

Craig Hemmens, JD, PhD
*Chair and Associate Professor
Department of Criminal Justice
Administration
Boise State University*

More Pre-publication
REVIEWS, COMMENTARIES, EVALUATIONS . . .

"THE FIRST COMPREHENSIVE BOOK ON CHILD VICTIMIZATION. . . . Represents the cutting edge of child victimization research. . . . Useful for professionals in law enforcement, health care, and social services. RECOMMENDED. The authors cover topics relevant to current events, such as how terrorism, or clergy sexual abuse, affects children. They describe how the Internet can make children vulnerable. And they describe how professionals can intervene on behalf of children via the legal or health care systems."

Kathleen Kendall-Tacket, PhD
Research Associate Professor
of Psychology,
Crimes Against Children Research
Center
University of New Hampshire

"This book helps bring the study of child victimization into the twenty-first century. It helps illuminate important issues in child victimization that are still mostly unrecognized. I'LL RETURN TO THIS BOOK AGAIN AND AGAIN FOR NEW IDEAS FOR PRACTICE, PROGRAMS, AND POLICY."

Theodore Cross, PhD
Research Professor
Crimes Against Children
Research Center
University of New Hampshire

HMTP

The Haworth Maltreatment & Trauma Press®
An Imprint of The Haworth Press, Inc.

New York • London • Victoria (AU)
www.HaworthPress.com

The Victimization of Children: Emerging Issues

The Victimization of Children: Emerging Issues has been co-published simultaneously as *Journal of Aggression, Maltreatment & Trauma*, Volume 8, Numbers 1/2 (#15/16) and 3 (#17) 2003.

The *Journal of Aggression, Maltreatment & Trauma* Monographic "Separates"

Robert Geffner, PhD, ABPN, Senior Editor

Below is a list of "separates," which in serials librarianship means a special issue simultaneously published as a special journal issue or double-issue *and* as a "separate" hardbound monograph. (This is a format which we also call a "DocuSerial.")

"Separates" are published because specialized libraries or professionals may wish to purchase a specific thematic issue by itself in a format which can be separately cataloged and shelved, as opposed to purchasing the journal on an on-going basis. Faculty members may also more easily consider a "separate" for classroom adoption.

"Separates" are carefully classified separately with the major book jobbers so that the journal tie-in can be noted on new book order slips to avoid duplicate purchasing.

You may wish to visit Haworth's website at . . .

http://www.HaworthPress.com

. . . to search our online catalog for complete tables of contents of these separates and related publications.

You may also call 1-800-HAWORTH (outside US/Canada: 607-722-5857), or Fax 1-800-895-0582 (outside US/Canada: 607-771-0012), or e-mail at:

docdelivery@haworthpress.com

The Victimization of Children: Emerging Issues, edited by Janet L. Mullings, PhD, James W. Marquart, PhD, and Deborah J. Hartley, MS (Vol. 8, No. 1/2 [#15/16] and 3 [#17], 2003). *"A fascinating, illuminating, and often troubling collection of research on child victimization, abuse, and neglect. This book . . . is timely, thought-provoking, and an important contribution to the literature. No other book on the market today provides such an authoritative overview of the complex issues involved in child victimization." (Craig Hemmens, JD, PhD, Chair and Associate Professor, Department of Criminal Justice Administration, Boise State University)*

Intimate Violence: Contemporary Treatment Innovations, edited by Donald Dutton, PhD, and Daniel J. Sonkin, PhD (Vol. 7, No. 1/2 [#13/14], 2003). *"Excellent. . . . Represents 'outside the box' thinking. I highly recommend this book for everyone working in the field of domestic violence who wants to stay fresh. Readers will be stimulated and in most cases very valuably informed." (David B. Wexler, PhD, Executive Director, Relationship Training Institute, San Diego, CA)*

Trauma and Juvenile Delinquency: Theory, Research, and Interventions, edited by Ricky Greenwald, PsyD (Vol. 6, No. 1 [#11], 2002). *"Timely, concise, compassionate, and stimulating. . . . An impressive array of authors deals with various aspects of the problem in depth. This book will be of considerable interest to clinicians, teachers, and researchers in the mental health field, as well as administrators and juvenile justice personnel handling juvenile delinquents. I highly commend Dr. Greenwald on a job well done." (Hans Steiner, MD, Professor of Psychiatry and Behavioral Sciences, Stanford University School of Medicine)*

Domestic Violence Offenders: Current Interventions, Research, and Implications for Policies and Standards, edited by Robert Geffner, PhD, and Alan Rosenbaum, PhD (Vol. 5, No. 2 [#10], 2001).

The Shaken Baby Syndrome: A Multidisciplinary Approach, edited by Stephen Lazoritz, MD, and Vincent J. Palusci, MD (Vol. 5, No. 1 [#9], 2001). *The first book to cover the full spectrum of Shaken Baby Syndrome (SBS). Offers expert information and advice on every aspect of prevention, diagnosis, treatment, and follow-up.*

Trauma and Cognitive Science: A Meeting of Minds, Science, and Human Experience, edited by Jennifer J. Freyd, PhD, and Anne P. DePrince, MS (Vol. 4, No. 2 [#8] 2001). *"A fine collection of scholarly works that address key questions about memory for childhood and adult traumas from a variety of disciplines and empirical approaches. A must-read volume for anyone wishing to understand traumatic memory." (Kathryn Quina, PhD, Professor of Psychology & Women's Studies, University of Rhode Island)*

Program Evaluation and Family Violence Research, edited by Sally K. Ward, PhD, and David Finkelhor, PhD (Vol. 4, No. 1 [#7], 2000). *"Offers wise advice to evaluators and others interested in understanding the impact of their work. I learned a lot from reading this book." (Jeffrey L. Edleson, PhD, Professor, University of Minnesota, St. Paul)*

Sexual Abuse Litigation: A Practical Resource for Attorneys, Clinicians, and Advocates, edited by Rebecca Rix, MALS (Vol. 3, No. 2 [#6], 2000). *"An interesting and well developed treatment of the complex subject of child sexual abuse trauma. The merger of the legal, psychological, scientific and historical expertise of the authors provides a unique, in-depth analysis of delayed discovery in CSA litigation. This book, including the extremely useful appendices, is a must for the attorney or expert witness who is involved in the representation of survivors of sexual abuse." (Leonard Karp, JD, and Cheryl L. Karp, PhD, co-authors, Domestic Torts: Family Violence, Conflict and Sexual Abuse)*

Children Exposed to Domestic Violence: Current Issues in Research, Intervention, Prevention, and Policy Development, edited by Robert A. Geffner, PhD, Peter G. Jaffe, PhD, and Marlies Sudermann, PhD (Vol. 3, No. 1 [#5], 2000). *"A welcome addition to the resource library of every professional whose career encompasses issues of children's mental health, well-being, and best interest . . . I strongly recommend this helpful and stimulating text." (The Honorable Justice Grant A. Campbell, Justice of the Ontario Superior Court of Justice, Family Court, London, Canada)*

Maltreatment in Early Childhood: Tools for Research-Based Intervention, edited by Kathleen Coulborn Faller, PhD (Vol. 2, No. 2 [#4], 1999). *"This important book takes an international and cross-cultural look at child abuse and maltreatment. Discussing the history of abuse in the United States, exploring psychological trauma, and containing interviews with sexual abuse victims,* Maltreatment in Early Childhood *provides counselors and mental health practitioners with research that may help prevent child abuse or reveal the mistreatment some children endure."*

Multiple Victimization of Children: Conceptual, Developmental, Research, and Treatment Issues, edited by B. B. Robbie Rossman, PhD, and Mindy S. Rosenberg, PhD (Vol. 2, No. 1 [#3], 1998). *"This book takes on a large challenge and meets it with stunning success. It fills a glaring gap in the literature . . . " (Edward P. Mulvey, PhD, Associate Professor of Child Psychiatry, Western Psychiatric Institute and Clinic, University of Pittsburgh School of Medicine)*

Violence Issues for Health Care Educators and Providers, edited by L. Kevin Hamberger, PhD, Sandra K. Burge, PhD, Antonnette V. Graham, PhD, and Anthony J. Costa, MD (Vol. 1, No. 2 [#2], 1997). *"A superb book that contains invaluable hands-on advice for medical educators and health care professionals alike . . ." (Richard L. Holloways, PhD, Professor and Vice Chair, Department of Family and Community Medicine, and Associate Dean for Student Affairs, Medical College of Wisconsin)*

Violence and Sexual Abuse at Home: Current Issues in Spousal Battering and Child Maltreatment, edited by Robert Geffner, PhD, Susan B. Sorenson, PhD, and Paula K. Lundberg-Love, PhD (Vol. 1, No. 1 [#1], 1997). *"The Editors have distilled the important questions at the cutting edge of the field of violence studies, and have brought rigor, balance and moral fortitude to the search for answers." (Virginia Goldner, PhD, Co-Director, Gender and Violence Project, Senior Faculty, Ackerman Institute for Family Therapy)*

Published by

The Haworth Maltreatment & Trauma Press, 10 Alice Street, Binghamton, NY 13904-1580 USA

The Haworth Maltreatment & Trauma Press is an imprint of The Haworth Press, Inc., 10 Alice Street, Binghamton, NY 13904-1580 USA.

The Victimization of Children: Emerging Issues has been co-published simultaneously as *Journal of Aggression, Maltreatment & Trauma*, Volume 8, Numbers 1/2 (#15/16) and 3 (#17) 2003.

The development, preparation, and publication of this work has been undertaken with great care. However, the publisher, employees, editors, and agents of The Haworth Press and all imprints of The Haworth Press, Inc., including The Haworth Medical Press® and The Pharmaceutical Products Press®, are not responsible for any errors contained herein or for consequences that may ensue from use of materials or information contained in this work. Opinions expressed by the author(s) are not necessarily those of The Haworth Press, Inc.

Cover design by Lora Wiggins

Library of Congress Cataloging-in-Publication Data

The victimization of children : emerging issues /Janet L. Mullings, James W. Marquart, Deborah J. Hartley, editors.
    p. cm.
    "Co-published simultaneously as Journal of aggression, maltreatment & trauma, Volume 8, numbers 1/2 (#15/16) and volume 8, number 3 (#17) 2003."
    Includes bibliographical references and index.
    ISBN 0-7890-2406-3 (hard cover : alk. paper)–ISBN 0-7890-2407-1 (soft cover : alk. paper)
    1. Child abuse. 2. Children–Crimes against. 3. Child abuse–United States. 4. Children–Crimes against–United States. 5. Children–Legal status, laws, etc.–United States. I. Mullings, Janet L II. Marquart, James W. (James Walter), 1954-. III. Hartley, Deborah J. IV. Journal of aggression, maltreatment & trauma.
    HV6626.5.V53 2004
    362.76–dc22
                                        2003027510

The Victimization of Children: Emerging Issues

Janet L. Mullings, PhD
James W. Marquart, PhD
Deborah J. Hartley, MS
Editors

The Victimization of Children: Emerging Issues has been co-published simultaneously as *Journal of Aggression, Maltreatment & Trauma*, Volume 8, Numbers 1/2 (#15/16) and 3 (#17) 2003.

HMTP

The Haworth Maltreatment & Trauma Press®
An Imprint of The Haworth Press, Inc.

New York • London • Victoria (AU)
www.HaworthPress.com

Indexing, Abstracting & Website/Internet Coverage

This section provides you with a list of major indexing & abstracting services. That is to say, each service began covering this periodical during the year noted in the right column. Most Websites which are listed below have indicated that they will either post, disseminate, compile, archive, cite or alert their own Website users with research-based content from this work. (This list is as current as the copyright date of this publication.)

(continued)

(continued)

Special Bibliographic Notes related to special journal issues (separates) and indexing/abstracting:

- indexing/abstracting services in this list will also cover material in any "separate" that is co-published simultaneously with Haworth's special thematic journal issue or DocuSerial. Indexing/abstracting usually covers material at the article/chapter level.
- monographic co-editions are intended for either non-subscribers or libraries which intend to purchase a second copy for their circulating collections.
- monographic co-editions are reported to all jobbers/wholesalers/approval plans. The source journal is listed as the "series" to assist the prevention of duplicate purchasing in the same manner utilized for books-in-series.
- to facilitate user/access services all indexing/abstracting services are encouraged to utilize the co-indexing entry note indicated at the bottom of the first page of each article/chapter/contribution.
- this is intended to assist a library user of any reference tool (whether print, electronic, online, or CD-ROM) to locate the monographic version if the library has purchased this version but not a subscription to the source journal.
- individual articles/chapters in any Haworth publication are also available through the Haworth Document Delivery Service (HDDS).

The Victimization of Children: Emerging Issues

CONTENTS

ABOUT THE EDITORS

Janet L. Mullings, PhD, is Associate Professor of Criminal Justice at Sam Houston State University in Huntsville, Texas. Additionally, she serves as the Director of Research for the National Institute for Victim Studies at Sam Houston State University. Dr. Mullings' research areas include child abuse and neglect, childhood maltreatment experiences among adult and juvenile offenders, and resiliency among abused and neglected children. She has published in such journals as *Child Abuse & Neglect, Deviant Behavior, Women & Criminal Justice, Journal of Criminal Justice, The Prison Journal, Crime and Deliquency, Criminal Justice Policy Review, Substance Use & Misuse,* and *Journal of Criminal Justice Education.*

James W. Marquart, PhD, is a tenured Full Professor of Criminal Justice at Sam Houston State University in Huntsville, Texas. Additionally, he serves as the Director for the National Institute for Victim Studies at Sam Houston State University. He has long-term research and teaching interests in prison organizations, capital punishment, criminal justice policy, and research methods. He has also published a number of articles on social control and change in prison settings. His books include *The Rope, The Chair, and The Needle: Patterns of Capital Punishment in Texas, 1923-1990; The Keepers: Prison Guards and Contemporary Corrections;* and *An Appeal to Justice: Litigated Reform of Texas Prisons.* The latter, with Ben M. Crouch, receiving the Outstanding Book Award from the Academy of Criminal Justice for 1991. He has also published in such journals as *Criminology, Deviant Behavior, Crime and Delinquency, Child Abuse & Neglect, Ageing and Society, The Prison Journal, Justice Quarterly,* and *Law and Society.* His current research involves investigating youth advocacy and alcohol policy, child maltreatment among institutionalized populations, and inappropriate staff-inmate relationships in prison settings.

Deborah J. Hartley, MS, is a Doctoral student at the College of Criminal Justice at Sam Houston State University in Huntsville, Texas, and

Research Assistant for the National Institute for Victim Studies at Sam Houston State University. Her research interests include the victimization of women and children, corrections, and substance abuse. She has published in such journals as *Substance Use & Misuse* and *The Prison Journal.*

ABOUT THE CONTRIBUTORS

Katherine J. Bennett, PhD, is Associate Professor at Armstrong Atlantic State University in Savannah, Georgia. She has a PhD in Criminal Justice from the College of Criminal Justice, Sam Houston State University, Huntsville, Texas. Research interests and areas of publications include legal issues in corrections, reintegrative shaming theory, and juvenile curfews.

Bette L. Bottoms, PhD, is Associate Professor of Psychology at the University of Illinois at Chicago (UIC). She received her PhD in Social Psychology from the State University of New York at Buffalo. Her research on childrens eyewitness testimony has been funded by the U.S. Department of Health and Human Services and the National Institute of Mental Health. She has authored scholarly articles and co-edited three books, including the recently released *Children, Social Science, and Law* (Cambridge). She is a recipient of the Saleem Shah Early Career Award for Contributions to Psychology and Law Research from the American Psychology-Law Society and the American Academy of Forensic Psychology, and four teaching awards from UIC. In addition, she is Past President of the American Psychological Association's Division 37 Section on Child Maltreatment.

Christina M. Bruhn, MSW, is Research Specialist at the Children and Family Research Center and a doctoral candidate at the University of Illinois at Chicago, Jane Addams College of Social Work. She had extensive background in working with people with disabilities and in the child welfare system and is the mother of a child with a disability.

Sarah M. Buel, JD, is Lecturer in Law at the University of Texas School of Law. She received her BA, *cum laude* from Harvard Extension School, and her JD, *cum laude* from Harvard Law School. She is a former domestic violence, child abuse and juvenile prosecutor, and an advocate since 1977.

Henrietta Filipas, MA, is a doctoral student in clinical psychology at the University of Illinois at Chicago. She conducts research related to child abuse as well as understanding the experiences of adult rape victims, and has published in the *Journal of Interpersonal Violence, Violence and Victims*, and the *Journal of Traumatic Stress*.

David Finkelhor, PhD, is Director of the Crimes against Children Research Center, Co-Director of the Family Research Laboratory, and Professor of Sociology at the University of New Hampshire. He has been studying the problems of child victimization, child maltreatment, and family violence since 1977. He is well known for his conceptual and empirical work on the problem of child sexual abuse, reflected in publications such as *Sourcebook on Child Sexual Abuse* (Sage, 1986) and *Nursery Crimes* (Sage, 1988). He has also written about child homicide, missing and abducted children, children exposed to domestic and peer violence and other forms of family violence. In his recent work, he has tried to unify and integrate knowledge about all the diverse forms of child victimization in a field he has termed Developmental Victimology. He is editor and author of 10 books and over 75 journal articles and book chapters. He has received grants from the National Institute of Mental Health, the National Center on Child Abuse and Neglect, and the US Department of Justice, and a variety of other sources. In 1994, he was given the Distinguished Child Abuse Professional Award by the American Professional Society on the Abuse of Children.

Jeff Maahs, PhD, is Assistant Professor in the Department of Sociology and Anthropology at the University of Minnesota Duluth. Dr. Maahs completed his doctoral work at the University of Cincinnati. He has authored several publications in criminology related journals and edited books. His main areas of interest are criminological theory, especially as it relates the development of offending behavior over time, corrections (private prisons, the roles and attitudes of corrections officers, probation outcomes, correctional officer use of force), and legal aspects of criminal justice (search and seizure, prison litigation).

Gerard J. McGlone, SJ, PhD, is currently a Clinical and Research Fellow at Johns Hopkins University, School of Medicine. Dr. McGlone is also a Jesuit priest, a staff therapist, and has been coordinator of Research at the National Institute for the Study, Prevention and Treatment of Sexual Trauma in Baltimore, Maryland.

Kimberly J. Mitchell, PhD, is Research Assistant Professor of Psychology at the Crimes against Children Research Center located at the University of New Hampshire. She received her PhD in Experimental Psychology from the University of Rhode Island in January of 1999 with concentrations in quantitative methods, women's health, and family violence. Dr. Mitchell's research interests include youth Internet victimization, exposure to violence, and fear of crime. She is co-author of *Online sexual solicitation of youth: Risk factors and impact* (2001), *Online victimization: A report on the nation's youth* (2000), *Risk of crime victimization among youth exposed to domestic violence* (2001), and has written several other collaborative papers about the incidence, risk, and impact of child victimization.

Rebecca Murray, PhD, earned her doctorate in Clinical Psychology from Georgia State University. She is Assistant Professor in the Department of Psychology at Georgia Southern University where she teaches a number of undergraduate and clinical graduate courses, publishes clinically relevant research, and maintains a part-time private practice.

Judith A. Myers-Walls, PhD, Associate Professor and Extension Specialist, is a certified family life educator. She is on the faculty in the Department of Child Development and Family Studies at Purdue University. The major focus of her job is to translate research findings in the area of human development (primarily child development and parenting) for use by the general public. She trains other professionals, writes pamphlets, delivers workshops, works with mass media, develops curricula, and reviews materials. Dr. Myers-Walls has conducted several studies to investigate how children and parents talk about war and peace issues. Some of her publications include three books: *Young Peacemakers Project Book, Peace Works*: *Young Peacemakers Project Book II, Families as Educators for Global Citizenship,* and a web site: www.ces.purdue.edu/terrorism/children.

Michael Nielsen, PhD, is Associate Professor of Psychology at Georgia Southern University. He received his PhD in Social Psychology from Northern Illinois University. He has written widely on psychological aspects of religion and has presented his research internationally. He also writes for the general public, maintaining award-winning Psychology of Religion pages and writing a regular column on psychology, religion and social issues for Sunstone magazine. He is Past President of the Mormon Social Science Association.

Vincent J. Palusci, MD, MS, is Director of the Child Protection Team at DeVos Children's Hospital at Spectrum Health in Grand Rapids, Michigan, and Associate Professor of Pediatrics and Human Development at the Michigan State University College of Human Medicine. As a pediatrician, Dr. Palusci has specialized in the care of children and adolescents who have been abused and neglected and has expanded the role of health care providers in caring for victims of maltreatment within the hospital and community. He is a Fellow of the American Academy of Pediatrics, a member of the Ray E. Helfer Society, and a member of Michigan's State Child Death Review Team and Chairman of its Citizen's Review Panel on Child Fatality. With Stephen Lazoritz, MD, he co-edited *The Shaken Baby Syndrome: A Multidisciplinary Approach,* published by The Haworth Press.

Derek J. Paulsen, PhD, is currently Assistant Professor in the Department of Criminal Justice and Police Studies at Eastern Kentucky University. He has published numerous articles dealing with violent crime issues that have appeared in such journals as *Homicide Studies, Gender Issues,* and *Journal of Criminal Justice and Popular Culture.* Dr. Paulsen is also the lead author of the forthcoming book *Crime Mapping and Spatial Analysis of Crime: Theory and Practice.* In addition to his interests in violent crime issues, his research interests include GIS and spatial aspects of crime and the media coverage of crime.

Janis Wolak, JD, is Research Assistant Professor of Sociology at the Crimes against Children Research Center located at the University of New Hampshire. She received her JD from Southwestern University School of Law in 1978. Her research interests include youth victimization, youth Internet use, and police reporting. She is co-author of *Online victimization: A report on the nation's youth* (2000), *Police reporting and professional help-seeking by child victims of violent crime* (2001), along with several other collaborative papers about youth and the Internet.

Preface

SUMMARY. Child victimization is a serious and on-going problem in the United States and throughout the world. In 2000, an estimated 900,000 children were victims of abuse and neglect in the United States. New and different responses to child maltreatment will have to be developed and implemented in response to the increasingly diverse contexts and situations within which maltreatment occurs. Emerging trends in adult-child boundary violations are explored within this volume from a cross-section of disciplines, including law, sociology, criminal justice, psychology, and health services. The selections analyze issues critical to child maltreatment and offer intriguingly different perspectives of present and future issues related to child abuse. *[Article copies available for a fee from The Haworth Document Delivery Service: 1-800-HAWORTH. E-mail address: <docdelivery@haworthpress.com> Website: <http://www.Haworth Press.com> © 2003 by The Haworth Press, Inc. All rights reserved.]*

KEYWORDS. Child physical and sexual abuse, child neglect, domestic violence

In 2000, an estimated 900,000 children were victims of abuse and neglect in the United States (U.S. Department of Health and Human Services, 2002). Figure 1 illustrates the trend in child maltreatment between 1990 and 2000. The 2000 victimization rate shows a small but noticeable

[Haworth co-indexing entry note]: "Preface." Mullings, Janet L., James W. Marquart, and Deborah J. Hartley. Co-published simultaneously in *Journal of Aggression, Maltreatment & Trauma* (The Haworth Maltreatment & Trauma Press, an imprint of The Haworth Press, Inc.) Vol. 8, No. 1/2, (#15/16) 2003, pp. xxv-xxxii; and: *The Victimization of Children: Emerging Issues* (ed: Janet L. Mullings, James W. Marquart, and Deborah J. Hartley) The Haworth Maltreatment & Trauma Press, an imprint of The Haworth Press, Inc., 2003, pp. xix-xxvi. Single or multiple copies of this article are available for a fee from The Haworth Document Delivery Service [1-800-HAWORTH, 9:00 a.m. - 5:00 p.m. (EST). E-mail address: docdelivery@ haworthpress.com].

one-year increase in victimization over the 1999 rate per 1000 children. The new data from 2001 show this same trend; however, this increase may have been unduly influenced by population estimates (U.S. Department of Health and Human Services, 2002, 2003). Comprehending facts and figures about the incidence of child maltreatment in America can be overwhelming. Is abuse increasing or decreasing? Is the latest bump in the rate of victimization "real," or is the increase the result of different reporting standards? Indeed, the research of Murray Strauss and Richard Gelles (1986) remind us of the danger of reading too much into official statistics on child abuse.

Our goal in this volume is not to challenge or even dwell on discrepancies between subjective self-reports and objective reality. Rather, our goal is to make the reader aware of the changing context of child maltreatment. Generally, the primary role of adults in society is to protect and nurture children. At the same time, a boundary exists that socially, psychologically, and legally demarcates the division between adulthood and childhood. Child maltreatment occurs when traditional boundaries be-

FIGURE 1. Trend in Child Victimization Rates, 1990-2000

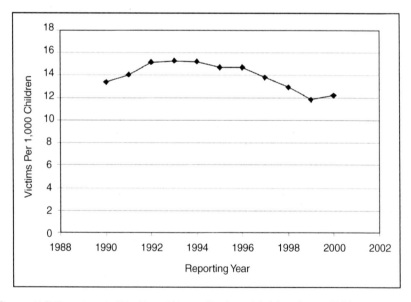

Source: U.S. Department of Health and Human Services, Administration on Children, Youth and Families. *Child Maltreatment 2000*. (Washington, DC: U.S. Government Printing Office, 2002).

tween adult and child are blurred or broken. In its most fundamental sense and for all times and places, child abuse is a boundary violation or a situation in which an adult disrupts, eliminates, or minimizes the traditional social, psychological, and legal distances between themselves and a child. More broadly, boundary violations occur when, for example, a therapist has sexual relations with a patient, or a high school coach becomes romantically involved with a student. The boundary can also be broken when a parent physically abuses or neglects their child.

The setting and context for adult-child boundary violations is changing and expanding. As technology further develops (e.g., the Internet), so too will the opportunity for adult-child boundary violations. If we get mired in extensive dialogue on the veracity of self-report data, we will fail to appreciate or understand the one objective reality about child abuse: constant change. As new ideologies (e.g., lowering the age of majority) and technologies develop, so too will the shape and contours of child maltreatment. In his classic book *Wayward Puritans*, Kai Erikson (1966) clearly illustrated that the devil comes in many shapes and forms, and the boundaries of deviant behavior were fluid depending on the historical era; that is, deviance (and criminality) was a moving target. In short, it is up to us to fully examine these changing contexts and situations in an effort to understand where and how adult-child boundary violations occur. Accordingly, new and different responses to child maltreatment will have to be developed and implemented in response to the increasingly diverse contexts and situations within which these violations occur.

In the ensuing selections of this volume, new and emerging trends in adult-child boundary violations are explored from a cross-section of disciplines, including law, sociology, criminal justice, psychology, and health services. The selections analyze issues critical to child maltreatment and offer intriguingly different perspectives of present and future issues related to child abuse.

The first section deals with emerging issues in child victimization. Kimberly J. Mitchell, David Finkelhor, and Janis Wolak present original research findings in "Victimization of Youths on the Internet." The chapter presents findings from the Youth Internet Safety Survey. The survey is a nationally representative study of 1501 youth, aged 10-17, that use the Internet regularly. Nineteen percent of the youth reported that in the previous year, they were the victims of an unwanted sexual solicitation. One-quarter reported an unwanted exposure to sexual material, and 6% had been harassed online. The data further suggested that youth encounter a substantial quantity of offensive episodes while online. Mitchell and colleagues conclude that a comprehensive strategy is needed to respond to the problem that would reduce the quantity of offensive behavior, better shield youth from its occurrence, increase the level of reporting, and provide more help to youth and families to protect them from any consequence.

In "Children as Victims of War and Terrorism," Judith A. Myers-Walls explores the tragic consequences of war and terrorism. Sadly, war and terrorism victimize all people in a country, group, or area, but disputes in recent decades (e.g., Somalia, Chechnya, Yugoslavia) are especially likely to impact children and families. Children can experience wars by being in the war zone, by being in countries that deploy military personnel to a war zone, by suffering from the consequences of military expenses and economic warfare, by experiencing war and terrorism from a distance through media, or by suffering from indoctrination and the building of enemy images. Myers-Walls reviews what researchers have discovered about the unique risks associated with each of those categories and recommends promising solutions.

The current paradigm concerning research on child maltreatment involves the collection of individual incidents of this activity. Researchers then transform individual-level data into percentages, rates, or other numerical forms for statistical analysis. In "No Safe Place: Assessing Spatial Patterns of Child Maltreatment Victimization," Derek J. Paulsen argues that the traditional paradigm of research might not be the most informative methodology. He also suggests that little is known about spatial patterns of child maltreatment. Paulsen thus examines the spatial patterns of child maltreatment victimization and their ecological causes. Specifically, his original research seeks to determine the answer to three important questions regarding the spatial nature of child maltreatment victimization: First, are child maltreatment victimizations concentrated within certain parts of cities? Second, are there different spatial patterns for child abuse, child neglect, and juvenile assault victimization locations? Finally, how well does ecological theory explain the incidence of child abuse, child neglect, and juvenile assault victimization at the neighborhood level? He concludes with a discussion of how spatial analysis of child maltreatment expands our understanding of the issue.

Bette L. Bottoms, Michael Nielsen, Rebecca Murray, and Henrietta Filipas examine "Religion-Related Child Physical Abuse: Characteristics and Psychological Outcomes." Their research is very timely given the recent scandal of priest sexual abuse within the American Catholic Church. Bottoms and her colleagues contend that religious beliefs can foster, encourage, and even justify child abuse. Religious motivations for child abuse and neglect, however, have been virtually ignored in social science research. In this chapter, the authors compare victims' retrospective reports of religion-related physical child abuse to other reported cases of child physical abuse. They describe in statistical detail the nature and circumstances of the abuse, characteristics of victims and perpetrators, and the spiritual and psychological impact of the abuse. The authors point out that although the basic characteristics of religion-related physical abuse are similar to non-religion-related physical abuse, religion-related abuse has significantly more negative implications for its victims' long-term psychological well-being.

In "The Pedophile and the Pious: Towards a New Understanding of Sexually Offending and Non-Offending Roman Catholic Priests," Gerard J. McGlone provides essential background information and a historical understanding of this serious problem within the Roman Catholic and other faith-based communities in the United States.

Selections in the next section focus on recent trends in response to child victimization. Medical professionals are among the first to respond to claims of child maltreatment. Vincent J. Palusci's selection, entitled "The Role of Health Care Professionals in the Response to Child Victimization," serves as an introduction to the many roles of health care professionals in the assessment, care, and treatment of child victimization. Palusci concentrates on those professionals caring for the physical health of victims of child abuse and neglect, although there are many similarities between child maltreatment and other family violence victims. In reviewing the health impact of maltreatment and the historical contributions of health care professionals, Palusci discusses the roles that health care disciplines play in clinical care, training, research, and advocacy, and their interaction with the community's child welfare, legal, and criminal justice systems.

Christina M. Bruhn addresses "Children with Disabilities: Abuse, Neglect, and the Child Welfare System." She notes that children in state custody as a result of abuse and neglect are more likely to have problems with health, cognitive development, and psychosocial development than children in the general population and, on average, are more likely to suffer from chronic health problems than children in poverty. This is the case because children in state custody are likely to have been exposed to maternal substance abuse, community and domestic violence, and poverty. These conditions, particularly poverty, may result in numerous risks to a child's development. Finally, children with disabilities are more likely to experience abuse than children in the general population. Given these high proportions of children in child welfare systems with such conditions, greater attention must be paid to the service needs of such children and the state of service delivery. Children are entitled to appropriate services via a number of separate mandates. Such services have the potential to enhance developmental outcomes. However, recognition of the needs of children in out-of-home care occurs at painfully low rates, and linkage to and delivery of appropriate services occurs at even lower rates. This may be the case for a variety of reasons, including those having to do with the structure of policies. Recommendations for policy review at state and federal levels are offered along with direction for future research.

The chapters in the last section of the book explore emerging legal issues pertaining to child victimization. Jeff Maahs examines "Fetal Homicide: Emerging Statutory and Judicial Regulation of Third-Party Assaults Against the Fetus." Under common law, a crime resulting in the death of a fetus that was viable but not "born alive" was viewed as a transgression less serious than murder. Accordingly, courts did not allow parents to bring wrongful death suits for the death of a fetus. In the past decade, however, several states have amended their criminal or civil statutes to include the specific crime of "feticide" or "fetal homicide," and the federal government is considering similar legislation. Maahs examines the history and current status of criminal and civil law regarding the third-party killing of a fetus.

A critical legal issue involves child-victim testimony in the courtroom. The right of the accused to confront witnesses against them is one of our most cherished constitutional rights. A potential problem arises, however, when the witness is a child victim. In "Legal and Social Issues Surrounding Closed-Circuit Television Testimony of Child Victims and Witnesses," Katherine J. Bennett explores the issues surrounding child victim testimony. Facing the alleged offender in court and the experience itself of testifying in an open court with dozens of onlookers are acutely difficult. The effect on children may be traumatic, with the potential to produce substantial psychological and emotional harm.

In the past decade, various court procedures have been implemented in the United States in an effort to minimize these effects. Court procedures can include erecting screens to shield the child victim or witness, presenting videotaped testimony, or testifying via one-way or two-way closed-circuit television. Closed-circuit television testimony (CCVT), which is especially controversial, involves both legal issues surrounding the constitutionality of such testimony and social issues regarding its effectiveness. Substantial variation across states in provisions for

CCVT for child witnesses is problematic. Consideration is given to how social science research directly influenced the Supreme Court's decision in *Maryland v. Craig* (1990), and the current state of research regarding use of CCTV and court outcomes.

In the final chapter, "Addressing Family Violence Within Juvenile Courts: Promising Practices to Improve Intervention Outcomes," Sarah M. Buel examines teen-perpetrated domestic violence. She suggests that family violence is prevalent within juvenile court caseloads, yet often is not identified within intake and disposition. Buel discusses model programs emerging in juvenile courts specifically addressing these issues. Additionally, a comparative analysis of the drug court trend is explored in the context of its applicability for specialized family violence applications in the Juvenile Court. Lastly, this chapter provides an overview of the King County (Washington) Juvenile Court's Step-Up program and the Santa Clara County (California) Juvenile Court's Family Violence program, followed by the process by which the Travis County (Texas) Juvenile Court has implemented a program similar to these models.

In conclusion, child victimization is a serious and on-going problem in the United States and throughout the world. There will be no shortage of issues to be discussed, researched, and debated, especially as new situations and contexts for child victimization emerge. Whether or not the incidence of child victimization goes up or down, we hope that the chapters in this publication will make a positive contribution to the understanding of the dynamics of child victimization in the present and future.

Janet L. Mullings
James W. Marquart
Deborah J. Hartley

REFERENCES

Erikson, K. T. (1966). *Wayward puritans: A study in the sociology of deviance*. New York: Wiley.

Maryland v. Craig, 497 U.S. 836; 110 S.Ct. 3157; 111 L.Ed.2d 666 (1990).

Strauss, M. A., & Gelles, R. J. (1986). Societal change and change in family violence from 1975 to 1985 as revealed by two national surveys. *Journal of Marriage and the Family, 48*, 465-479.

U.S. Department of Health and Human Services, Administration of Children, Youth and Families. (2002). *Child Maltreatment 2000*. Washington, DC: U.S. Government Printing Office.

U.S. Department of Health and Human Services, Administration on Children, Youth and Families. (2003). *Child Maltreatment 2001*. Washington, DC: U.S. Government Printing Office.

EMERGING ISSUES
IN CHILD VICTIMIZATION

Victimization of Youths on the Internet

Kimberly J. Mitchell
David Finkelhor
Janis Wolak

SUMMARY. The Youth Internet Safety Survey is a nationally representative study of 1501 youth, aged 10-17, who use the Internet regularly. In
the past year, 19% of youth reported an unwanted sexual solicitation, 25%
reported an unwanted exposure to sexual material, and 6% had been ha-

Address correspondence to: Kimberly J. Mitchell, PhD, Crimes Against Children Research Center, University of New Hampshire, 126 Horton Social Science Center, Dur-
ham, NH 03824 (E-mail: Kimberly.Mitchell@unh.edu).
The authors would like to thank not only the Center for its research funding, but also
Tobias Ball for help in preparing this paper.
Funded by the U.S. Congress through a grant to the National Center for Missing & Exploited Children. The National Center for Missing & Exploited Children is the national clearinghouse and resource center funded under Cooperative Agreement #98-MC-CX-K002
from the Office of Juvenile Justice and Delinquency Prevention, U.S. Department of Justice.

[Haworth co-indexing entry note]: "Victimization of Youths on the Internet." Mitchell, Kimberly J., Da-
vid Finkelhor, and Janis Wolak. Co-published simultaneously in *Journal of Aggression, Maltreatment &
Trauma* (The Haworth Maltreatment & Trauma Press, an imprint of The Haworth Press, Inc.) Vol. 8, No. 1/2
(#15/16), 2003, pp. 1-39; and: *The Victimization of Children: Emerging Issues* (ed: Janet L. Mullings,
James W. Marquart, and Deborah J. Hartley) The Haworth Maltreatment & Trauma Press, an imprint of
The Haworth Press, Inc., 2003, pp. 1-39. Single or multiple copies of this article are available for a fee
from The Haworth Document Delivery Service [1-800-HAWORTH, 9:00 a.m. - 5:00 p.m. (EST).
E-mail address: docdelivery@haworthpress.com].

Digital Object Identifier: 10.1300/J146v08n01_01

rassed online. Data suggest that youth encounter a substantial quantity of offensive episodes, and a comprehensive strategy to respond to the problem would aim to reduce the quantity of offensive behavior, better shield youth from its occurrence, increase the level of reporting, and provide more help to youth and families to protect them from any consequence. *[Article copies available for a fee from The Haworth Document Delivery Service: 1-800-HAWORTH. E-mail address: <docdelivery@haworthpress. com> Website: <http://www.HaworthPress.com> © 2003 by The Haworth Press, Inc. All rights reserved.]*

KEYWORDS. Internet, adolescence, pornography, victimization, harassment, online safety

INTRODUCTION

The Internet is quickly becoming an integral element in the lives of many children, adolescents, and adults. Internet use has dramatically increased throughout the entire United States population over the last several years (U.S. Department of Commerce, 2002). This increase is readily apparent among youths, a population known for enthusiastically embracing new technology. In 1998 and 2001, an increase from 4.1% to 14.3% was seen among 3-4 year olds; 16.8% to 38.9% among 5-9 year olds; 39.2% to 65.4% among 10-13 year olds; and 51.2% to 75.6% among 14-17 year olds. The Internet provides youths with many exciting experiences, including education, entertainment, and communication, opportunities that this population readily embraces. A great majority of teens (12-17 years old) use the Internet to communicate, with 92% reporting sending or reading e-mail, 74% sending Instant Messages, and 55% visiting chat rooms (Lenhart, Raine, & Lewis, 2001). Many also go online to gather information. Sixty-nine percent use the Internet to look for information on hobbies, 68% for news, 66% to research a product or service before buying it, 47% check sports scores, 26% look for health information, and 18% look for information on a topic that is hard to talk about. Finally, youths also use the Internet for entertainment, with 84% surfing the Web for fun, 83% visiting entertainment sites, 66% playing or downloading games, and 59% listening to music.

Unfortunately, the Internet can also be a tool for bothering, harassing, and/or committing crimes against children. It is not uncommon to hear media reports of youths being sexually solicited or harassed online or having easy access to pornography, whether they want it or not. These occurrences have led to a concern among families, professionals, and policy makers, leading them to question what can be done to help protect youth from these types of situations. The first step toward a complete understanding of youth and their experiences and safety online is to get a get a complete picture of what youth experience and how often.

The present study, funded by the U.S. Congress through the National Center for Missing & Exploited Children, was developed to address this issue. The Youth Internet Safety Survey (YISS) relies upon interviews with youths and parents about experiences using the Internet. Specifically, it provides a base national estimate of how many youths (aged 10-17) experienced unwanted exposure to sexual material, sexual solicitations, and harassment on the Internet "in the past year." The study also examines characteristics of the youths, perpetrators, incidents, and impacts of such experiences, along with household rules and concerns.

This study does not seek to contradict or lessen the benefits the Internet can offer, but it does draw attention to the potential dangers associated with its use. The Internet is certain to continue to play a large role in the lives of Americans, specifically children and adolescents. Therefore, it is important to highlight the need for private and public initiatives to raise awareness and provide solutions.

METHODS

Participants

The Youth Internet Safety Survey,[1] sponsored by the National Center for Missing & Exploited Children, conducted telephone interviews between August 1999 and February 2000 to gather information from a national sample of 1501 young people (796 boys and 705 girls), ages 10-17, who were regular Internet users. Table 1 details the demographic characteristics of the sample. In the survey "regular" Internet use was defined as "using the Internet at least once a month for the past six months on a computer at home, school, a library, someone else's home, or some other place." The researchers chose this definition to exclude "occasional" Internet users and, at the same time, to include a range of both "heavy" and "light" users. Prior to each youth interview, a shorter interview was conducted with a parent or guardian in the household. Thus, the study was able to determine regular Internet use by youth initially by ques-

TABLE 1. Youth and Household Characteristics[†] ($N = 1501$)

Characteristic	% All Youth
Age of youth	
• 10	4%
• 11	8%
• 12	11%
• 13	15%
• 14	16%
• 15	18%
• 16	17%
• 17	13%
Sex of youth	
• Male	53%
• Female	47%
Race of youth	
• Non-Hispanic White	73%
• Black or African American	10%
• American Indian or Alaska Native	3%
• Asian	3%
• Hispanic White	2%
• Other	7%
• Don't know/Refused	2%
Marital status of parent/guardian	
• Married	79%
• Divorced	10%
• Single/Never married	5%
• Living with partner	1%
• Separated	2%
• Widowed	2%
Youth lives with both biological parents	64%
Highest level of completed education in household	
• Not a high school graduate	2%
• High school graduate	21%
• Some college education	22%
• College graduate	31%
• Post college degree	22%
Annual household income	
• Less than $20,000	8%
• $20,000 to $50,000	38%
• $50,000 to $75,000	23%
• More than $75,000	23%
Type of community	
• Small town	28%
• Suburb of large city	21%
• Rural area	20%
• Large town (25,000 to 100,000)	15%
• Large city	14%

[†] All the data in this table are based on questions asked of the parent/guardian with the exception of the information on race.
Note: Categories that do not add to 100% are due to rounding and/or missing data.

tions to the parent or guardian, before confirming this regularity during the youth interview.

The survey sample does not represent all youths within the United States because Internet use was not evenly distributed among the population during the time period in question. Internet users tended to have higher incomes and more education than non-Internet users, and among lower income groups, Internet users were more likely to be White, although racial difference was disappearing at higher income levels (National Public Radio, 2000). However, the sample is representative of the population of *Internet-using youths* in the United States and can therefore be used to extrapolate population estimates to this population (see Appendix A).

Procedures

Households with children in the target age group were identified through another much larger household survey, the Second National Incidence Study of Missing, Abducted, Runaway, and Thrownaway Children (NISMART 2), conducted by the Institute of Survey Research at Temple University between February and December 1999. This was a random digit dial sample of United States household phone numbers randomly generated using GENESYS, a commercial database maintenance and retrieval system (Hammer, Finkelhor, & Sedlak, 2002). NISMART 2 interviewers screened more than 180,000 telephone numbers to identify 16,000 households with children aged eighteen and younger. Telephone numbers for households including young people aged nine through seventeen were forwarded to interviewers for the YISS.

Staff of the experienced national survey research firm Schulman, Ronca, and Bucuvalas, Inc., conducted interviews for the YISS. They first screened for regular Internet use by a child in the household aged 10-17. In doing so, they defined Internet use itself as "connecting a computer or a TV to a phone or cable line to use things like the World Wide Web and e-mail." The interviewers identified the children who used the Internet most often in the household and then asked to speak with the parents or guardians who knew the most about these children's Internet use. They then conducted short interviews with these individuals about household rules and parental concerns about Internet use, as well as about demographic characteristics. Finally they asked permission to speak with the previously identified youths. The interviewers assured parents and guardians of the confidentiality of the interviews, told them that young participants would receive checks for $10, and informed them frankly that the interviews would include questions about "sexual material your child may have seen."

With parental consent, the interviewers described the study to the children and obtained their verbal consent. The subsequent youth interviews lasted about half an hour. They were scheduled at the convenience of youth participants and arranged for times when they could talk freely and confidentially. Researchers constructed questions that invited mostly short, one-word youth responses that would not reveal anything meaningful to persons overhearing any portions of the conversations. Where the study required longer answers, they were prefaced with the statement, "This may be something private. If you feel you can talk freely, or move to a place where you can talk freely, please tell me what happened." The interviewers did not press youths for answers. They promised complete confidentiality and told them that they could skip any questions that they did not want to answer and could stop the interview at any time. As promised, youth respondents received checks for $10, as well as brochures about Internet safety.

RESULTS

Participation Rate

In total, 6594 household phone numbers were forwarded from the NISMART-2 survey to YISS researchers. All of these numbers were dialed. No contact was made with 3148 (47.7%) of the households, including un-active residential phone numbers at the time of the survey, households with a non-English-speaking caregiver or a caregiver that was unavailable for an extended period of time, and households that did not answer the phone or were in call-back status at the end of the data collection period. Of the 3446 households where contact was made, 874 (25.4%) refused to screen for the study. Seventy-five percent of these households ($N = 2572$) completed the eligibility screen for the study. The majority of households qualified for study participation, representing 72% ($N = 1857$) of those screened. Eighty-two percent ($N = 1501$) of eligible households completed the survey (Finkelhor, Mitchell, & Wolak, 2000). The 18% of eligible households that did not participate are as follows: 5% of parents in eligible households refused to complete the adult questionnaire, 11% completed the interview and then refused to allow their child to participate, 2% of youth refused to participate after the adult had granted permission, and 1% of eligible households were in 'call-back' status when the survey period ended.

Patterns of Youth Internet Use

Of the 1501 youths interviewed, nearly three-quarters (74%) had access to the Internet at home. Youths also used the Internet in a number of other locations, including school (73%), other households (68%), and public libraries (32%). The great majority (86%) used the Internet in more than one location. At the time of the interviews, most youths (76%) had last used the Internet during the previous week, with 10% reporting Internet use in the previous two weeks and 14% in the previous month or more. In a typical week 29% spent one day or less online, 40% used the Internet two to four days, and 31% went online five to seven days. Sixty-one percent of the interviewed youth spent one hour or less online on a typical day when they used the Internet, with 26% spending one to two hours and 13% spending more than two hours in a typical day.

Overall Incidence of Online Victimization

The study asked youths about unwanted sexual solicitations or approaches, unwanted exposures to sexual material, and harassment during the year prior to the interview. Figure 1 shows the incidence of each type of online victimization.

FIGURE 1. Online Victimization in the Past Year

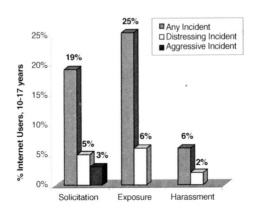

Sexual Solicitation and Approaches

With so many young people socializing on the Internet, a key law-enforcement concern has been the access and anonymity that the Internet gives to persons who might want to exploit youths sexually. The YISS confirms that large numbers of youths are sexually propositioned online, although such propositions do not always come in the form of the most frightening law-enforcement stereotypes. Namely, these stereotypes often involve youths who meet an adult stranger online, meet them in person, and are subsequently sexually assaulted.

To assess the problem of sexual exploitation on the Internet, the survey asked youths about four kinds of potentially dangerous online incidents: (1) sexual approaches, when "someone on the Internet tried to get them to talk about sex when they did not want to" or "asked for sexual information about them when they did not want to answer such questions, very personal questions like what their body looked like or sexual things they had done"; (2) sexual solicitations from people online who "asked them to do something sexual they did not want to do," such as asking them to engage in "cybersex"; (3) close friendships formed online with adults, including those involving sexual overtures; and (4) encouragements by people they met online to run away, a ploy apparently favored by some individuals looking for vulnerable youth. In the context of these questions, sexual solicitations and approaches were defined as "requests to engage in sexual activities or sexual talk or to give personal sexual information that were *unwanted or*, whether wanted or not, *made by an adult*" (see Appendix B for further details).

According to this definition, the survey determined that approximately one in five of the youths interviewed (19%) had received an unwanted sexual solicitation or approach in the previous year. Not all of these episodes were disturbing to the recipients; however, 5% of youths (one in four of those solicited) reported a solicitation that left them feeling very or extremely upset or afraid; the study termed these cases *distressing incidents.*

In order to assess solicitations that appeared to pose a higher risk to youths based on their potential to carry over into offline contact, the study identified *aggressive sexual solicitations*, defined as "solicitations involving *offline contact* with the perpetrator through regular mail, by telephone, or in person, or attempts or requests for offline contact." Three percent of youths (one in seven of all the solicitations) reported these more serious aggressive sexual solicitations.

Unwanted Exposure to Sexual Material

While it is easy to access pornography on the Internet, what makes the Internet appear particularly risky to many parents is the impression that young people can encounter pornography there inadvertently. It is common to hear stories about children researching school reports or looking up movie stars and finding themselves subjected to offensive depictions or descriptions.

To assess the problem of unwanted exposure to sexual material, the survey asked youths about two kinds of online experiences: (1) while "conducting an online search or surfing the web, finding themselves in a website that showed pictures of naked people or of people having sex when they did not want to be in that kind of site"; and (2) "opening an e-mail or Instant Message or a link in a message that showed them actual pictures of naked people or people having sex that they did not want." In the context of the survey, *unwanted exposure to sexual material* was defined thus: "without seeking or expecting sexual material, being exposed to pictures of naked people or people having sex when doing online searches, surfing the web, opening e-mail or e-mail links" (see Appendix B for further details).

One quarter (25%) of the surveyed youths had at least one such unwanted exposure to pictorial sexual material in the previous year. Seventy-one percent of these exposures occurred while the youths were searching or surfing the Internet, and 28% occurred while they were opening e-mails or clicking on links in e-mail or Instant Messages. Because exposure to sexual images, even when unwanted, is not necessarily offensive, the study designated a category of *distressing exposures* to identify specific situations in which youths found an exposure to such materials very or extremely upsetting. Six percent of youths reported *distressing exposures* to sexual material on the Internet in the previous year.

Harassment

Although less publicized than sexual solicitation and unwanted exposure to sexual material, other threatening and offensive behaviors have been directed on the Internet to youths, including threats to assault or harm them, their friends, their families, or their property and efforts to embarrass or humiliate them. Once again, the concern of parents and other officials is that the anonymity of the Internet may make it a fertile territory for such behaviors.

To assess the problem of harassment on the Internet, the survey asked youths about two kinds of incidents: (1) "feeling worried or threatened because someone was bothering or harassing them online"; and (2) "having someone using the Internet to threaten or embarrass them by posting or sending messages about them for other people to see." Accordingly, the study defined *harassment* as "threats or other offensive behavior (not sexual solicitations) sent online to the youth or posted online for others to see" (see Appendix B for further details).

Six percent of youths were the targets of threats or other kinds of offensive behavior that we termed harassment. A third of these youths, or 2% of the total sample, reported *distressing incidents*, that is, harassment that left them feeling very or extremely upset or afraid.

Targets of Victimization

Youth Targets for Sexual Solicitations

Girls were targeted for sexual solicitation at almost twice the rate of boys (66% versus 34%), but, given that girls are often thought to be the exclusive targets of sexual solicitation, the sizable percentage of boys is important (see Figure 2). More than three quarters of targeted youth (77%) were age fourteen or older (see Figure 3). Only 22% were ages 10-13, but this younger group reported 37% of the distressing episodes, suggesting that younger children have a harder time shrugging off such solicitations.

Youth with Unwanted Exposures to Sexual Material

Unlike the sexual solicitation incidents mentioned above, boys were slightly more likely to have experienced an unwanted exposure to sexual material than girls (57% to 42%) (see Figure 2). Nearly two-thirds (63%) of unwanted exposure incidents occurred to youths fifteen years of age or older (see Figure 3). Eleven- and twelve-year-olds accounted for 7% of the unwanted exposures, while none of the ten-year-olds reported unwanted exposures. The somewhat greater exposure of boys may reflect their tendency to allow curiosity to draw them closer to such encounters. However, the relatively small difference should not be over-emphasized. Nearly a quarter of both boys and girls had such exposures.

FIGURE 2. Target Gender by Type of Online Victimization

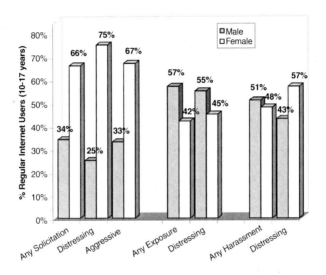

Youth Targets for Harassment

Boys and girls were targeted about equally for harassment (51% and 48%) (see Figure 2). Seventy percent of the episodes occurred to youth fourteen and older (see Figure 3). Eighteen percent of targeted youths were ages ten, eleven, or twelve.

Perpetrators of Victimizations

Perpetrators of the Sexual Solicitations

It must be kept in mind that, given the anonymity the Internet provides, individuals may easily hide or misrepresent themselves. This information gathered about perpetrators was derived from the self-reports of youths; thus, no substantiated reports of perpetrator characteristics are available. Further, virtually all perpetrators of sexual solicitation (97%) were persons that the youths originally met online, so it is possible that the reality of who these perpetrators were might be different from that reported here.

Adults were responsible for 24% of sexual solicitations and 34% of the aggressive solicitations (see Figure 4). Most of the adult solicitors

FIGURE 3. Target Age by Type of Online Victimization

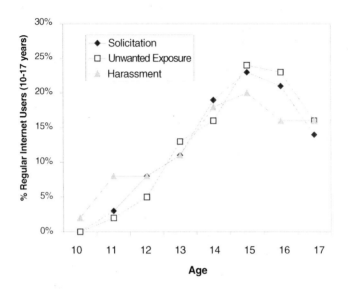

were reported to be ages 18-25, with only about 4% of all solicitors known to be older than twenty-five. Juveniles made up 48% of the overall and 48% of the aggressive solicitations. Slightly more than two-thirds of the solicitations and approaches came from males, while one-quarter of the aggressive episodes came from females (see Figure 5). In 13% of instances, the youth knew where the solicitors lived. Youths stated that the solicitors lived nearby (within an hour's drive or less) in only 4% of incidents.

As the study demonstrates, few of the sexual trawlers on the Internet fit the media stereotype of an older, male predator. Many are young, and some are women. In a large percentage of cases (27%), youths did not know the ages of the persons making the overtures. And in 13% of cases, they did not know the genders. In almost all of the cases in which the youths gave ages or genders for perpetrators, they had never met the perpetrators in person, thus leaving the accuracy of the identifying information in question.

Perpetrators of Harassment

More than one quarter of the perpetrators of harassment (28%) were offline friends or acquaintances of the targeted youth. A majority (54%)

FIGURE 4. Perpetrator Age by Type of Online Victimization

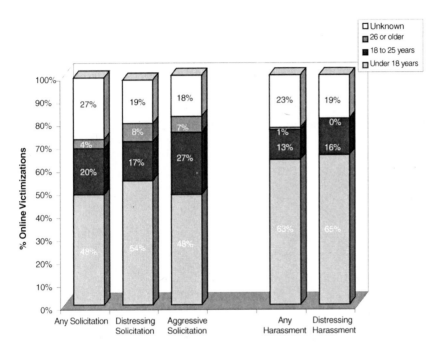

were reported to be males, but 20% were reportedly females (see Figure 5). In 26% of instances, the gender of the perpetrators was unknown. Nearly two-thirds (63%) of harassment perpetrators were other juveniles (see Figure 4). Almost a quarter of harassment perpetrators (24%) lived near the youths (within an hour's drive). In distressing episodes, 35% of perpetrators lived near the youths. In contrast to the sexual solicitation episodes, in which only 3% of perpetrators were known to the youths offline, approximately one quarter of the harassment episodes involved known persons and persons living relatively close to the youths.

Characteristics of Victimizations

Solicitation Incident Characteristics

Based on the descriptions given to interviewers, many of the sexual propositions appear to be solicitations for "cybersex," which is a form of fantasy sex involving interactive chatroom sessions in which the participants describe sexual acts and sometimes disrobe and masturbate. In

FIGURE 5. Perpetrator Gender by Type of Online Victimization

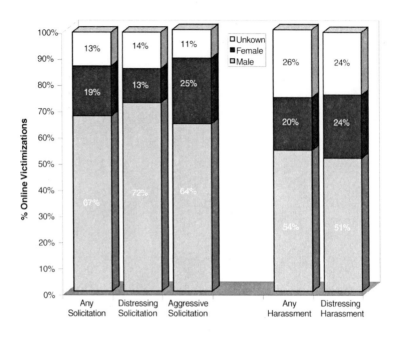

70% of the sexual solicitation incidents, the youths were at home when they were solicited, and in 22% of incidents they were at other people's homes (see Table 2). In 65% of incidents, the youths met the persons who solicited them in chatrooms; in 24% of episodes the meetings occurred through Instant Messages. In 10% of incidents, the perpetrators asked to meet the youths somewhere. Six percent of the youths received regular mail, 2% received telephone calls, and 1% received money or gifts. In one instance, a youth received a travel ticket. The study labeled all such incidents as aggressive solicitations. In most incidents, the youths ended the solicitations, using a variety of strategies like logging off, leaving the sites, or blocking the persons who made the solicitations.

Exposure Incident Characteristics

Ninety-four percent of the unwanted images seen by the youths consisted of naked persons (see Table 3). Thirty-eight percent showed people having sex, and 8% involved violence in addition to nudity and/or sex. Most of the unwanted exposures (67%) occurred at home, but 15% occurred at school, and 3% in libraries. Unfortunately, the study did not

TABLE 2. Solicitation Incident Characteristics

Episode Characteristics	All Incidents (N = 293)	Aggressive Incidents (N = 44)	Distressing Incidents (N = 72)
Gender of solicitor			
• Male	67%	64%	72%
• Female	19%	25%	13%
• Don't know	13%	11%	14%
Age of solicitor			
• Younger than 18 years	48%	48%	54%
• 18 to 25 years	20%	27%	17%
• Older than 25 years	4%	7%	8%
• Don't know	27%	18%	19%
Relation to solicitor			
• Met online	97%	100%	96%
• Knew in person before incident	3%	-----	3%
Incidents in which youth knew where person lived	**13%**	**29%**	**17%**
• Person lived near youth (1 hour drive or less)	4%	11%	7%
Location of computer when incident occurred			
• Home	70%	66%	51%
• Someone else's home	22%	27%	36%
• School	4%	2%	5%
• Library	3%	5%	4%
• Some other place	1%	-----	1%
Place on Internet that incident first happened			
• Chat room	65%	52%	60%
• Using Instant Messages	24%	36%	26%
• Specific web page	4%	7%	7%
• E-mail	2%	2%	1%
• Game room, message board, newsgroup, or other	3%	-----	2%
• Don't know/refused	2%	2%	1%
Forms of offline contact[†,‡]			
• Asked to meet somewhere	10%	66%	20%
• Sent regular mail	6%	39%	9%
• Called on telephone	2%	14%	4%
• Came to house	< 1%	2%	-----
• Gave money, gifts, or other things	1%	5%	1%
• Bought plane, train, or bus ticket	< 1%	2%	-----
• None of the above	84%	-----	70%
How situation ended			
• Logged off computer	28%	25%	35%
• Left site	24%	16%	22%
• Blocked perpetrator	14%	25%	17%
• Told them to stop	13%	11%	5%
• Changed screen name, profile, or E-mail address	5%	13%	13%
• Stopped without youth doing anything	4%	9%	5%
• Called police or other authorities	1%	2%	3%
• Other	20%	20%	18%

[†] Multiple responses possible.
[‡] Only youths who did not know the solicitors prior to the incidents were asked this question (N = 284 for all incidents, N = 44 for aggressive incidents, and N = 70 for distressing incidents).
Note: Categories that do not add to 100% are due to rounding and/or missing data.

establish how many of the exposures involved child pornography. Important as this question is, the researchers had decided that youth respondents could not reliably determine the ages of individuals appearing in the pictures that they viewed.

For the youths who encountered the unwanted material while surfing the web, it came up as a result of searches (47%), misspelled addresses (17%), and links in web sites (17%). For youths who encountered the

TABLE 3. Exposure Incident Characteristics

Episode Characteristics	All Incidents (N = 393)	Distressing Incidents (N = 92)
Location of computer		
• Home	67%	61%
• School	15%	16%
• Someone else's home	13%	16%
• Library	3%	3%
• Some other place	2%	3%
Type of material youth saw or heard[†]		
• Pictures of naked person(s)	94%	92%
• Pictures of people having sex	38%	42%
• Pictures that also included violence	8%	9%
How youth was exposed		
• Surfing the Web	71%	72%
• Opening E-mail or clicking on E-mail link	28%	30%
Youth could tell site was X-rated before entering	17%	12%

Surfing Exposure	All (N = 281)	Distressing (N = 66)
How web site came up		
• Link came up as result of search	47%	36%
• Misspelled web address	17%	18%
• Clicked on link when in other site	17%	24%
• Other	15%	18%
• Don't know	3%	3%
• Youth has gone back to web site	2%	-----
• Youth was taken into another X- rated site when exiting the first one	26%	33%

E-mail Exposure	All (N = 112)	Distressing (N = 26)
• Youth received E-mail at a personal address	63%	58%
• E-mail sender unknown	93%	96%

[†] Multiple responses possible.
Note: Categories that do not add to 100% are due to rounding and/or missing data.

TABLE 4. Harassment Incident Characteristics

Episode Characteristics	All Incidents (N = 96)	Distressing Incidents (N = 37)
Gender of harasser		
• Male	54%	51%
• Female	20%	24%
• Don't know	26%	24%
Age of harasser		
• Younger than 18 years	63%	65%
• 18 to 25 years	13%	16%
• Older than 25 years	1%	-----
• Don't know	23%	19%
Relation to harasser		
• Met online	72%	65%
• Knew in person before incident	28%	35%
Incidents in which youth knew where person lived	**35%**	**43%**
• Person lived near youth (1 hour drive or less)	24%	35%
Location of computer[†]		
• Home	76%	81%
• Someone else's home	13%	5%
• School	6%	5%
• Library	1%	3%
• Some other place	2%	3%
• Wasn't using computer[‡]	2%	3%
Place on Internet that incident first happened		
• Using Instant Messages	33%	41%
• Chat room	32%	22%
• E-mail	19%	22%
• Specific web page	7%	8%
• Game room, message board, newsgroup, other	6%	5%
• Don't know	2%	3%
Forms of Offline Contact[‡,£]		
• Sent regular mail	9%	4%
• Asked to meet somewhere	6%	4%
• Called on telephone	4%	-----
• Came to house	1%	-----
• Gave money, gifts, or other things	1%	-----
• Bought plane, train, or bus ticket	-----	-----
• None of the above	88%	96%
How situation ended		
• Logged off	19%	22%
• Blocked that person	17%	11%
• Left site	13%	16%
• Told harasser to stop	11%	16%
• Stopped without youths doing anything	10%	11%
• Changed screen name, profile, or E-mail address	3%	3%
• Called police or other authorities	2%	-----
• Other	27%	22%

[†] These youths had information posted about them online by other people.
[‡] Multiple responses possible.
[£] Only youths who did not know the harassers prior to the incidents were asked this question (N = 69 for all incidents and N = 24 for distressing incidents).
Note: Categories that do not add to 100% are due to rounding and/or missing data.

material through e-mail, 63% of unwanted exposures came to addresses used solely by the youths. In 93% of instances, the sender was unknown to the youth.

In 17% of all unwanted exposure incidents, the youths said that they did know the sites were X-rated before entering them (these were all encounters described earlier as unwanted or unexpected). This group of episodes was not distinguishable in any fashion from the other 83% of episodes, including the likelihood of being distressing. Almost half of these incidents (48%) were disclosed to parents. It is not clear to what extent it was curiosity or just navigational naiveté that resulted in the opening of the sites in spite of the prior knowledge.

Pornography sites are often programmed to make them difficult to exit. In fact, in some sites the exit buttons take viewers into other sexually explicit sites. In 26% of unwanted exposure incidents, youths reported that they were brought to other sex sites when they tried to exit the sites they were in. This happened in one-third of distressing incidents.

Harassment Incident Characteristics

Slightly more than three quarters of the youths who reported harassment incidents were logged on at home when the harassments occurred (see Table 4). These harassments primarily took the form of Instant Messages (33%), chat room exchanges (32%), and e-mails (19%). Twelve percent of the harassment episodes involving perpetrators who were not face-to-face acquaintances of the youths included attempts at offline contact by telephone or regular mail or requests to meet in person.

Youth Disclosure

Youth Disclosure of Online Sexual Solicitations

In almost half of the incidents (49%), the youths did not tell anyone about the episodes; even when the episodes were aggressive, youths did not tell in 36% of incidents (see Figure 6). In 24% of incidents, the youths disclosed the incidents to parents, and in 29%, to friends or siblings. Only 10% of incidents were reported to authorities, such as teachers, Internet service providers, or law-enforcement. Even with aggressive episodes, only 18% were reported to authorities.

It is remarkable that so few episodes of sexual solicitation, even those that were quite distressing, prompted the youths to confide in other persons or to make reports to authorities. This phenomenon

FIGURE 6. Youth Disclosure by Type of Victimization

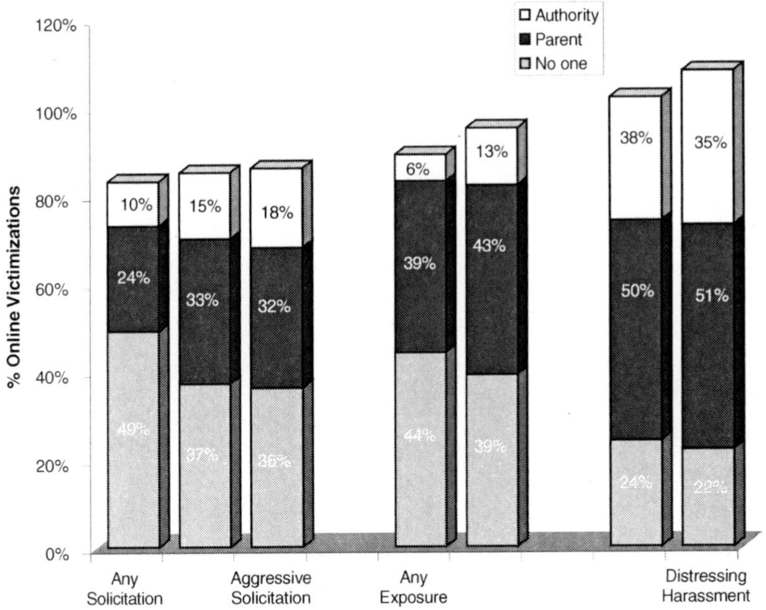

may reflect the fact that in some cases the youths were not alarmed. Others probably did not know or doubted that anything could be done. But the response may also reflect embarrassment or shame because the youths may have believed they had gone into places on the Internet of which parents, law-enforcement, or even friends would disapprove. Some may also have been concerned that their access to the Internet would be restricted if they told parents about such incidents.

Youth Disclosure of Unwanted Exposure to Sexual Materials

Parents found out or were told in 39% of the episodes of unwanted exposure to sexual materials (see Figure 6). In 44% of incidents, youths disclosed the episodes to no one. In only a few cases were authorities notified, most frequently teachers or school officials (3% of incidents) and Internet service providers (3%). Only 2% of youths encountering unwanted exposures said that they returned later to the sites of the exposures. None of the youths with distressing exposures returned.

The fact that so many youths did not disclose the incidents of exposure to anyone, including friends, even to laugh about them or talk about them as adventures, is noteworthy. This phenomenon probably reflects some degree of guilt on the part of many youths.

Youth Disclosure of Harassment

Parents found out or were told about episodes of harassment half the time (see Figure 6). Slightly more than a third of youths told friends. Twenty-one percent of the episodes were reported to Internet service providers, 6% to teachers, and 1% to law enforcement agencies. Twenty-four percent of harassment incidents were undisclosed. It is noteworthy that, compared to sexual solicitations and exposures, a larger proportion of the harassment episodes were reported to parents and to authorities.

Impact of Victimizations

Impact of Solicitations on Youths

In 75% of incidents, youths had no or only minor reactions, saying that they were not very upset or afraid in the wake of the solicitations (see Figure 7). However, in 20% of incidents, youths reported being very or extremely upset, and in 13% they reported being very or extremely afraid. In 36% of the aggressive solicitations, youths were very or extremely upset and in 25% very or extremely afraid. In 17% of incidents, youths were very or extremely embarrassed. This was true in 32% of aggressive incidents. In one quarter of the incidents, youths reported at least one symptom of stress (staying away from the Internet; not being able to stop thinking about the incident; feeling jumpy or irritable; and/or losing interest in things) "more than a little" or "all the time." The aggressive episodes were more distressing, with at least one symptom of stress reported in 43% of such episodes. Seventeen percent of the youths who were solicited had five or more symptoms of depression at the time they were interviewed, twice the rate of depressive symptoms in the overall sample.

Most of the youths who were solicited appeared to brush off the encounters, treating them as minor annoyances. Nonetheless, there was a core group of youths who experienced high levels of "upset" and/or "fear" and for whom the experience may have provoked stress responses. It is reassuring that most solicited youths were not affected, but given the estimated large proportions that were solicited, the group with strongly negative reactions is quite substantial (see Appendix A).

Impact of Exposure

Twenty-three percent of youths were very or extremely upset by exposures to sexual material (see Figure 7). This figure amounts to 6% of regular Internet users. Twenty percent of youths were very or extremely embarrassed. Twenty percent reported at least one symptom of stress "more than a little" or "all the time" following the incident (staying away from the Internet; not being able to stop thinking about the incident; feeling jumpy or irritable; and/or losing interest in things).

Impact of Harassment

Thirty-one percent of the harassment episodes were very or extremely upsetting, and 19% were very or extremely frightening (see Figure 7). Eighteen percent were very or extremely embarrassing. Al-

FIGURE 7. Impact by Type of Victimization

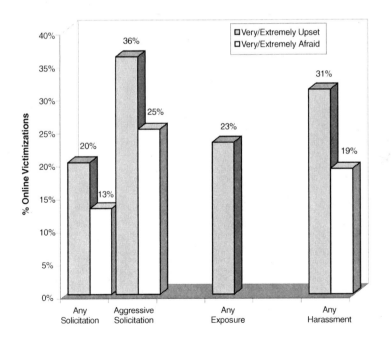

most one-third of the harassed youths (32%) reported at least one symptom of stress "more than a little" or "all the time" following the incident (staying away from the Internet; not being able to stop thinking about the incident; feeling jumpy or irritable; and/or losing interest in things). Almost one half of the youths with distressing experiences had at least one symptom of stress. Eighteen percent of the harassed youths were depressed at the time of their interview, more than twice the rate for the overall sample. Most of the harassed youths described the episodes as mildly distressing, but an important subgroup was quite distressed.

Youth at Risk for Internet Victimization

Youth at Risk for Sexual Solicitation

Identifying the vulnerable population of youths is an important first step in the development of effective prevention and intervention programs surrounding online sexual solicitations. Logistic regression findings from these data (Mitchell, Finkelhor, & Wolak, 2001) suggest that youths at risk tend to be troubled,[2] older (14-17) female teens who use the Internet more often than others,[3] enter chat rooms, talk with strangers online, engage in high online risk behaviors,[4] and use the Internet in households other than their own (see Figure 8). These findings suggest that troubled youth and youth with high Internet use and risk behavior may be at increased risk for victimization and are worth targeting for prevention efforts. Yet caution needs to be taken not to focus exclusively on these groups of youths: 42% of youths reporting sexual solicitations were *not* troubled high-rate or risky Internet users.

Youth at Risk for Unwanted Exposure to Sexual Materials

An important step necessary to inform the national debate about policies regarding youths and Internet pornography is to identify youths at risk for unwanted exposure to sexual materials on the Internet. Published findings from a logistic regression analysis from the present dataset reveal that these youths are similar to those at risk for sexual solicitation: They are typically troubled, older (ages 14-17) teens who use the Internet more frequently than others, use e-mail and chat rooms, use the Internet in households other than their own, talk with strangers online, and engage in high online risk behavior (Mitchell, Finkelhor, & Wolak, 2003) (see Figure 9). Again, as is the case with youths at risk for online sexual solicitation, we must take caution not to create too narrow a focus on youths who are troubled and have high and risky Internet use:

FIGURE 8. Risk Factors for Unwanted Sexual Solicitation

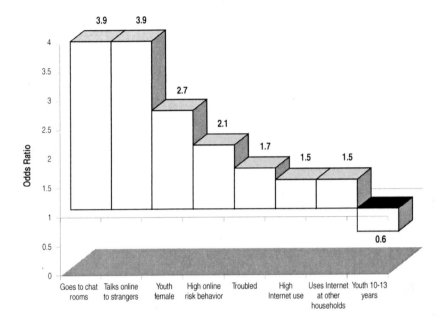

In the cases of unwanted exposure, nearly half (45%) of youths report-ing exposure were *not* troubled high-rate Internet users or high online risk takers.

Risks and Remedies

Our lack of knowledge about the dimensions and dynamics of the problems this new technology has created for young people is, of course, a barrier to devising effective solutions. But even in the absence of knowledge, there has been no dearth of suggestions about things to do. Parents have been urged to supervise their children and talk with them about perils and dangers, and organizations have been established to monitor and investigate suspicious episodes. Have any of these reme-dies been taken to heart?

The survey asked a variety of questions of both parents and children to find out more about the prospects for prevention. The study tried to determine to what degree parents are monitoring and advising their children about Internet activities and asked about parents' and youths'

FIGURE 9. Risk Factors for Unwanted Exposure to Sexual Materials

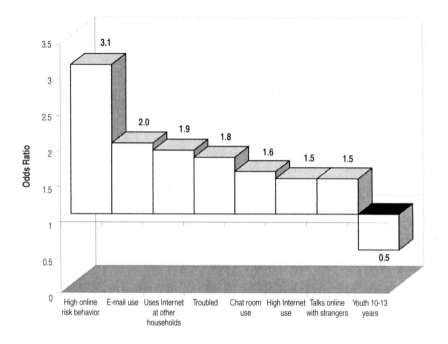

knowledge about what remedies or information sources are available for them when they run into problems.

Parental Concern

Parents and youth both believed that adults should be concerned about the problem of young people's exposure to sexual material on the Internet. As might be expected, parents thought adults should be more concerned than youths thought adults should be, with 84% of parents saying that adults should be extremely concerned, compared to 46% of the youths (see Figure 10). Some inflation of concern might be expected in a survey with this topic, but other surveys confirm that this an issue of substantial immediacy for parents and youths (e.g., Turow, 2000).

Use of Filtering and Blocking Software

Thirty-three percent of households surveyed were currently using filtering or blocking software at the time of the interviews (see Figure 11).

FIGURE 10. Parental Concern About Youth Online Exposure to Sexual Materials

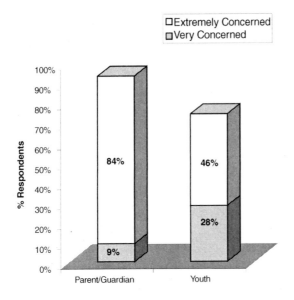

The most common option used by far is the access control offered by America Online (AOL) to its subscribers, used by 12% of the households with home Internet access, or 35% of households using filtering or blocking software. Interestingly, another 5% of the households in the sample had used some kind of filtering or blocking software during the year but were no longer doing so, a statistic suggesting some possible dissatisfaction with its use.

Knowledge of Help Sources

As noted earlier, youths reported relatively few of the Internet episodes (solicitations, unwanted exposures to sexual material, or harassment) to official sources. One possibility is that youths and their families are not familiar enough with places that are interested in or receptive to such reports. Almost a third of the interviewed parents or guardians claimed that they had heard of places where troublesome Internet episodes could be reported, but only approximately 10% of them could cite specific names or authorities (see Figure 12). Only 24% of youths stated that they had heard of places to report, and only 17%

FIGURE 11. Family Use of Filtering and Blocking Software

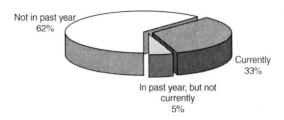

Not in past year 62%

Currently 33%

In past year, but not currently 5%

could actually name such places (see Figure 13). Reporting the episodes to the Internet service providers, most often AOL, was the option most often considered.

DISCUSSION

By providing more texture and details to the picture of the cyber-hazards facing youth, the national Youth Internet Safety Survey has much to contribute to current public policy discussions about what to do to improve the safety of young people (see Appendix C for study limitations). What follows are some key conclusions and recommendations based on the important findings from the study:

1. *A large percentage of youths appear to be encountering offensive experiences on the Internet.*

The percent of youths encountering offensive experiences (19% solicited sexually, 25% exposed to unwanted sexual material, 6% harassed) are figures for one year only. The number of youths encountering such experiences from the time that they start using the Internet until they are 17, which might include five or more years of Internet activity, would certainly be higher.

2. *The offenses and offenders seem even more diverse than previously thought.*

The perpetrators highlighted in this study were not merely adult males trolling for sex. Much of the offending behavior came from other youths. There was also a substantial amount committed by females. In

FIGURE 12. Has Parent Heard of Places to Report Internet Victimization?

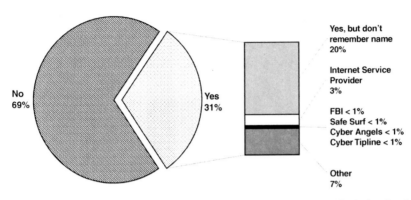

FIGURE 13. Has Youth Heard of Places to Report Internet Victimization?

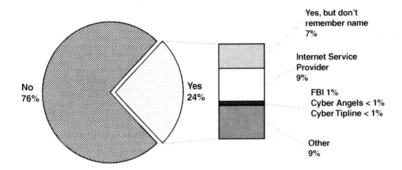

addition, the non-sexual offenses (e.g., harassment episodes) were numerous and quite serious. We need to keep this diversity in mind. Sexual victimization on the Internet should not be the only thing that grabs public attention.

3. *Most sexual solicitations fail, but their quantity is potentially alarming.*

Based on current Internet use statistics, we estimate that 4.5 million young people ages 10-17 are propositioned on the Internet every year. If even some small percentage of these encounters results in offline sexual assaults or illegal sexual contact, a percentage smaller than we could detect in this survey, it would amount to several thousand incidents. The good news is most young people seem to know what to do to deflect these sexual "come-ons." But there are youths who may be especially vulnerable through ignorance, neediness, disability, or poor judgment. The wholesale solicitation for sex on the Internet is worrisome for that reason.

4. *The primary vulnerable population is teenagers.*

For solicitations, as well as unwanted exposures to sexual materials and harassment, most of the targets identified in the survey were teens, especially teens fourteen and older. Because children and teenagers are different victim populations, it is thus misleading to say that child molesters are moving from the playground to the living room, trading in their trench coats for digicams, as some have characterized it. Pre-teen children use the Internet less, in more limited ways (Richardson, 1999; Roberts, Foehr, Rideout, & Brodie, 1999), and are less independent. It does not appear that much predatory behavior over the Internet involves conventional pedophiles targeting eight-year-old children with their modems, at least not yet. Because the target population for this Internet victimization is teens, prevention and intervention present a different sort of challenge. Teens are more independent, and they do not necessarily listen to what parents and other "authorities" tell them.

5. *The sexually explicit material on the Internet is very intrusive.*

Great numbers of youthful Internet users are exposed to sexually explicit materials when they are not looking for them, through largely innocent misspellings and opening of e-mails, web sites, and other documents. These explicit materials on the Internet are not discretely segregated and signposted, as in a bookstore, and they are not easy to avoid. Some graphic imagery is easy to stumble upon; youths can come across it inadvertently while searching for other materials.

6. *Most youths brush off these offenses, but some are quite distressed.*

Most youths are not bothered much by what they encounter on the Internet, but there is an important subgroup who are quite distressed by the exposure, as well as the threats and solicitations. We cannot assume that this distress is merely a transient effect. Intrusive thoughts, physical discomfort, and other stress symptoms reported by youths are warning signs. The residual effects of distressing Internet encounters, which are hard to predict, may depend partly on variables like age, prior experience–both with the Internet and with sexual matters–family attitudes, the degree of surprise, and the kinds of exposure. Anticipating and trying to respond to negative impacts is something that needs more consideration.

7. *Many youths do not tell anyone about their encounters on the Internet.*

Nearly half of the sexual solicitations were not disclosed to anyone. Parents, who would certainly want to know, are not being informed about many of these episodes. And some youth are not even telling their friends. Thus, they are not getting chances to reflect upon, process, or get ideas about how to deal with these encounters.

Some of the non-disclosure in cases of sexual solicitation is certainly due to embarrassment or guilt, as the higher disclosure rates for nonsexual encounters suggest. The Internet is providing places to talk about difficult subjects, but, ironically, at the same time it may be increasing the number of difficult subjects to talk about.

8. *Youth and parents rarely report these experiences and do not often know where to report them.*

Most parents and youths interviewed by the survey did not know where to report or get help for Internet offenses, and the low rate of reporting for actual offenses confirms this lack of awareness. Even the most serious episodes were rarely reported. Because the Internet is new territory, most people do not yet know who the policing authorities are; this may, in fact be part of the attraction. But victims and their parents need to know how to get help, and people perpetrators do need to know that there are consequences.

IMPLICATIONS AND RECOMMENDATIONS

Some recommendations follow from these major findings and conclusions:

1. *Those concerned about preventing sexual exploitation on the Internet need to talk specifically in their materials about the di-*

versity of hazards, including threats from youthful and female offenders.

A stereotype of the adult Internet "predator" or "pedophile" has come to dominate much of the discussion about Internet victimization. While such figures exist and may be among the most dangerous of Internet threats, the YISS revealed a more diverse array of individuals who are making offensive and potentially exploitative online overtures. We should not ignore them. We have to remember that in a previous generation, campaigns to prevent child molestation characterized the threat predominately as "playground predators" so that for years the problem of youthful, acquaintance, and intrafamily perpetrators went unrecognized. One of the reasons for the mistaken characterization of child molesters in an earlier era was that people extrapolated the problem entirely from what came to the attention of law enforcement. A similar process could currently be underway in the case of Internet victimization, but it is probably early enough to reverse. Today, those concerned with preventing Internet exploitation must be careful not to make, consciously or inadvertently, a characterization of the threat that fails to encompass all of its forms.

2. *Prevention planners and law enforcement officials need to address the problem of non-sexual, as well as sexual, victimization on the Internet.*

An additional problem with the "Internet predator" stereotype mentioned above is that it does not give enough attention to non-sexual forms of Internet victimization. The current study shows that non-sexual threats and harassment constitute another common peril for youth that can be as distressing as, or even more distressing than, sexual overtures. Experience in crime prevention has shown that concerns about sexual threats often eclipse other equivalently serious crimes. Those who would prevent Internet victimization should make a concerted effort to ensure that non-sexual threats and harassment are included among the Internet safety agenda of educators, mental health practitioners, legislators, and law enforcement agencies.

3. *More of the Internet-using public need to know about the existence of help sources for Internet offenses, and the reporting of offensive Internet behavior needs to be made even easier, more immediate, and more important.*

Multiple strategies are needed to increase reporting. The Internet-using public needs to be made aware of reporting options in as many ways as possible, through the Internet as well as through other avenues. The public also needs to be briefed on the reasons why they should make such reports and on the importance of keeping the Internet a safe and comfortable place for everyone to use. Although people balk at being tattle-tales, citizen vigilance and community involvement have been traditional keys to community safety; the same community involvement would serve Internet safety interests as well.

4. *Different prevention and intervention strategies need to be developed for youth of different ages.*

Most of the encounters reported to the current study occurred to teenagers, specifically older teens. The threat, then, differs from conventional child molestation, and the potential victims differ from the 7-13-year-old targets of this kind of molestation. Older teens have more independence, more experience, and different relationships with adults and their families. For example, advice telling parents to check the Internet and e-mail activity of older teens regularly may amount to saying that parents should read their teens' mail, and such invasions of privacy will seem unrealistic in many families. Good protection strategies, especially for teens, cannot rely too heavy-handedly on parental control; they should, instead, invite the youth themselves to develop prevention strategies in conjunction with those offered by parents and other authorities.

5. *Youths themselves need to be mobilized in campaigns to help clean up the standards of Internet behavior and take responsibility for youth-oriented parts of the Internet.*

Much has been learned over the years about reducing crime, social deviance, and public disorder in communities. For example, greater community policing and cleaning up of minor kinds of neighborhood disorder and decay have helped reduce crime. Crime-watch campaigns that deputize and empower community members to be on the watch for crime have worked to reduce theft. In the field of education, school revitalization campaigns have had similar success in improving decorum and reducing anti-social behaviors in school communities. We should adapt the same kinds of initiatives to the Internet, which, after all, is itself a community, albeit one with special properties. We might, for example, apply the experiences of those trying to prevent sexual harassment in the larger world by launching campaigns to raise awareness about Internet threats and their effects, and help youths themselves enforce proper conduct among peers. Because such youth-oriented campaigns might have some success with at least some forms of Internet victimization, and they may well be worth a try.

6. *We need to train mental health, school, and family counselors about these new Internet hazards and about how these hazards contribute to personal distress and other psychological and interpersonal problems.*

The current study revealed that substantial numbers of young people do experience distress because of Internet encounters. Unfortunately, in most cases, these youths are not getting help. Mental health and other counselors need to learn to be alert and ask questions to induce young people to talk about such encounters. They need to know how young people use the Internet, so that they can understand their problems; they also need to be trained to treat the kinds of distress and conflicts that have connections with negative Internet experiences. Educational packages for schools and for the professional development of all kinds of youth workers would help inform counselors about the threats and suggest methods for intervention. Unfortunately, at the training conferences being offered today, most of the Internet education seems directed at law enforcement. We need to develop workshops for educators, practitioners, psychologists, and social workers as well.

7. *Much more research is needed on the developmental impact of unwanted exposure to pornographic images among children of different ages.*

The Internet is almost certainly increasing the frequency and the explicitness of unwanted exposures to sexual images, but even more importantly, it is certainly increasing the number of youths exposed involuntarily and unexpectedly. Although this topic has commanded some public attention, to date there has been little research on it. And even if the vast majority of such encounters are trivial or innocuous, it would be important to know under what conditions such encounters can be influential or stressful and what kinds of interventions are useful to preventing negative influence. The domain of influences could be broad, including attitudes about sex, attitudes about the Internet itself, and family dynamics. Studying these matters in an ethical and dispassionate way is not easy, but it can be done. We should make it a priority to do so.

8. *More understanding is needed about families' knowledge of, attitudes about, and experience with filtering and blocking software.*

The study found that only a minority of families with children was using blocking or filtering software, even though most interviewed parents said that adults should be very or extremely concerned about the problem of Internet victimization. Blocking and filtering software is one main line of defense available to families concerned about the problem. It is, in fact, the one being strongly advocated by people opposed to legislative solutions. Why, then, is it not being used more?

The lack of filtering or blocking software use may reflect a lack of knowledge about its availability, suspicions about its utility, or the unsuitability of such software in the context of real family dynamics and Internet use practices. For example, the introduction of such software may provoke conflicts between adults and youth or at least excite fears about such conflicts. It is interesting that 5% of the families interviewed during the survey had used filtering or blocking software in the past year and then discontinued its use.

Before recommending that more families utilize such software, we should know more about its operation and suitability. If a lack of knowledge is the problem, then education and awareness can be the answer. If the software does not suit the concerns of families or is difficult to use in real family contexts, then new designs or approaches may be needed. We need detailed, real-life evaluation research about available Internet blocking and filtering technologies.

9. *Laws are needed to ensure that offensive acts that are illegal in other contexts will also be illegal on the Internet.*

Some of the offensive behaviors revealed in this study–especially sexual solicitations by adults of minors and some of the threatening harassment–are probably illegal under current law. But questions have been raised about whether and how various criminal statutes apply to Internet behavior because most law was written prior to the development of the Internet. Although it is a daunting task, criminal statutes need to be reviewed systematically with the Internet in mind to make sure that relevant statutes cover Internet behaviors.

10. *Concern about Internet victimization should not eclipse prevention and intervention efforts to combat other conventional forms
of youth victimization.*

This study has revealed how many offensive and distressing experiences youths encounter on the Internet. But Internet victimization has
not become, nor is it threatening to become, the most serious crime peril
in children's lives, just the newest. Among the regular Internet users in
the survey, 30% had been physically attacked in real life by other
youths in the last year, 1% had been physically abused by an adult, and
1% had been sexually assaulted (see Bruhn, this volume). As far as the
study could determine, however, none of these serious offenses had any
connection with the Internet. And none of the Internet threats documented by the study actually materialized into a face-to-face violent offense. Certainly we need to mobilize about Internet victimization because
it is a new threat that causes distress, that could mushroom, and that could
otherwise escape attention. But the conventional crime perils in the lives
of children and youth are all too real and continuing. As reported by the
National Crime Victimization Survey, youth the age of the respondents in
the YISS have conventional violent crime victimization rates–rape, robbery, and aggravated assault–that are twice that of the adult population
(Hashima & Finkelhor, 1999). Children and adolescents are the most
criminally victimized segment in our society. So, as much as possible, efforts to address Internet victimization should try to combine with, and not
displace, efforts to prevent youth crime victimization in general.

NOTES

1. The survey was conducted under the supervision of the University of New Hampshire's Institutional Review Board and conformed to the rules mandated by research
projects funded by the U.S. Department of Justice.
2. *Troubled* is a composite variable that includes items from a negative life event
scale (death in the family, moving to a new home, parents' being divorced or separated,
and/or parents losing a job); from the physical and sexual assault items on a victimization scale; and from a depression scale (five or more depression symptoms in the past
month). Those with a composite value of one standard deviation above the mean or
higher were coded as having this characteristic, while the rest were coded as zero.
3. *High Internet use* is a composite variable consisting of high experience with the
Internet (4 or 5 on a scale of 1 to 5); high importance of Internet in child's life (4 or 5 on
a scale of 1 to 5), spending four or more days online in a typical week; and spending
two or more hours online in a typical day. Youths with a composite value one standard
deviation above the mean or higher were considered high Internet users.
4. *High online risk behavior* is a composite variable of the following dichotomous
activities pertaining to behavior online: posting personal information; making rude or
nasty comments; playing a joke on or annoying someone; harassing or embarrassing

someone; talking about sex with someone the youth never met in person; and going to X-rated sites on purpose. Youths with a composite value two standard deviations above the mean or higher were considered high online risk takers.

REFERENCES

Bruhn, C. M. (2003). Children with disabilities: Abuse, neglect, and the child welfare system. *Journal of Aggression, Maltreatment, & Trauma, 8*(1/2), 173-203.

Finkelhor, D., Mitchell, K. J., & Wolak, J. (2000). *Online victimization: A report on the nation's youth.* Alexandria, VA: National Center for Missing & Exploited Children (Order #62).

Hammer, H., Finkelhor, D., & Sedlak, A. J. (2002). *NISMART-2 Household Survey Methodology Technical Report.* Washington, DC: U.S. Department of Justice, Office of Justice Programs, Office of Juvenile Justice and Delinquency Prevention.

Hashima, P., & Finkelhor, D. (1999). Violent victimization of youth versus adults in the National Crime Victimization Survey. *Journal of Interpersonal Violence, 14,* 799-819.

Lenhart, A., Rainie, L., & Lewis, O. (2001). *Teenage life online: The rise of the instant-message generation and the internet's impact on friendships and family relationships.* Washington, DC: Pew Internet & American Life Project. Available online at: http://www.pewinternet.org/reports/toc.asp?Report=36.

Mitchell, K. J., Finkelhor, D., & Wolak, J. (2001). Online sexual solicitation of youth: Risk factors and impact. *Journal of the American Medical Association, 285*(23), 3011-3014.

Mitchell, K. J., Finkelhor, D., & Wolak, J. (2003). The exposure of youth to unwanted sexual material on the Internet: A national survey of risk, impact and prevention. *Youth & Society, 34*(3), 330-358.

National Public Radio. (2000). *NPR/Kaiser/Kennedy School Kids and Technology Survey.* Retrieved November 5, 2001, from http://www.npr.org/programs/specials/poll/technology/technology.kids.html.

Richardson, A. (1999). *Interactive consumers: The monthly topical data report from Cyber Dialogue.* New York, NY: Cyber Dialogue, Inc.

Roberts, D. F., Foehr, U. G., Rideout, V. J., & Brodie, M. (1999). *Kids and media at the new millennium: A comprehensive national analysis of children's media use.* The Henry J. Kaiser Foundation. A Kaiser Family Foundation Report. Retrieved November 5, 2001, from http://www.kff.org/content/1999/1535/KidsReport%20FINAL.pdf.

Turow, J., & Nir, L. (2000). *The Internet and the family 2000: The view from parents, the view from kids.* The Annenberg Public Policy Center of the University of Pennsylvania. Report Series No. 33. Retrieved November 5, 2001, from http://www.appcpenn.org/internet/family/finalreport_fam.pdf.

U.S. Department of Commerce. (2002). *A nation online: How Americans are expanding their use of the internet.* Washington, DC: Economics and Statistics Administration & National Telecommunications and Information Administration. Available online at: http://www.ntia.doc.gov/ntiahome/dn/index.html.

APPENDIX A. Prevalence of Internet Use

Estimates of the prevalence of regular Internet use for youth ages ten through seventeen were created from data gathered during eligibility screening for the survey. These data allowed for the calculation of numbers and ages of children in households that screened out of the survey as having no Internet use, as well as numbers and ages of children in households that screened into the survey. National estimates of regular Internet use by age are presented in Table Appendix A.1 below. The middle column in the table represents the percentage of youth in the U.S. in each age group who used the Internet regularly in 1999, based on the screening for this survey. The estimated number of Internet users in column three was derived by multiplying the percentage of Internet users in each age group by the 1999 census figures for the population for that age group (not shown). Population estimates for specific online victimizations of youth are provided in Table Appendix A.2. See the box titled "How Many Youth Had Online Episodes" for information about the limitations of these estimates.

TABLE Appendix A.1. National Estimates of Regular Internet Use by Age[1]

AGE	% INTERNET USERS	ESTIMATED # INTERNET USERS[2]
10 years old	52%	2,100,000
11 years old	64%	2,490,000
12 years old	77%	2,970,000
13 years old	81%	3,150,000
14 years old	79%	3,080,000
15 years old	86%	3,270,000
16 years old	83%	3,260,000
17 years old	87%	3,490,000
TOTAL		23,810,000

[1] Confidence intervals were not calculated for these figures.
[2] Estimates are rounded to the nearest ten thousand.

TABLE Appendix A.2. Population Estimates and Confidence Intervals for On-line Victimization of Youth[1]

Online Victimization	% Regular Internet Users	95% Confidence Interval	Estimated Number of Youth[2]	95% Confidence Interval[2]
Sexual Solicitations and Approaches				
• Any	19%	17% - 21%	4,520,000	4,050,000 - 4,990,000
• Distressing	5%	4% - 6%	1,190,000	930,000 - 1,450,000
• Aggressive	3%	2% - 4%	710,000	510,000 - 910,000
Unwanted Exposure to Sexual Material				
• Any	25%	23% - 27%	5,950,000	5,430,000 - 6,470,000
• Distressing	6%	5% - 7%	1,430,000	1,140,000 - 1,720,000
Harassment				
• Any	6%	5% - 7%	1,430,000	1,140,000 - 1,720,000
• Distressing	2%	1% - 3%	480,000	310,000 - 650,000

[1] Estimates and confidence intervals are based on an estimated number of 23,810,000 regular Internet users between the ages of 10 and 17.

How Many Youth Had Online Episodes?

Because this sample of youth was designed to be representative of all regular Internet users ages ten through seventeen in the U.S., it is tempting to try to translate percentages from this survey into actual numbers or population estimates. For example, the 19% of the sample who experienced a sexual solicitation or approach in the last year can be multiplied against our estimate that 23.81 million youth between ten and seventeen are regular Internet users to yield a population number of 4.52 million youth who might have had such an episode.

However, this precision can be somewhat misleading. Sample surveys have margins of error, which are described in scientific terms as "95% confidence intervals." These confidence intervals express the range of numbers within which the "true" number is likely to fall in 95 out of 100 attempts to estimate it with a sample of this size. So in this sample of 1501, it is 95% likely that the true number of youth experiencing a sexual solicitation or approach in the previous year falls in a range that could be almost half a million youth more or less than our estimate of 4.52 million. These ranges are provided for seven of the major episode types in Table Appendix A.2. Unfortunately, in this case the imprecision for such estimates is compounded by the fact that the figure for regular Internet users is **also** an estimate with its own margin of error (not calculated for this report) and not a number obtained from an actual census count.

Thus, because both the parameters needed to make a population estimate have large elements of imprecision and because population estimates can take on an aura of exactitude that is sometimes misleading, we have in this report followed the convention with most social scientific surveys of this size and reported the results primarily in terms of percentages (in this case of regular Internet users). We recommend this approach to other interpreters of this survey.

APPENDIX B. Definitions and Instrumentation

The aspects of youth online victimization that this study focused on were sexual solicitations and approaches, unwanted exposure to sexual materials, and harassment. The incidence rates for sexual solicitation, unwanted exposure to sexual materials, and harassment were estimated based on a series of screener questions about unwanted experiences while using the Internet. Two of the screeners concerned harassment, four involved unwanted exposure to sexual materials, three focused on sexual solicitation, and one asked if anyone online had encouraged the youth to run away from home. More extensive follow-up questions were asked about up to two of the unwanted incidents per youth, and these follow-up questions were used to classify the reported episodes further into the categories reported on in this chapter.

Follow-up questions were limited to only two reported incidents because of time constraints. Consequently, some incidents reported by young people were not followed up upon, and these were omitted from incidence rates. If a youth reported more than one incident in a particular category, the follow-up questions referred to the "most bothersome" incident or, if none was "most bothersome," the most recent incident. The limits on follow-up questions probably led to some undercounting of incidents, particularly episodes of unwanted exposure to sexual materials.

APPENDIX C. Limitations of the Study

Every scientific study has limitations and defects. Readers should keep some of these important things in mind when considering the findings and conclusions of this study:

1. We cannot be certain how candid our respondents were. Although we used widely accepted social science procedures, our interviews involved telephone conversations with young people on a sensitive subject, a factor that could easily result in less-than-complete candor.

2. The young people to whom we did not talk may be different from the youth we talked to. There were parents who refused to participate or refused to allow us to talk to their children, and there were youth who refused to participate, and those we could never reach. Our results might have been different if we had been able to talk to all these people.

Appendix D. Recommended Resource Materials

1. The National Center for Missing & Exploited Children (www.missingkids.org) provides materials and maintains an online reporting system, the CyberTipline, at www.cybertipline.com, for reporting online victimizations.

2. Federal Bureau of Investigation's Innocent Images Program: www.fbi.gov/hq/cid/cac/innocent. htm.

3. Information and Resources about the Commission on Online Child Protection (COPA): www.COPAcommission.org.

4. National Resource Council project on tools and strategies for protecting kids from pornography: http://www4.nas.edu/cpsma/cstb/itas.nsf.

5. Internet Safety Education for Parents and Youth: www.getnetwise.com.

6. CyberAngels: Internet Safety Organization: www.cyberangels.org.

Children as Victims of War and Terrorism

Judith A. Myers-Walls

SUMMARY. War and terrorism victimize all people in a country, group, or area, but disputes in recent decades are especially likely to impact children and families. Children can experience wars by being in the war zone, by being in countries that deploy military personnel to a war zone, by suffering from the consequences of military expenses and economic warfare, by experiencing war and terrorism from a distance through media, or by suffering from indoctrination and the building of enemy images. This paper reviews what researchers have discovered about the unique risks associated with each of those categories and recommends promising solutions. *[Article copies available for a fee from The Haworth Document Delivery Service: 1-800-HAWORTH. E-mail address: <docdelivery@haworth press.com> Website: <http://www.HaworthPress. com> © 2003 by The Haworth Press, Inc. All rights reserved.]*

KEYWORDS. Children, terrorism, war, peace, parents, military

War and terrorism victimize all people in a country, group, or area, but disputes in recent decades are especially likely to impact children and families. UNICEF (1986) estimated that 80% of the casualties in

---

Address correspondence to: Judith A. Myers-Walls, Child Development and Family Studies, Purdue University, Fowler Memorial House, 1200 West State Street, West Lafayette, IN 47907-2055 (E-mail: myerswal@cfs.purdue.edu).

[Haworth co-indexing entry note]: "Children as Victims of War and Terrorism." Myers-Walls, Judith, A. Co-published simultaneously in *Journal of Aggression, Maltreatment & Trauma* (The Haworth Maltreatment & Trauma Press, an imprint of The Haworth Press, Inc.) Vol. 8, No. 1/2 (#15/16), 2003, pp. 41-62; and: *The Victimization of Children: Emerging Issues* (ed: Janet L. Mullings, James W. Marquart, and Deborah J. Hartley) The Haworth Maltreatment & Trauma Press, an imprint of The Haworth Press, Inc., 2003, pp. 41-62. Single or multiple copies of this article are available for a fee from The Haworth Document Delivery Service [1-800-HAWORTH, 9:00 a.m. - 5:00 p.m. (EST). E-mail address: docdelivery@haworthpress.com].

http://www.haworthpress.com/web/JAMT
© 2003 by The Haworth Press, Inc. All rights reserved
Digital Object Identifier: 10.1300/J146v08n01_02

foreign wars were women and children. Some believe that this victimization is not accidental. "There is no doubt that in today's conflicts, children are targets, not incidental victims" (UNICEF, 1999a, p. 234). The terrorist acts of September 11, 2001, represented a different type of risk, however. Even though only a few children died or were injured in the incident, children all around the world were and are victims of fear, trauma, and confusion. Even when they are not at immediate physical risk, children, as the most dependent and vulnerable members of a society, feel the disruption, threat, loss, hatred, and fear connected with war and terrorism personally and have only limited coping strategies. This paper presents an overview of the ways that children can be victims of war, terrorism, and other political violence and summarizes some of the research that has addressed those situations.

Although war and terrorism are seen by some as separate phenomena, the distinction may be primarily a semantic one when the impact on children is considered. Whether a conflict is consider "war" or "terrorism" often depends on the perspective of the observer. What distinguishes war and terrorism from other kinds of violence, however, is their political nature and foundation in intergroup conflict. Ed Cairns (1996) uses the term "political violence" to encompass wars and terrorist activities along with civil disputes and inter-communal violence. The important differentiation to make when defining types of violence is between interpersonal and inter-group conflict. Some of this distinction can be traced to Henri Tajfel (1981), whose work with social identity theory highlighted the unique properties of conflicts among groups when compared to conflicts between individuals. Those unique properties are included in Cairns' definition of political violence as "violence perpetrated by one set or group of people on another set or group of people who were often strangers to each other before the violence occurred" (p. 10). Cairns' conceptualization suggests that the research on war, terrorism, and other political violence can be considered together as an interrelated body of work. Although countless volumes have been written addressing political violence, children have been almost invisible in that literature until recently.

HOW WAR AND TERRORISM IMPACT CHILDREN

Children can experience the victimization of war and terrorism at a number of levels. They can be in the war zone and be in direct, physical danger. They can be in countries or areas from which men and women–the parents, friends, and relatives of children–are sent into battle in another country or area. They can suffer from the consequences of military expenses and economic warfare. They may experience war and terrorism from a distance through the media and formal and informal instruction. Or they could suffer from the indoctrination and the building of enemy images. This paper will review what researchers have discovered about the unique risks associated with each of those categories and will recommend promising solutions.

Children in War Zones

In war zones, children may be killed or injured directly by hostilities or may be victims of mines and unexploded armaments, sometimes years after an active conflict has ended. UNICEF (1999a) has estimated that two million children have been killed in armed conflict in the past decade, and at least six million children have been seriously injured or permanently disabled as a result of war. As mentioned above, children are sometimes intended victims.

In addition to facing physical dangers, people in war zones find that life is disrupted and that the public sector breaks down (Cairns, 1996). This breakdown seems to be most difficult for families with limited resources (Armenian, 1989; Bryce, Walker, & Peterson, 1989), because "social class does not take a vacation in a war zone" (Garbarino, Kostelny, & Dubrow, 1991a, p. 150). Speaking of Yugoslavia in 1994, Andjelka Milic (2001) reported "the breakdown impacted the manufacturing sector, police, banks, insurance companies, health services, and trade" (p. 114). The result is that families in war zones lose their livelihoods and routines, and they find themselves needing to assume the functions of essential institutions; yet many families are themselves disrupted because members are in the military service, are displaced, have died, have abandoned the family, are abused, or are emotionally paralyzed. The disruption also seems to lead to an increase in accidents and other risks (Cairns, 1996).

The theme of disruption was central in comments by Serbian children shortly after the NATO bombing of Belgrade, Yugoslavia, in 1999 (Myers-Walls, Myers-Bowman, Walker, & Khosravi, 2000). Those children described war by saying things like, "Everything is destroyed–houses, flats, bridges, factories, cinemas, railroad tracks," and "You don't live as nice as you do in peace." The disruption of war was a central theme even when the parents of the Serbian children described peace. They used the disruption of war as a contrast to define peace: "[In peace] you can live normally, move normally, work; Children play without a care."

James Garbarino, Kathleen Kostelny, and Nancy Dubrow (1991b) have documented the impact on children in several regions that have been touched by war. They found that "today's wars are likely to put children in the front lines because there are no real front lines, only shifting zones of conflict" (p. 6). They speak of the outcomes of living with danger and the chronic threat of violent assault. In a war zone, people are in danger because of where they live, what groups they belong to, and how they are identified socially: "You are in jeopardy just because you are who you are when you happen to be the wrong person in the wrong place at the wrong time–all of the time" (p. 13). Growing up in a war zone disrupts attachment relationships and leads to emotional exhaustion because of the constant exposure to fear, hatred, and loss.

Some children even become perpetrators of political violence. They may be asked to serve the war effort in support roles as cooks, porters, messengers, spies, or lookouts (Azmon, 2001; UNICEF, 1999a). Girls may be recruited for sexual purposes. Some children are forcibly recruited into service, and others volunteer, although it is often difficult to distinguish between the two. This is because participation in an activity, whether voluntary or not at the beginning, tends to become internalized, and the child grows in commitment to the group (Bandura, 1990; Cairns, 1996; Staub, 1989). Several authors have outlined the process that is likely to be followed in converting children into warriors (Bandura, 1990; also see Cairns, 1996). Garbarino and his colleagues (1991b) have studied this phenomenon and report that the youth themselves may be brutalized and tortured and thus desensitized to brutality, and taught the lessons that anything is possible and that the unthinkable is thinkable. Then efforts are made to teach the young people that the "other side" is subhuman and/or evil. That indoctrination enables the young people to commit any atrocity against the enemy because they learn that enemy lives are of no value.

Even if the children are liberated from military servitude, reintegration can be very difficult. UNICEF (2001) arranged for testimony from one such child from Sierra Leone, Alhaji, who was kidnapped when he was ten years old. "We were trained for a week to shoot and dismantle AK47 guns. Thereafter I was used to fight when we were attacked." He killed people, burned down houses, destroyed property, and cut limbs. Even after being liberated from two years of forced service, "the community school children were not friendly to us. They kept calling us 'rebel children'" (UNICEF, 2001). This type of scenario is unfortunately a widespread problem. UNICEF worked in 2000 and 2001 with child soldiers in at least eight different areas: Sudan, Rwanda, Sri Lanka, Burkina Faso, Angola, Sierra Leone, Congo, and Uganda.

In an Optional Protocol to the Convention on the Rights of the Child on the Involvement of Children in Armed Conflict (UNICEF, 1999a), UNICEF expressed concerns about both direct and indirect participation of children and youth under eighteen in armed conflict. The original Convention on the Rights of the Child suggested that the minimum age for military service should be fifteen, but recent work has suggested that the age should be higher. UNICEF (1999a) stated in the draft Optional Protocol:

> In the view of the Committee, the involvement in hostilities of persons who have not attained the age of 18 is harmful for them physically and psychologically, and affects the full enjoyment of their fundamental rights. For this reason, it is the belief of the Committee that persons below 18 should never be involved in hostilities. (p. 219)

The committee suggested that this guideline should be applied both to forcing young people to participate and to the recruitment and voluntary enlistment of young people in the military. As of September 2002, 111 countries had signed the Optional Protocol, and 43 had ratified it. United Nations procedures require that ten ratifications are necessary for the document to enter into force, and this protocol met those qualifications in February of 2002 (UNICEF, 2003). (Note that the United States signed but did not ratify the Optional Protocol in July of 2000.)

In summary, the risks for children in war zones include the danger of injury and death, living with constant threat, the disruption of society in war zones, and the risk of being forced to fight in the war. As a result of these risks and their consequences, the United Nations recommends that no children under the age of eighteen should be combatants in war and encourages special attention to children living in war zones.

Children in Countries Sending Men and Women to War

Many of the soldiers going to war are parents. Although the vast majority of U.S. soldiers during the Vietnam War were single, two-thirds of today's soldiers are married (Axtman, 2001). In addition, there are many cases in which both husband and wife have enlisted in the military. Given these situations, military spouses and parents must prepare for sudden separation from their children with little or no warning before the conflict begins. They need to prepare for and then deal with single parenting, challenges related to childcare, reorientation of family lines of authority, and the stress and anxiety of knowing that at least one family member is or will be in danger. This often leads the remaining parents and children to experience an "anticipation of loss" (McCubbin, Dahl, & Hunter, 1976). Children prepare for and then watch as their parents leave home and family, and they usually have little idea where they are going or when or if they will return.

During World War II, researchers found that children were more damaged by the separation from parents or by the parents' and other relatives' own reactions to stress than by the situation itself (Carlsmith, 1973; Freud & Burlingham, 1943). Other authors have concluded that the impact of war on children is minimized if the children remain in close contact with their most important attachment figures (Punamaki, 1987). A book of diaries of children in war zones reveals some of children's feelings about family members going to war. A twelve-year-old Dutch child whose father was fighting in World War II said, "I said a prayer for Father and I hope God heard it in spite of all the noise" (Holliday, 1999, p. 34).

In recent years, some researchers have found that military separations have resulted in reduced employment rates for women, probably because of childcare challenges, and they have also found increased divorce rates after deployment, especially if it was the woman who was deployed (Angrist & Johnson, 1998). In addition, some families are forced to deal with losses related to death or injury. Unfortunately, there is very little good information about how children deal with the death of family members during war. In the absence of better data, it is reasonable to conclude that these stresses and losses impact spouses, children, and parents. Their reactions are complicated by the simultaneous but conflicting emotions of pride, resentment, and longing for the family member to return. Families also face the myriad public attitudes, assumptions, and disagreements associated with the war.

Families need to face the fact that their loved ones not only are at risk of becoming victims of aggression but also may commit that aggression themselves. They may even face the possibility of defining young children as dangerous enemies and may make them targets. Yael Azmon (2001) explored these issues in her examination of some of the public discourse during the Intifada in Israel from 1982 to 1993. She described a situation that was reported in the media in which a young girl, dressed in pink and approximately five years old, appeared to be directing the movement of the military by reporting who was coming and going. The dilemma was whether the soldiers on lookout should target the little girl or not. While some parents of young soldiers responded with letters to their sons saying that they wanted them to shoot in similar situations so that they would come home alive, another responded by saying, "I live in constant fear that the living body of my son will return home and inside it are extinguished sensitivities which died in the war of the stone against the bullet" (Azmon, 2001, p. 174). After the soldiers return home, friends and family members need to deal with the difficulties of reintegrating individuals who have changed, in part because they have witnessed horrors and faced the unthinkable (Hogancamp & Figley, 1983).

In summary, children are faced with risks when their family members and friends–and especially their parents–are deployed to military duty. The children face uncertainty and secrecy, separation from parents, potential losses due to injury or death of loved ones, the stress experienced by the remaining family members, and the dilemmas of mixed feelings and political disagreements.

Children and Military Funding and Expenses

Children who are not in the line of fire may still be victims of the fiscal choices taken by opposing nations or by their own countries to support the war efforts. UNICEF (1999a) reports that "thousands of children are killed every year as a direct result of fighting, from knife wounds, bullets, bombs and landmines, but many more die from malnutrition and disease caused by armed conflicts" (p. 239). Although some people believe that war is good for an economy, Melman (1982) called that the "guns-create-butter" myth. For example, the economic sanctions directed toward Iraq after the Persian Gulf War are said to have hit children especially hard. Anthony Arnove (2000) has pointed out that the current sanctions target the weakest and most vulnerable members of Iraqi society, including the elderly, the infirm, and the children. Many Iraqi children have died in the past decade because of the restrictions on the importing of medicines, food, and other necessities. In August 1999, UNICEF (1999b) reported that the under-five mortality rate had doubled since 1990 and that the sanctions were significantly to blame for that rise. In addition, the sanctions had disrupted the health, growth, and development of surviving children because of the blockading of pencils, computer equipment, spare parts, and air-conditioned trucks, items that are necessary to conduct everyday life. At the time of the writing of this document, those sanctions were still in force as the U.S. contemplated an attack on Iraq.

The sanctions have had an economic impact not only on Iraq, but also on the United States. It has been estimated that hundreds of millions of dollars have been spent each year just on monitoring Iraqi imports and exports, maintaining the no-fly zone, and supporting a military presence in the region (Myers, 1999). The increases in U.S. military spending being proposed at the time of this writing in response to the attacks of September 11, 2001, will make it more difficult to meet the needs of education and health care in the U.S. and other countries during a time of an economic downturn.

Costa Rica is a country that has made the decision not to have a standing army, and that decision seems to have had significant benefits for children and families. Although the social outcomes are difficult to connect directly to the lack of an army, it is interesting to note comparisons between Costa Rica and Nicaragua, a neighbor with a history of major military commitments. While Costa Rica's infant mortality rate is 10.87/1000 and life expectancy is 78.89 years, Nicaragua's figures are 32.52/1000 and 69.37 years. The literacy rate in Costa Rica is over 95% compared to 68% in Nicaragua (Central Intelligence Agency, 2002). It seems that Costa Rica has made resources available for health and education rather than military efforts.

> UNICEF (1999a) has addressed the need to monitor military expenditures: Governments should honour the commitments made at the World Summit on Social Development to support the concept of human security. Toward that end, firm action is required to shift the allocation of resources from arms and military expenditures to human and social development. (p. 255)

In conclusion, the military-related fiscal choices made by countries create additional situations in which children may suffer. Economic sanctions punish children first, and high economic expenditures by countries limit the resources available to support the care and education of children and their families.

Children as Observers of War and Terrorism

Children need not be near a war zone to feel its impact. They learn about events by experiencing media and by sensing and observing the reactions of the adults in their lives. Modern mass media carry news of armed conflicts around the world in seconds. That news may come complete with vivid images and sounds or may be sanitized and controlled. This "reality violence" began with the coverage of the Vietnam

War in the 1960s and has continued since that time (McCleneghan, 2002).

Researchers have reported that this televised violence frightens many children. Approximately one-third of children of elementary age in the U.S. and Europe have reported that they have been frightened or upset by a news story on television (Cantor & Nathanson, 1996; Valkenburg, Cantor, & Peeters, 2000). Older children in this age range respond especially strongly to violence between strangers and foreign wars.

Because the flow of information is often indirect, there are many opportunities for confusion and misunderstandings among children. Some children have difficulty knowing the difference between reality and fantasy in the media. This aspect of children's understanding of news media impact has not been explored in detail by researchers, but an example of such confusion appeared in a report in the Asian edition of *Wall Street Journal* after the terrorist attacks of 2001. This story documented the experience of an eight-year-old child in the international school in Hong Kong. On September 12, 2001, he said that he was tired because he stayed up late watching a movie and wanted to see how it ended–the movie of a plane crashing into a building (Voigt, 2001). A parent reported to the author of this chapter that a five-year-old became confused by the news shortly after the terrorist attacks, because he was not familiar with the word "hijacker." He did know the word "kayaker," though, and was concerned about the safety of the boaters on the river.

The media saturation can also lead children to feel vulnerable, no matter how far away from the war they are. This exposure can lead to what one reporter called the "mean world syndrome" (Lowry, 2002). Others have said the exposure can teach the viewer that the world is a dangerous place (Hesse, 1989).

Fear is a major and intentional outcome of war and terrorism. Even though the actual fighting of the Persian Gulf War in the early 1990s was taking place halfway around the world, U.S. children reported a variety of feelings in response (Myers-Walls, 1991, 1992). They spoke of very graphic fears and nightmares after that conflict, including thinking the "war planes" were flying over their school, people were breaking into their houses, and their parents were taken away from their families. More than 73% of the children reported fear and worry. The second most common response reported by the children was anger (44%), and the third was sadness (32%). The parents of those children agreed; they reported that "worry about the war coming to the U.S." was present for over one-fourth of their children, making it the most common response for both parents and children, but the parents reported a much lower level. The second most common child reaction reported by the parents was worry about people in general or people they did not know (22%). Increased pride in the U.S. and patriotism was reported almost as often (18%). The parents did not recognize the anger or sadness of the children, although they did note the concern about people they did not know. The children never mentioned the patriotism that was listed by the parents. So it appears that children had a number of reactions to the media reports of the conflict that their parents did not recognize. In addition, parents also tended to misread some of the children's reactions.

Fear of war and destruction was a major theme in research with children and war in the 1970s and 1980s. The Cold War dominated the news, and half of the children in some studies believed a war would come (Berger Gould, Moon, & Van Hoorn, 1986; Schwebel, 1965). The fear of terrorism may today replace the fear of nuclear war in the lives of children. Those fears impact mental health:

> Wars, hot or cold, . . . give rise to social problems that are incontrovertibly related to individual behavior. They influence morality and hence interpersonal relations; they shake security and thus shape perceptions of the social scheme and expectations for the future . . . An insecure world is bound to take its toll of health. (Schwebel, 1965, p. 119)

In summary, because they are bombarded with media images and the reactions of people around them, even children who are far from active hostilities are at risk for stress and despair. There can be significant impact on the mental and emotional health of children around the world.

Children and Enemy Images

Even with no contact with the war zone or the news of it and even when no armed conflict is taking place, children can be victims of the rhetoric and the building of an enemy image that accompany international tensions. This indoctrination can be a major problem in war zones as well, of course. Children are not born knowing enemies. As Petra Hesse (1989) argues, "We go through a long and subtle process of political and ideological education in childhood and adolescence during which we learn to identify the heroes and villains in our own country and in international politics" (p. 1). Some authors have presented this process as a balance between the "tribal" and the "global" (Azmon, 2001). Do people focus on the needs and protection of those who belong to the "tribe," or do they focus on the needs and protection of all people? If the focus is the "tribe," how is membership determined? Children are likely to be able to outline these prejudices before they can understand them and their implications.

Children learn from an early age what an enemy or "bad guy" is. They describe him (and it is often a male) as "dirty," "stupid," or "terrible" (Povrzanovic, 1997). This "training" takes place even in the toys and entertainment directed at children (Hesse, 1989; Vriens, 1999). One teenager from Northern Ireland reflected on the frustrations of dealing with the hatred and mixed messages that accompany this process of creating enemy images:

> There's always the 'them' and 'us' factor. Why should religion have to matter? . . . From an early age we are taught that it is not what is outside a person but what is inside that counts. Why does this not seem to matter where religion is concerned? (Holliday, 1999, p. 204)

Painting a population as the enemy holds dangers both for the hater and the object of hate. Children who are taught to hate may carry that hatred for a very long time. Andjelka Milic (2001), a Serbian, described some of the pain and shame that came with her nation's being portrayed as evil. She felt that she would no longer be included as part of the academic community, even though she had been a respected sociologist: "After all, I was from Belgrade, Serbia. That was a country and people all the world media declared as criminals, warmongers and primitives" (p. 116). If this is the reaction of an educated adult, how will children respond?

Many children ask the question, "Why do they hate us?" That question, in fact, is the title of the book of stories and diaries from children in war zones assembled by Laurel Holliday (1999) and also the theme of several media reports in the U.S. after the terrorist attacks of September 2001. Some authors have warned that the enemy image may become a central part of a person's understanding of self: "[T]hose raised in the greatest conflict . . . have organized their self-definitions (identity) around participation in the conflict" (Elbedour, Bastien, & Center, 1997, p. 227). In other words, children in areas of high conflict may decide who they are by comparing themselves to those they hate. In fact, they may feel that they do not have an identity without an enemy. A danger is that the hatred that is built in the child's early years could continue throughout the person's lifetime.

Garbarino and colleagues have reported that the ability to find meaning in a difficult situation is one important method of survival, but that it
can have significant costs when one deals with war and terrorism. It may
"set in motion the dark forces of the human spirit . . . The same ideology
that gives meaning to life in a war zone may also lead to a process of de-
humanization" (Garbarino et al., 1991b, p. 22). The result of this building
of an enemy image is the prolongation of wars and conflicts.

In conclusion, enemy images and hatred of the "other" can color a
child's thinking for many years or even a lifetime. Those labels and
emotions can also make continued war and conflict more likely.

REDUCING THE RISKS OF WAR AND TERRORISM
FOR CHILDREN

What can be done to reduce the various risks for children from war
and terrorism? There is a huge literature on child coping and resilience,
but only a very small amount deals with children and political violence.
Lösel and Bliesener (1990) listed several characteristics or conditions
that seem to be associated with children's survival in the face of stressful early experience. The list presented by these authors also is not entirely adequate for the situation at hand, but it provides some helpful
guidance and is consistent with the recommendations made by many
other authors. The Lösel and Bliesener list includes taking action to
cope rather than just reacting; being of at least average intelligence;
having a sense of self-esteem and personal power; having a stable emotional relationship with at least one parent; being in an open, supportive,
educational environment; and receiving social support from people outside the family. It is clear that these assets are in short supply in war
zones, but any attempt to recover them is likely to have significant benefits for children in those settings. This list of assets can also be helpful
to consider for children experiencing war and its consequences from a
distance.

Certainly the most effective strategy for supporting children and protecting them from the ravages of war and terrorism would be to reduce
the prevalence of international armed conflict. Realizing that this is not
a likely or easy solution, it cannot be ignored that most of the negative
outcomes of political conflict would be eliminated if children were not
recruited or accepted in the military, if their parents were not sent to
war zones, or if military expenditures were redirected to peaceful purposes. If governments and ethnic, political, religious, or regional groups

would decide that using violence to solve their differences is not acceptable, the very long-term, devastating effects on children would be eliminated.

In lieu of the abolition of war, however, there are steps that can be taken to help children and families deal with the stresses that are associated with armed conflicts and to lessen the likelihood that they will occur. These recommendations are derived from the literature related to child coping and resilience and on the research regarding children and political violence cited above. It is important to note that most of that research has investigated children and families in the Americas and Europe.

Listening and Talking to Children

As mentioned above, studies have shown that all but the youngest children have some awareness of war and have some reactions to it, even if they are far from the war zone (Myers-Bowman, Walker, & Myers-Walls, 2000). Children know that war is something very unpleasant, and they may react to even the idea of war with fears, nightmares, and worries. The common child response to traumatic events is not the same as the adult response, however. War is likely to affect both children and adults, but children often react to trauma by trying to return to normal as soon as possible. They find comfort in routine. The danger is that adults may misread this reaction and think that the children are not impacted by the events or that they have recovered from them very quickly. So the adults may not communicate with the children about the traumatic event, trying instead to avoid bringing up a subject that they believe is not an issue for the children and that is uncomfortable for the adults. When the children see that the adults are not talking about the issue, they assume that it is not acceptable to discuss it. These misunderstandings set up a sort of cycle of silence, and neither children nor their caregivers adequately cope with the trauma within the family (Dyregrov, 1998; Jacobs, 1988). Adults need to be approachable, sensitive, and responsive in order to avoid this cycle.

As Lösel and Bliesener (1990) and Punamaki (1987) noted, a good relationship with parents or other supportive adults is important for children to survive in the wake of traumatic experiences. If parents need to be sensitive, observant, supportive, and communicative to avoid the cycle of silence, it is logical to conclude that it may not be possible for children to survive or thrive when faced with war and terrorism unless the needs of their parents and other caregivers are also met. As is true for many other experiences (for example, divorce, death, and parental employment), children are likely to cope as well or as poorly as their parents or caregivers (National Institute of Mental Health [NIMH], 2001). So to meet the needs of children, support services should be provided to parents as well as children so that they can fulfill their roles as supporters and caregivers of their children. This is especially true in regions of active conflict where normal services are disrupted. Where families are divided and parents are not present, other caregivers must be available to the children as attachment figures and confidantes.

When children do talk about the conflict, they need to know not only that they can feel safe and comfortable to talk, but also that they can get information and clarification (Lösel & Bliesener, 1990; NIMH, 2001). Because the issues and vocabulary related to international and intercommunal conflicts are complex and confusing, it is very common for children to have misunderstandings. In many cases, they may be unnecessarily afraid, or they may reach inaccurate conclusions. The euphemisms and slang terms used by adults, such as "friendly fire," "collateral damage," and "smart bombs" can be very confusing to children, who are likely to interpret those terms literally. It is a real benefit for children to be able to share their thoughts, reactions, and questions with adults who care about them.

Some kinds of communication are especially important. For example, it is critical that parents and other adults provide training and background in media literacy so that children can decipher and interpret the messages they receive (Heins & Chow, 2002). Because children feel vulnerable in the face of war and terrorism, it is also important for adults to provide some level of reassurance and safety. It is difficult, however, for adults to reassure children when the parents also feel at risk and are not sure that they or their children really are safe. In times of insecurity and threat (or at any time, for that matter), adults cannot guarantee that there will be no dangerous consequences for the children. It is important, however, that the parents reassure the children in a realistic and honest way. Adults will not be able to promise that nothing bad will ever happen or that the child will always be safe. However, they may be able to say that the adults who care about the children the most will do everything they can to keep the children safe. They can assure the children that the parents' love will be with them, no matter what happens. This is also an appropriate time for parents who have an identified religious faith to share their faith and their beliefs about a higher power or force and its presence and protection.

Recognizing the Complexity of Children's Responses

It is sensible to think that children's primary responses to war and terrorism–whether they experience the conflict directly or indirectly–would be dominated by fear and anxiety. That outcome was confirmed in the study conducted by Myers-Walls and colleagues of U.S. children aged three to twelve after the Persian Gulf War (Myers-Walls, 1991, 1992). The study seems to indicate that children's reactions to international conflicts are not as simple or self-focused as some adults assume. If the only presumed reaction is fear, then reassurance from adults should be sufficient support. The reactions of sadness and anger and the concern about the well-being of other people, however, suggest that children have additional needs. They need to have an opportunity to grapple with the inherent unfairness of war and the reality of violent human conflict. This requirement can be very difficult for adults themselves to face, especially if they are also traumatized by the situation or if they are unsure about their own positions. But adults who do tackle the issues and try to unravel the complexities of conflict and violence may actually find their own awareness and sensibility raised, and therefore they can play a role in making such violence less likely in the future. As Hungarian author Péter Somlai (2001) concludes, "Children's naïve questions become the nagging conscience of an adult society which has lost sight of its values" (p. 21).

Allowing Children to Be Actors

Children can be victims of war and terrorism at many different levels. Viewing children only as victims is not an entirely fair or helpful approach, however. War and terrorism are huge, challenging situations, and children are not in control of the overall outcome. Kathleen Walker (2002) found, however, that even some children in a war zone felt empowered to make peace. Lösel and Bliesener (1990) listed taking action as a central coping strategy. Some children do feel out of control and helpless in war situations, and those who do feel that way will feel the stress more acutely (Norris, Byrne, Diaz, & Kaniasty, 2002). Others, however, feel empowered to take some kind of action, and some experts recommend that helping children feel in control of some aspect of the situation is a central management strategy (NIMH, 2001). Some researchers have found that many children "see themselves as active agents, and this image of themselves and their state is more salient for them than as vulnerable victims in need of protection, or as requiring services" (Taylor, Smith, & Nairn, 2001, p. 32). As Walker (2002) quoted a nine-year-old boy as saying, "We might be a big influence, since kids are the main thing that motivates humans" (p. 101).

Parents and other adults can support this desire for involvement by helping children find actions that they would like to take. Children have indicated an interest in everything from public demonstrations and media efforts to trying to be peaceful with friends to talking to their parents about war and peace. Many children seem to be more comfortable with direct interpersonal actions than with larger-scale activities. Some studies have shown that even college students who have completed peace studies courses are more likely to apply the learning to their own lives than to try to address militarism or war on an international scale (Eckhardt, 1984; Harris, 1995). Young people's desire for "participation rights" (Tayor et al., 2001) dictates that parents should not feel responsible for making choices about activities for their children. It suggests that the children need opportunities themselves to identify and choose activities that will help them gain a sense of efficacy and power. However, parents can facilitate children's contact with and awareness of opportunities and approaches for making a difference in the world and putting their beliefs in action (Haessley & Myers-Walls, 2001; Myers-Walls, 2001).

Parents also have responsibility for modeling action by taking action themselves. Children will not understand how to be active forces in the world or learn to value such action if their parents or other mentors do not demonstrate that approach. Parents and children also can take action together. There are indications that parents who attempt to improve the world may increase the sense of hope in their children that the world can be better. Those parents tell the children that it is worthwhile to try to effect change. Hope is one of the most valuable gifts that children can receive from their parents.

Teaching Peacemaking Skills

In order to make war and terrorism less prevalent in the future and thereby protect children, the next generation of children will need the opportunity to learn alternatives to violence. This is also another way to take action. Children who feel that they know other alternatives besides violence may feel less victimized in difficult situations. Studies have shown that teaching conflict resolution and related peacemaking strategies increases resilience in children and improves their social and emotional competency and academic performance. It also has a positive impact on school climate (Bodine & Crawford, 1998; Jones & Kmitta, 2000; Sandy & Cochran, 2000).

Many of the aforementioned studies involve school programs led by teachers or other facilitators. Parents can also provide a teaching and modeling environment that is more likely to lead to peace and nonviolence than to supporting war and terrorism. Judith Myers-Walls and Karen Myers-Bowman (1999) have argued that this approach to nonviolent parenting could be called Socially Conscious Parenting and deserves consideration as an alternative school of thought in parenting education. Socially Conscious Parenting, as they define it, includes the following characteristics: awareness and sharing of power, nurturance and empathy, communication skills, responsibility and empowerment, problem-solving and conflict resolution, connections and personal impact, and hope and commitment to the future. Materials that can be classified as Socially Conscious Parenting have been said to include "(a) a clear statement of values and beliefs, (b) a focus on and interaction with the larger social context and environment, and (c) a commitment to social action and change" (p. 78). Other authors have talked about a similar approach called Parenting for Peace and Justice (McGinnis & McGinnis, 1990).

To help parents learn peacemaking skills, parenting educators will need preparation in those methods. They may need help to learn both the philosophy and techniques for communicating the values and methods to parents. High quality evaluation studies of the teaching approaches are also necessary. It is critical to help educators and parents recognize that parenting is more that just managing children's behavior; it is also passing on values and shaping the future world.

Studying the Effects of War and Terrorism

In spite of the demonstrated impact on children of war, the threat of war, and losses related to war, and in spite of the need to identify effective intervention strategies to help both children and their parents overcome the related traumas, there is only minimal research attention to war, terrorism, and children. One reason for that shortage is the difficulty of conducting research in war zones in which transportation, communication, and even electrical power and water may be disrupted. Researchers in war zones may have a commitment to and interest in the outcome of such research; they themselves are often traumatized and may have lost the resources and connections necessary to function as social scientists (Milic, 2001), or the ethical dilemmas of doing such research may have raised insurmountable barriers (Cairns, 1996). Other researchers in war zones who have found the ability and resources to conduct research have concentrated on political and economic issues and have not seen the need for attention to the children and their experiences.

The National Center for Post-Traumatic Stress Disorder reviewed 177 articles on the effects of natural and human-caused disasters and listed very few that dealt with children or war and terrorism (Hamblen, 2002). The studies used 130 different research samples that included over 50,000 individuals, but only 9% of those articles addressed mass violence (a category including, but apparently larger than, war and terrorism). Other articles considered natural disasters (62%) and technological disasters (29%). A mere 16% of the studies in any of the categories dealt with children or youth. Although information on these issues is sorely needed, it is in short supply.

Some of the few studies that have been conducted are cited in this manuscript. Further studies are needed that include information gathered from children directly, studies of children from countries or factions on multiple sides of conflicts, outcome studies assessing the effectiveness of interventions, and studies that include the family context. Clearly, parents are critical to the coping of children, but they have very seldom been included in studies.

Researchers should be encouraged to address this shortage and should be given support to do so. Funding that can be garnered to support research with a very fast response period in a time of war or conflict is especially lacking but important.

CONCLUSION

War and terrorism are tragic forces. Children are especially likely to fall victim to the indoctrination, trauma, confusion, and fatal consequences of these conflicts. Professionals, families, and the public could choose to despair in the shadow of the overwhelming issues. Or they could choose to take action. That action could be conducting research and discovering new information. Some may choose to help families deal with the stress and trauma of war and terrorism, and others may work to lead nations and factions to consider alternatives to violence. The form of action is probably less important than the fact that action of some kind is taken.

REFERENCES

Angrist, J. D., & Johnson, J. H. (1998). Effects of work-related absences on families: Evidence from the Gulf War. *National Bureau of Economic Research, Working Paper 6679.*

Armenian, H. K. (1989). Perceptions from epidemiological research in an endemic war. *Social Science and Medicine, 28*(7), 643-7.

Arnove, A. (Ed.). (2000). *Iraq under siege: The deadly impact of sanctions and war.* Cambridge: South End Press.

Axtman, K. (2001, October 4). Military bases get families ready for war. *Christian Science Monitor.* Retrieved January, 2002, from http://www.csmonitor.com/2001/1004/p3s1-usmi.htm.

Azmon, Y. (2001). War, mothers, and a girl with braids: Involvement of mothers' peace groups in the national discourse in Israel. In J. A. Myers-Walls, P. Somlai, & R. Rapoport (Eds.), *Families as educators for global citizenship* (pp. 165-176). Aldershot: Ashgate.

Bandura, A. (1990). Mechanisms of moral disengagement. In W. Reich (Ed.), *Origins of terrorism: Psychologies, ideologies, theologies, states of mind* (pp. 161-191). New York: Cambridge University Press.

Berger Gould, B., Moon, S., & Van Hoorn, J. (Eds.). (1986). *Growing up scared? The psychological effect of the nuclear threat on children.* Berkley, CA: Open Books.

Bodine, R., & Crawford, D. (1998). *The handbook of conflict resolution education: A guide to building quality programs in schools.* San Francisco: Jossey-Bass.

Bryce, J. W., Walker, N., & Peterson, C. (1989). Predicting symptoms of depression among women in Beirut: The importance of daily life. *International Journal of Mental Health, 18*(1), 57-70.

Cairns, E. (1996). *Children and political violence.* Cambridge, MA: Blackwell.

Cantor, J., & Nathanson, A. I. (1996). Children's fright reactions to television news. *Journal of Communication, 46*(4), 139-152.

Carlsmith, L. (1973). Some personality characteristics of boys separated from their fathers during World War II. *Win, 1,* 466-477.

Central Intelligence Agency. (2002). *The world factbook 2002.* Retrieved January 10, 2003, from http://www.odci.gov/cia/publications/factbook/geos/cs.html and http://www.odci.gov/cia/publications/factbook/geos/nu.html.

Dyregrov, A. (1998, November). *The worst memory in my head: Families and war.* Plenary delivered at the annual conference of the National Council of Family Relations, Milwaukee, WI.

Eckhardt, W. (1984). Peace studies and attitude change: A value theory of peace studies. *Peace and Change, 4*(1), 6-71.

Elbedour, S., Bastien, D. T., & Center, B. A. (1997). Identity formation in the shadow of conflict: Projective drawings by Palestinian and Israeli Arab children from the West Bank and Gaza. *Journal of Peace Research, 34*(2), 217-231.

Freud, A., & Burlingham, D. (1943). *War and children.* New York: Medical War Books.

Garbarino, J., Kostelny, K., & Dubrow, N. (1991a). What can children tell us about living in danger. *American Psychologist, 46*(4, April), 376-83.

Garbarino, J., Kostelny, K., & Dubrow, N. (1991b). *No place to be a child: Growing up in war zone.* Lexington, MA: D.C. Heath and Company.

Haessley, J., & Myers-Walls, J. A. (2001). Religion, spirituality, and the family: Challenges for global citizenship. In J. A. Myers-Walls, & P. Somlai, with R. N. Rapoport (Eds.), *Families as educators for global citizenship* (pp. 177-190). Aldershot: Ashgate.

Hamblen, J. (2002). *Terrorist attacks and children.* National Center for Post-Traumatic Stress Disorder. Retrieved January 10, 2003, from http://www.ncptsd.org/facts/disasters/fs_children_disaster.html.

Harris, I. (1995). Teachers' response to conflict in selected Milwaukee schools. In H. Ledgren (Ed.), *Peace education and human development* (pp. 197-219). Lund, Sweden: Department of Educational and Psychological Research.

Heins, M., & Chow, C. (2002). *Media literacy: Alternative to censorship.* New York: Free Expression Policy Project.

Hesse, P. (1989). *The world is a dangerous place: Images of the enemy on children's television.* Cambridge, MA: Harvard University Center for Psychological Studies in the Nuclear Age.

Hogancamp, V. E., & Figley, C. R. (1983). War: Bringing the battle home. In C. R. Figley, & H. I. McCubbin (Eds.), *Stress in the family: Volume II: Coping with catastrophe* (pp. 148-165). New York: Brunner/Mazel.

Holliday, L. (1999). *Why do they hate me? Young lives caught in war and conflict.* New York: Pocket Books.

Jacobs, J. B. (1988). Families facing the nuclear taboo. *Family Relations, 37,* 432-6.

Jones, T. S., & Kmitta, D. (2000). *Does it work? The case for conflict resolution education in our nation's schools.* Washington, D.C.: Conflict Resolution Education Network (CREnet).

Lösel, R., & Bliesener, T. (1990). Resilience in adolescence: A study on the generalizability of protective factors. In K. Hurrelmann, & F. Lösel (Eds.), *Health hazards in adolescence* (pp. 299-320). New York: Walter de Gruter.

Lowry, B. (2002, October 16). Newscasts too often employ scare tactics. *Los Angeles Times.* Retrieved January 10, 2003, from http://www.childrennow.org/newsroom/news-02/cam-ra-10-16-02.htm.

McCleneghan, J. S. (2002). "Reality violence" on TV news: It began with Vietnam. *Social Science Journal, 39*(4), 593-598.

McCubbin, H. I., Dahl, B. B., & Hunter, E. J. (1976). *Families in the military system.* Beverly Hills, CA: Sage.

McGinnis, K., & McGinnis, J. (1990). *Parenting for peace and justice.* Maryknoll, NY: Orbis.

Melman, S. (1982). Teaching about reversing the arms race. *Teachers College Record, 84*(1), 38-49.

Milic, A. (2001). Reflections from a war zone: A partial essay and memorial tribute. In J. A. Myers-Walls, P. Somlai, & R. Rapoport (Eds.), *Families as educators for global citizenship* (pp. 113-116). Aldershot: Ashgate.

Myers, S. L. (1999, August 13). In intense but little-noticed fight, allies have bombed Iraq all year. *New York Times*, p. A6.

Myers-Bowman, K. S., Walker, K., & Myers-Walls, J. A. (2000, November). *Children's reactions to international conflict: A cross-cultural analysis.* Poster presented at the annual meeting of the National Council on Family Relations, Minneapolis, MN.

Myers-Walls, J. A. (1991, November). *Parents, children, and the Persian Gulf War.* Presented as part of the symposium Operation Desert Storm: Impact on the Home Front, National Council on Family Relations, Denver, CO.

Myers-Walls, J. A. (1992, January). *Parents, children, and the fear of war: Emphasis on the Persian Gulf War.* Presented at "Family: Resources and Responsibilities in a Changing World," Seminar and Conference: Preparing for International Year of the Family at Family Life Education for Peace, University of Peace, Costa Rica.

Myers-Walls, J. A. (2001). The parents' role in educating about war and peace. In J. A. Myers-Walls, P. Somlai, & R. Rapoport (Eds.), *Families as educators for global citizenship* (pp. 191-202). Aldershot: Ashgate.

Myers-Walls, J. A., & Myers-Bowman, K. S. (1999). Sorting through parenting education resources: Values and the example of socially conscious parenting. *Family Science Review, 12*(2), 69-86.

Myers-Walls, J. A., Myers-Bowman, K. S., Walker, K., & Khosravi, R. (2000, November). *Passing on the peace: Parents and children describe war and peace.* Paper presented at the annual meeting of the National Council on Family Relations, Minneapolis, MN.

National Institute of Mental Health. (2001). *Helping children and adolescents cope with violence and disasters.* Bethesda, MD: National Institutes of Mental Health (NIH Publication No. 01-3518).

Norris, F. H., Byrne, C. M., Diaz, E., & Kaniasty, K. (2002). *The range, magnitude, and duration of effects of natural and human-caused disasters: A review of the empirical literature.* National Center for Post-Traumatic Stress Disorder. Retrieved January 10, 2003, from http://www.ncptsd.org/facts/disasters/fs_range.html.

Povrzanovic, M. (1997). Children, war and nation: Croatia 1991-4. *Childhood, 4*(1), 81-102.

Punamaki, R. L. (1987). *Childhood under conflict: The attitudes and emotional life of Israeli and Palestinian children.* Tampere: Tampere Peace Research Institute, Research Reports.

Sandy, S. V., & Cochran, K. M. (2000). Conflict resolution: From early childhood to adolescence. In M. Deutsch, & P. T. Coleman (Eds.), *The handbook of constructive conflict resolution: Theory and practice* (pp. 316-342). San Francisco: Jossey-Bass.

Schwebel, M. (1965). Effects of the nuclear threat on children and teenagers: Implications for professionals. *American Journal of Orthopsychiatry, 52*, 608-618.

Somlai, P. (2001). Global citizenship: An essay on its contradictions. In J. A. Myers-Walls, P. Somlai, & R. Rapoport (Eds.), *Families as educators for global citizenship* (pp. 13-22). Aldershot: Ashgate.

Staub, E. (1989). *The roots of evil: The origins of genocide and other group violence.* New York: Cambridge University Press.

Tajfel, H. (1981). *Human groups and social categories.* Cambridge: Cambridge University Press.

Taylor, H., Smith, A. B., & Nairn, K. (2001). *Rights important to young people: Secondary student and staff perspectives*. Denedin, New Zealand: University of Otago Press.

UNICEF. (1986, March 10). *Children in situations of armed conflict*. New York: Author.

UNICEF. (1999a). *Children in conflict*. New York: UNICEF Staff Working Paper EPP-99-001.

UNICEF. (1999b, August 12). *Iraq survey shows 'humanitarian emergency.'* UNICEF, press release (Cf/doc/pr/1999/29).

UNICEF. (2001). *Security council meeting on children and armed conflict*. UNICEF. Retrieved January 10, 2003, from http://www.unicef.org/exspeeches/01espalhaji.htm.

UNICEF. (2003). *Optional protocols to the convention on the rights of the child*. UNICEF. Retrieved January 10, 2003, from http://www.unicef.org/crc/oppro.htm/.

Valkenburg, P. M., Cantor, J., & Peeters, A. L. (2000). Fright reactions to television–A child survey. *Communication Research, 27*(1), 82-99.

Voigt, K. (2001, September 21). Talking to kids about tragedy. *The Asian Wall Street Journal*, W3.

Vreins, L. (1999). Children, war, and peace. In A. Raviv, L. Oppenheimer, & D. Bar-Tal (Eds.), *How children understand war and peace* (27-58). San Francisco: Jossey-Bass.

Walker, K. K. (2002). *Peace starts with a "P": Parents' and children's perceptions of peace*. Unpublished doctoral dissertation, Kansas State University.

No Safe Place:
Assessing Spatial Patterns
of Child Maltreatment Victimization

Derek J. Paulsen

SUMMARY. Little is known about spatial patterns of child maltreatment. The purpose of this exploratory research is to analyze the spatial patterns of child maltreatment victimization and their ecological causes. Specifically, this research seeks to determine the answer to three important questions regarding the spatial nature of child maltreatment victimization: First, are child maltreatment victimizations concentrated within certain parts of a city? Second, are there different spatial patterns for child abuse, child neglect, and juvenile assault victimization locations? Finally, how well does ecological theory explain the incidence of child abuse, child neglect, and juvenile assault victimization at the neighborhood level? *[Article copies available for a fee from The Haworth Document Delivery Service: 1-800-HAWORTH. E-mail address: <docdelivery@haworth press.com> Website: <http://www.HaworthPress.com> © 2003 by The Haworth Press, Inc. All rights reserved.]*

KEYWORDS. Child abuse, child neglect, spatial analysis, ecological theory

---

Address correspondence to: Derek J. Paulsen, Department of Criminal Justice and Police Studies, Eastern Kentucky University, Stratton 467, 521 Lancaster Avenue, Richmond, KY 40475-3102 (E-mail: Derek.Paulsen@eku.edu).

[Haworth co-indexing entry note]: "No Safe Place: Assessing Spatial Patterns of Child Maltreatment Victimization." Paulsen, Derek J. Co-published simultaneously in *Journal of Aggression, Maltreatment & Trauma* (The Haworth Maltreatment & Trauma Press, an imprint of The Haworth Press, Inc.) Vol. 8, No. 1/2 (#15/16), 2003, pp. 63-85; and: *The Victimization of Children: Emerging Issues* (ed: Janet L. Mullings, James W. Marquart, and Deborah J. Hartley) The Haworth Maltreatment & Trauma Press, an imprint of The Haworth Press, Inc., 2003, pp. 63-85. Single or multiple copies of this article are available for a fee from The Haworth Document Delivery Service [1-800-HAWORTH, 9:00 a.m. - 5:00 p.m. (EST). E-mail address: docdelivery@haworthpress.com].

http://www.haworthpress.com/web/JAMT
© 2003 by The Haworth Press, Inc. All rights reserved.
Digital Object Identifier: 10.1300/J146v08n01_03

Child maltreatment is an act that occurs on a daily basis in almost every community in this country. It occurs behind closed doors in the supposed safe haven of homes, in the public arena of schools and day care centers, and in state-controlled areas such as safe houses and juvenile facilities. Victimization crosses over the bounds of race, gender, class, and geography to affect every community in some manner. While many people would prefer to believe that child maltreatment is a private matter and one whose causes lie in personal family conflict, more and more research points to the causes of child maltreatment being related to neighborhood characteristics (Coulton, Korbin, & Su, 1999; Coulton, Korbin, Su, & Chow, 1995; Deccio, Horner, & Wilson, 1994; Drake & Padney, 1996; Garbarino & Crouter, 1978; Garbarino & Kostelny, 1992; Garbarino & Sherman, 1980; Vinson, Baldry, & Hargreaves, 1996; Zuravin, 1989). This research seeks to determine the extent to which child maltreatment is spatially concentrated within certain geographic areas and explore the role that neighborhood characteristics play in child maltreatment victimization.

BACKGROUND ON CHILD MALTREATMENT

Before delving into how neighborhood characteristics impact child maltreatment, it is beneficial to begin with a discussion of the definition and extent of child maltreatment. While each state is free to define child maltreatment in the manner that it decides, the federal government provides a minimum set of criteria that characterize the acts of maltreatment. In general, child maltreatment is defined as "any recent act or failure to act on the part of a parent or caretaker which results in death, serious physical or emotional harm, sexual abuse or exploitation" (Henderson, 2000, p. 82). As this definition implies, there are four major varieties or types of child maltreatment: physical abuse, child neglect, sexual abuse, and emotional abuse. While each of these four types of child maltreatment is closely related, each is also separate and distinct from the others. Physical abuse is characterized by the infliction of physical injury through punching, beating, kicking, shaking or other means of harm. Importantly, the definition does consider intention; a caretaker need not intend to injure the child, as physical abuse can result from over-discipline or physical punishment. Child neglect, characterized by a failure to provide for a child's basic needs, can take the form of physical, emotional, or educational neglect. Examples of child neglect include failure to provide adequate health care, abandonment, allowance of chronic truancy, and inattention to a child's psychological needs. Sexual abuse is characterized by any number of improper sexual acts involving a child including fondling of genitals, intercourse, incest, rape, sodomy, and commercial exploitation through prostitution or production of pornographic materials. Finally, emotional abuse, characterized as psychological or mental injury to a child, includes any such acts or omissions that may cause serious behavioral, cognitive, or emotional problems (Henderson, 2000).

While laws and social actions aimed at reducing and preventing the incidence of child maltreatment have improved significantly over the last seventy years, the incidence of child maltreatment in the United States is still staggeringly high. The following findings reported by Henderson (2000) indicate the depth of the problem with child maltreatment within the United States. In 1997 alone, child protective services investigated over two million reports of child maltreatment involving over three million children. Importantly, substantiated maltreatment cases actually decreased slightly from 1,030,751 in 1996 to 984,000 in 1997, this after increasing a full 18% from 1990 to 1996. The most common type of child maltreatment is child neglect, which accounts for fully 54% of all victims, followed by child abuse with 24%, sexual abuse with 13%, and either emotional or medical neglect with 8%. While a significant percent of all child maltreatment results in some form of injury, 1,196 of the over 980,000 victims died as a result of their maltreatment. In terms of the age of victims, over 50% of all victims were seven years old or younger, with 25% of all victims under the age of four. The breakdown of victims by gender and racial type shows that females are slightly more likely than males to be victims, accounting for 52% of all victims, and that the vast majority of all reported cases of child maltreatment (67%) involve victims who are white. Finally, the vast majority of all child maltreatment offenders are either parents (75%) or other family members (10%). Overall, the picture of child maltreatment in this country is one in which victimization is still prevalent despite the best efforts of many.

EXPLANATIONS OF CHILD MALTREATMENT

Because of the high incidence of child maltreatment in the United States, there has been no shortage of research dealing with the causes of child maltreatment victimization. In general, causation research can be grouped into three different categories: psychological, sociological, and social-psychological explanations. While psychological and sociological theories focus on differing micro and macro explanations of child maltreatment, social psychological theories constitute, in effect, a middle ground between psychological and sociological theories. As such, it attempts to understand the interaction between the abuser, the victim, and their immediate environment. The main theory within this social psychological perspective is ecological theory, which, importantly, is the explanation undergirding the present research. Ecological theory focuses on how various neighborhood characteristics such as poverty, population mobility, and housing status impact residents' propensity towards child maltreatment. Specifically, these neighborhood characteristics make child maltreatment more likely by preventing the development of formal and informal social networks that provide both emotional support and social control within a neighborhood. As Zuravin (1989) argues,

> High risk neighborhoods are characterized by demographic, social and physical characteristics that negatively impact on family and individual stress levels by decreasing the availability as well as the adequacy of support systems. Low risk neighborhoods are socially rich areas; they are neighborhoods in which families are embedded in informal helping networks and can easily access formal systems of assistance. (p. 102)

Thus neighborhoods that suffer from high levels of economic disadvantage and residential instability are more likely not to develop solid social networks; this condition increases the risks of child maltreatment within their boundaries.

Considerable research testing ecological theory has found a number of neighborhood characteristics strongly associated with a high incidence of child maltreatment. Specifically, child maltreatment rates have been associated with poverty (Coulton et al., 1995; Garabino & Sherman, 1980; Gelles, 1992; Zuravin, 1989), unemployment (Steinberg, Catalano, & Dooley, 1981), and overall community disorganization (Garabino & Kostelny, 1992; Zuravin, 1989). However, while considerable research supports the ecological theory of child maltreatment, several problems exist within the current literature. Most importantly, the models that have been used to test ecological theory have, in general, been incomplete. The majority of the research has focused largely on economic factors such as neighborhood poverty and income levels, while ignoring characteristics associated with neighborhood instability (Zuravin, 1989). However, the degree of instability within a neighborhood is vitally important to the rationale of ecological theory because instability (as measured by such characteristics as residential mobility, housing tenure, and the number of vacant homes and owner-occupied homes in a given neighborhood) in concert with neighborhood economic factors significantly impacts the development of informal support networks in neighborhoods (Bursik & Grasmik, 1993). Neighborhoods high in economic disadvantage but low in instability factors have been shown to have lower criminal victimization rates than those neighborhoods that have high amounts of both poverty and instability (Bursik & Grasmik, 1993). In effect, neighborhood instability factors can act as limits of victimization through their impact on the development of informal support networks.

One problem confronting our understanding of child maltreatment in terms of ecological theory is that past research has tended to give most of its attention to associations between maltreatment and neighborhood economics and has, by and large, neglected connections between maltreatment and neighborhood instability. The research has thus understood and applied ecological theory unevenly or only in part. A more complete ecological model would be one based on criminological research that combines measures of both neighborhood disadvantage and neighborhood instability factors (Sampson & Groves, 1989). In order to remedy this problem, this research will employ an ecological model based on prior criminological research that employs both neighborhood disadvantage and neighborhood instability measures (Rosenfeld, Bray, & Eglen, 1999).

A second problem confronting our understanding of child maltreatment in terms of ecological theory is the paucity of research supporting the way in which the theory explains different types of child maltreatment (Drake & Padney, 1996). Virtually all research into child maltreatment has grouped different types of child maltreatment (child neglect and child abuse) together into one aggregate measure rather than separate them out into individual measures. However, this methodology ignores the potential that these distinctly different types of child maltreatment are associated with different aspects of ecological theory (Drake & Padney, 1996). In grouping different forms of child maltreatment together as one measure, researchers are masking potential differences in causation that might be determined by separating them. This problem is made all the more glaring by research indicating that the neighborhood characteristics associated with child abuse and child neglect are fundamentally different (Drake & Padney, 1996; Zuravin, 1989). Specifically, prior research has indicated that child neglect is more strongly associated with neighborhood disadvantage than is child abuse (Drake & Padney, 1996; Zuravin, 1989). Moreover, little research has attempted to determine the degree that ecological variables are associated with child maltreatment and other forms of juvenile victimization such as juvenile assault victimization (Coulton et al., 1995). The present research will attempt to remedy such problems by determining the degree to which different forms of child victimization are associated with ecological factors, and what if any potential differences in ecological characteristics are associated with these different victimization types.

A final problem with the current literature on child maltreatment is the lack of any analysis of potential spatial patterns of child maltreatment. While research on child maltreatment has been conducted at various levels of measurement amenable to spatial analysis, with the exception of one national level study, research has thus far ignored spatial aspects of child maltreatment (Turnbull, 2000). The long productive history of spatial pattern research with criminology has yielded sound insights and understanding of victimization patterns (Messner, Anselin, Baller, Hawkins, Deane, & Tolnay, 1999); the same methodology can be applied profitably to research on child maltreatment. Specifically, the analysis of spatial patterns can provide valuable information concerning areas of high and low concentration of child victimization as well as any spatial differences that exist between different types of victimization. These spatial patterns can, in turn, be overlaid with measures of ecological characteristics to determine what, if any, associations may exist between spatial patterns of ecological factors and spatial patterns of victimization. Furthermore, assessing spatial patterns of individual victimization locations provides a better understanding of spatial processes than analyzing aggregate measures of victimization. The present research will accordingly attempt to remedy this gap in the literature by analyzing child victimization locations to determine whether any spatial patterns exist, to what degree these patterns vary by victimization type, and what association, if any, there is between spatial patterns of neighborhood ecological characteristics and victimization locations.

Overall, this research is exploratory in nature and seeks to answer three main research questions concerning child maltreatment: First, are child victimizations concentrated within certain parts of a city? Second, are there different spatial patterns for child abuse, child neglect, and juvenile assault victimization locations? Finally, how well does ecological theory explain the incidence of child abuse, child neglect, and juvenile assault victimization at the neighborhood level?

METHODS

Child abuse and child neglect victimizations were singled out as the main variables of analysis in this study because they are the most prevalent type of maltreatment and are most likely to be reported to official departments. In addition, juvenile assault victimization was included in this study to determine the degree to which characteristics of juvenile assault victimization are similar to child maltreatment victimization. Juvenile assault was chosen because of its relative frequency and the various common elements it shares with child abuse and child neglect in terms of victim and offender relationship. For purposes of this analysis, juvenile assault is defined as all criminal assaults in which a minor was the victim. The data used in this study come from Charlotte, North Carolina, a large city in the southeastern United States with a population of approximately 550,000. Data concerning child abuse, child neglect, and juvenile assault victimization come from official police records and represent all incidents occurring in the year 2000 that were serious enough to warrant an official response. While official data on child abuse and child neglect are often derided as underestimating the incidence of victimization (Newberger, Reed, Daniel, Hyde, & Kotelchuck, 1977; O'Toole, Turbett, & Nalpeka, 1983), recent research indicates that findings based on official records are almost identical to those based on survey research (Drake & Pandey, 1996). Furthermore, official records are a commonly used measure for child maltreatment research and are considered highly valid (Garbarino & Sherman, 1981; Pelton, 1981; Zuravin, 1989).

The data informing this research were received from the Charlotte police in a standard Geographic Information Systems (GIS) format, from which the information on child abuse, child neglect, and juvenile assault victimization was selected out from all crimes occurring in the year 2000. A total of 156 child abuse, 134 child neglect, and 410 juvenile assault incidents were included in the analysis. Importantly, all of these incidents were independent incidents in which no other crime was reported. While co-occurrences of child abuse, child neglect and juvenile assault may have actually occurred, officially only one of the crimes was reported to the police. The information on individual victimization was then separated into two discrete data sets to be used in the analysis. The first of these sets, to be used in the spatial analysis of incident locations, comprised all individual incidents in a GIS format. A GIS is a relational database that allows any incident with an address to be displayed geographically on a map. As the data supplied by the Charlotte Police was already in a GIS format, no further preparation for the individual incident location spatial analysis was necessary.

The analysis of this spatial dataset was conducted using two different spatial analysis techniques, hot spot analysis and kernel density interpolation. Hot spot analysis determines statistically significant concentrations of point patterns, much like a multivariate cluster analysis. Specifically, nearest neighbor hierarchical clustering (Nnh) determines groups of points that are spatially closer than would be expected to occur by chance alone (Levine, 1999). In conducting an Nnh hot spot analysis using Crimestat software, the user is required to specify two important criteria prior to beginning the analysis. First, the minimum number of points for the hot spot is selected. This determination sets the least amount of points required for a hot spot to be created. In these analyses the minimum number of points was set at five incidents, a figure that is commonly used in exploratory hot spot analysis (Levine, 1999). Second, the user must select the probability level for defining the threshold distance between the points in the hot spot (Levine, 1999). This selection determines the probability that the hot spot could be due to chance. In this analysis the probability level was set at the .05 level. In contrast to hot spot analysis, kernel density interpolation is used to create a point pattern density map showing where there are statistically significant high densities of points (Levine, 1999). The kernel density interpolation for the present study was conducted using ESRI's Spatial Analyst extension for Arcview 8.1 (Environmental Systems Research Institute, 2001). The method of kernel density interpolation chosen for the analysis was a single kernel interpolation, an analysis type which is commonly used in these types of analyses because it allows for a smoother density creation (Levine, 1999).

The second data set that was created involved aggregating all of the incident location data to the census tract level for use in traditional statistical analysis. Creation of this data set was accomplished through a multi-step process. First, in order to determine the number of child abuse, child neglect, and juvenile assault victimization incidents per census tract, all incident level data were joined with census tracts using a GIS. This process allows for individual incidents to be joined with census tract numbers based on the census tract that the incidents are located within on a map. The data were then exported to a statistical package, where variables representing ecological characteristics were then added to the data set. In selecting variables to be used in the analysis, this study paid careful attention to select variables that represented both the economic disadvantage and residential instability components crucial to a complete and comprehensive ecological explanation. Variables included in the analysis were based on variables used in research by Rosenfeld and colleagues (1999) involving violent victimization. The variables considered in the analysis included family poverty rates, the number of female-headed households with children under 18, the number of unemployed males, vacancy rates, owner occupancy rates, lengths of household tenure, the number of households receiving public assistance, the prevalence of populations between the ages of fifteen and twenty-four, and the incidence of black population (see Table 1 for full explanation of variables).

In accordance with the methodology used in the research by Rosenfeld et al. (1999), the present study calculated variables and conducted a factor analysis using principal component analysis for later use in multiple regression analysis. The research produced two factors with eigenvalues above one, accounting for approximately 63% of the variance. Six different variables loaded significantly on these two factors. The variables that loaded on the first factor, which was renamed "neighborhood disadvantage," were family poverty rates, the number of female-headed households with children under eighteen, the number of households receiving public assistance, and the prevalence of populations between the ages of 15-24. Only two variables, rates of owner occupied housing and vacant home rates, loaded on the second factor, which was renamed "neighborhood instability." These two factor scores, as well as the percent of pop-

TABLE 1. Variables Used in Analysis

Variable Name	Variable Description
Family Poverty Rate	Family households with incomes above the poverty line.
Female-Headed Households	% of total households headed by females with children under the age of 18.
Male Unemployment	% of males over 16 that are unemployed.
Vacancy Rate	% of total housing units that are vacant.
Owner Occupancy Rate	Rate per 1,000 of owner occupied households.
Household Tenure	% of population in the same house 5 years ago.
Households Receiving Public Assistance	% of total households receiving public assistance.
Population between 15-24	% of family households between 15-24.
Black Population	% of total population that is black.

ulations that are black, were used as independent variables in a multiple regression analysis. Finally, the dependent variables for the multiple regression analysis were created. In following standard convention in creating child maltreatment rates, child neglect and child abuse rates are per 1,000 housing units within each census tract (Drake & Padney, 1996). In contrast, the juvenile assault rate is per 1,000 juveniles (under 18) per census tract. All of the data in this aggregate set were then joined with a map of census tracts in order to make the data available for spatial analysis.

RESULTS

In considering the results of the analysis, the discussion will first start with the spatial analysis and then move on the statistical analysis. Figure 1 provides a geographical version of a frequency distribution, showing the spatial distribution of child abuse, child neglect, and juvenile assault incident locations in Charlotte. In comparing these distributions, it is apparent that child neglect incidents have the most spatially compact distribution, with child abuse incidents being more spatially dispersed and juvenile assault incidents having the greatest spatial distribution. Despite the differences in their spatial distribution, all three incident types have their greatest concentration of incidents near the center areas of Charlotte. This phenomenon appears to show that there is some degree of spatial consistency, at least in terms of areas of highest concentrations of incidents, between the three distinct victimization types.

Figure 2 provides a view of the spatial distribution of victimization rates by census tract for child abuse, child neglect, and juvenile assault incidents. It is apparent from this map that there are definite spatial differences in terms of rates of victimization for these three incident types. Child abuse appears to have the greatest spatial distribution of census tracts with high victimization rates, with census tracts with high victimization rates distributed throughout the Charlotte area. Similarly spatially distributed, but not to the same degree as child abuse, high juvenile assault victimization rates appear most concentrated in the downtown Charlotte area and directly to the north of downtown. In contrast to child abuse and juvenile assault, child neglect victimization appears to be centered in a narrow area around the downtown area of Charlotte. It is important to note that while there appear to be marked differences in the spatial distribution of victimization rates, there are some important similarities in

FIGURE 1. Comparison of Incident Locations by Victimization Type

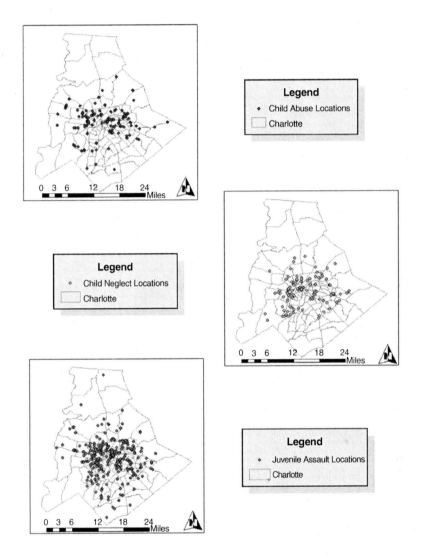

the victimization rates as well. Specifically, victimization rates are low for all three incident types on the outer areas of Charlotte, such as the northern boundary of the county.

Figures 3 and 4 provide a more statistically significant analysis of the spatial patterns of the three incident types by showing the areas of great-

FIGURE 2. Comparison of Victimization Rates per Census Tract

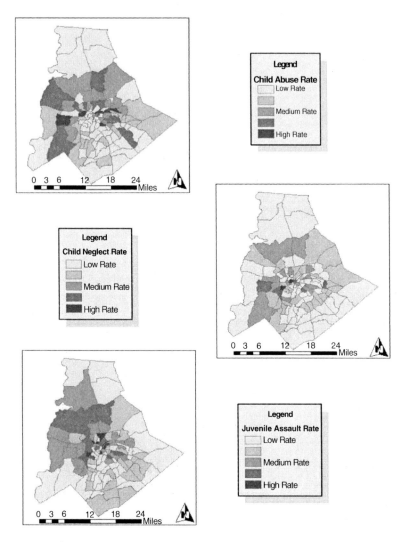

est concentration, or "hot spots" of incident locations. Figure 3 shows the hot spot locations for each incident type overlaid with the distribution of the actual incident locations. Child abuse has eight hot spots, indicating a moderate degree of spatial concentration. In contrast, child neglect has only four hot spots, indicating that it is not very spatially concentrated.

FIGURE 3. Comparison of Hot Spot Locations by Victimization Type

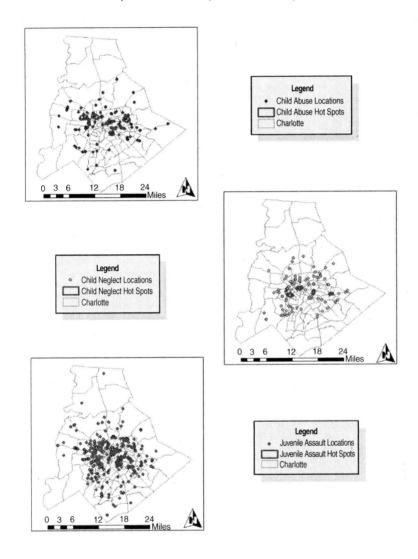

Finally, juvenile assault has nineteen hot spots, indicating a strong degree of spatial concentration. In comparing the location of the hot spots, Figure 4 indicates a considerable degree of spatial overlap between the different incident types. Specifically, seven of eight child abuse hot spots, two of four child neglect hot spots, and twelve of nineteen juvenile as-

FIGURE 4. Overlay of Different Hot Spot Locations

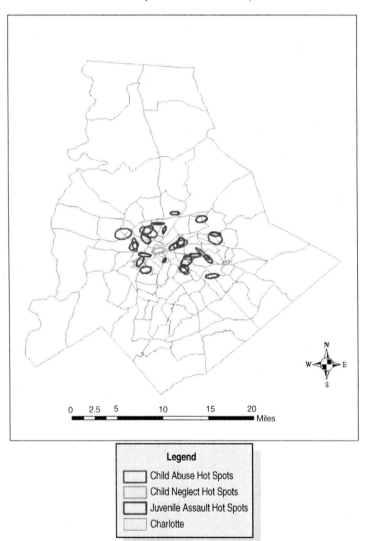

sault hot spots overlap with other incident hot spots. In terms of spatial patterns, child abuse and juvenile assault appear to be the most similar, with seven child abuse hot spots overlapping ten juvenile assault hot spots. In contrast, of the four child neglect hot spots, only two overlap with either child abuse or juvenile assault, indicating a definite spatial difference in its incident pattern. Importantly, there is only one location in which all three hot spots overlap, indicating that there are definite spatial differences in the distributions of these incident types.

Figure 5, the final representation of the spatial distribution of incident patterns, shows the kernel density of each incident type. The purpose of this map is to indicate the areas where the highest density of incident locations occurs. In looking at these maps, it is apparent that there are definite spatial differences in the amount and location of incident density areas. Child abuse has several fairly spatially close, high-density incident locations, indicating a moderate degree of spatial concentration. In contrast, child neglect has only a few high-density locations that are more spatially dispersed than child abuse, indicating only a mild degree of spatial concentration. Finally, juvenile assault is the most spatially concentrated of the three incident types, with one major area of high-density incident locations. Importantly, in comparing the density maps of the three incident types, the research suggests, as it does with the hot spot locations, that child abuse and juvenile assault are spatially similar in distribution.

Overall, the spatial analysis provides important information concerning two of the main questions this research sought to determine. First, child maltreatment victimizations do appear to be concentrated within certain parts of Charlotte. Specifically, all three incident types are more heavily concentrated near the city center or downtown area, with little concentration on the outer areas of the city. Secondly, there do appear to be different spatial patterns for the different incident types, although not to a large degree. Importantly, child abuse and juvenile assault incidents appear to occur in similar spatial patterns, which appear to be spatially dissimilar to the patterns of child neglect. Both the hot spot analysis and kernel density interpolation analysis appear to indicate that child neglect incidents have a slightly different spatial pattern than either child abuse or juvenile assault victimizations.

ECOLOGICAL THEORY ANALYSIS

Table 2 provides basic descriptive statistics for census tracts in which incidents of each incident type occurred as well as those where no victimizations occurred. This table indicates that census tracts where these incidents occurred are fairly similar in their composition, with the exception of a few areas. Specifically, the poverty rates, number of female-headed households, and prevalence of black population

FIGURE 5. Comparison of Victimization Density Levels by Victimization Type

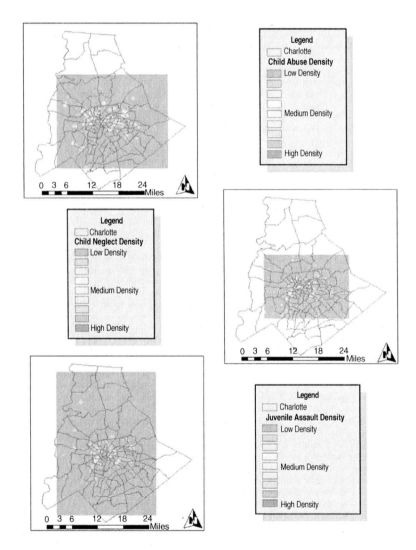

are all substantially lower in census tracts where juvenile assaults oc-curred than in those tracts where child abuse or child neglect victimiza-tions occurred. It is important to note that in comparison to census tracts where no victimizations occurred, victim tracts have much higher pov-erty rates, total populations, and black populations.

TABLE 2. Basic Descriptives for Census Tracts Containing Victims of Different Types

Neighborhood Characteristic	Child Abuse Tracts	Child Neglect Tracts	Juvenile Assault Tracts	No Victim Tracts
Total Population	4576	4576	4307	4027
Total Households	1753	1753	1679	1583
Family Poverty Rate per 1,000 Households	39.95	39.95	33.54	21.54
% of Total Households that Are FHH w/Children	10.5	10.5	8.5	8.3
% of Males Unemployed	2.6	2.6	2.48	2.85
% of Total Households Getting Public Assistance	8.2	8.2	6.86	6.8
% of Population Between 15-24	3.5	3.5	2.71	2.5
% of Population that Is Black	42.8	42.8	34.62	31.3
Total Census Tracts	59	59	90	111

Table 3 provides the results of the multiple regression analysis. Standardized betas are provided, as well as significance levels and adjusted r-squares. These results indicate striking differences in the level of explanation that is provided for each victimization type. None of the factors had any significant effect on child neglect rate, although neighborhood disadvantage ($p = .062$) was close to being significant at the .05 level. This finding means that child neglect rates are not significantly related to neighborhood disadvantage, neighborhood instability, or the percent of population that is black. In contrast, the variance of child abuse rates at the census tract level is significantly impacted by neighborhood disadvantage ($\beta = .383$) characteristics. These findings are consistent with previous studies (Coulton et al., 1995; Drake & Padney, 1996; Zuravin, 1989). However, as with child neglect rates, neighborhood instability and black population have little impact on the variance in child abuse rates at the census tract level. Finally, the results indicate that juvenile assault rates are significantly impacted by both neighborhood disadvantage ($\beta = .288$) and black population ($\beta = .385$), with black population having the larger impact. Importantly, neighborhood instability has little to no impact at all on any of the three victimization types. Moreover, neighborhood instability does not even appear to approach significance in any of the three regression analyses; this indicates its true lack of impact in the analysis.

TABLE 3. Multiple Regression Results

Variables	Child Abuse β (p-value)	Child Neglect β (p-value)	Juvenile Assault β (p-value)
Neighborhood Disadvantage	.383**	.288(.062)	.288*
Neighborhood Instability	−.029(.740)	−.006(.947)	−.009(.911)
Black Population	.167(.167)	.211(.170)	.385**
Adjusted R-square	.258***	.203***	.395***

* Chi square $p < .05$
** Chi square $p < .01$
*** Chi-square $p < .001$

It is important to note that the adjusted R^2 for these three models are all fairly low, ranging from only .203 for child neglect to .395 for juvenile assault. This result indicates that the model explained a relatively small percent of the total variance in these victimization types, ranging from only 20% for child neglect to 25% for child abuse and 39% for juvenile assault. Overall, this finding indicates that the model was a much better fit for explaining the variance in juvenile assault rates at the census tract level than either child abuse or child neglect rates.

The final aspect of the ecological theory analysis involved determining the spatial relationship between victimization hot spot locations and neighborhood disadvantage and neighborhood instability scores at the census tract level. Figure 6 shows the spatial relationship between hot spot locations for all three victimization types and neighborhood disadvantage scores. Importantly, all of the hot spot locations for both child abuse and juvenile assault are located within census tracts that scored between medium and high disadvantage. In contrast, two of the four child neglect hot spots are located in census tracts that scored at the lower end of the disadvantage range. It is also important to note that two census tracts to the west of downtown Charlotte that had the highest disadvantage scores had no victimization hot spots at all. This finding appears to indicate that some other factors present in those census tracts, but untested in this analysis, help to minimize victimization.

Figure 7 shows the spatial relationship between neighborhood instability scores and victimization hot spot locations. Importantly, all three victimization types appear to be in census tracts that score low on neighborhood instability. These spatial analysis results appear to confirm the multiple regression analysis results. Specifically, child abuse and juvenile assault hot spots are strongly associated with neighborhood disad-

FIGURE 6. Comparison of Hot Spot Locations by Neighborhood Disadvantage
Score

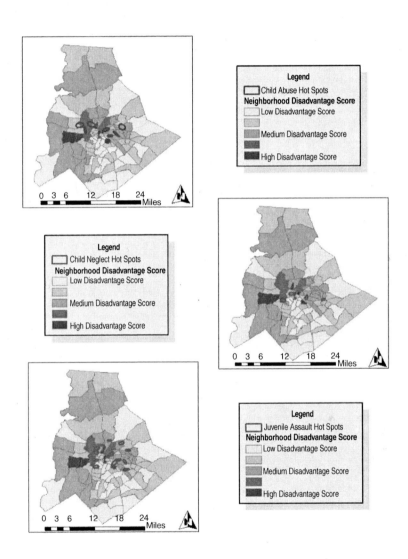

FIGURE 7. Comparison of Hot Spot Locations by Neighborhood Instability Score

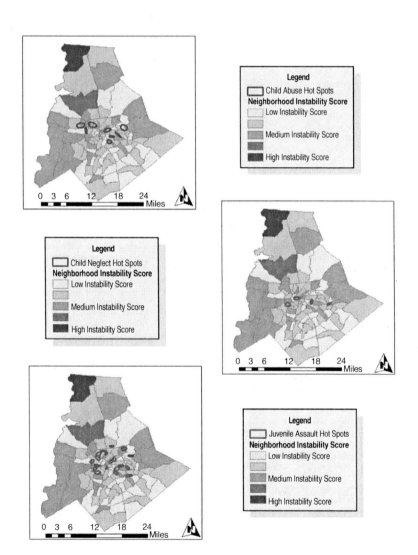

vantage scores, with child neglect hot spots being less so; in addition, all three victimization types are unrelated to neighborhood instability scores.

DISCUSSION

The results of the present study provide several important findings and insights concerning the understanding of child maltreatment. First, the results are consistent with the literature, in that economic factors appear to be highly related to child abuse rates (Coulton et al., 1995; Drake & Padney, 1996; Zuravin, 1989). However, in contrast with prior research, child neglect rates are not significantly associated with economic factors (Drake & Padney, 1996). This finding seems to indicate that there are different social processes associated with child abuse and child neglect victimization. These results are particularly important, considering that the ecological theory model fully tested both economic and instability factors, whereas prior research has largely failed to consider instability factors.

A second important finding is the spatial difference in child abuse and child neglect locations. These spatial analysis results appear to further confirm that there are different social processes associated with child abuse and child neglect victimization. These spatial and ecological differences point to the need for different policies for addressing the problems of child abuse and child neglect. Furthermore, the spatial analysis points to the potential requirement that victims' services for child abuse and child neglect be centered in different locations to serve their victim population more fully. This last point confirms the utility of spatial analysis of these types of incidents and begs for replication of these analyses in other locations.

A third major finding centers around the spatial and ecological similarities between child abuse and juvenile assault victimization. The results seem to indicate that spatially and socially, these two different victimization types may be more closely related than first assumed. These two victimization types, while not considered similar in the research literature, appear to be associated with similar social processes resulting in spatially similar patterns. More research needs to be conducted in this area to determine the nature and extent of the similarities of these two incident types.

A fourth major finding surrounds the failure of neighborhood instability to be a significant predictor for either child abuse or child neglect. These findings bring into question the validity of ecological theory in the study of child maltreatment. Given the current findings and the large amount of research relating economic factors to child maltreatment, it appears that there may be some other social processes at work in child maltreatment. More research needs to be conducted using a full ecological model to determine further the extent that ecological variables are at work in child maltreatment.

A final important finding concerns the incidence of census tracts having high scores of neighborhood disadvantage, yet low amounts of victimization. While neighborhood disadvantage was found to be highly associated with child abuse and juvenile assault victimization, some areas with high neighborhood disadvantage had low densities of victimization. These findings, only apparent through spatial analysis, appear to support the idea that some other factors are present in some neighborhoods that protect them from high victimization, despite high levels of disadvantage. More research needs to be conducted to try to determine what other social, cultural, or other factors may be present in these areas that insulate them from high concentrations of victimization.

While this study is admittedly limited by its use of official data and its relatively small geographical focus, its implications are potentially far reaching. Specifically, the results of this study point to the utility of using full ecological models in the study of child maltreatment as well as the benefits to be gained from disaggregating victimization types. Furthermore, this research heralds the insights that can be gained into social processes by conducting small area spatial analysis. It is hoped that through replication in other cities, further understanding can be gained into the research questions this research generates.

REFERENCES

Bursik, R. J., & Grasmik, H. G. (1993). *Neighborhoods and crime.* New York: Lexington.

Coulton, C., Korbin, J., & Su, M. (1999). Neighborhoods and child maltreatment: A multi-level study. *Child Abuse and Neglect, 23*(11), 1019-1040.

Coulton, C., Korbin, J., Su, M., & Chow, J. (1995). Community level factors and child maltreatment rates. *Child Development, 66,* 1262-1276.

Deccio, G., Horner, W., & Wilson, D. (1994). High risk neighborhoods and high-risk families: Replication research related to the human ecology of child maltreatment. *Journal of Social Service Research, 18,* 123-127.

Drake, B., & Padney, S. (1996). Understanding the relationship between neighborhood poverty and specific types of child maltreatment. *Child Abuse & Neglect, 20,* 1003-1018.

Environmental Systems Research Institute. (2001). *ArcGIS Spatial Analyst 8.1* [Computer Software]. Redlands, CA: Author.

Garbarino, J., & Crouter, A. (1978). Defining the community context for parent-child relations: The correlates of child maltreatment. *Child Development, 49,* 604-616.

Garbarino, J., & Kostelny, K. (1992). Child maltreatment as a community problem. *Child Abuse & Neglect, 16*, 455-464.

Garbarino, J., & Sherman, D. (1980). High-risk neighborhoods and high-risk families: The human ecology of child maltreatment. *Child Development, 55*, 188-198.

Gelles, R. (1992). Poverty and violence towards children. *American Behavioral Scientist, 35*(3), 258-274.

Henderson, H. (2000). *Domestic violence and child abuse sourcebook*. Detroit: Omingraphics.

Levine, N. (1999). *Crimestat: A spatial statistics program for the analysis of crime incident locations*. Washington, DC: The National Institute of Justice.

Messner, S., Anselin, L., Baller, R., Hawkins, D., Deane, G., & Tolnay, S. (1999). The spatial patterning of county homicide rates: An application of exploratory spatial data analysis. *Journal of Quantitative Criminology, 15*(4), 423-450.

Newberger, E., Reed, R., Daniel, J., Hyde, J., & Kotelchuck, M. (1977). Pediatric social illness: Toward an etiological classification. *Pediatrics, 60*, 178-185.

O'Toole, R., Turbett, P., & Nalpeka, C. (1983). Theories, professional knowledge, and diagnosis of child abuse. In D. Finkelhor, R. Gelles, G. Hotaling, & M. Strauss (Eds.), *The dark side of families: Current family violence research* (pp. 349-362). Newbury Park, CA: Sage.

Pelton, L. (1981). *The social context of child abuse and neglect*. New York: Human Sciences Press.

Rosenfeld, R., Bray, T., & Egland, A. (1999). Facilitating violence: A comparison of gang motivated, gang affiliated, and non-gang youth homicides. *Journal of Quantitative Criminology, 15*(4), 495-515.

Sampson, R., & Groves, W. (1989). Community structure and crime: Testing social disorganization theory. *American Journal of Sociology, 94*, 775-802.

Steinberg, L., Catalano, R., & Dooley, D. (1981). Economic antecedents of child abuse and neglect. *Child Development, 52*, 975-985.

Turnbull, S. L. (2000). The spatial dimensions of child abuse and neglect. In L. Turnbull, E. Hendrix, & B. Dent (Eds.), *Atlas of crime: Mapping the criminal landscape* (pp. 100-108). Phoenix, AZ: Oryx Press.

Vinson, T., Baldry, E., & Hargreaves, J. (1996). Neighborhoods, networks and child abuse. *British Journal of Social Work, 26*, 23-54.

Zuravin, S. (1989). The ecology of child abuse and neglect: Review of the literature and presentation of data. *Violence and Victims, 4*, 101-120.

Religion-Related Child Physical Abuse: Characteristics and Psychological Outcomes

Bette L. Bottoms
Michael Nielsen
Rebecca Murray
Henrietta Filipas

SUMMARY. Religious beliefs can foster, encourage, and justify child abuse, yet religious motivations for child abuse and neglect have been virtually ignored in social science research. In this paper, we compare victims' retrospective reports of religion-related child physical abuse to other reported cases of child physical abuse. We describe in statistical detail the nature and circumstances of the abuse, characteristics of victims and perpetrators, and the spiritual and psychological impact of the abuse. Results indicate that although the basic characteristics of religion-related physical abuse are similar to non-religion-related physical abuse, religion-related abuse has sig-

Address correspondence to: Bette L. Bottoms, University of Illinois at Chicago, Department of Psychology (m/c 285), 1007 West Harrison Street, Chicago, IL 60607-7137 (E-mail: bbottoms@uic.edu).

The authors thank Leslie Hollins, Sara B. Kay, Kristina Almassy, Sharanya Gururajan, Monica Antoun, Anisha Shetty, and Krissie Fernandez for dedicated research assistance.

[Haworth co-indexing entry note]: "Religion-Related Child Physical Abuse: Characteristics and Psychological Outcomes." Bottoms, Bette L. et al. Co-published simultaneously in *Journal of Aggression, Maltreatment & Trauma* (The Haworth Maltreatment & Trauma Press, an imprint of The Haworth Press, Inc.) Vol. 8, No. 1/2 (#15/16), 2003, pp. 87-114; and: *The Victimization of Children: Emerging Issues* (ed: Janet L. Mullings, James W. Marquart, and Deborah J. Hartley) The Haworth Maltreatment & Trauma Press, an imprint of The Haworth Press, Inc., 2003, pp. 87-114. Single or multiple copies of this article are available for a fee from The Haworth Document Delivery Service [1-800-HAWORTH, 9:00 a.m. - 5:00 p.m. (EST). E-mail address: docdelivery@haworthpress.com].

Digital Object Identifier: 10.1300/J146v08n01_04

nificantly more negative implications for its victims' long-term psychological well-being. *[Article copies available for a fee from The Haworth
Document Delivery Service: 1-800- HAWORTH. E-mail address:
<docdelivery@haworthpress.com> Website: <http://www.HaworthPress.com>
© 2003 by The Haworth Press, Inc. All rights reserved.]*

KEYWORDS. Child abuse, religion, physical abuse, corporal punishment, child victims

Religion provides specific directives for positive moral action and
the promotion of human welfare. It may be difficult to realize, then, that
religious beliefs can also foster, encourage, and justify abusive behavior. The myriad connections between religion and child abuse led Donald Capps, a past president of the Society for the Scientific Study of
Religion, to entitle his presidential address, "Religion and Child Abuse,
Perfect Together." Although religious himself, Capps (1992) sorrow-
fully traced the indisputable connection between traditional religion
and violence against children. Similar points have been made by Capps
(1995), Straus (1994), Pagelow and Johnson (1988), and by Greven
(1991) in his sobering book, *Spare the Child: The Religious Roots of
Punishment and the Psychological Impact of Physical Abuse.*

In this paper, we explore the complex role of religion in child abuse
cases reported retrospectively by young adults in a survey. We sought to
understand the nature, circumstances, and emotional, psychological,
and spiritual outcomes of religion-related physical abuse as compared
to other physical abuses. We are among the first researchers to conduct
a systematic examination from the victims' perspective of religion-related
child physical abuse as compared to other forms of physical abuse. Herein,
we review the limited literature on the ways in which religious beliefs can be
involved in child physical abuse and the impact of this abuse on psychological well-being and spirituality. We then delineate our hypotheses
regarding the impact of religion-related abuse, and subsequently present the methods and findings of our study.

RELIGION AND CHILD PHYSICAL ABUSE

Religious groups often play an active, positive role in the prevention
of child abuse and treatment of abuse victims. Yet, as Greven (1991)
points out, encouragement for violent, physically abusive child-rearing
techniques can be traced to Biblical passages such as, "He that spareth

his rod hateth his son: but he that loveth him chasteneth him betimes," and "Withhold no correction from the child: for if thou beatest him with the rod, he shall not die. Thou shalt beat him with the rod, and shalt deliver his soul from hell" (Proverbs 13:24 and 23:13-14, respectively). Directives such as these and a belief in a vengeful God who would punish earthly pleasure with the ultimate torture of hell drive some parents to use corporal punishment to enforce parental authority and to prohibit supposed sinful behavior (Bottoms, Shaver, Goodman, & Qin, 1995; Ellison & Sherkat, 1993). Sin (e.g., disobedience) is considered the vehicle to hell, and parents may believe that it is better to inflict temporary pain than allow their children to burn in eternal hell. Some believers (and even mental health professionals; Friesen, 1992) even equate children's misbehavior with the actual activity of Satan or other evil spirits who literally possess the children and who must be exorcized by beatings. Thus, physical abuse is sometimes perpetrated by parents or by religious leaders or teachers who believe they are helping to deliver children from sin.

Because of media attention, the public is generally aware of cases in which fringe religious groups and isolationalist cults practice beatings in the name of Godly discipline (e.g., Malcarne & Burchard, 1992). When discovered, such cults' abusive practices and even their particular religious beliefs are immediately highlighted in the news media, and criticized and rejected by society with much self-righteousness. Yet "cult" beliefs and practices may differ only in degree from those of mainstream religious groups such as Methodists, Baptists, and Catholics, who believe the physical punishment of children is religiously sanctioned, especially those who are Biblical literalists (Ellison, Barthkowski, & Segal, 1996a, 1996b; Wiehe, 1990).

Social scientists have contributed to a growing, but still conceptually and empirically thin, literature that identifies ways in which religiosity and belief systems promote and justify abuse, especially by increasing parents' risk for perpetrating and rationalizing child abuse. Capps (1992, 1995) articulates clearly how the values of fundamental Christianity can be seen as supportive of the physical and emotional abuse of children. In studies of parenting practices, Jackson, Law, Thompson, Christiansen, Colman, and Wyatt (1999) found that religious ideology was a critical factor in predicting proneness to abuse, and Neufeld (1979) found similarities in parental attitudes between abusive parents and parents who hold fundamentalist Christian values. Shor (1998) determined that religious values may be related to child maltreatment in ultra-orthodox Jewish families. Others have drawn similar conclusions about the connection between religion and beliefs in corporal punishment (e.g., Ellison et al., 1996a, 1996b; Ellison & Sherkat, 1993; Flynn, 1996; Maurer, 1982; Nelsen & Kroliczak, 1984). Although there has been little research on this topic, the relation between religion and abuse does not go unnoticed, even among the devout: A church-funded survey of nearly 650 members of the Christian Reformed Church revealed that while church attendance was inversely related to reported perpetration of child abuse, a majority of members believed "the church does little to prevent abuse," that "Christians too often use the Bible to justify abuse," and that "Church leaders are not prepared to help members of their churches who are victims of abuse" (Rice & Annis, 1992).

Thus, child abuse is indeed occurring within the context of religion. But what are its particular circumstances, and what are its effects on child victims? Bottoms et al. (1995) conducted one of the largest studies to date of religion-related child abuse, a survey of mental health professionals (psychologists, psychiatrists, and social workers) who had encountered the following types of cases in their clinical practices: child abuse perpetrated by persons with religious authority, religiously motivated medical neglect, and severe forms of abuse and even murder perpetrated by parents and religious groups who believed they were ridding children of evil (see also Bottoms, Shaver, & Goodman, 1996; Goodman, Bottoms, Redlich, Shaver, & Diviak, 1998). Sixty-six percent of their cases in the latter category included physical abuse, but almost half of the cases were characterized by sexual abuse, and nearly a third involved neglect, either in addition to or instead of physical abuse. Also, many of their cases of physical abuse were quite extreme; for example, they reported one case in which an "eyeball was plucked out of a youth's head during an exorcism ceremony," and another in which a "father performed an exorcism on his children by dismembering and then boiling them." Thus, their category of physical abuse is not precisely like the cases we focus on in the present paper; nonetheless, given the overlap and the lack of other information in the literature, it is informative to consider a profile of their cases. In particular, 43% of the cases involved fundamentalist or fringe Christian religions, 38% involved other Protestants, and 16% involved Catholics. The abuse was usually perpetrated by parents (85% of cases). On average, victims were abused between the ages of 5 and 11 years of age. Psychological sequellae included depression in half the cases, with a third of the victims having suicidal ideation. Other symptoms included phobias, social withdrawal, inappropriate aggression, and dissociative disorders. Even though the abuses were often quite violent, corroborative evidence was present only about half of the time, and trials (12%) and convictions (9%) were rare. Social service agencies performed investigations in 56% of the cases, but less than a fifth of the cases involved police, and only 6% involved prosecutors.

There are few other studies of the circumstances or psychological impact of religion-related physical abuse, but some studies provide insights regarding the effects of abuse on children's spirituality. In a study of children in grades 4 through 8, Nelsen and Kroliczak (1984) revealed that when parents use the threat "God will punish you" as a disciplinary tool, children tend to engage in more self-blame and are more obedient. Studies of children sexually abused by priests have revealed that the trauma can have a negative impact upon the victims' religion and spirituality (e.g., Rossetti, 1995; see also McGlone, this volume). Also, child abuse generally (not necessarily abuse related to religion) influences victims' religious and spiritual practices. For example, Johnson and Eastburg (1992) found that although physically and sexually abused children saw their parents as more wrathful, this malevolent perception did not extend to God. Even so, other research suggests that by the time victims reach adulthood, their relationship with and perception of God is conflicted at best. For example, Ryan (1998) concluded that the effect of child abuse on adult spirituality is complex, with some survivors reporting that retaining their religious beliefs helped them to heal from abuse, while others feel angry at God, abandoned by God, and view God as punitive. In a study of over 1000 veterans, Lawson, Drebing, Berg, Vincellette, and Penk (1998) found that men with a history of sexual or other child abuse were more likely than nonabused men to engage in prayer and spiritual activities, yet they also reported feeling greater spiritual injury and instability in spiritual behaviors and experiences. Doxey, Jensen, and Jensen (1997) concluded that sexual abuse was associated with a decrease in religiosity. Kane, Cheston, and Greer (1993) found that female sexual abuse survivors feel that God is disapproving and ashamed of them.

The results of these studies provide evidence that spiritual damage is linked to abuse. Few studies, however, distinguish religion-related abuse from abuse without religious connotations, so our understanding of the impact of religion-related abuse on spirituality is incomplete. As Durkheim (1915/1965) speculated, one of the major functions of religion is to provide us with meaning, the sense of which offers us comfort when we are vulnerable. If abuse is perpetrated in the name of God, its victim may be robbed of the meaning and comfort that spirituality can provide, which might intensify the trauma of the abuse and compromise coping efforts. Thus, any negative impact on spirituality or religiosity might itself add to the psychological impact of the abuse. In our study, we measured both current psychological functioning as well as spirituality.

A PROFILE OF NON-RELIGION-RELATED CHILD PHYSICAL ABUSE

Although little is known specifically about the circumstances and outcomes of religion-related child physical abuse, much is known about child physical abuse in other contexts (for example, see Bruhn, this volume). It is important to consider a profile of physical abuse as a basis for understanding the additive or exacerbating effects of abuse-linked religious ideology or context.

Physical abuse affects hundreds of thousands of children each year, and accounts for about a quarter of all child abuse reports (U.S. Department of Health and Human Services, 2000). A comprehensive review by Kolko (2002) indicated that rates of reported abuse do not generally differ by age or gender, though younger children may sustain the most severe injuries (Lung & Daro, 1996). Nearly all child physical abuse is perpetrated by parents and other loved ones. Ecological models proposed to explain physically abusive parenting (e.g., Belsky, 1993; Lynch & Cicchetti, 1998) stress the importance of family interactional and contextual variables, such as cultural and community factors. Other models focus on parent factors such as perceptions of and attributions for children's behaviors; expectations, developmental knowledge, and problem solving skills; beliefs about the appropriateness of using physical discipline; and tolerance for stress and ability to inhibit aggression, etc. (Azar & Gehl, 1997; Milner, 2000; Simons, Whitbeck, Conger, & Chyi-In, 1991; Wolfe, 1999; see Kolko, 2002, for review). Researchers such as Kolko (2002) have noted the need for a better understanding of the host of factors that contribute to excessive parental negativity toward children's misbehavior. We propose religious beliefs as one important factor. Religion can contribute to the likelihood of abuse by providing knowledge and attitudes that directly support abusive behaviors. This likelihood of abuse is probably greatest when other risk factors are also present.

The detrimental effects of physical abuse on psychological health in childhood and adulthood are well documented. Of course, how any one individual adjusts psychologically after having been abused as a child depends on numerous factors (e.g., Winton & Mara, 2001), but generally, children who are battered can develop an assortment of physiological, intellectual, psychological, and behavioral problems in response to the stress of their abuse (for review, see Kolko, 2002). For example, abused children often have lower self-esteem than their peers (Allen & Tarnowski, 1989; Oats, Forrest, & Peacock, 1985), although Kolko notes that the long-term impact on self-esteem needs further investigation. Externalizing problems such as increased aggression are commonly associated with physical abuse, but so too are some internalizing problems such as depression and hopelessness (e.g., Pelcovitz, Kaplan, Goldenberg, & Mandel, 1994). The limited longitudinal and retrospective cross-sectional data that are available reveal that adult survivors of child abuse also differ from non-abused adults. For example, childhood abuse leads to later life aggression, violence, and criminal behavior (Dodge, Pettit, & Bates, 1997; Maxfield & Widom, 1996; Quas, Bottoms, & Nunez, 2002); antisocial personality disorder (Luntz & Widom, 1994); anxiety and emotional behavioral problems (Silverman, Reinherz, & Giaconia, 1996); depression (Brown, Cohen, Johnson, & Smailes, 1999; Levitan et al., 1998; Silverman et al., 1996), and suicidal ideation (Brown et al., 1999; Bryant & Range, 1997; Levitan et al., 1998; Silverman et al., 1996).

Thus, the factors that lead parents to abuse their children and the psychological effects of physical abuse are many and varied. We propose that parents' religious attitudes and beliefs (e.g., spare the rod, spoil the child) are among the attitudinal factors that can contribute to the likelihood of familial abuse. Further, we believe that for reasons outlined next, the long-term emotional toll of religion-related child physical abuse will be similar in type to that of non-religion-related physical abuse, but compounded, because of the added stress and guilt associated with religious justifications for maltreatment.

OVERVIEW AND PREDICTIONS

Given the fact that religion-related justifications for abuse abound and sometimes manifest in cases of physical abuse, and that abuse related to religion may be particularly detrimental to children's well-being, it is surprising that little research has been conducted to explore its characteristics or consequences. Many questions about religion-related abuse exist. What are the circumstances of this form of abuse–who are its victims, its perpetrators? What is its impact on religiosity and spiritual beliefs? Does this type of abuse have distinct psychological consequences? To address these important questions, we undertook a retrospective survey study of three groups of young adults: (a) adult survivors of religion-related child physical abuse, (b) adult survivors of non-religion-related child abuse, and (c) a control group of individuals who had not suffered any form of childhood abuse. We queried all individuals about their current psychological and emotional well-being, including self-esteem, and we asked the two victim groups about the nature and circumstances of their abuse experiences.

In keeping with the literatures reviewed above, we theorize that religious overtones add an additional layer of complexity and harm to child abuse experiences. Victims of religion-related abuse must deal with the trauma associated not only with parental betrayal but also perhaps the additional despair related to perceived betrayal by God. This may inhibit a child's ability to cope with maltreatment. Therefore, we hypothesized that individuals in our study who experienced religion-related abuse would experience more emotional and psychological distress and have lower self-esteem than victims of other forms of physical abuse. We expected both groups of victims to exhibit more emotional and psychological difficulties than the control group. Further, we predicted that religion-related abuse victims would report greater spiritual injury and be less religious than individuals who had suffered non-religion-related childhood abuse. We did not expect to find differences in the basic circumstantial characteristics of the two types of physical abuse in terms of form or frequency of abuse, its likelihood of being disclosed or otherwise discovered, characteristics of victims and perpetrators, etc. Instead, we expected both forms of physical abuse to fit the profile of physical abuses found in many other studies (for review, see Kolko, 2002), with the exception that, as found in the Bottoms et al. (1995) work, we expected more religion-related abuse to be perpetrated by religious leaders.

METHOD

Participants

Fifty-four men and 72 women from the University of Illinois at Chicago (a large, racially and ethnically diverse, urban university) volunteered to serve as participants in exchange for Introductory Psychology course credit. Twenty-six (54% women) had experienced childhood physical abuse that was in some way related to religion as defined below; 46 (61% women) experienced non-religion-related physical abuse, and 54 (57% women) experienced no abuse of any kind and served as the control group. The groups were statistically similar in terms of all demographic variables we measured (all $ps > .20$), including age ($M =$ 19.4 years), year in college (51% freshmen, 35% sophomores, 14% juniors or seniors), marital status (99% single), race/ethnicity (16% African American, 26% Asian American, 43% Caucasian, 13% Hispanic/Latino/Latina, 2% other), mother's education (Mdn = at least one year of college), father's education (Mdn = college degree), and estimated parental income (Mdn = $60,000-$69,000, on an eight-point scale ranging from $0 to $80,000+ in increments of $10,000).

Materials

Demographic Questionnaire. A demographic questionnaire requested the information reported in the "participants" section above.

Religiosity Measures. Several items measured participants' involvement in religion and their religious attitudes. First, participants indicated their religious affiliation, then rated the importance of their religious beliefs on a scale ranging from 1 (Not at all important) to 5 (Extremely important). (Participants who considered themselves "spiritual" without believing in a specific deity were asked to frame this and the other religious items in terms of spirituality rather than religion.) Another item asked participants to rate the importance of religion to their self-concept, using a 1 (Not at all) to 5 (Extremely) scale. The frequency with which participants attended religious services, and the frequency of their prayers, were rated on separate scales ranging from 1 (Less than once a year) to 8 (Once a day). Finally, Christian orthodoxy was assessed using the short version of the Christian Orthodoxy Scale (Hunsberger, 1989), which consists of three items that address core Christian doctrines described in the Apostles Creed and Nicene Creed such as "Jesus Christ is the divine Son of God," and three that describe the rejection of those doctrines such as "Despite what many people believe, there is no such thing as a God who is aware of our actions." Responses were given on a seven-point scale, ranging from -3 (Strongly disagree) to $+3$ (Strongly agree). Appropriate items were reverse-coded so that higher scale scores reflect greater orthodoxy. Responses were recoded from 1 to 7, and item scores were summed, producing a theoretical range from 6 to 42 (higher scores indicating greater orthodoxy).

Abuse Experiences Survey. As part of a larger survey study, experiences of physical abuse were assessed with our Abuse Experience Survey.[1] The question used to determine whether participants had suffered childhood physical abuse was based on definitions used by Straus and Gelles (1988) and was similar to a question used previously to assess physical abuse with a similar university sample (Epstein & Bottoms, 2002): "When you were a child or teenager (age 17 years or younger), did any person who was at least 5 years older than you ever do any of the following types of things to you for any reason: (a) hit, slapped, spanked, lashed, grabbed, shoved, choked, punched, kicked, bit, burned, beat, stabbed, or whipped you and it left you with welts, bruises, bleeding, or other marks or injuries; (b) punished or disciplined you with a belt, cord, or other hard object; or (c) threatened you with a weapon?" Participants were also asked, "Do you consider your experience 'abuse'?" We labeled respondents to be physical abuse victims even if they failed to consider the experience to have been "abuse" themselves. This method helps to avoid underestimating the true number of abuse victims, because some individuals who have had abusive experiences fail to self-label as victims (e.g., Silvern, Waelde, Baughan, Karel, & Kaersvang, 2000).

The participant then moved on to a series of specific questions about the experience. As evident in our description of the results below and therefore not detailed here, a variety of survey questions tapped information about the nature and circumstances of the abuse, characteristics of the victims and the perpetrator(s), etc. To classify cases as religion-related, the survey included this question: "Do you think this experience had anything at all to do with religion?" We considered their abuse to have been religion-related if they chose any one or more of the following possible answers: "(a) it happened in a religious setting; (b) person(s) who did it to you had some religious authority or was in any religious leadership position; (c) the person(s) told you God would punish you if you told about it; (d) it was done to punish or discipline you in a way that was suggested by a religious text or spiritual being; (e) person(s) who did it thought you were possessed by devils or evil spirits; (f) person(s) who did it thought God or another spiritual figure or religious text told him/her to do it for reasons other than discipline or possession; (g) you were told God or another spiritual being would love you more because of the experience; (h) other religious reason." (In a few cases, cases were classified as religion-related when respondents failed to choose "a" but later on the survey indicated a religious setting for the abuse, or failed to choose "b" but later indicated that the perpetrator had religious authority.)

Brief Symptom Inventory (BSI). The BSI is a well-validated 53-item inventory used to assess psychological symptom patterns among patient and non-patient populations (Derogatis & Spencer, 1982). It is a brief form of the SCL-90-R. Participants use a five-point Likert scale to rate the extent to which the BSI items (describing various emotional states, feelings, and behavior) apply to themselves. The BSI provides a Global Severity Index (average response per item), a Positive Symptom Total (the number of positive or symptomatic responses overall), and a Positive Symptom Distress Index (ratio of the BSI Global Severity Index score and the BSI Positive Symptom Total, which is intended to indicate the severity of symptoms indicated). Component subscales measure nine primary symptom dimensions: hostility, depression, somatization, obsessive-compulsive tendencies, phobic anxiety, interpersonal sensitivity, anxiety, paranoid ideation, and psychoticism.

Center for Epidemiological Studies Depression Scale (CESD). The CESD consists of 20 items designed to assess recent experience of depression (Radloff, 1977). Participants respond to items in Likert-scale fashion, indicating the extent to which each statement describes their experience during the past week. The test yields an overall score, with a score of 16 indicating the possibility of depression and a score of 23 used to indicate clinically significant levels of depression.

Rosenberg Self-Esteem Scale (Rosenberg, 1965). The Rosenberg Self-Esteem Scale is one of the most popular and well-validated measures of self-esteem, with excellent internal consistency and test-retest reliability. Respondents use a four-point scale ranging from 1 (strongly agree) to 4 (strongly disagree) to answer items such as "I feel that I am a person of worth, at least on an equal basis with others." Items are coded such that higher numbers indicate higher levels of self-esteem, and summed.

Procedure

All measures were randomly ordered within one stapled packet, except that the demographic form was always placed first. Participants completed the packet in small groups during an experimental session in a large room where at least two chairs separated them from each other. Signed informed consent forms were returned separately from surveys to ensure complete anonymity.

RESULTS

We begin by presenting data regarding the nature of the abuses suffered by the two groups of victims (religion-related physical abuse victims and non-religion-related physical abuse victims), including the form of the physical maltreatment, the number of times the abuse allegedly occurred, and whether the abuse was disclosed or otherwise discovered. Then we examine characteristics of the alleged victims and perpetrators, such as the relationship between them, their religious affiliation, the victim's age, and the perpetrator's gender. Finally, we test our main hypotheses regarding the long-term impact of physical abuse: We examine the spiritual, emotional, and psychological impact of the abuse as perceived by the victims, followed by current psychological well-being as measured by our standardized psychological tests. All analyses, except those of current psychological well-being, were one-way analyses of variance (ANOVAs) or chi square analyses (as appropriate) comparing the two abuse groups. (Controls were not included in those analyses because they did not suffer abuse and therefore could not describe abuse experiences.) Analyses of well-being compared the three groups of participants (victims of religion-related physical abuse, victims of non-religion-related physical abuse, and non-abused controls). Main effects of abuse type in these latter analyses were followed by Tukey tests of pairwise comparisons of means or tests with Scheffe corrections, as appropriate (Keppel, 1982).

Characteristics of the Alleged Abuses

Form of Physical Abuse. The specific forms of the physical maltreatment suffered were statistically similar in both victim groups (see Table 1). That is, the two groups did not differ with regard to their likelihood of having been: (a) "hit, slapped, spanked, lashed, grabbed, shoved, choked, punched, kicked, bit, burned, beat, stabbed, or whipped you and it left you with welts, bruises, bleeding, or other marks or injuries," $\chi^2(1, N = 72) = .05$, $p = .82$; (b) "punished or disciplined with a belt, cord, or other hard object," $\chi^2(1, N = 72) = 3.00$, $p = .08$; or (c) "threatened with a weapon," $\chi^2(1, N = 72) = 2.78$, $p = .10$.

Reflecting the degree to which our society accepts the physical abuse of children, only about a quarter of the participants who we labeled victims believed that their experiences were abusive. Among those who experienced non-religion-related abuse, 22% considered the actions to be abusive, compared to 35% of those in the religion-related abuse group, a difference that was not statistically significant, $\chi^2(1, N = 72) = 1.42$, $p = .23$.

TABLE 1. Characteristics of the Abuse as a Function of Condition (Percentage of Cases)

	Condition	
	Religion-related abuse	Non-religion-related abuse
Specific form of the physical abuse		
Hit, slapped, spanked, etc.	69%	72%
Punished with objects	77%	57%
Threatened with a weapon	12%	2%
Other	0%	2%
Frequency of abuse		
Once	16%	4%
Twice	8%	4%
3 - 5 times	12%	39%
6 - 10 times	8%	30%
11 - 20 times	16%	7%
21 or more times	40%	15%

Involvement of Religion in the Abuse. How was religion involved in the cases? According to victims' responses to the non-mutually exclusive items used to identify cases as religion-related, in 31% of cases the perpetrator was a religious leader. (In light of recent scandal and publicity, it is important to note that sexual abuse is not the only form of abuse perpetrated on children by religious authorities.) In 31% of the religion-related abuse cases, the abuse was punishment or discipline that the perpetrator justified with religious texts, and in 12% of the cases, it was done for reasons other than punishment or discipline (but still believed by perpetrators to be ordered by God or a religious text). In 20% of cases, the perpetrator told the victim that God would punish her/him if the abuse was disclosed. Eight percent of the cases involved physical abuse done to rid the child of supposed devils or evil spirits, a form of religion-related physical abuse specifically studied by Bottoms et al. (1995, 1996). In 35% of the cases, the abuse occurred in a non-secular setting. When asked in a separate question to identify the setting of abuse, 12% of victims specified a church, 23% indicated a parochial or church-affiliated school, and 8% named some other religious meeting place. Like all forms of child abuse, however, it was still most likely to happen in the home (73% of cases; more than one setting could have been indicated).

Frequency of Abuse. The physical abuse reported was not typically a one-time occurrence (see Table 1). In fact, 40% of the religion-related abuse occurred over 20 times. To gain clarity about the nature of differences in frequency that might exist between the two types of abuse, we converted these data to a scale ranging from 1 (once) to 6 (21 or more times). We acknowledge the imperfect nature of this conversion, which collapses across many numbers at the higher end of the scale, but results from an analysis of this scale are actually conservative in this regard. An ANOVA revealed that the religion-related cases occurred, on average, with statistically similar frequency ($M = 4.20$, $SD = 1.94$) as other abuse cases ($M = 3.76$, $SD = 1.27$), $F(1, 69) = 1.33$, n.s.

Disclosure and Case Outcome. Not surprisingly, most abuse victims told no one about their experiences, perhaps out of fear or simply because they did not believe that the actions were abusive. There was no significant difference in the percentage of religion-related abuse victims (42%) and other victims (61%) who failed to disclose the abuse, $\chi^2(1, N = 71) = 2.39$, $p = .12$. Disclosures that were made by victims of religion-related or other physical abuse, were made to parents (31% and 18%), another relative (15% and 11%), a friend (27% and 21%), or a teacher (4% and 7%), respectively, all χ^2s $(1, N = 71) \leq 1.47$, $ps \geq .23$.

In addition, most respondents (69% of religion-related abuse victims and 75% of others) indicated that no one discovered the abuse (apart from disclosure), $\chi^2(1, N = 71) < 1$, n.s. In only 27% of religion-related cases and 25% of other cases did someone try to stop the abuse, $\chi^2(1, N = 70) < 1$, n.s.

A formal investigation by the police, social services, or district attorney's office was rare, occurring in only four of the religion-related cases and three of the other cases. In two of the former, there was a formal determination that the abuse occurred. In one of the latter, a conviction was obtained.

Characteristics of Victims and Perpetrators

Victim Age. There was no significant difference in the age at which the abuse began for victims of religion-related abuse ($M = 6.46$ years, $SD = 3.43$) and non-religion-related abuse ($M = 6.39$ years, $SD = 2.86$), $t(63) < 1$, n.s. The abuse lasted around 6 years, on average, ending by the age of 12.5 years ($SD = 3.91$) for victims of religion-related abuse and by 12 years ($SD = 3.43$) for other victims, $t(63) < 1$, n.s., as in the study by Bottoms et al. (1995).

Victims' Religious Affiliation and Religiosity. The victims from the two abuse groups did not differ significantly in terms of denominational affiliation. As shown in Table 2, over a third of the sample was Roman Catholic (whereas Catholics comprise around 25% of the general population). The next most popular category was mainstream Protestant (20% or less), then "Christian." The two groups also failed to differ with regard to perceived importance of religious beliefs, importance of religion to self-concept, frequency of attending religious services, frequency of prayer, and scores on the Christian Orthodoxy Scale, all $ts(\geq66) \leq 1.31$, n.s. (see Table 2). In short, the participants were much more similar than dissimilar in terms of their religious beliefs and practices.

TABLE 2. Victim and Perpetrator Characteristics as a Function of Condition

	Condition	
	Religion-related abuse	Non-religion-related abuse
Victims' religious affiliation (percentage of victims)[1]		
Fundamental protestant	4%	2%
Protestant	17%	20%
Catholic	38%	35%
Christian	17%	13%
Measures of religiosity (mean ratings)		
Importance of religious beliefs	3.80 (1.12)	3.42 (1.18)
Importance of religion to self-concept	3.04 (1.17)	2.77 (1.16)
Frequency of attending religious services	4.20 (1.83)	3.58 (2.10)
Frequency of prayer	5.96 (2.57)	5.42 (2.80)
Christian Orthodoxy Scale	33.31 (10.09)	31.80 (10.56)
Relationship of perpetrators to victims (percentage of cases)[2]		
Parent or step-parent	73%	91%
Grandparent	12%	7%
Other relative	15%	4%
Teacher	19%	2%
Perpetrators' religious affiliation (percentage of cases)[3]		
Fundamental protestant	0%	0%
Protestant	23%	7%
Catholic	59%	52%
Christian	9%	17%

Note. Standard deviations are noted parenthetically. For religiosity measures, higher values indicate more religiousness.
[1] The two victim samples also included Hindu ($N = 2$), Islam ($N = 1$), Judaism ($N = 1$), atheist ($N = 4$), and other ($N = 6$).
[2] In addition, a sibling and some other person were each the abuser in 2.2% of the non-religion-related abuse cases.
[3] The two perpetrator samples also included Hindu ($N = 2$), Islam ($N = 2$), and atheist ($N = 6$).

Relationship of Perpetrator to Victim. As is true in most cases of child physical abuse, parents were the most common perpetrators. This was more likely to be true, however, in cases of non-religion-related abuse than in religion-related abuse, $\chi^2(1, N = 71) = 4.09, p = .04$ (see Table 2). In no cases was the abuse perpetrated by a stranger or mere acquaintance. The two abuse groups did not differ significantly in the likelihood that the abuser was another family member such as a grandparent, $\chi^2(1, N = 71) = 0.51, p = .48$, or other relative, $\chi^2(1, N = 71) = 2.55, p = .11$. A teacher was more likely to have been the abuser in religion-related abuse cases than in non-religion-related abuse cases, $\chi^2(1, N = 71) = 6.16, p = .01$, probably reflecting the involvement of teachers at religious schools. We were particularly interested in instances of abuse perpetrated by religious authorities. In one religion-related abuse case, the abuser was a Sunday school teacher, and in three cases (12%), the abuser was a priest. No cases were specified as having been perpetrated by a nun, minister, rabbi, or religious healer.

We were also interested in the perceived emotional relationship between the victim and perpetrator, and so we asked the victims to rate the degree to which they felt emotionally close to the abuser both before and after the abuse, on a scale ranging from 1 (Not at all close) to 5 (Extremely close). We performed a 2 (abuse type) $\times$ 2 (time: before vs. after the abuse) ANOVA on these scale scores, with time as a within-subjects variable. There was no significant difference in perceived closeness reported overall by victims of religion-related ($M = 3.67, SD = 0.26$) and non-religion-related abuse ($M = 3.97, SD = 0.20$), $F(1, 69) < 1$, n.s. As would be expected, however, there was a significant main effect for time, with respondents feeling closer to the abuser before the abuse ($M = 4.07, SD = 1.26$) than they did following the abuse ($M = 3.65, SD = 1.58$), $F(1, 69) = 9.26, p = .003$. There was no statistically significant interaction between these two factors, $F(1, 69) < 1$, n.s.

Perpetrator Gender. There was no statistically greater likelihood of a man (77%) or woman (62%) being a perpetrator in religion-related cases, as compared to the other cases (61% and 64%, respectively), χ^2s $(1, N = 70) \leq 1.79, ps \geq .18$. These results are consistent with our finding that parents were most likely to be the abusers, and suggests that the parents worked together in performing the abuse.

Perpetrator Religion. Abusers' religious affiliations did not differ significantly between the two abuse categories, $\chi^2(7, N = 64) = 6.29, p = .51$ (see Table 2). Unsurprising for this particular Midwest sample, the abuser was most likely to be Catholic–in over half of both kinds of cases. In light of previous writings (e.g., Capps, 1992, 1995), it is surprising that no perpetrators were reported to have been "fundamentalist." This might be a function of inaccurate reporting tendencies. That is, fundamentalist might be a category unlikely to be used by our young victims, who may have chosen to leave this item blank or use identifiers like "Christian."

Spiritual, Emotional, and Psychological Effects of the Abuse

Perceived Effects on Religiosity. Respondents indicated whether the abuse caused them to change their religious beliefs. Victims of religion-related abuse (69%) were significantly less likely than other victims (94%) to report that the abuse had no effect, $\chi^2(1, N = 72) = 7.55, p < .01$. Twelve percent of the religion-related victims indicated that the abuse made them more religious, 16% less religious or atheistic, and 4% indicated that it made them switch religions. It is interesting that fully 28% of the religion-related abuse victims told us that they felt that the physical abuse was "acceptable or justified for religious reasons." Perhaps this is a necessary coping mechanism for reducing the cognitive dissonance that would otherwise result from identifying one's parents or trusted religious leaders or teachers as abusers, or from believing that religious teachings are not helpful or comforting. This finding warrants further examination in future research.

Perceived Emotional Effects. We asked respondents to tell us how emotionally upset they were by the abuse on a scale ranging from 1 (not at all upset) to 5 (highly upset). There was no difference in the average ratings given by non-religion-related ($M = 3.33, SD = 1.49$) and religion-related abuse victims ($M = 3.04, SD = 1.45$), $t(70) < 1$, n.s. Separately, we asked respondents whether they experienced any "lasting effects" of the experience. Most respondents (76% of non-religion-related and 54% of religion-related abuse victims) reported none, a difference that only approached statistical significance $\chi^2(1, N = 71) = 3.55$, $p = .06$. The most common type of lasting effect noted was "emotional or psychological harm," which was indicated by 17% of non-religious and 23% of religion-related abuse victims, $\chi^2(1, N = 71) < 1$, n.s. Only 2% of victims from the non-religion-related group reported "positive spiritual effects," as compared to 19% of religion-related abuse victims, $\chi^2(1, N = 71) = 6.16, p = .01$. None of those who reported positive spiritual effects changed their religious affiliation; whatever positive effects that might have occurred took place within their faith tradition, not as a result of changing their affiliation. The rate at which victims reported "negative spiritual effects" did not differ between the non-religion-related (4%) and religion-related (8%) abuse groups, $\chi^2(1, N = 71) < 1$, n.s. No participants reported lasting physical impairment.

Current Self-Esteem and Psychological Well-Being. We analyzed scores on the Rosenberg Self-Esteem scale, the Center for Epidemiological Studies Depression Scale, and the Brief Symptom Inventory scales in separate ANOVAs comparing all three groups (religion-related abuse victims, non-religion-related abuse victims, and the non-abused control group).[2]

First, with regard to participants' general self-esteem, there was only a non-significant trend in the expected direction. Victims of religion- related abuse reported slightly lower levels of self-esteem ($M = 30.50$, $SD = 6.16$) as compared to victims of non-religion-related abuse ($M = 33.13$, $SD = 5.65$) and the control participants ($M = 33.37$, $SD = 5.70$), $F(2, 123) = 2.37$, $p = .10$.

Next, we examined participants' current level of depression. CES-D scores revealed the effects we hypothesized: 42% of religion-related abuse victims, but only 15% of other victims and 20% of the control group could be classified as clinically depressed using the recommended criterion score of 23, $\chi^2(2, N = 126) = 7.25$, $p = .03$. Follow-up chi square analyses with Scheffé corrections (as recommended by Sheshkin, 2000) revealed that the differences between the religion-related abuse group and each of the other two groups were both statistically significant, χ^2s ≥ 4.24, $ps \leq .02$. A similar but non-significant trend emerged in level of depression as measured by the BSI-Depression subscale (see Table 3). The religion-related abuse group reported slightly higher levels of depression ($M = 1.15$, $SD = 0.85$) than did the other abuse group ($M = 0.80$, $SD = 0.88$) and the control group ($M = 0.85$, $SD = 0.76$), $F(2, 123) = 1.72$, $p = .18$.

Table 3 illustrates all means from the BSI measures. In terms of the component subscales, as predicted, victims of religion-related abuse faired more poorly than other victims and than control participants in terms of anxiety, $F(2, 123) = 4.33$, $p = .02$; phobic anxiety, $F(2, 123) = 3.87$, $p = .02$; hostility $F(2, 123) = 4.04$, $p = .02$; psychoticism, $F(2, 123) = 3.79$, $p = .02$; and paranoid ideation, $F(2, 123) = 3.46$, $p = .04$. A similar trend approached significance for obsessive-compulsive tendencies, $F(2, 123) = 2.34$, $p = .10$. In fact, the religion-related victims' mean score for obsessive-compulsiveness approached the mean score of psychiatric outpatients (1.57; Derogatis & Spencer, 1982). For somatization, there was also an overall group effect, $F(2, 123) = 3.15$, $p = .05$, with the religion-related group mean for somatization approaching the mean score for psychiatric outpatients (.83; Derogatis & Spencer, 1982). However, Tukey comparisons revealed that their score differed significantly only from the non-religion-related group, not from the control group. Mean differences for interpersonal sensitivity failed to reach statistical significance, $F(2, 123) = 1.53$, $p = .22$.

Not surprisingly, given these component results, general symptomology, as measured by the BSI Global Severity Index was, overall, greatest among people who had suffered religion-related abuse than among the other two groups of people, $F(2, 123) = 4.40$, $p = .01$. There was a similar, but only marginally significant effect, on the Positive Symptom Distress Index scores, $F(2, 123) = 2.83$, $p = .06$. Nevertheless, the analysis of individual subscales on the BSI demonstrates that, above and beyond possible effects of abuse frequency, religion-related abuse is associated with more negative effects in many areas of mental health than is abuse that has no religious component.

TABLE 3. Mean Scores on the Brief Symptom Inventory as a Function of Condition

	Condition		
	Religion-related abuse	Non-religion-related abuse	Control
Global Severity Index	1.16_a (.84)	$.71_b$ (.62)	$.78_b$ (.55)
Positive Symptom Total	28.88_a (16.6)	20.65_b (13.07)	23.26_{ab} (12.25)
Positive Symptom Distress Index	1.96_a (.51)	1.73_a (.65)	1.64_a (.48)
Primary Symptom Dimension Subscales			
Depression	1.15_a (.85)	$.80_a$ (.88)	$.85_a$ (.76)
Anxiety	1.13_a (1.11)	$.59_b$ (.68)	$.73_b$ (.60)
Phobic anxiety	$.72_a$ (.96)	$.29_b$ (.54)	$.37_b$ (.52)
Obsessive compulsiveness	1.54_a (.96)	1.06_a (.85)	1.26_a (.93)
Somatization	$.81_a$ (1.04)	$.41_b$ (.51)	$.52_{ab}$ (.53)
Hostility	1.39_a (1.21)	$.82_b$ (.75)	$.95_b$ (.68)
Paranoid ideation	1.41_a (1.06)	$.93_b$ (.94)	$.89_b$ (.67)
Psychoticism	1.06_a (.88)	$.59_b$ (.74)	$.64_b$ (.67)
Interpersonal sensitivity	1.31_a (1.08)	$.95_a$ (.95)	$.95_a$ (.86)

Note. Standard deviations are noted parenthetically. Means within a row that share letters in their subscripts do not differ from each other at $p < .05$. Higher values indicate greater distress.

DISCUSSION

In a 1988 review article, Gorsuch asked, "Is religion an important psychological variable?" When considering the abuse of children, our data indicate that it is, and that religion-related abuse should be considered distinct from other forms of child abuse. The religion-related cases in our sample were defined as such because the perpetrator of the physical abuse was a religious leader or religious teacher, believed he or she was directed by God or a religious text, and/or perpetrated the abuse in a religious context, all of which are circumstances that could lead victims to feel as though the abuse was sanctioned by a church or even God.

Our hypotheses were largely supported by our data. In particular, as expected, we found that abuse related in some way to religious beliefs or practices was quite similar to non-religion-related abuse in terms of its basic form, frequency of occurrence, likelihood of having been disclosed or otherwise discovered by anyone or acted upon by legal or social service authorities (which rarely occurred), victim characteristics (age, religious affiliation, and religiosity), and perpetrator characteristics (religious affiliation, gender). The only reliable difference in the nature of the cases involved the relationship of victim to perpetrator: Although all cases were more likely to be perpetrated by a parent than by anyone else, this was somewhat more likely in non-religion-related cases, and teachers were more likely to be perpetrators in religion-related cases than in other cases.

We expected to find more spiritual injury and decreased religiosity among religion-related abuse victims. These hypotheses were not supported: There were no significant group differences in terms of perceived importance of religion generally and to the self-concept, frequency of attending religious services and of praying, and religious beliefs as measured by the Christian Orthodoxy Scale. Thus, findings of decreased spirituality or religiosity noted in victims of child sexual abuse (e.g., Doxey et al., 1997; Lawson et al., 1998) may not generalize to victims of child physical abuse.

Of most importance were our hypotheses regarding long-term psychological impact. We found that victims from the two abuse groups did not differ in the extent to which they reported having been emotionally upset by the abuse. In fact, victims of religion-related abuse were more likely than victims of other physical abuse to say that their experience had lasting positive spiritual effects. The two groups also failed to differ in terms of general self-esteem, contrary to our expectations. However, other standard measures of psychological well-being revealed significant differences such that victims of religion-related abuse had greater psychological symptomology than did victims of other physical abuse or non-abused controls. In particular, victims of religion-related abuse displayed more depression, anxiety, hostility, psychoticism, phobic anxiety, and paranoid ideation (although the latter two effects weakened after covarying for proxy measures of abuse severity). Those victims were also higher in somatization than victims of non-religion-related abuse, but did not differ from the control group in that regard. As noted in our introduction, several of these sequellae were also found in the Bottoms et al. (1995) study of religion-related child abuse. Although prior research has shown that many of these emotional difficulties, including hostility, anxiety, depression, and suicidal ideation, result from child physical abuse without religious components, the victims of non-religion-related abuse in our study did not differ significantly from the control group on any dimension of well-being. (This is cause for some caution in interpreting our results, because it is possible that our non-religion-related abuse comparison group was more highly functioning than such victims in the general population. However, if this were true, then one would expect religion-related abuse group to also be proportionally higher functioning.)

What could explain the poorer psychological outcomes for the religion-related victims compared to the other two groups? As we theorized in the introduction, religious contexts and justifications may add an additional layer of complexity and harm to the experience of child physical abuse. Additional research is necessary to determine the specific nature of this additional complexity, but like others (Bottoms et al., 1995; Goodman et al., 1998), we speculate that there is an additional sense of betrayal involved, and much internal cognitive dissonance and perhaps guilt as victims deal not only with the physically abusive actions, but also with the confusing relation of the actions to religion, which they are taught to believe and follow. This may interfere with normal coping mechanisms. Young victims may come to believe (or are told to believe) that the abuse is parentally and/or supernaturally sanctioned or required, or is a punishment for their own sins. Fully 28% of our victims had, in fact, come to believe that the abusive experiences were justified for religious reasons. Only 35% of them considered their experiences to have been abusive.

To understand the differential psychological effect of religion-related abuse, it is also worthwhile to consider theories proposed by researchers such as Pargament and Kirkpatrick. First, Pargament (1997) has demonstrated that, for some people, religion is a source of meaning that helps them cope with daily and existential concerns. We suggest that victims of religion-related abuse, whose relationship to or views of God could be disturbed by the abuse experience, might be deprived of the benefits of viewing God as a coping resource. Victims abused by a person with religious authority have also lost that spiritual leader as a source of social support. Second, according to Kirkpatrick (1997, 1998), God serves as an attachment figure for some individuals, especially those who are not securely attached to parents. In the typical religion-related abuse case in our sample, one or both parents were the perpetrator, the perpetrators invoked religion or God to legitimize their actions, and the victims felt more distant emotionally from the perpetrators after the abuse. Thus, our victims might have felt deprived of secure attachments with parents and with God, and might have had fewer social psychological resources for effective coping. Although we failed to find decreased religiosity or religious practices among victims of religion-related abuse, we did not directly measure the use of religion as a coping mechanism or source of social support, nor did we measure feelings of attachment to parents or God. Of interest, Kennedy and Drebing (2002) similarly found no relation between current religious behaviors and past experiences of abuse (non-religion-related abuse), but they did find that self-reported frequency of abuse was related to feelings of alienation from God.

Strengths and Limitations

Our study is one of very few studies, if any, to use data reported directly by victims (as opposed to data reported by their therapists or by the authorities, for example, as in Bottoms et al., 1995 and Bottoms et al., 1996) to compare child physical abuse that is religion-related with abuse that is not. Our methodology is solid in many ways: We used appropriate comparison and control groups, well-conceived and validated measures, and a sample that was diverse and therefore representative in terms of socioeconomic status and race/ethnicity. Even so, there are many questions we were unable to address, and our findings should be considered in light of our study's limitations. For example, we investigated only one form of religion-related abuse, ignoring other forms that are also of importance, such as religion-related medical neglect and sexual abuse perpetrated by persons with religious authority (but these have been covered in some depth in other articles, e.g., Bottoms et al., 1995). Further, even though our sample was diverse in some ways, it was also small in size, young, and included only victims from a non-clinical, urban, Midwest setting. Our findings might not represent the experiences of individuals who suffered extremely severe abuse or emotional sequellae and who therefore are less likely to appear in a sample of highly functioning college students (e.g., Duncan, 1999). Nor might they be generalizable to other locales. We also have no way of moving from our data to base rates in the general population, so we cannot provide any insight into the incidence or prevalence of this form of abuse. Further, as is true for any study using retrospective self-report methodology, people are not always accurate in reflecting upon their past experiences, their motivations, or their cognitive processes (Azar, 1997). We have necessarily accepted the accuracy of information provided by respondents, but victims' perceptions and recollections might not all be accurate. It is also worth noting that we measured victims' perceptions and psychological well-being at only one point in time, when the victims are relatively young; we do not know what longer term effects might be. Finally, no one study can measure all important variables. Although we included several measures of abuse severity, including one (frequency) which did differ between the two abuse groups, we do not know if there are additional unmeasured variables which might help explain the differences we observed in mental health status of the victims from the two abuse groups. Obviously, random assignment to abused and nonabused groups is not, and never will be, feasible. For all these reasons, our study is an important start in documenting that differences exist in the mental health outcomes of religion-related and other forms of physical abuse, but it is only a start. Future research must be conducted to determine if the differences we observed can be replicated, and if so, additional research should use a theoretically oriented approach to understand the specific reasons for those differences. Even so, we believe our study makes an important contribution to a controversial field by providing scientific findings that can lead to a better understanding of religion-related abuse. Understanding necessarily precedes and informs identification, treatment, and prevention efforts, especially efforts to work with parents or others who need to learn non-abusive methods for disciplining children. We are pleased that some churches are already engaging in such intervention efforts.

CONCLUSION

A regrettable picture has been developed by our study: Physically abusive actions taken against a child for religious reasons are generally not severe enough to attract the attention of authorities (as indicated by our data on disclosure and discovery), and not often considered by its victims to be abusive, but nonetheless might have long-lasting negative consequences for psychological well-being. As Greven (1991) notes, abusive parenting styles have been driven by mainstream religious beliefs for centuries. They are part of our Euro-American heritage, and if religion-related child abuse is not acknowledged now as a problem by our society, it will be our legacy to the future. The freedom to choose religions and to practice them will, and should, always be protected by our constitution. The freedom to abuse children in the course of those practices ought to be curtailed.

NOTES

1. The larger parent survey consisted of four parts, each addressing a different form of child maltreatment (physical, sexual, emotional, and neglect). For the present paper, we analyzed data from participants who suffered only child physical abuse (or, for the control group, no abuse). Thus, we were able to examine the nature and effects of child physical abuse specifically rather than in combination with other forms of abuse. That is, religious beliefs can contribute to single or multiple forms of child abuse (Bottoms et al., 1995), and the presence or absence of various combinations of abuse has differential effects on victims (Goodman et al., 1998). Even so, we acknowledge different and uncontrolled levels of emotional abuse among our cases, consistent with arguments that all forms of child abuse involve some level of psychological maltreatment (Brassard, Germain, & Hart, 1987; Claussen & Crittenden, 1991; Garbarino, 1980; Garbarino & Vondra, 1987). It is also important to note that the distribution of respondents across our three groups is not at all indicative of incidence or prevalence; it results from purposeful sampling from among a much larger number of students who participated in the parent study.

2. We also performed analyses of covariance (ANCOVA) comparing only the two abused groups while statistically controlling for two variables that might reflect abuse severity: (a) frequency of abuse, as measured by the six-point frequency scale described in the results section (and which did not differ significantly between the two groups), and (b) whether or not a parent or parents were the perpetrators of the abuse (which did differ significantly between the groups, with parents more likely to be the perpetrators in cases of non-religion-related abuse). These ANCOVAs revealed few differences in the results presented herein: After covarying for the two factors simultaneously, (a) the significant effects of abuse type on phobic anxiety and on somatization weakened to marginal levels of significance, $F(1, 66) = 3.04, p = .09$ and $F(1, 66) = 3.07, p = .08$, respectively; and (b) the significant effect on paranoid ideation became non-significant, $F(1, 66) = 1.95, p = .17$.

REFERENCES

Allen, D. M., & Tarnowski, K. G. (1989). Depressive characteristics of physically abused children. *Journal of Abnormal Child Psychology, 17*, 1-11.

Azar, B. (1997). Poor recall mars research and treatment: Inaccurate self-reports can lead to faulty research conclusions and inappropriate treatment. *The APA Monitor, 28*, 1.

Azar, S. T., & Gehl, K. S. (1997). Physical abuse and neglect. In R. T. Ammerman, & M. Hersen (Eds.), *Handbook of prescriptive treatments for children and adolescents* (pp. 329-345). Boston: Allyn & Bacon.

Belsky, J. (1993). Etiology of child maltreatment: A developmental-ecological analysis. *Psychological Bulletin, 114*, 413-434.

Bottoms, B. L., Shaver, P. R., & Goodman, G. S. (1996). An analysis of ritualistic and religion-related child abuse allegations. *Law and Human Behavior, 20*(1), 1-34.

Bottoms, B. L., Shaver, P. R., Goodman, G. S., & Qin, J. (1995). In the name of God: A profile of religion-related child abuse. *Journal of Social Issues, 51*(2), 85-111.

Brassard, M., Germain, R., & Hart, S. (1987). *Psychological maltreatment of children and youth*. New York: Pergamon Books.

Brown, J., Cohen, P., Johnson, J. G., & Smailes, E. M. (1999). Childhood abuse and neglect: Specificity of effects on adolescent and young adult depression and suicidality. *Journal of American Academy of Child and Adolescent Psychiatry, 38*, 1490-1505.

Bruhn, C. M. (2003). Children with disabilities: Abuse, neglect, and the child welfare system. *Journal of Aggression, Maltreatment & Trauma, 8*(1/2), 173-203.

Bryant, S. L., & Range, L. M. (1997). Type and severity of child abuse and college students' lifetime suicidality. *Child Abuse & Neglect, 21*(12), 1169-1176.

Capps, D. (1992). Religion and child abuse: Perfect together. *Journal for the Scientific Study of Religion, 31*(1), 1-14.

Capps, D. (1995). *The child's song: The religious abuse of children*. Louisville, KY: Westminster John Knox Press.

Claussen, A. H., & Crittenden, P. M. (1991). Physical and psychological maltreatment: Relations among types of maltreatment. *Child Abuse and Neglect, 15*, 5-18.

Derogatis, L. R., & Spencer, P. M. (1982). *The Brief Symptom Inventory (BSI): Administration, scoring, & procedures manual-I*. Baltimore, MD: Johns Hopkins University School of Medicine.

Dodge, K. A., Pettit, G. S., & Bates, J. E. (1997). How the experience of early physical abuse leads children to become chronically aggressive. In *Developmental perspectives on trauma: Theory, research, and intervention* (Vol. 8, pp. 263-288). Rochester, NY: University of Rochester Press.

Doxey, C., Jensen, L., & Jensen, J. (1997). The influence of religion on victims of childhood sexual abuse. *International Journal for the Psychology of Religion, 7*, 179-186.

Duncan, R. (1999, July). *Childhood maltreatment and college drop-out rates: Implications for researchers and educators*. Presented at the 7th Annual Colloquium of the American Professional Society on the Abuse of Children, San Antonio, TX.

Durkheim, E. (1915/1965). *The elementary forms of the religious life*. New York: Free Press.

Ellison, C. G., Bartkowski, J. P., & Segal, M. L. (1996a). Do conservative Protestant parents spank more often? Further evidence from the national survey of families and households. *Social Science Quarterly, 77*, 663-673.

Ellison, C. G., Bartkowski, J. P., & Segal, M. L. (1996b). Conservative Protestantism and the parental use of corporal punishment. *Social Forces, 74*(3), 1003-1028.

Ellison, C. G., & Sherkat, D. E. (1993). Conservative Protestantism and support for corporal punishment. *American Sociological Review*, *58*(1), 131-145.

Epstein, M. E., & Bottoms, B. L. (2002). Forgetting and recovery of abuse and trauma memories: Possible mechanisms. *Child Maltreatment*, *7*, 210-225.

Flynn, C. P. (1996). Normative support for corporal punishment: Attitudes, correlates, and implications. *Aggression and Violent Behavior*, *1*(1), 47-55.

Friesen, J. G., Jr. (1992). Ego-dystonic or ego-alien: Alternate personality or evil spirit? *Journal of Psychology and Theology*, *20*, 197-200.

Garbarino, J. (1980). Defining emotional maltreatment: The message is the meaning. *Journal of Psychiatric Treatment and Evaluation*, *2*, 105-110.

Garbarino, J., & Vondra, J. (1987). Psychological maltreatment: Issues and perspectives. In M. Brassard, R. Germain, & S. Hart (Eds.), *Psychological maltreatment of children and youth* (pp. 25-44). New York: Pergamon.

Goodman, G. S., Bottoms, B. L., Redlich, A., Shaver, P. R., & Diviak, K. (1998). Correlates of multiple forms of victimization in religion-related child abuse cases. *Journal of Aggression, Maltreatment, & Trauma*, *2*, 273-295. [Reprinted in B. B. R. Rossman, & M. S. Rosenberg (Eds.). (1998). *Multiple victimization of children: Conceptual, developmental, research, and treatment issues* (pp. 273-295). Binghamton, NY: The Haworth Press, Inc.]

Gorsuch, R. L. (1988). Psychology of religion. *Annual Review of Psychology*, *39*, 202-221.

Greven, P. (1991). *Spare the child: The religious roots of punishment and the psychological impact of physical abuse*. New York: Knopf.

Hunsberger, B. (1989). A short version of the Christian orthodoxy scale. *Journal for the Scientific Study of Religion*, *28*, 360-365.

Jackson, S., Law, L., Thompson, R. A., Christiansen, E. H., Colman, R. A., & Wyatt, J. (1999). Predicting abuse-prone parental attitudes and discipline practices in a nationally representative sample. *Child Abuse & Neglect*, *23* (1), 15-29.

Johnson, B. W., & Eastburg, M. C. (1992). God, parent and self concepts in abused and nonabused children. *Journal of Psychology and Christianity*, *11*(3), 235-243.

Kane, D., Cheston, S. E., & Greer, J. (1993). Perceptions of God by survivors of childhood sexual abuse: An exploratory study in an underresearched area. *Journal of Psychology and Theology*, *21*(3), 228-237.

Kennedy, P., & Drebing, C. E. (2002). Abuse and religious experiences: A study of religiously committed evangelical adults. *Mental Health, Religion, & Culture*, *5*, 225-237.

Keppel, G. (1982). *Design and analysis: A researcher's handbook*. Englewood Cliffs, NJ: Prentice-Hall.

Kirkpatrick, L. A. (1997). A longitudinal study of changes in religious belief and behavior as a function of individual differences in adult attachment style. *Journal for the Scientific Study of Religion*, *36*, 207-217.

Kirkpatrick, L. A. (1998). God as a substitute attachment figure: A longitudinal study of adult attachment style and religious change in college students. *Personality and Social Psychology Bulletin*, *24*, 961-973.

Kolko, D. J. (2002). Child physical abuse. In J. E. B. Myers, L. Berliner, J. Briere, C. T. Hendrix, C. Jenny, & T. A. Reid. *The APSAC handbook on child maltreatment* (pp. 21-54). Thousand Oaks, CA: Sage.

Lawson, R., Drebing, C., Berg, G., Vincellette A., & Penk, W. (1998). The long term impact of child abuse on religious behavior and spirituality in men. *Child Abuse & Neglect, 22*(5), 369-380.

Levitan, R. D., Parikh, S. V., Lesage, A. D., Hegadoren, K. M., Adams, M., Kennedy, S. H., & Goering, P. N. (1998). Major depression in individuals with a history of childhood physical or sexual abuse: Relationship to neurovegetative features, mania and gender. *American Journal of Psychiatry, 155*(12), 1746-1752.

Lung, C. T., & Daro, D. (1996). *Current trends in child abuse reporting and fatalities: The results of the 1995 annual fifty state survey.* Chicago: National Committee to Prevent Child Abuse.

Luntz, B., & Widom, C. S. (1994). Antisocial personality disorder in abused and neglected children grown up. *American Journal of Psychiatry, 151*, 670-674.

Lynch, M., & Cicchetti, D. (1998). An ecological-transactional analysis of children and contexts: The longitudinal interplay among child maltreatment, community violence, and children's symptomatology. *Development and Psychopathology, 10*(2), 235-257.

Malcarne, V. L., & Burchard, J. D. (1992). Investigations of child abuse/neglect allegations in religious cults: A case study in Vermont. *Behavioral Sciences & the Law, 10*(1), 75-88.

Maurer, A. (1982). Religious values and child abuse. *Child & Youth Services, 4*, 57-63.

Maxfield, M. G., & Widom, C. S. (1996). The cycle of violence: Revisited six years later. *Archives of Pediatrics and Adolescent Medicine, 150*, 390-395.

McGlone, G. J. (2003). The pedophile and the pious: Towards a new understanding of sexually offending and non-offending Roman Catholic priests. *Journal of Aggression, Maltreatment, & Trauma, 8*(1/2), 115-131.

Milner, J. S. (2000). Social information processing and child physical abuse: Theory and research. In D. J. Hansen (Ed.), *Nebraska symposium on motivation, Vol. 46, 1998: Motivation and child maltreatment* (pp. 39-84). Lincoln, NE: University of Nebraska Press.

Nelsen, H. M., & Kroliczak, A. (1984). Parental use of the threat "God will punish": Replication and extension. *Journal for Scientific Study of Religion, 23*(3), 267-277.

Neufeld, K. (1979). Child-rearing, religion, abusive parents. *Religious Education, 74*(3), 235-243.

Oats, R. K., Forrest, D., & Peacock, A. (1985). Self-esteem of abused children. *Child Abuse & Neglect, 9*, 159-163.

Pagelow, M. D., & Johnson, P. (1988). Abuse in the American family: The role of religion. In A. L. Horton, & J. A. Williamson (Eds.), *Abuse and religion: When praying isn't enough.* (pp. 1-12). Lexington, MA: Lexington Books.

Pargament, K. I. (1997). *The psychology of religious coping.* New York: Guilford.

Pelcovitz, D., Kaplan, S., Goldenberg, B., & Mandel, F. (1994). Posttraumatic stress disorder in physically abused adolescents. *Journal of American Academy of Child and Adolescent Psychiatry, 33*(3), 305-312.

Quas, J. A., Bottoms, B. L., & Nunez, N. (Eds.). (2002). Linking juvenile delinquency and child maltreatment: Causes, correlates, and consequences [Special issue]. *Children's Services: Social Policy, Research, and Practice, 5*(4).

Radloff, L. S. (1977). The CES-D Scale: A self-report depression scale for research in the general population. *Journal of Applied Psychological Measurement, 1*, 385-401.

Rice, R. R., & Annis, A. W. (1992). *A survey of abuse in the Christian Reformed Church*. Grand Rapids, MI: Social Research Center of Calvin College.

Rosenberg, M. J. (1965). *Society and the adolescent self-image*. Princeton, NJ: Princeton University Press.

Rossetti, S. J. (1995). The impact of child sexual abuse on attitudes toward God and the Catholic Church. *Child Abuse & Neglect, 19*(12), 1469-1481.

Ryan, P. L. (1998). Spirituality among adult survivors of childhood violence: A literature review. *The Journal of Transpersonal Psychology, 30*(1), 39-51.

Sheshkin, D. J. (2000). *Handbook of parametric and nonparametric statistical procedures* (2nd ed.). Boca Raton, FL: Chapman & Hall/CRC.

Shor, R. (1998). The significance of religion in advancing a culturally sensitive approach towards child maltreatment. *Families in Society, 79*(4), 400-409.

Silverman, A. B., Reinherz, H. Z., & Giaconia, R. M. (1996). The long-term sequelae of child and adolescent abuse: A longitudinal community study. *Child Abuse & Neglect, 8*(8), 709-723.

Silvern, L., Waelde, L. C., Baughan, B. M., Karel, J., & Kaersvang, L. J. (2000). Two formats for eliciting retrospective reports of child sexual and physical abuse: Effects on apparent prevalence and relationships to adjustment. *Child Maltreatment, 5*, 236-250.

Simons, R. L., Whitbeck, L. B., Conger, R. D., & Chyi-In, W. (1991). Intergenerational transmission of harsh parenting. *Developmental Psychology, 27*, 159-171.

Straus, M. (1994). *Beating the devil out of them: Corporal punishment in American families*. San Francisco: Jossey-Bass.

Straus, M. A., & Gelles, R. J. (1988). How violent are American families? Estimates from the National Family Violence Survey and other studies. In G. T. Hotaling, D. Finkelhor, J. T. Kirkpatric, & M. A. Straus (Eds.), *Family abuse and its consequences: Violence in American families* (pp. 14-36). New York: Anchor/Doubleday.

U.S. Department of Health and Human Services. (2000). *Child maltreatment 1998: Reports from the states to the National Child Abuse and Neglect Data System*. Washington, DC: U.S. Government Printing Office.

Wiehe, V. R. (1990). Religious influence on parental attitudes toward the use of corporal punishment. *Journal of Family Violence, 5*, 173-186.

Winton, M. A., & Mara, B. A. (2001). *Child abuse and neglect: Multidisciplinary approaches*. Needham Heights, MA: Allyn & Bacon.

Wolfe, D. (1999). *Child Abuse: Implications for child development and psychopathology* (2nd ed.). Thousand Oaks, CA: Sage.

The Pedophile and the Pious:
Towards a New Understanding
of Sexually Offending and Non-Offending
Roman Catholic Priests

Gerard J. McGlone

SUMMARY. This chapter is an attempt at providing heretofore unpublished and essential background information and historical understanding about clerical sexual abuse, which might allow some to contextualize differently the serious problem in the Roman Catholic and other faith based communities in the United States. Discussion indicates some variables that might provide researchers with clear markers for differentiation. Directions for future research are discussed. *[Article copies available for a fee from The Haworth Document Delivery Service: 1-800- HAWORTH. E-mail address: <docdelivery@haworthpress.com> Website: <http:// www.Haworth Press.com> © 2003 by The Haworth Press, Inc. All rights reserved.]*

KEYWORDS. Assessment, historical roots, pedophile, ephebophile, priests, Roman Catholic, sexually offending

Address correspondence to: Gerard J. McGlone, PhD, Johns Hopkins University, School of Medicine, 740 North Calvert Street, Baltimore, MD 21202 (E-mail: Gjmcglone@aol.com).

[Haworth co-indexing entry note]: "The Pedophile and the Pious: Towards a New Understanding of Sexually Offending and Non-Offending Roman Catholic Priests." McGlone, Gerard J. Co-published simultaneously in *Journal of Aggression, Maltreatment & Trauma* (The Haworth Maltreatment & Trauma Press, an imprint of The Haworth Press, Inc.) Vol. 8, No. 1/2 (#15/16), 2003, pp. 115-131; and: *The Victimization of Children: Emerging Issues* (ed: Janet L. Mullings, James W. Marquart, and Deborah J. Hartley) The Haworth Maltreatment & Trauma Press, an imprint of The Haworth Press, Inc., 2003, pp. 115-131. Single or multiple copies of this article are available for a fee from The Haworth Document Delivery Service [1-800-HAWORTH, 9:00 a.m. - 5:00 p.m. (EST). E-mail address: docdelivery@haworthpress.com].

http://www.haworthpress.com/web/JAMT
© 2003 by The Haworth Press, Inc. All rights reserved.
Digital Object Identifier: 10.1300/J146v08n01_05

Sexual abuse of children by members of the Roman Catholic clergy is an enormously tragic, complex, and intriguing problem in today's society. In less than one year's time, this crisis has seen the fall of one of the most powerful American Catholic Church figures, Cardinal Bernard Law of Boston. The gross mismanagement of both the victims and the perpetrators has been chronicled (Boston Globe Staff, 2002). Since the early 1980s, many priests and brothers have been labeled "pedophiles" by the media. Sensationalism and intrigue surround most of these stories, but few accounts offer any help in understanding the problem. Scientific terms are bantered about with little regard for their meaning and little care for their importance. In the Church, those on the right and left use this crisis to promote their own agendas. In order to progress beyond its current status, the problem demands a full exploration of its context, along with rigorous scientific investigation. This chapter will attempt to evaluate and add to the base of existing knowledge about the Roman Catholic priest sex offender by exploring the psychosexual and psychological profiles of this group and comparing them with priests who have no known history of sexually abusive behaviors (for a discussion of religion-related child physical abuse, see Bottoms, Nielsen, Murray, & Filipas, this volume).

The problem of clerical sexual abuse is one that springs from an ecclesiastical cultural environment that has enormous power and influence upon an individual. Certain individuals–the clear majority of priests–are able to relate normally and healthfully out of this atmosphere, whereas others cannot. Clerical sexual abuse comes from this setting and takes place within a relationship of power and dominance. The clarity with which one sees the full dimensions of the current problem rests not only in understanding the distinctions of terms, but also the distinctions of meaning. Clearly, some priests have taken their role and misused it to such an extent that a victim's concept and very experience, if not the full reality, of the sacred is sacrificed and, in some cases, destroyed. This experience, harm, and pain must never escape attention, and this attentiveness might lead to a better understanding of this substantial problem.

The study of clerical sexual abuse must begin with a clarification of terms that are used throughout this chapter. According to the American Psychiatric Association's (APA) *Diagnostic and Statistical Manual of Mental Disorders* (DSM-IV), a pedophile is "an individual who is attracted to a prepubescent child (generally under the age of 13)" (2000, p. 571). Most classic pedophiles seem to be fixated upon a certain age and type of child, and sometimes have victims that number into the hundreds (Schwartz & Cellini, 1995). The number of actual Roman Catholic priest pedophiles seems to be 0.2-0.3% of all Catholic clergy (Jenkins, 1996; Plante, 1999; Sipe, 1995). In contrast, an *ephebophile* is an individual who is attracted sexually to a postpubertal child or adolescent in the age range of 14-18. This is not a diagnosis from the DSM-IV but rather a useful and commonly used classification, since 80% of the known priest offender population fall into this grouping. A recent analysis by *The New York Times* would put this figure in question, however (Goodstein, 2003). Ephebophiles tend to have significantly fewer victims and seem less fixated than pedophiles (Goodstein, 2003).

For the purposes of this discussion, a *sex offender* or a sexually offending individual is a person who is either an ephebophile or a pedophile, or one who engages in these types of behaviors and who might better be classified with a Nonspecific Paraphilia, according to current diagnostic codes employed by the DSM-IV. The DSM-IV (APA, 2000) identifies paraphilic behaviors as those that are significantly distressful, cause impairment, involve non-consenting individuals, and which lead to legal and social complications. Typically, a priest who admits to perpetrating an offense on an adolescent does not fit easily into the DSM-IV diagnostic codes; indeed, several factors seem to be different. The object choice is often over the age of 13, the number(s) of victims is often lower, and the victim's gender is typically male; however, all too often the sexual behavior/fantasy experienced is undefined sexual exploration that does not fit into any easily defined classification or sexual fetish. Hence, the broader definition used here is an attempt to gain a wider understanding or description of the heterogeneity of this group of individuals.

Obtaining reliable data on prevalence and incidence rates in this field is extremely difficult and confusing. There are many problems with both the tendency to underreport and the tendency to miscalculate (Finkelhor, Hotaling, Lewis, & Smith, 1990; Follingstad & DeHart, 2000; Goodstein, 2003). Information becomes even more difficult to find when there is no consistent reporting on the type of abuse committed, the relationship of the victim to the perpetrator, and the extent and content of the abuse (Conte & Savage, 2003; Demarest, 1999; Haugaard, 2000). When distinguishing between a pedophile and an ephebophile, most researchers use the prevalence rates of victims to speculate about the prevalence among perpetrators (Finkelhor & Dziuba-Leatherman, 1994). For female victims, it seems safe to conclude that, at present, a 28-45% prevalence rate for sexual abuse exists in the general population, whereas for male victims this rate seems to be between 8-16% (Mendel, 1995; Schwartz &

Cellini, 1995). These numbers seem to hold up across many samples. Generally 90% of perpetrators in the general population are male, and the prevalence rate for perpetrators may range from 5-9% of the entire male population (Schwartz & Cellini, 1995). General figures about the rate of prevalence with this population of male ephebophiles approximate 0.8-2.1% (Plante, 1999). This could be much higher considering recent documentation and research (Plante, 1999). These researchers seem to suggest–which at best is a guess–that these figures might more accurately be doubled if we take into account the overwhelming evidence suggesting that males tend not to report abuse as much as females do. All of these figures are not "true" prevalence rates but are what is known as "detected" rates of prevalence for this population.

Hence, due to underreporting and miscalculations, great concern and caution need to be exercised because of the high prevalence of male-to-male contact among this clerical offender population (Plante, 1999). Reliable statistical figures for sex offenders among the nearly 53,000 Catholic clergy (priests and brothers) in the United States are extremely difficult to ascertain (see Table 1). The Center for Applied Research in the Apostolate at Georgetown University estimates the total number of priests to be about 47,000. It estimates that 67% of these priests are diocesan with the remaining one-third being religious order priests. Some estimate from 0.2-4.0% (Jenkins, 1996), or minimally between 100 and 2,000 priests, are sex offenders; the latest *New York Times* survey puts the total percentage at 1.8% (Goodstein, 2003), while others believe the numbers are as high as 2,000 to 3,000 priests (Plante, 1999; Sipe, 1995).

While some question these percentages and numbers (Economus, 1996; Sipe, 1995), almost no one doubts that more than 80% of these known priest-offenders are classified as ephebophiles, a fact that is often underreported and unanalyzed (Jenkins, 1996; Loftus, 1999; Plante,

TABLE 1. Prevalence of Sexual Activity Among Catholic Clergy

Researchers	Pedophiles	Ephebophiles	Sexually Active[a]
Loftus & Camargo (1992)	2.7%	8.4%	27.8%
Connors (1994)	0.2%-0.3%	5-8%	Not reported
Sipe (1990, 1995)	2%	4%	40-50%
Jenkins (1996)	0.3%	2-4%	Not reported

[a]Sexually active refers to a priest who is engaged genitally with a consenting adult in a non-pastoral setting. This is an attempt to avoid confusion with sexual harassment cases.

1999). Goodstein (2003), however, seems to report a more even split in these data. The inability to clearly distinguish these two types of sexual offenders (the pedophile versus the ephebophile) prevents the public and, therefore, most Catholics, from fully understanding the breadth and depth of the problem (Golden, 2000; Haugaard, 2000). Likewise, this inability can confuse researchers and theoreticians as to the phenomenon encountered in the Church today.

Little is known about sexually offending priests because of many factors, not the least of which has been the Catholic Church's unwillingness and/or inability to sponsor and lead genuine research in this area (Loftus, 1999; Plante, 1999). Access to subjects has been a primary stumbling block in previous research (Loftus, 1999) as well as in this research project. Jenkins (1996), and more recently Plante (1999) and Cozzens (2000b), detailed the complexities of the social situation within which the Church is attempting to respond. The relatively recent publicity about this problem highlights the paucity of basic information available (Boston Globe Staff, 2003; Goodstein, 2003; Plante, 1999). Many writers have chronicled this phenomenon (Foggo, 2000; Plante, 1999; Sipe, 1999; "The sex abuse file," 2000; Wilkes, 2000; Wills, 2000). More often than not, they are vivid descriptions of the divergent political agendas that obscure the problem of clerical sexual abuse (Jenkins, 1996; Goodstein, 2003).

It becomes essential to depict the historical roots of the problem and to have a clear classification as to the phenomenon that is being critiqued, namely, clearly distinguishing between pedophiles and ephebophiles (Connors, 1994; Jenkins, 1996; Plante, 1999), and between those cases with males versus females as victims. Collecting preliminary and descriptive data is essential in order to advance basic knowledge in the field (Bryant, 1999; Loftus, 1999). Most current knowledge about priest sex offenders comes from the treatment centers that have encountered these individuals, but data from these centers reveal a significant selection bias and lacks some independence and objectivity because of the inherent flaws in using a convenience sample. Some would also suggest that they work for the Church and have a fiscal interest in helping the Church prevail in lawsuits. Priests are sent to these centers for various reasons depending upon the views, perspective, and experiences of the bishop or religious superior who is charged with this responsibility. In addition, the Church is also funding the treatment. Likewise, some treatment centers adhere to a 12-Step model for treatment, while others have various psychological orientations. Little independent research has been conducted (Loftus, 1999; McGlone, 2001), and many researchers from the treatment centers are calling for this important new data (Loftus, 1999; Plante, 1999; Rossetti, 2000). Even so, some treatment centers have been instrumental in detailing cases and unfolding this important new field of study. They have provided important data, and their initial findings have allowed the scientific community to begin searching for the similarities and differences between clerical and other sex offenders (Plante, 1999). It should be noted that Connors (1994) detailed his clinical impressions in a speech whereas the only comprehensive descriptive and scientific study was done by Loftus and Camargo (1992).

To understand the problem of priest sex offenders, it must be seen within its uniquely Catholic context. This is not to suggest that this problem only exists in the Roman Catholic Church (Bottoms, 2002; Interfaith Sexual Trauma Institute [ISTI], 1995. It clearly does not, but certain features of the problem seem different. Three important aspects of the Roman Catholic clergy must therefore be discussed: (a) historical and theological background, (b) celibacy and the priesthood, and (c) psychosexual understandings (Cozzens, 2000b; Jordan, 2000; Wills, 2000).

THE PRIESTHOOD'S
HISTORICAL AND THEOLOGICAL BACKGROUND

Throughout its nearly 2,000-year history, the Catholic Church has attempted to fulfill one essential mission: to proclaim Christ Jesus and the Gospel. Within this mission, priests have come to be seen as one essential instrument among many. In both early and current theology, the priest is viewed as being like Christ. In theological terminology commonly employed before the Second Vatican Council in the early 1960s, a priest was seen as an *"Alter Christus,"* or *"Another Christ"* (Cozzens, 2000b; Wills, 2000). These theological roots date back to the Hebrew scripture in which the sons of Aaron and the descendants of Abraham used priests "appointed on behalf of men in relation to God, to offer gifts and sacrifices for sins" (Ratzinger, 1994, p. 386). From the perspective of Catholic belief, Christ came into salvation history to end, once and for all, the endless Hebrew sacrificing. Christ's sacrifice of himself before God's throne is complete in the very person and sacrifice of Christ on the cross. Theologically, this eucharistic memorial is celebrated at every Mass in the actions of the priest and the community. From this belief system, it follows logically that the priest imitates the sacrifice of Christ, and each member of the community participates through this priestly mission.

Over time, the priest's role became more and more significant both within ecclesiastical and civil structures while the participation of the community diminished. Church history details the extraordinary powers and functions that priests began to assume–functions that derived not from holiness or the priestly mission, but from the political and economic realities of particular time periods (Chamberlin, 1993; Wills, 2000). This point is illustrated in the many stories of priests exercising civic authority over towns and territories during the medieval period (Manchester, 1992).

The combination of secular and spiritual powers throughout history created both enormous privileges and problems for the priest (Cozzens, 2000b; Manchester, 1992). Church histories show that the order or rank of priest became more significant; in this belief system, the priest functioned out of an office or role that could not allow him to be anything but that which the office or role dictated. As early as the fifth century, Saint Gregory of Nazianzus put it aptly:

Who then is the priest? He is the defender of truth, who stands with angels, gives glory to archangels, causes sacrifices to rise to the altar on high, shares Christ's priesthood, refashions creation, restores it in God's image, recreates it for the world on high and, even greater, is divinized and divinizes. (Ratzinger, 1994, p. 393)

Saint Gregory began to put into focus the enormous task, expectation, and pressure that face the priest in his attempt to be similar to this *Alter Christus* or *Christ*-like figure: "the priest continues the work of redemption on earth" (Ratzinger, 1994, p. 398). The priest may attempt to do this by imitating Christ completely and, eventually in the history of the western Catholic Church, only celibately.

Theology surrounding the priesthood changed after the Council of Trent in the 16th century. The priest's very being was defined as being forever changed as a result of simply being ordained into the "order" of "priest." In this Catholic framework, ordination to the priesthood is such an otologically significant and altering event that, even if a priest decides to renounce his duties, he may never technically resign from being a priest. "He cannot become a layman again in the strict sense, because the character imprinted by ordination is forever" (Ratzinger, 1994, p. 395). In just being ordained a priest, as stated in Genesis 14:18, "one is considered a priest forever in the order of Melchizedek."

CELIBACY AND THE PRIESTHOOD

The current stipulation that requires celibacy for Roman Catholic priests should be evaluated within the broad context of its history as a discipline (National Conference of Catholic Bishops, 1994). The purpose and aim of celibacy is to imitate Christ as an *Alter Christus*. Historically, celibacy has always been part of the history of the priesthood: It was seen as a gift to be exercised as an option by those so graced or called into this state of living as Christ had lived. Not until the Gregorian reforms in the 12th century, however, when the Church needed to protect its property and rights from the eldest son's medieval hereditary rights, did this change. Essentially, mandatory celibacy as a discipline for all priests came into being to address a growing economic and property rights crisis. What was originally considered a gift and a path freely chosen *by some* became a required discipline *for all* who desired to exercise priestly ministry.

PSYCHOSEXUAL UNDERSTANDING OF CELIBACY

A list of specific problem areas inherent in any study about Roman Catholic priests must begin with the fact that celibates are indeed sexual creatures. Ignatius of Loyola, founder of the Jesuit order, was often cited by many of his companions as saying that, in the matter of celibacy or chastity, one must simply do one thing and that is, "Imitate the angels" (Loyola, 1540/1980). Ignatius gives one good example among many as to the paradigm that has been in force throughout the Church's history (Cozzens, 2000b; Wills, 2000). This reality demands attention to the fact that modern theory and research offer no theoretical underpinnings to understand what constitutes healthy or "normal" development for sexual celibates (Cozzens, 2000a; Loftus, 1999; Sipe, 1995). McGlone (2001) explored these normative aspects in detail and has reported the results elsewhere (McGlone, in press; McGlone & Viglione, 2002).

These points begin to describe a broader and far more interesting context within which the problem of clerical sexual abuse must be placed: The role and function of the priest are significantly different from the role and function of most individuals in the Church and in society. A priest's role springs from ancient images of an intermediary who acted with influence and power unmatched in most societies. This theology not only served the priest but also the layperson: "if I, as a priest, am closer to God, perhaps I do not suffer the slings and arrows of ordinary creatures; if I, as a layperson, have such an intermediary who is so close to God, I tend to view myself as safer in the eternal plan of salvation and damnation."

One key factor often mentioned by various studies is the problem that clergy of any faith face because of the special role accorded them by others (Bottoms et al., 2003; ISTI, 1995; Plante, 1999). This role tends to prevent the priest from functioning in relationships that provide intimacy, support, and natural comfort. Some speculate that the priest avoids being intimate because of this unique pastoral role and the way he is being viewed by people: "if I am dealt with as an ordinary human, I lose my authority and power as priest. If I become intimate, I run the risk of being sexually active." This tendency is noted time and time again as a deficiency and inability to relate or, more psychologically, as an inability to sustain relationships that are enduring and that demand intimacy, time, and a basic ability to be object-related (Cozzens, 2000b). Cozzens (2000b) pointed out how this understanding of the priest's role is changing in today's Church but also points out the problems associated with these changes. Such a transitional understanding can and does pose specific and new challenges for the priest and the Church (Rossetti, 2000; Schuth, 1999).

Some writers have also suggested that this inability to relate to others in a healthy fashion is expressive of a narcissistic personality disorder that seems to be common among members of the clergy across faiths but also in the Catholic clergy (Meloy, 1986). Nelson (1989) contradicted this assertion and found no maladjustment in the mental health of Roman Catholic priests in general. Perhaps a middle ground could be asserted that in some cases the priest's behavior is a result of a behavior style learned in seminary and religious formation, while for others it springs out of a personality disorder or structure. In some cases, like the priest sex offender, there could have been a combination of both factors.

The Misuse of Power by Clergy

The use or misuse of power by priests has been a consistent and important issue throughout the history of Roman Catholic priesthood (Plante, 1999; Pope, Sonne, & Holroyd, 1993; Wills, 2000). Clergy in any religion often hold a special place in people's eyes (Bottoms, 2002; Winston, 1995). Within the Catholic context, the position of the priest as this "other Christ" or *Alter Christus* creates a tendency to see the priest as different, special, or closer to God, which often has the result of making him appear less human and less able to sin as humans sin (Winston, 1995). Priests are often seen within this context with different and even special ethical and moral power, especially in regard to issues relating to sexuality (Sipe, 1995). Therefore, it seems shocking and a betrayal of trust when graphic stories of sexual misconduct among the clergy appear in the national and local press (Berry, 1992; Burkett & Bruni, 1993). It is not a specifically or even uniquely "Catholic" problem as research indicates (Bottoms, 2002); it also affects Protestant churches and Jewish synagogues.

The role of the priest and the misuse of power becomes a crucial point in the discussion of this topic. Some speculate that this misuse of power might be one aspect of both environmental and internal factors that belie an out-of-control state. In other words, inappropriate sexual acts of abuse (an exercise of control and power over an innocent individual) might be an attempt to control and/or deal with an inner sense of powerlessness (Pope et al., 1993).

The Typical Scenario

A number of authors have detailed how the Roman Catholic Church has responded to allegations made against its own clergy and how these alleged, admitted, and/or convicted perpetrators have been sent away to some "secret" treatment center or new assignment (Berry, 1992; Boston Globe Staff, 2002; Burkett & Bruni, 1993).

Jason Berry (1992), in his groundbreaking book about Father Gilbert Gauthe, summoned national attention to the issue while depicting the typical scenario that has been repeated again and again. Recent public outcry and anger both within and outside the Church seems most directed towards the bishops and cardinals, the church leaders who have failed to shepherd and failed to protect (Boston Globe Staff, 2002).

The purpose served by the media in such cases is a hotly debated topic. On one hand, the media's tendency to sensationalize has led to inaccurate portrayals of priest pedophiles and ephebophiles and clearly inaccurate reports on the magnitude and size of the problem; on the other hand, subsequent to the initial case of Father Gauthe, many more cases have been discovered and reported only by the media (Frazier, 2000; Jordan, 2000; Wills, 2000). These cases also highlight the fact that most priest perpetrators of sexual abuse have never been convicted of any crime (Economus, 1996; Jenkins, 1996). It cannot be denied any longer that without the free press these stories would never have been told.

Each story, of course, gives one perspective that comes from either the more conservative or liberal side of the press (Jenkins, 1996). According to Jenkins, who details this situation in a fairly convincing fashion, each political agenda, whether it be from the left or the right, attempts to manipulate and sway public opinion to its own end: The left tries to further its agenda of doing away with celibacy, linking it to the current sexual abuse problem, and the right uses the problem to attack homosexuals who are members of the clergy. Others suggest that this shows that a current problem has not only been over-sensationalized but has also been used by people within the Church structure for their own political ends (Cozzens, 2000a; Plante, 1999). Agenda driven critiques cannot help but muddy the waters of an already tragic and confusing situation. These realities beg a further question: What else might be going on?

The Effects of Priestly Abuse

Priestly perpetration has enormous associations and implications for the victims, especially if those victims are children (Sargent, 1989; Terr, 1990). The priest represents more than just himself to a child. God, Christ, and the Church, as well as the priest, become the abusers (Lebacqz & Barton, 1991). Gaylor (1988) points out, "priests are God's representatives on earth. The symbolic aspect of the title 'Father' should not be overlooked in understanding the position the priest has in relation to the child" (p. 14). She further details the enormous internal conflict the child must experience when, after being sexually abused by the priest during the week, he/she witnesses "his/her parents bowing, kneeling, genuflecting, praying, receiving sacraments, and graciously thanking the priest for his involvement" on Sunday (Gaylor, 1988, p. 14).

The significance of the priest perpetrators' role cannot be underestimated (Lebacqz & Barton, 1991; Plante, 1999). Because children are often taught to see their clergy as representatives of God (Gaylor, 1988), it would make sense for a child to view his or her priest as God-like. Thus, if God is viewed as being holy, this representative of God must be equally as holy (Plante, 1999).

In the Catholic belief system, God is the Father, and a patriarchal theology and spirituality justifies this identification. In this same church, only males are priests and a priest is called Father. It seems evident, then, that since God is Father, and the priest is called Father and is viewed as Godlike by the child, that the sexual abuse perpetrated upon someone who believed in such figures could have a shattering and devastating effect. It clearly could affect the person's perception of God (Poling, 1991), sense of self, and ability to develop intimate relationships with others (Pope et al., 1993). Clerical sexual abuse seems similar to the trauma that may be experienced when a person is abused by a close relative (McLaughlin, 1994).

Children often do not tell about being sexually abused, especially if the abuser is a member of the family (Finkelhor, Araji, Baron, Browne, Peters, & Wyatt, 1986; Sargent, 1989). When a "Father," or "God's representative," abuses a child, the shame associated with the abuse tends to keep the child silent about the event(s) (McLaughlin, 1994). Those who have broken their silence are often not believed as children or as adults. Many tried to tell church leaders about their abuse (Berry, 1992; Burkett & Bruni, 1993), resulting only in stories of mistreatment, not being believed, being accused of lying, and re-victimization through attempts to silence their stories with threats of retribution from the Church and her leaders.

One rather staggering fact that adds to the silence of victims is the out-of-court settlements that follow these cases around the country (Burkett & Bruni, 1993; Cozzens, 2000b). Experts ten years ago conservatively placed the monetary figure associated with these settlements to be around $500 million (Berry, 1992; Burkett & Bruni, 1993). There are no reliable figures for the total costs spent by the Church. Current reports are estimating the figures to be more around one billion dollars, with some speculating that lawsuits could go as high as five billion in the next five years (Lyons, 2003). Out-of-court settlements also prevent many priest offenders from being convicted of their crimes or from serving time in prison (Berry, 1992; Economus, 1996).

Church leaders have the opportunity to add a valuable voice to the current debate, to re-gain a traditional "Catholic" pursuit by actively supporting researchers in the pursuit of "reason" and demonstrating the value of the intellectual life and its "traditions," by sponsoring important and timely data-gathering in this area. While Diocesan lawyers and officials may reject this outright, recent press statements by people appointed by the bishops seem to suggest a desire and focus to lead the way in research and getting the facts straight. The Roman Catholic church community and all faith based communities can only help themselves with this new knowledge and also can begin to effect changes in a society tortured by abuse, trauma, and violence at large.

Recent research demonstrates that clerical sexual trauma may have some unique effects (Fortin & Chamberland, 1995; McLaughlin, 1994). Spiritual relationships with God and the church may be severely damaged if not permanently broken. McLaughlin (1994) reports that such damage may depend upon whether the victim was a child or an adult at the time of the traumatic event. Abused children often struggle with the sense that they must be very bad for God to allow the abuse to happen in the first place (Sargent, 1989). Abused Catholics, as adults, struggle with trusting an institution they were taught was the only true representation of God on earth (Burkett & Bruni, 1993). Developmental delays are often present in adults abused as children, and fears of re-victimization prevent many from even entering a church again (Terr, 1990). "To simplify: The priest = the church, the church = God, therefore the priest = God. To go to the place where the trauma occurred means risking re-victimization by the church or by God" (McLaughlin, 1994, p. 157). Each individual seems to possess unique resources within themselves that might both help and hinder their appropriation of the trauma (Finkelhor, 1984). Effects of any trauma, therefore, must be seen on an individual basis because of the individual's ability to react differently to seemingly similar events (Herman, 1992). This frame of reference, then, broadened to the general population of sex offenders, poses a significant research and assessment problem for a priest population that has, in many writers' eyes, clearly distinguished itself as not being like the general population of sex offenders (Bryant, 1999; Plante, 1999; Loftus, 1999). This was so for several reasons: (a) the unique educational background of priests, (b) the unique and extraordinary environment of seminary and/or religious formation programs that most priests are trained within or are exposed to throughout their years of training, (c) the demands of celibacy that force a solitary lifestyle upon individuals in a public setting, and (d) a general lack of research and, therefore, information as to how normal sexual desires may be displaced or suppressed/sublimated within healthy ministerial and/or apostolic endeavors.

A final component of these problem areas is the lack of descriptive data (Loftus, 1999; Plante, 1999). Basic data about the individual and the environment must be obtained before theories can be formulated about the interaction that might exist between an individual's personality makeup and a particular environment. Data about the individual and the environment must be validated and proven reliable. Currently, little data exist in this regard and, as one researcher has put it, even those data are paltry (Loftus, 1999; Plante, 1999). New data about offenders and non-offenders suggest that the problem might be far more serious and complicated than anyone had anticipated (Boston Globe Staff, 2002; Goodstein, 2003; Plante, 1999; Sipe, 1999). Recent stories in Australia and England point to higher than reported numbers of victims and perpetrators (Plante, 1999; Sipe, 1999; "The sex abuse file," 2000). Furthermore, we are only beginning to comprehend what personality traits, social influences, and what sort of past abuse history might combine or interact to create and predict various types of perpetrators (McGlone, 2001, in press). This point cannot be over-stated.

REFERENCES

American Psychiatric Association. (2000). *Diagnostic and statistical manual of mental disorders* (4th ed., Text Revision). Washington, DC: Author.

Berry, J. (1992). *Lead us not into temptation: Catholic priests and the sexual abuse of children*. New York: Doubleday.

Boston Globe Staff. (2002). *Betrayal. The crisis in the Catholic Church*. Boston, MA: The Boston Globe Publishing Co.

Bottoms, B. (2002, August). *Maltreatment of children by clergy*. Paper presented at the Family Research Laboratory Annual Conference, Portsmouth, NH.

Bottoms, B. L., Nielsen, M., Murray, R., & Filipas, H. (2003). Religion-related child physical abuse: Characteristics and psychological outcomes. *Journal of Aggression, Maltreatment & Trauma, 8*(1/2), 87-114.

Bryant, C. (1999). Psychological treatment of priest sex offenders. In T. G. Plante (Ed.), *Bless me Father for I have sinned: Perspectives on sexual abuse by Roman Catholic Priests* (pp. 87-110). Westport, CT: Praeger.

Burkett, E., & Bruni, F. (1993). *A gospel of shame: Children, sexual abuse, and the Catholic church*. New York: Viking.

Chamberlin, E. R. (1993). *The bad popes*. New York: Barnes & Noble.

Connors, C. (1994). Keynote address to National Catholic Council on Alcoholism. Washington, DC: St. Luke's Institute.

Conte, J., & Savage, S. (2003). Concluding observations. *Journal of Interpersonal Violence, 18*(4), 452-468.

Cozzens, D. (2000a, August 5). The priest's crisis of soul: 3. Telling the truth. *The Tablet*.

Cozzens, D. B. (2000b). *The changing face of the priesthood: A reflection on the priest's crisis of soul*. Collegeville, MN: The Liturgical Press.

Demarest, S. A. (1999). Foreword. In T. G. Plante (Ed.), *Bless me Father for I have sinned: Perspectives on sexual abuse committed by Roman Catholic Priests* (pp. ix-xiii). Westport, CT: Praeger.

Economus, T. (1996, September). Panel presentation at the LINK-UP Conference, Chicago, IL.

Finkelhor, D. (1984). *Child sexual abuse: New theory and research*. New York: Free Press.

Finkelhor, D., Araji, S., Baron, L., Browne, A., Peters, S. D., & Wyatt, G. E. (1986). *A sourcebook on child sexual abuse.* Newbury Park, CA: Sage.

Finkelhor, D., & Dziuba-Leatherman, J. (1994). Victimization of children. *American Psychologist, 49*(3), 173-183.

Finkelhor, D., Hotaling, G., Lewis, I. A., & Smith, C. (1990). Sexual abuse in a national survey of adult men and women: Prevalence, characteristics, and risk factors. *Child Abuse and Neglect, 14,* 19-28.

Foggo, D. (2000, October 22). Senior clergy face police inquiry over paedophile cover-ups. *The Sunday Telegraph,* p. 7.

Follingstad, D. R., & DeHart, D. D. (2000). Defining psychological abuse of husbands toward wives: Contexts, behaviors, and typologies. *Journal of Interpersonal Violence, 15*(9), 891-920.

Fortin, A., & Chamberland, C. (1995). Preventing the psychological maltreatment of children. *Journal of Interpersonal Violence, 10*(3), 275-295.

Frazier, J. B. (2000, October 11). Catholic Church issues apology in abuse case. *San Diego Union-Tribune,* p. A3.

Gaylor, A. L. (1988). *Betrayal of trust: Clergy abuse of children.* Madison, WI: Freedom from Religion Foundation, Inc.

Golden, O. (2000). The federal response to child abuse and neglect. *American Psychologist, 5*(9), 1050-1053.

Goodstein, L. (2003, January 12). Decades of damage: Trail of pain in church crisis leads to nearly every Diocese. *The New York Times,* p. 1.

Haugaard, J. J. (2000). The challenge of defining child sexual abuse. *American Psychologist, 55*(9), 1036-1039.

Herman, J. L. (1992). *Trauma and recovery.* Boston: Basic Books.

Interfaith Sexual Trauma Institute (ISTI). (1995, February). Discovery conferences: *Addressing sexual abuse within the church.* Los Angeles, CA.

Jenkins, P. (1996). *Pedophiles and priests: Anatomy of a contemporary crisis.* New York: Oxford University Press.

Jordan, M. D. (2000). *The silence of Sodom: Homosexuality in modern Catholicism.* Chicago: The University of Chicago Press.

Lebacqz, K., & Barton, R. G. (1991). *Sex in the parish.* Louisville, KY: Westminster/John Knox Press.

Loftus, J. A. (1999). Sexuality in priesthood: Noli Me Tangere. In T. G. Plante (Ed.), *Bless me Father for I have sinned: Perspectives on sexual abuse by Roman Catholic Priests* (pp. 7-20). Westport, CT: Praeger.

Loftus, J. A., & Camargo, R. J. (1992). *Child sexual abuse among troubled clergy: A descriptive summary.* Resources in Education (ERIC Document Reproduction Services No. ED 354-420), Greensboro, NC: ERIC/CASS University of North Carolina.

Loyola, I. (1540/1980). *Autobiography of Saint Ignatius Loyola.* St. Louis, MO: Seminar on Jesuit Spirituality.

Lyons, D. (2003, June 9). Sex, God, and greed. *Forbes Magazine, 171*(12), p. 66.

Manchester, W. (1992). *A world lit only by fire: The medieval mind and the Renaissance: Portrait of an age.* Boston, MA: Little & Brown.

McGlone, G. J. (2001). Sexually offending and non-offending Roman Catholic priests: Characterization and analysis. Unpublished doctoral dissertation, University of Michigan, Ann Arbor.

McGlone, G. J. (in press). Normal and celibate: Myths and misconception while rediscovering our tradition. *Human Development*.

McGlone, G. J., & Viglione, D. J. (2002, September). *Dependency and narcissism in sexually offending and non-offending Roman Catholic clergy.* Paper presented at the International Congress on Rorschach and other Projective Methods, Rome, Italy.

McLaughlin, B. R. (1994). Devastated spirituality: The impact of clergy sexual abuse on the survivor's relationship with God and the church. *Sexual Addiction and Compulsivity, 1*(2), 145-159.

Meloy, J. R. (1986). Narcissistic psychopathology and the clergy. *Pastoral Psychology, 35*(1), 50-55.

Mendel, M. P. (1995). *The male survivor: The impact of sexual abuse.* Thousand Oaks, CA: Sage Publications.

National Conference of Catholic Bishops. (1994). *Restoring trust: A pastoral response to sexual abuse, Vol. 1.* Washington, DC: The Bishops' Ad Hoc Committee on Sexual Abuse.

Nelson, D. C. (1989). *The psychological correlates of adjustment in Roman Catholic priests.* Unpublished doctoral dissertation, California School of Professional Psychology, San Diego, CA.

Plante, T. G. (Ed.). (1999). *Bless me Father for I have sinned: Perspectives on sexual abuse committed by Roman Catholic priests.* Westport, CT: Praeger.

Poling, J. (1991). *The abuse of power: A theological problem.* Nashville, TN: Abingdon Press.

Pope, K. S., Sonne, J. L., & Holroyd, J. (1993). *Sexual feelings in psychotherapy: Explorations for therapists and therapists-in-training.* Washington, DC: American Psychological Association.

Ratzinger, J. C. (1994). *Catechism of the Catholic Church.* (1994). Vatican City, Italy: Libreria Editrice Vaticana.

Rossetti, S. J. (2000). Priesthood in transition. *Human Development, 21*(2), 29-34.

Sargent, N. M. (1989). Spirituality and adult survivors of child sexual abuse: Some treatment issues. In S. M. Sgroi (Ed.), *Vulnerable populations: Sexual abuse treatment for children, adult survivors, offenders, and persons with mental retardation, Vol. 2* (pp. 167-202). New York: Lexington Books.

Schuth, K. (1999). *Seminaries, theologates, and the future of church ministry: An analysis of trends and transitions.* Collegeville, MN: The Liturgical Press.

Schwartz, B. K., & Cellini, H. R. (1995). *The sex offender: Corrections, treatment, and legal practice.* Kingston, NJ: The Civic Research Institute, Inc.

Sipe, A. W. R. (1990). *A secret world: Sexuality and the search for celibacy.* New York: Brunner/Mazel.

Sipe, A. W. R. (1995). *Sex, priest, and power: Anatomy of a crisis.* New York: Brunner/Mazel.

Sipe, A. W. R. (1999). The problem of prevention in clergy sexual abuse. In T. G. Plante (Ed.), *Bless me Father for I have sinned: Perspectives on sexual abuse committed by Roman Catholic priests* (pp. 111-134). Westport, CT: Praeger.

Terr, L. (1990). *Too sacred to cry: Psychic trauma in childhood.* New York: Basic Books.

The sex abuse file. (2000, September 16). *The Tablet.*

Wilkes, P. (2000, July 22). The priest's crisis of soul: 1. This strange culture. *The Tablet.*

Wills, G. (2000). *Papal sin: Structures of deceit.* New York: Doubleday.

Winston, D. (1995, March 6). Fallen clergy: Hypocrisy writ large. *Philadelphia Inquirer*, p. 1.

RECENT TRENDS IN RESPONSE TO CHILD VICTIMIZATION

The Role of Health Care Professionals in the Response to Child Victimization

Vincent J. Palusci

SUMMARY. This chapter serves as an introduction to the many roles of health care professionals in the assessment, care, and treatment of child victimization. It concentrates on those professionals caring for the physical health of victims of child abuse and neglect, although there are many similarities between child maltreatment and other family violence victims. In reviewing the health impact of maltreatment and the historical contributions of health care professionals, it discusses the roles that

Address correspondence to: Vincent J. Palusci, MD, MS, Associate Professor of Pediatrics and Human Development, Michigan State University College of Human Medicine, DeVos Children's Hospital Child Protection Team, 100 Michigan Street, MC-178, Grand Rapids, MI 49503 (E-mail: Palusci@msu.edu).

This chapter is dedicated to the memory of Robert Kirschner, MD, a forensic pathologist whose work addressed the needs of victimized children and families around the world.

[Haworth co-indexing entry note]: "The Role of Health Care Professionals in the Response to Child Victimization." Palusci, Vincent J. Co-published simultaneously in *Journal of Aggression, Maltreatment & Trauma* (The Haworth Maltreatment & Trauma Press, an imprint of The Haworth Press, Inc.) Vol. 8, No. 1/2, (#15/16) 2003, pp. 133-171; and: *The Victimization of Children: Emerging Issues* (ed: Janet L. Mullings, James W. Marquart, and Deborah J. Hartley) The Haworth Maltreatment & Trauma Press, an imprint of The Haworth Press, Inc., 2003, pp. 133-171. Single or multiple copies of this article are available for a fee from The Haworth Document Delivery Service [1-800-HAWORTH, 9:00 a.m. - 5:00 p.m. (EST). E-mail address: docdelivery@haworthpress.com].

health care disciplines play in clinical care, training, research, and advocacy and their interaction with the community's child welfare, legal, and criminal justice systems. *[Article copies available for a fee from The Haworth Document Delivery Service: 1-800-HAWORTH. E-mail address: <docdelivery@haworthpress.com> Website: <http://www.HaworthPress.com> © 2003 by The Haworth Press, Inc. All rights reserved.]*

KEYWORDS. Health care services, medical education, training, research, advocacy

INTRODUCTION

The victimization of children through abuse and neglect remains an all-too-common occurrence (Administration for Children, Youth and Families, US Department of Health and Human Services, 1992; Anne E. Casey Foundation, 2001; Migley, Wiese, & Salmon-Cox, 1996). With three million reports and over 900,000 substantiated victims of child maltreatment annually, the United States child abuse and neglect reporting system continues to document our nation's maltreatment of children (National Committee to Prevent Child Abuse, 1998; US Department of Health and Human Services, Children's Bureau, 2001).

Based on sheer numbers, child maltreatment can be thought of as the second most common chronic disease of childhood in a disease model, following asthma/allergies. However, detailed epidemiologic information regarding the incidence of child abuse and its long-term effects remains less clear. National incidence studies and the National Child Abuse and Neglect Data System (NCANDS) have noted that over three million children suspected of suffering from child abuse and neglect are reported annually, with one to three thousand deaths (McClain, Sacks, Froehlke, & Ewigman, 1993; Michigan Child Death State Advisory Team, 2001; Overpeck, Brenner, Trumple, Trifiletti, & Berendes, 1998; Sedlak & Broadhurst, 1996; United States Advisory Board on Child Abuse and Neglect, 1995; Wang & Daro, 1998). Other than documentation of fatalities, however, information regarding the physical injuries and health effects from abuse in children has not been systematically collected on a national basis (American Academy of Pediatrics [AAP], 1966; Ards & Harrell, 1993; Ewigman, Kivlahan, & Land, 1993; Fingerhut, 1989; Herman-Giddens et al., 1999; Jason, 1983; Jason, Gilliland, & Tyler, 1983).

Health care professionals have historically taken a significant, though not predominant, role in the evaluation of child victimization. Physicians and nurses have a long history of participating as team members in the interdisciplinary assessment of child maltreatment (AAP, 2001a; Bross, Krugman, Lenherr, Rosenberg, & Schmitt, 1988; Shelman & Lazoritz, 1998). Early child welfare advocacy efforts in the United States in the 1800s highlighted the physical and emotional effects of abuse in New York City, resulting in the establishment of multidisciplinary committees consisting of social workers, physicians, nurses, and other child advocates to address this multidimensional problem (Lazoritz, 1990; Shelman & Lazoritz, 1998). Abraham Jacobi, a forefather of modern pediatric medicine, joined the Committee for the Prevention of Cruelty to Children in New York City in 1878 (Burke, 1998). Physicians intermittently noted the health effects of abuse and neglect through the years, with early identification of maltreatment injuries in the medical literature by John Caffey (Caffey, 1946, 1972, 1974). In the 1950s, Woolley and Evans in Detroit noted the presence of bone injuries that were inconsistent with parental explanations (Helfer, Kemp, & Krugman, 1997).

Discussions of diagnoses in the medical literature consistently began to remark upon injuries from physical abuse, with Silverman's identification of fractures (Silverman, 1953, 1972) and Henry Kempe's landmark article naming the "Battered Child Syndrome" (Kempe, Silverman, Steele, Droegemueller, & Silver, 1962) prominent among them. Since that time, the increasing numbers of medical articles on maltreatment have concentrated on physical abuse in the 1960s and 1970s, sexual abuse in the late 1970s and 1980s, and neglect in the 1990s (AAP, 1993a, 1998b, 1999a; Cupoli & Sewell, 1988; Dube & Hebert, 1988; Dubowitz, 1999; Duhaime, Alario, & Lewander, 1992; Finkelhor, 1979; Ommaya, Fass, & Yarnell, 1968; Reece & Ludwig, 2001; Rimsza & Niggermann, 1982; Schmidt, 1980; Woodling & Heger, 1986). A better understanding of these health effects led to clearer definitions of child victimization, which were adopted by the World Health Organization (see Table 1) (World Health Organization, 1999).

Medical practitioners, including physicians, nurses, and allied health professionals, have identified a wide range of conditions that can result from abuse and neglect (see Table 2) (American Medical Association [AMA] Council on Scientific Affairs, 1985; American Professional Society on the Abuse of Children [APSAC], 1996; Jenny, Taylor, & Cooper, 1996). Specialized imaging and diagnostic technologies, from the x-ray to sophisticated computer-assisted imaging techniques such as CT scans and magnetic resonance imaging (MRI), have been developed

TABLE 1. World Health Organization Definitions*

Child Abuse–Child abuse or maltreatment constitutes all forms of physical and/or emotional ill-treatment, sexual abuse, neglect or negligent treatment or commercial or other exploitation, resulting in actual or potential harm to the child's health, survival, development, or dignity in the context of a relationship of responsibility, trust or power (p. 15).

Physical Abuse–Physical Abuse of a child is that which results in actual or potential physical harm from an interaction or lack of an interaction, which is reasonably within the control of a parent or person in a position of responsibility, power or trust. There may be a single or repeated incidents (p. 15).

Emotional Abuse–Emotional abuse includes the failure to provide a developmentally appropriate, supportive environment, including the availability of a primary attachment figure, so that the child can establish a stable and full range of emotional and social competencies commensurate with her or his personal potentials and in the context of the society in which the child dwells. There may also be acts towards the child that cause or have a high probability of causing harm to the child's health or physical, mental, spiritual, moral or social development. These acts must be reasonably within the control of a parent or person in a position of responsibility, power or trust. Acts include restriction of movement, patterns of belittling, denigrating, scapegoating, threatening, scaring, discriminating, ridiculing or other non-physical forms of hostile or rejecting treatment (p. 15).

Neglect and negligent treatment–Neglect is the failure to provide for the development of the child in all spheres: health, education, emotional development, nutrition, shelter and safe living conditions, in the context of resources reasonably available to the family or caretakers and causes or has a high probability of causing harm to the child's health or physical, mental, spiritual, moral or social development. This includes the failure to properly supervise and protect children from harm as much as is feasible (p. 15).

Sexual abuse–Child sexual abuse is the involvement of a child in sexual activity that he or she does not fully comprehend or is unable to give informed consent to, or that violates the laws or social taboos of society. Child sexual abuse is evidenced by this activity between a child and an adult or another child who by age or development is in a relationship of responsibility, trust or power, the activity being intended to gratify or satisfy the needs of the other person. This may include but is not limited to:
   The inducement or coercion of a child to engage in any unlawful activity
   The exploitative use of a child in prostitution or other unlawful sexual practices
   The exploitative use of children in pornographic performances and materials (p. 15-16).

Exploitation–Commercial or other exploitation of a child refers to the use of the child in work or other activities for the benefit of others. This includes, but is not limited to, child labour and child prostitution. These activities are to the detriment of the child's physical or mental health, education, or spiritual, moral or social-emotional development (p. 16).

*World Health Organization (WHO). (1999). *Report of the consultation on child abuse prevention.* Geneva, Switzerland: Author. Retrieved February 19, 2003 from http://www.who.int/mipfiles/2017/childabuse.pdf.

---

in the last century to aid in the diagnosis of such conditions and have proved invaluable in visualizing internal bleeding and injury. Physicians have also honed their skills in medical photography and colposcopy to better visualize external injuries and provide more precise clinical documentation of those injuries for use by the child welfare and legal systems (Kleinman, 1989, 1998; Kleinman, Marks, & Blackbourne, 1986; McCann, 1990; Ricci, 1988, 2001). They have also developed specialized skills needed to identify the particular patterns of abusive injuries to the skin, head, abdomen, and genitals (AAP Section on Radiology, 1991; Emans, Woods, Flatt, & Freeman, 1987; Jenny et al., 1996) and to detect sexually transmitted diseases microbiologically (AAP, 1998a, 2000; Centers for Disease Control and Prevention [CDC], 1998; Giedinghagen, Hoff, &

TABLE 2. Physical Health Effects of Child Abuse and Neglect

Premature Death

Neurologic Handicap and Disability
    Intracranial bleeding
    Diffuse axonal injury
    Mental retardation
    Cerebral palsy
    Hydrocephalus
    Seizures
    Developmental delays in language, cognition, learning
    Attention-Deficit Disorders with and without hyperactivity
    Blindness
    Deafness
    Inability to swallow, eat
    Weakness or loss of sensation
    Loss of posture, balance, or ambulation

Abdominal organ dysfunction
    Intestinal perforation, malabsorption, hemorrhage
    Jaundice from liver injury
    Toxemia from kidney failure
    Peritonitis

Skin infection, disfigurement, and scarring from lacerations and burns
Loss of function, growth abnormalities, and disfigurement from bony fracture
Disfigurement, infertility and genitourinary infections from trauma and sexually transmitted infections

Biery, 1992; Hammerschlag, 1998; Ingram, Everett, Flick, Russell, & White-Sims, 1997; Ingram, Everett, Lyna, White, & Rockwell, 1992; Ison, 1990; Robinson, Watkeys, & Ridgway, 1998; Shapiro, Schubert, & Siegel, 1999; Sicoli, Losek, Hudlett, & Smith, 1995; Siegel, Schubert, Myers, & Shapiro, 1995).

These developments highlight the multiple roles and cross-disciplinary activities of medical professionals in the assessment of suspected maltreatment (Briere, Berliner, Bulkley, Jenny, & Reid, 1996). While physicians have had the primary role and responsibility for providing medical evaluation, nurses have increasingly been called upon to perform more than routine nursing services in the evaluation of suspected abuse. "Sexual Assault Nurse Examiners" or "SANE" nurses have been used increasingly to provide medical examinations for the collection of forensic evidence of suspected sexual and physical assault (AAP, 1994, 1996; Little, 2001; Sattler, 1998). Nurses also visit homes of new parents to help reduce the risk of child maltreatment (Eckenrode, Ganzel, Henderson, Smith, & Olds, 2000; Olds, 1992).

Within the ranks of physicians, pediatricians, family doctors, and emergency medicine physicians have traditionally provided assessments for abused children (Ricci, 1986). Physician assistants have also been specifically trained for examinations of children, albeit with physician supervision. More recently, specialists such as radiologists, gynecologists, pediatric critical care medicine specialists, ophthalmologists, surgeons, psychiatrists, and pathologists have taken on new specialized roles in the evaluation of particular aspects of child abuse and neglect (Levin, 1990). The development of the subspecialty of pediatrics called "Forensic Pediatrics" has added additional expertise in training, research, and advocacy and in areas of clinical diagnostics such as the performance of colposcopy or videocolposcopy (Muram & Jones, 1993; Palusci & Cyrus, 2001). All of these cross-disciplinary activities of various professionals require collaboration and coordination within a hospital or a university-based setting, but such collaboration has also occurred outside of the health care system, such as in the correctional system (AAP, 2001b).

Despite the abilities and experience of doctors and nurses, the evaluation of child abuse does not depend solely on the diagnosis of a health care professional (Flaherty & Weiss, 1990; Fontana, 1989). Health care professionals have increasingly come to appreciate our child welfare system and the roles of nonmedical professionals in protecting children (Bearup & Palusci, 1999; Briere et al., 1996; Faller & Henry, 2000; Johnson, 1993b; Kienberger Jaudes & Martone, 1992; Krugman, 1984; Lamb, 1994; Lazoritz & Palusci, 2001; Swenson & Spratt, 1999; Takayama, Wolfe, & Coulter, 1998; Tjaden & Anhalt, 1994). Medical specialists, who have gained increasing expertise in understanding criminal and social work practices, have utilized medical social workers in hospital and outpatient settings to "triage" victims and to coordinate services for abused children effectively. Social workers can perform specialized psychosocial assessments and "forensic" interviewing (Ceci & Hembrooke, 1998; Walker, 1994).

Beyond the traditional medical model, multidisciplinary teams have been formed to address the training, education, research, and clinical needs at specialized institutions such as children's hospitals and universities (Bross, Chadwick, Philip, & Newberger, 1993). The first such "child protection teams" were formed in the 1950s in San Diego and Colorado, and many children's hospitals and university settings now utilize some form of child protection team to coordinate and provide services for children, both within the hospital and in the greater community (AAP, 1993b; Bell, 2001; Bross et al., 1993; Bross et al., 1988; Kolbo & Strong, 1997; Krugman, 1984; Thomas, Leventhal, & Friedlander, 2001).

CLINICAL ASSESSMENT

In health care, a clinical assessment of child victimization begins with a medical encounter that usually follows a predictable pattern of information-gathering, physical assessment, testing, and clinical diagnosis followed by treatment and/or referral (see Table 3) (AAP, 1999a; AMA Council on Scientific Affairs, 1985; Bays & Chadwick, 1993; Johnson, 1999; Palusci, Cox, Cyrus, Heartwell, Vandervort, & Pott, 1999; Shapiro, 2000; Zitelli & Davis, 1987). However, the specific procedures followed for this clinical assessment often depend upon the field of practice of the professional making the assessment. First, the main reason for the medical encounter or "chief complaint" is recorded from the child or family, followed by delineation of appropriate elements of the medical history. The health care professional then examines the patient utilizing a variety of techniques and procedures that, while gleaned from adult medicine, have been specifically adapted to meet the special needs of children (Adams & Knudson, 1996).

In cases of child victimization, the content and methods used to obtain the patient's history and the techniques used for physical examination are further specialized to concentrate on areas of increased risk (AAP, 1994, 1999a; Blythe & Orr, 1995; Brewster et al., 1998; Brown, Cohen, Johnson, & Salzinger, 1998; Bureau of Communicable Disease Epidemiology, 1989; Dubowitz, Black, & Harrington, 1992; Finkelhor, 1999; Hager, Emans, & Muram, 2000; Hobbs & Wynne, 1996; Kadish, 1998; New York City Health & Hospitals Corporation, 1991; New York State Department of Social Services, 1985). The examining practitioner arrives at an assessment or diagnosis, usually utilizing schema of diagnostic categories, such as the International Classification of Disease (US Department of Health and Human Services, CDC, & National Center for Health Statistics, 1998) or a specialized diagnostic scheme for certain types of abuse (Adams, Harper, Knudson, & Revilla, 1994). A presumptive diagnosis leads the practitioner to request diagnostic tests for the child, such as imaging, blood work, or microbiologic cultures, if such tests are indicated. The presumptive diagnosis also leads the practitioner at the time of the encounter to begin treatment of any acute injury, ensure protection of the child from further harm, and arrange referrals to appropriate physical or mental health specialists for further evaluation and treatment (Council of the American Academy of Child and Adolescent Psychiatry, 1997; Tilelli, Turek, & Jaffe, 1980). Practitioners also have legal responsibilities to report their concerns of child abuse and neglect to appropriate state agencies in all fifty states in

TABLE 3. Medical Diagnostic Evaluation in Child Victimization Emphasizing Identification of Cause and Sequellae of Physical Injury

History–Questions asked by healthcare professionals of the child and caretakers during medical encounter
Chief Complaint (Why are you here today?)
History of Present Illness 　Circumstances surrounding injury 　Physical symptoms such as pain, bleeding, sensory problems, etc. 　Events leading to seeking medical care 　Timing
Past Medical History 　Birth history (weight, gestational age, complications, delivery type) 　Developmental history (physical growth, gross and fine motor skills, language, social interaction)
Sexual and pubertal development; menstrual/gynecological history in females
Prior medical treatments, surgery, medications, hospitalizations, mental health services
Prior evaluations for victimization
Chronic medical conditions, particularly bleeding, neurologic, metabolic, growth disorders
Immunizations received
Known allergies
Psychosocial history (caretakers, school attendance, housing, income, family structure)
Physical Examination–Procedures done by the physician, nurse, or other practitioner based on history 　Vital signs (pulse, respiration rate, height, weight, head circumference, Glasgow Coma Scale) 　Skin (bruising, burns, pattern marks, contusions, tenderness) 　Head (presence of skin swelling, bruising, skull deformity, fontanels) 　Eyes (pupillary response, sclera, retina, periorbital tissues) 　Ears (earlobes, canals, tympanic membranes) 　Nose (bleeding, nares, deformity) 　Mouth, throat (condition of teeth, tonsils, pharynx, frenula) 　Neck (flexibility, lymph glands, thyroid) 　Chest (rib deformities, air movement and congestion, tenderness) 　Heart (heart sounds, rhythm) 　Abdomen (tenderness, organ swelling, bowel sounds) 　Genitals (penis, scrotum, testes, urethra in males; labia, hymen, urethra, vagina in females) 　Anorectal (perineum, internal and external anal sphincters, ruggal folds, tone) 　Extremities (movement, tenderness, swelling, joint involvement, pulses, ambulation) 　Neurological (alertness, reflexes, muscular strength and tone, cranial nerves
Laboratory–Tests performed as indicated by history and physical findings 　Complete blood count (white and red blood cells, hematocrit, platelet counts) 　Coagulation studies (prothrombin time, partial thromboplastin time, fibrinogen, bleeding time) 　Blood chemistries X-rays of affected areas or skeletal survey of all bones 　Computer-assisted tomography (CT) scan of brain, or other affected part 　Magnetic Resonance Imaging (MRI) of head or other affected part 　Specialized metabolic tests (collagen, organic and amino acids, others) 　Microbiologic cultures and tests for sexually transmitted infections
Diagnosis and Treatment–Identification of disease or trauma, reporting and provision for medical and 　emotional treatment, protection and referral

the United States (Fontana, 1989; U.S. Department of Health and Human Services, Children's Bureau, 2001).

The clinical assessment by health care practitioners generally follows the outline of history, physical, laboratory tests, diagnosis, and treatment. However, it is often modified according to the practitioner's specialty. For example, pathologists, who specialize in the examination of the child after death or in the analysis of laboratory tests, have less direct involvement. The role of forensic pathologists, who perform autopsies to identify the means, manner, and cause of death, includes examination of tissues (gross examination) as well as histologic or microscopic assessment with biochemical analysis and toxicologic assessment (Hicks & Gaughan, 1995). Pathologists may utilize x-rays to identify non-visible injuries and may preserve certain body parts for more specialized analysis (for example, electron microscopy and special stains). Extensive medical literature has developed regarding the identification of child abuse by the forensic pathologist and investigation by the medical examiner (Byard & Cohle, 1994; Kirschner, 1998; Kirschner & Wilson, 1994; Krugman, 1985; McClay, 1996; Missouri Department of Social Services, 1998).

Nurses have always played an important role in caring for the medical needs of maltreated children. Nurses perform their own assessments and have traditionally prepared children for examination by the physician, administered immunizations and other medications, and performed biophysical measurements of children who are brought in for medical care. As previously noted, nurses can make home visits to reduce the risk of abuse (Eckenrode et al., 2000; Olds, 1992). In hospital settings, nurses supervise inpatient units, provide medications, monitor vital signs, and perform other important day-to-day functions. During forensic assessments for child abuse, nurses have taken on additional roles in interviewing children (as in forensic interviewing), preparing them for special medical procedures, and reducing their anxiety and pain (Briere et al., 1996; Britton, 1998; Dubowitz, 1998; Sattler, 1998). In the area of child sexual abuse, "SANE" nurses and those with advanced degrees have also been allowed to perform forensic examinations and have developed protocols for the identification and retrieval of forensic evidence after sexual contact (Little, 2001). Several of these have been modeled after those designed for adult women, but the research supporting interventions is more limited than for children (Rhodes & Levinson, 2003; Wathen & MacMillan, 2003).

Several strategies have been reported regarding assessments of children for child abuse by primary care providers, and many continue to note the importance of primary care practice in protecting children (Bureau of Communicable Disease Epidemiology, 1989; New York City Health & Hospitals Corporation, 1991; New York State Department of Social Services, 1985; Shapiro, 2000). The primary care provider often has first contact with children who have been victimized by child abuse and neglect and have the greatest opportunities to identify, treat, and report child abuse and neglect and to prevent further maltreatment. General practitioners, family practitioners, pediatricians, and physician assistants work "on the front lines," seeing large numbers of children; the average pediatrician, for example, may see thirty to forty children a day, four to six days a week, resulting in 3,000 to 5,000 patient visits per year. Given that child abuse and neglect affects 1-2% of children per year, this results in two to four patients per month per pediatrician who present with victimization (U.S. Department of Health and Human Services, Children's Bureau, 2001). Primary care providers have the added advantage of having extended or longitudinal contact with families and have the opportunity to understand the more global medical and mental health needs of the adults as well as the children in a family (Council of the American Academy of Child and Adolescent Psychiatry, 1997). Family practitioners, general practitioners, and physician assistants generally care for fewer children than do pediatricians, and the number of their encounters with maltreated children is therefore reduced.

Table 4 displays some of the potential roles that a health care professional may have in responding to the victimization of a child. While the term "medical specialist" can apply to any physician who has completed medical school and general internship requirements, primary care providers usually refer child victims to specialists in fields such as forensic pediatrics, surgery, pathology, critical care medicine, or gynecology for consultation. Developmentalists, geneticists, dentists, and toxicologists also have an important but more limited role. All practitioners licensed as physicians or nurses by a state in the United States, even those who practice in medical specialties, have a responsibility to report suspected child abuse which may come before them in their professional practice (Fontana, 1989). Typically, however, the assessment of child victimization comprises a significantly smaller proportion of these practitioners' professional efforts, unless they have limited their practices to the care of children. Pediatric radiologists, surgeons, and critical care medicine specialists often encounter children with the physical injuries identified with maltreatment and have become knowledgeable in the diagnosis and treatment of abuse. The provision of their care is generally limited to specific areas; for example, pediatric critical care specialists generally see children with significant physical injuries, gynecologists may be called for cases of sexual assault, and pathologists are involved in identifying abnormalities after a child has died. Psychiatrists, radiologists, pathologists, and other non-pediatricians have also played significant roles in the development of the field (Leventhal,

TABLE 4. Potential Roles of Health Care Professionals in Responding to Child Victimization

Physicians

Primary Care Providers (Family Practice, Pediatrics, General Practice)
    Provide a medical home for children
    Identify potential physical and emotional signs of child maltreatment
    Provide anticipatory guidance about child development and maltreatment
    Report concerns to designated government agency
    Provide ongoing medical care for maltreated children
    Provide care to stabilize children with injuries and preserve evidence
    Refer to pediatric subspecialists and mental health providers as indicated
    Participate in multidisciplinary teams and health and education programs
    Receive training to improve skills in identification and reporting
    Attend court proceedings and provide testimony
    Advocate for the needs for children
Pediatric and Emergency Medicine Specialists (MD, DO, EMT, Other)
    Identify potential physical and emotional signs of child maltreatment
    Report concerns to designated government agency
    Provide care to stabilize children with injuries and preserve evidence
    Refer to pediatric subspecialists and mental health providers
    Receive training to improve skills in identification and reporting
    Attend court proceedings and provide testimony
    Advocate for the needs for children
Consultant and Forensic Pediatricians
    Identify potential physical and emotional signs of child maltreatment
    Attend to the child's needs and respond
    Report concerns to designated government agency
    Refer to pediatrics subspecialists and mental health providers
    Participate in multidisciplinary teams and health and education programs
    Receive training to improve skills in identification and reporting
    Provide education about victimization to trainees and community members
    Attend court proceedings and provide expert opinion testimony
    Coordinate and evaluate community programs for child victims
    Advocate for the needs for children

Nurses (RN, MSN, PhD, Other)
    Identify potential physical and emotional signs of child maltreatment in area of specialty
    Attend to the child's needs and respond to assessment of victimization
    Provide additional services for children commensurate with training and licensure
    Report concerns to designated government agency as required by law
    Participate in community multidisciplinary teams and health and education programs
    Receive training to improve skills in identification and reporting in area of specialty
    Provide education to medical trainees and community members in area of specialty
    Attend court proceedings and provide expert opinion testimony
    Advocate for the needs for children

Social Worker and Allied Health Professionals (MS, PhD, MSW, Other)
    Identify potential physical and emotional signs of child maltreatment in area of specialty
    Report concerns to designated government agency as required by law
    Participate in community multidisciplinary teams and health and education programs
    Receive training to improve skills in identification and reporting in area of specialty
    Provide education to medical trainees and community members in area of specialty
    Attend court proceedings and provide expert opinion testimony
    Advocate for the needs for children

Thomas, & Rosenfield, 1993; Levitt, Smith, & Alexander, 1994; Ludwig & Kornberg, 1992; Marshall, 1997; Reece, 1993).

Recent developments within the specialty of pediatrics include the identification of "child abuse and forensic pediatrics" (Jenny, 1999; Starling, Sirotnak, & Jenny, 2000). Those in "forensic pediatrics" have devoted a significant portion of their professional efforts and careers to the care and treatment of abused and neglected children. Many have received training beyond their residencies in general pediatrics or pediatric specialties to become experienced and/or expert in the special needs, diagnosis, and treatment of those who have been maltreated. Forensic pediatricians have additional experience in providing information for legal proceedings and for multidisciplinary settings in the community (DeJong & Rose, 1989; Hanes & McAuliff, 1997; Lyon, Gilles, & Cory, 1996; Myers, 1997). It has been said that "forensic" pediatricians, while not necessarily expert in all aspects of microbiology, photography, radiology, pathology, burns, or neurology, must be expert in all of these fields as they apply to the victimized child (Jenny, 1996, 1999). Many of these forensic pediatricians work at medical schools and university centers and have taken a lead in the development of the field, particularly with regard to research and training of future practitioners.

Some physicians specializing in the area of child maltreatment have recently been recognized with membership in the Ray E. Helfer Society, an honorary society for physicians who care for abused and neglected children. Named for the late Dr. Helfer, the society seeks to acknowledge physicians who have contributed significantly to research, clinical care, and education in the field (Runyan, 2001).

COMMUNITY ASSESSMENT

The identification, treatment, and prevention of child victimization ultimately rest with the family and the community. Health care professionals have an important role in community assessment of child abuse and neglect in collaboration with multiple community agencies (such as child advocacy centers and social services agencies) and governmental entities (such as police and child protective services) that have the resources, responsibility, and authority to improve and protect the lives of children (Briere et al., 1996.)

Communities have several organizational structures by which health care professionals can participate. Multiple community agencies exist which seek to prevent child victimization from occurring in the first place. County councils for the prevention of child abuse and neglect, social service agencies charged with providing childcare or foster care, and departments of social services that have the legal authority to investigate suspected child maltreatment are all interested in prevention to some degree. Health care professionals make important contributions to complement the activities of such organizations by designing programs for families and targeting those perceived to be at increased risk. Health care professionals have a unique ability to explain child development and the special health needs of children (particularly those with chronic medical conditions) to the community and to provide the scientific background and structure for the implementation and evaluation of community programs (Olds, 1992; Palusci et al., 1999; Showers, 1992).

Once children have been identified as being victimized, several community organizations can utilize the experiences of health care practitioners. Child Protective Services, with the ultimate responsibility for the protection of victims of child abuse and neglect, can employ the services of medical practitioners through direct contract or by way of community participation as in multidisciplinary team reviews. These reviews are usually protected by statute for family privacy and confidentiality of team discussions and enable the health care professional to provide a unique perspective on the child's medical conditions and expert knowledge to aid in the assessment by child protective services agencies of actual or potential harm to the child. Various strategies have been devised to provide medical services to child protective services agencies (Socolar, Fredrickson, Block, Moore, Tropez-Sims, & Whitworth, 2001).

Many such services occur in what are now called "child advocacy centers." Child advocacy centers (or CACs) began in the 1980s to provide specialized services for children, usually for concerns of sexual abuse. The CAC model utilizes professionals from a variety of disciplines, including police, child protective services agencies, social services, counselors, and physicians and nurses to provide "a coordinated response" to child abuse in a community (National Children's Alliance, 2001). These centers have developed both within and separate from hospitals. Physicians, nurses, and other health care professionals play roles in these centers by providing medical evaluations and participating in team discussions (Palusci et al., 1999). Based on a model developed in Huntsville, Alabama, child advocacy centers have developed in most, if not all states in the United States; regional facilities, such as the Midwest Regional Children's Advocacy Center in St. Paul, Minnesota, provide training and case review. These advocacy centers generally have a law enforcement or Child Protective Services focus in their investigations, but have increasingly involved medical and mental health professionals and services (Gordon & Palusci, 1991b; Lamb, 1994).

Community health care professionals can also participate in multidisciplinary reviews after the death of a child. The "child death review" movement (or CDR) began in 1978 as a response to the serious and significant misidentification of child abuse deaths in vital statistics records (Arizona Child Fatality Review Program, 2001; Durfee, Durfee, & West, 2002). The state of Missouri recognized that most or many child abuse fatalities were not properly labeled as such, and so began a movement to correctly label the cause of child abuse fatality and to prevent additional deaths through "social autopsy" (Missouri Department of Social Services, 1998). Guided by these principles, child protective services agencies, law enforcement, prosecutor's offices, public health officials, and medical professionals come together to review specific child fatalities in communities with the aim of developing prevention strategies. Other states have developed CDRs to include variable combinations of local, county-based or state-level review (Michigan Child Death State Advisory Team, 2001; Michigan Public Health Institute, 2001).

A prime tenant of child death review includes a review of actual case information that is often provided by direct service providers. Specific legal statutes protect the confidentiality of such discussions and protect the members of the teams from lawsuits for sharing information. Individual case reviews can provide impetus for community members to prevent child fatalities beyond those from child abuse and neglect. Accidents, suicides, and homicides, for example, are addressed in ways intended to improve services and to prevent further victimization. The National Center for Child Fatality Review (2001) has developed training guidelines for child death review members; however, child death review teams have varying goals and methods for review, and the results of review are variably transmitted to the community.

A program developed recently by the American College of Obstetricians and Gynecologists (ACOG) and the Maternal and Child Health Bureau looks specifically at fetal and infant mortality. This National Fetal and Infant Mortality Review Program (NFIMR) incorporates detailed medical record reviews and interviews of families with fetal or infant deaths, with the goal of decreasing perinatal mortality (NIFMR, 1999). These reviews, which are much more detailed than those of CDR, look at the mother's obstetrical and prenatal histories as well as postnatal or infant concerns. FIMR teams are more heavily weighted with medical professionals, especially obstetricians, pediatricians, neonatologists, perinatologists, and maternal-child nurses. Child victimization occurs in a less significant portion of cases, but FIMR also looks at the role of health care systems and access to care and its association with mortality. A recent initiative to link CDR with FIMR in many states has demonstrated the differences and similarities of these reviews. The interests of FIMR are limited to the deaths of children under the age of one year and are more "medical" with less "community involvement." Furthermore, FIMR places less emphasis on criminal issues than does CDR. However, the goals of the two review structures are similar, since both concern themselves with child victimization and child welfare in the community. Both CDR and FIMR also invite medical professionals to make unique contributions to the review based on their fields of practice and willingness to participate in community assessment.

LEGAL ISSUES

The practice of health care professionals is regulated by a series of laws in state public health statutes and through licensing requirements specific to individual medical disciplines. Hospitals and other health organizations have developed professional credentialing and practice standards to ensure safe, acceptable medical practice. Of particular concern to patients and their families is the issue of the privacy of medical information. This concern has resulted in the recent federal adoption of the Health Insurance Portability and Accountability Act of 1996; however, the confidentiality of medical records has always been important within the medical care system. Special protections for the confidential nature of patient records have historically been provided through state and federal statute, particularly regarding substance abuse, treatment for pregnancy and sexually-transmitted infections, mental health services, and HIV diagnosis and treatment.

It would appear that the need for patient and family confidentiality would run counter to the community's needs to identify child victims for the sake of protecting them. It was just this conflict between confidentiality and the need to protect children that gave rise to the states' adoption of mandated child reporting laws throughout the United States, modeled on the Child Abuse Prevention and Treatment Act of 1974. Although the forms of the legislation vary from state to state, these "child protection laws" stipulate that certain professionals must report their concerns of child abuse and neglect to appropriate governmental agencies. The reporting requirements of these laws supercede the confidentiality of medical records and the patient-provider relationship. The "mandated reporters" generally include physicians, nurses, and other professionals working in hospitals, in addition to a variety of other licensed professionals who include teachers, counselors, law enforcement officers, and mental health professionals. Specific protections are usually given for reports made "in good faith," and certain penalties are listed for the failure to report when child maltreatment would "reasonably" have been suspected. Penalties for not reporting range from monetary fines in some states to criminal charges in others, but usually include civil penalties so that the child and/or the child's family may litigate to redress financial losses sustained because of maltreatment that was not reported by the mandated professional. Other states have also provided mechanisms for the release of medical records to child protective services agencies or to police agencies as part of their investigations. Finally, courts may use their subpoena power to compel the disclosure of such confidential information during criminal and civil proceedings.

It is important to note that child abuse reporting is one of the few instances in which health care professionals are required to contact a governmental agency in the routine course of their practice. While disease reporting has traditionally existed within public health (particularly when a contagious infection may pose a hazard to the community's health), reporting actions that are deemed to be "crimes" have historically been less accepted by the medical community. Less clear statutory requirements have been enacted in the United States for the reporting of domestic violence and victimization of the elderly and vulnerable adults.

Reporting child victimization to governmental agencies begins a process during which an investigation occurs to identify the presence or absence of "evidence" to support or "substantiate" the suspicions. Evidence is defined within the legal system as something of a physical nature, but can include testimony and other information helpful to the court in the adjudication of criminal or civil actions (Kanda, Thomas, & Lloyd, 1985; Lyon, Gilles, & Cory, 1996). Case law has developed detailing what can be entered as evidence in a court proceeding (*Daubert v. Merrell Dow Pharmaceuticals, Inc.*, 1993; *Frye v. United States*, 1923). Physicians and other health care providers are routinely called to provide information regarding children, particularly with regard to statements made by the child, the medical history obtained, and any findings of physical examination (AAP, 1992). Physicians are also asked to provide their expert opinions of medical diagnoses and their interpretations of laboratory and x-ray findings in regard to the general health, prognoses, and long-term out-come decisions for the children (Goodwin, Friedman, & Bellefleur, 1991; Palusci & Stoiko, 2001). Providing evidence in a legal setting is an uncommon activity for other health care professionals, although those specializing in forensic pathology or forensic pediatrics have be-come accustomed to interacting with the legal system and with lawyers on these issues (Jenny, 1999).

While giving testimony in court, physicians and other health care pro-fessionals are often asked their opinion "within a reasonable degree of medical certainty" concerning the diagnosis of child abuse and neglect or victimization. Significant differences exist between standards for medi-cal diagnosis and those for civil or criminal adjudication. Medical diag-nosis is defined as "the act of distinguishing one disease from another" or "the determination of the nature of a case of disease" (Dorland, 1974, p. 435). A constellation of the patient's history, physical examination, and laboratory findings may result in multiple diagnoses, which may lead the practitioner to a treatment plan without absolute or even proba-ble certainty after diagnosis. These criteria differ significantly from le-gal standards, by which a level of certainty must be carefully crafted to include "credible" evidence, a "preponderance" of evidence, "clear and convincing" evidence, or evidence "beyond a reasonable doubt." These standards of evidence in the legal system are defined by a state's case law and/or statute and are distinct from those in medical practice, where the certainty of medical diagnosis may be "possible," "probable," or "de-finitive." As one might imagine, differences in interpretation of certainty lead to difficulty in communication between legal and medical practitio-ners. Recently, testimony provided by physicians has been sometimes considered as part of medical practice and providing "irresponsible testi-mony" may have negative repercussions for the physician (Chadwick & Krous, 1997; Higgins, 1998).

The ultimate action of a health care professional's involvement with the legal system to protect a child from further victimization occurs when the practitioner appears in court. Forensic pathologists and pediatricians are often called to testify about injuries to children. So, too, primary care providers and other health care professionals who provide medical care for children have more opportunity to receive subpoenas and attend court hearings. Those in adult medical practice may have more involvement with the legal system in determining disability or civil actions resulting from accidents or professional liability (Mohn, 2000). Despite the needs of the legal system for health care professionals to provide evidence in mal-treatment cases, it in fact remains a relatively uncommon phenomenon for them to be required to attend court hearings, even if they specialize in caring for maltreated children (Palusci, Hicks, & Vandervort, 2001).

Health care providers and physicians, however, have exhibited aversion to legal mandates for child abuse reporting and court attendance, and problems have been noted with mandated reporting of suspected maltreatment (Johnson, 1993a; Ladson, Johnson, & Doty, 1997; McDonald & Reece, 1979; Morris, Johnson, & Clasen, 1985; Saulsbury & Campbell, 1985; Warner & Hansen, 1994). Mandated reporters have expressed several reasons for not complying with state child abuse reporting statutes, including the time required, lack of knowledge, not wanting to act like "policemen," and differences in the professional cultures among medical and the legal and criminal justice systems. A fear or discomfort with the legal system may issue from inconvenience, dislike of the adversarial nature of court proceedings, fear of breaking patient/physician confidentiality, and the fear of detrimental effects on the providers' practice. Physicians may also feel that they are "harming" the children in question by participating in the potential break-up of the families, and some may feel inadequate or unprepared to appear in a court of law. Recommendations have been made to improve the experience of physicians and other health care professionals within the legal system, yet most feel that such participation extends beyond the normal scope of their practice. For this reason, many are unwilling or unable to provide vital information needed to assist the child welfare and legal systems in protecting children from further victimization (Pollak & Levy, 1989). Community support for health care professionals with the development of community agencies and services designed to advocate for the needs of witnesses and child victims has been helpful, particularly with the development of "victim witness systems" within prosecutor's offices and with the realization that a small number of cases actually require the appearance of the health care professional in court (Palusci et al., 2001).

ADVOCACY

Health care professionals have historically had an important role as advocates for the health and welfare of their patients (AAP, 2001a). Advocating for patients requires that practitioners best identify and respond to patients' needs by working with them, their families, and others in the community to assure the best possible outcomes. Advocating for patients requires understanding their reactions to medical procedures and minimizing further trauma caused by medical care (Berson, Herman-Giddens, &

Vincent J. Palusci   *151*

Frothingham, 1993; De San Lazaro, 1995; Mears, Helfin, & Finkel, 1997; Palusci & Cyrus, 2001; Steward, Schmitz, Steward, Joye, & Reinhart, 1995). Advocating for patients may involve the health care professional with government, particularly at the local community level. Additionally, health care professionals may approach their elected representatives, either as individuals or through professional organizations, to improve the laws and funding for a variety of programs that can help child victims.

Advocating for patients begins at home. Health care professionals begin advocating for their patients' needs through exemplary professional practice. By increasing their accessibility to patients (with convenient locations or office hours), improving their own affability and that of their offices toward children (with congenial staffs and inviting physical environments), or making care more affordable, professionals establish their professional practice as a "medical home" for children (AAP, 1999c). Physicians and other health care professionals best advocate for their patients' needs by maintaining their expertise through superior residency training and continuing medical education in child victimization and by maintaining board certification in the appropriate subspecialty applying to practice with children. Physicians, nurses, and other professionals can easily receive training in the area of child abuse and neglect from a variety of professional organizations such as the AMA and the AAP, and multidisciplinary organizations such as the American Professional Society on the Abuse of Children (APSAC).

Once health care professionals have provided the best possible care for the victims of child abuse and neglect, it then behooves them to ensure that the proper physical and mental health services are available for the children as needed upon referral (AAP, 1999c). For example, the primary care physician, while having concerns about abuse and neglect, may not have the diagnostic skills of a radiologist in identifying fractures or intracranial injury. The physician can take steps to ensure the availability of appropriately trained pediatric specialists or subspecialists who can identify, diagnose, and treat the sequelae of child victimization within their community.

Beyond physical health concerns, it is the health care professional's responsibility to ensure that there are appropriate mental health diagnostic and treatment services available for the child (Council of the Academy of Child and Adolescent Psychiatry, 1997). Such services may be centered at a psychiatric inpatient facility, but may also be available through outpatient facilities utilizing psychologists, social workers, and other professionals trained in providing short-term services which can be specialized to meet the developmental needs of children with physical abuse, sexual abuse, neglect, or failure to thrive.

It is difficult for individual practitioners to be able to ensure the availability of a complete spectrum of services for children, and it is obviously impossible to provide all services for all children in all communities. However, significant strides have been made in the regionalization of services with children's hospitals providing regional care and services that cannot be provided in each and every community (National Association of Children's Hospitals and Related Institutions, 2001). Child advocacy centers have also taken on a role in providing regionalized services, and it is a responsibility of the practitioners to learn about the availability of physical and mental health services at children's hospitals, advocacy centers, and other institutions within their regions (National Children's Alliance, 2001).

All of these services take money. Physicians and other health care practitioners traditionally have not taken a significant role in fundraising for services that are not reimbursed by traditional fee-for-service or third-party medical payors. Historically, healthcare professionals have shrunk from the limelight of fundraising and have allowed others, such as business executives and community leaders, to "lead the charge" in raising money for children. However, physicians and other healthcare professionals miss important opportunities if they fail to participate in such activities. Medical practitioners can provide unique insights into the condition of children and can aid community leaders in assessing those needs and determining the amount of financial and material support required. Healthcare providers can "raise the bar" of community support with their advocacy (AAP, 1999b, 1999c).

Perhaps even more important than raising money is raising awareness. While C. Henry Kempe first taught us about the battered child in 1962 and Ray Helfer showed the importance of understanding a child's perspective in 1984, we still have a long way to go in solving the problems of child neglect and victimization in our communities (Helfer, 1984; Kempe et al., 1962; National Research Council, 1993a). Many segments of our population do not understand the higher rates of poverty, unique health concerns, and other special circumstances of children (Anne E. Casey Foundation, 2001). Physicians and other health care professionals must advocate for their patients in the community by raising the awareness of those who do not understand children, be it in hospitals, offices, or governmental agencies.

Regional and statewide organizations that have recognized the special conditions of child victims. Professional organizations such as the

AAP and APSAC (2001) have historically advocated for the needs of children. The "National Call to Action" spearheaded by thirty or more organizations across the country has raised awareness of the needs of victimized children (National Call to Action, 2001). Child abuse and neglect has been called "a national emergency" (Administration for Children, Youth and Families, 1992), and multiple administrative departments of the United States Government have targeted child abuse and neglect through grants and other funding mechanisms to the community (National Research Council, 1993b). Physicians and other health care professionals have an obligation to participate with these organizations on a variety of levels as health care providers, leaders, and concerned members of communities to tailor services to the special needs of child victims.

TRAINING

Health care professionals have unique roles and responsibilities in the training of child welfare professionals, law enforcement, and child protection services workers, and all professionals who manage the day-to-day care of children. To fulfill their mandatory roles in reporting child abuse and neglect, teachers, child development specialists, mental health workers, and others who provide daycare, education, and counseling services need to understand the medical manifestations of child victimization. They also need to identify the physical as well as emotional signs of abuse and neglect so that they can provide for the optimal outcome and protection for children in their care.

Professionals from a variety of health care disciplines do provide specialized training nationally for medical and nonmedical providers through multidisciplinary organizations such as APSAC or medical organizations such as the AAP. Additionally, various child protective services agencies and consultants such as Cornell University render services to nonmedical providers and offer information about medical issues attendant upon child victimization. National conferences sponsored by the International Society for the Prevention of Child Abuse and Neglect, APSAC, and the National Children's Alliance also offer nonmedical providers training in recognizing and confronting medical manifestations of child abuse. Conferences such as those sponsored by the San Diego Children's Hospital; the Children's Advocacy Centers in Huntsville, Alabama; the Midwest Child Advocacy Center in Minneapolis; the University of Michigan; and other universities and institutions frequently provide specialized training in medical topics for nonmedical professionals (Gallmeier & Bonner, 1992).

Such training has been used as a means to improve reporting by mandated professionals (Gordon & Palusci, 1991a; Reiniger, Robison, & McHugh, 1995; Warner & Hansen, 1994). However, a recent Institute of Medicine review of the education and training of health professionals in family violence noted, "claims regarding what training is needed and how it should be carried out far outnumber the studies that provide empirical evidence to support them" (Cohn, Salmon, & Stobo, 2002, p. 84). The authors then systematically review the available evidence regarding training and assess the limited information regarding the impact of training on improving outcomes for child victims, making several recommendations to improve training in the medical field.

Medical professionals have a unique responsibility to train new professionals within the healthcare professions. Physicians, nurses, physician assistants, social workers, and others in the hospital setting need ongoing training and recertification in a variety of topics, including child victimization. Traditionally, medical students have received very few training hours in the diagnosis and treatment of child victimization, but this shortcoming has recently improved. During their second and third years of medical school, most medical students now generally receive information in the fields of child psychiatry and child development to better understand the behavioral and mental health effects of child victimization. During clinical years, medical students typically receive some training in the assessment of injury and the manifestations of child abuse and neglect. Graduate medical professionals who earn their primary degree (MD or DO) receive additional training as interns and resident physicians in institutions caring for children. Such training exposes the trainee to children with a variety of injuries and, while clinically based, provides experience in the identification, diagnosis, treatment, and reporting of child abuse and neglect.

Nurses also receive training in a variety of fields related to children. Nursing school offers the opportunity to care for children in various inpatient and outpatient settings and also provides academic training in the mandatory requirements of reporting child abuse and neglect. Training is generally provided for the psychosocial aspects of health care but is especially important in nursing training for the care and welfare of mothers and children.

After internship and residency training, pediatricians, family practitioners, and psychiatrists can take post-graduate fellowships in child abuse and neglect to learn the special medical techniques, community advocacy, and research skills needed to work effectively in the field. Training curricula have been developed for trainees at different educational levels (AAP, 1994; Dubowitz & Black, 1991; Hibbard, Serwint, & Connolly, 1987; Kini & Lazoritz, 1998; Palusci & McHugh, 1995). Such training can provide the skills needed for appearing in court, special information regarding the care of foster care children, and specialized skills such as colposcopy, videocolposcopy, neuroradiology, and the interpretation of photographs in the area of child abuse and neglect (Starling et al., 2000). However, few specialized training programs in forensic pediatrics or in the care of child abuse victims have existed at any given time. Recently, several programs have expanded beyond the ten to fifteen positions previously available at the post-residency level (Jenny, 1999).

An important but often neglected feature of child abuse and neglect training by physicians is the area of community education. Health professionals have a unique position in the community because they are respected for their knowledge and expertise. Accordingly, they can help communities to improve school, public health, and services for indigent populations. Health professionals are often asked to provide specialized information regarding the care and prevention of child abuse and neglect and can play a vital role in raising community awareness and helping other interested citizens to address the needs of children in our society. Pediatricians have played important roles in community training regarding adult and child victimization and violence overall (AAP, 1998b, 1999c, 1999d). Such training needs to be supported as a necessary community service by health care organizations, and the material content of such training needs to be tailored specifically to a nonmedical audience.

RESEARCH

Clinicians have traditionally played an important role in the advancement of the science of medicine. Medical scientists include physicians, nurses, psychologists, and other professionals in child development who can advance our knowledge in the identification, treatment, and prevention of child abuse and neglect. Specialized areas in bench and clinical research overlap with research in child victimization, particularly as it applies to brain development and neurologic outcomes. Researchers in the health sciences also work with others in fields such as sociology, law, social work, and criminal justice to expand our knowledge of how to prevent and respond to child victimization. Several areas of research are actively being investigated, while others are newly emerging. As we learn more about children, we learn more about their unique problems and the health professional's role in the assessment and prevention of child abuse and neglect and the interaction of medical variables with mental health and societal outcomes (Finkelhor, 1999; Theodore & Runyan, 1999).

Foremost among areas of continuing research is the delineation of the pathophysiology of abusive head trauma and Shaken Baby Syndrome (Duhaime et al., 1992; Duhaime, Gennarelli, Thibault, Bruce, Marguiles, & Wiser, 1987; Ewing-Cobbs et al., 1998; Lazoritz & Palusci, 2001). Medical practitioners have long been able to identify the type of brain injuries caused by inflicted trauma, yet true understanding of these injuries is being reached only with the advent of technologic advances in central nervous system imaging (Lazoritz, 1997; Lazoritz, Baldwin, & Kini, 1997). Biomechanics and the biophysical aspects of injury play an important role in health care research regarding both intentional and unintentional injuries and accidents (Hymel, Bandak, Partington, & Winston, 1998; Spivak, 1992). A body of research has grown regarding the accidents children sustain on playgrounds, in walkers, on swings, or in the home after falling down the steps or out of bed (Helfer, Kempe, & Krugman, 1997; Helfer, Slovis, & Black, 1977). Our limited understanding of the biomechanical properties of the infant's brain, skull, and neck has prevented our complete understanding of the forces required to cause abusive head trauma; this is an area requiring ongoing research, both in the clinic and in the basic science laboratory. A report of an entity called "Adult Shaken Baby Syndrome" suggests that such victimization is not limited to children (Pounder, 1997). While we have an initial understanding of the devastating neurologic impact of abuse, significant work remains to understand completely the short- and long-term outcomes of physical and emotional trauma and to translate that understanding for use by the child welfare and criminal justice systems (Duhaime, Christian, Moss, & Seidl, 1996; Kendall-Tackett, 2001; Nashelsky & Dix, 1995; National Institutes of Health, 1999) (for an in-depth discussion of victimization and the child welfare system, see Bruhn, this volume).

Research has demonstrated that most children who are sexually abused have normal or non-specific physical examination findings, but medical practitioners continue to work to identify genital injuries specific to such abuse (Adams et al., 1994; Adams & Knudson, 1996; Berenson, Chacko, Wiemann, Mishaw, Friedrich, & Grady, 2000; Heger, Ticson, Velasquez, & Bernier, 2002). Because the interpretation of injuries in such cases has both forensic significance, further medical research is important (Kerns, 1998; Palusci et al., 1999; San Lazaro, Steele, & Donaldson, 1996). Recent advances in our understanding of certain injuries in prepubertal females, for example, have dramatically changed our interpretation of physical findings in legal settings (DeJong & Rose, 1989). The diagnosis of sexual abuse relies on an understanding of child disclosures and behaviors, and research by physical and mental health care professionals also continues in these areas (DiPietro, Runyan, & Frederickson, 1997; Friedrich, Grambsch, Broghton, Kuiper, & Beilke, 1991).

Sexually transmitted infections (or sexually transmitted diseases, STDs) are another area of growing interest in child sexual victimization research. While much is known about the microbiology of STDs from studies in adults, little is understood about the incidence of their transmission before puberty and long-term outcomes (AAP, 1999a). Certain STDs such as gonorrhea and syphilis are thought to be definitely indicative of sexual contact in children after the neonatal period, while others such as chlamydia are less definitive for sexual contact (AAP, 1999a; Hammerschlag, 1998; Robinson et al., 1998; Siegel et al., 1995). Anogenital warts and herpes simplex are thought to have high rates of both sexual and nonsexual transmission, and vertical transmission during birth has been reported to result in disease several years later. The incubation, presentation, and significance of STD findings in prepubertal children need further delineation to improve our identification and treatment of sexual abuse victims (Kerns, 1998).

Surprisingly, the incidence and risk factors for child victimization are only now emerging. Despite the fact that the National Child Abuse and Neglect Data System (NCANDS) has over ten years of information from the states, and there have been three independent national incidence studies, a complete epidemiologic picture of child abuse and neglect in the United States remains and is still developing (Hennes, Kini, & Palusci, 2001; Jason, 1983). Limited secondary analyses of NCANDS have been used to explain the risk factors for occurrence and recurrence, but use of administrative data has its limitations (Fluke, Yuan, & Edwards, 1999; Palusci, 2002). Several studies have assessed risk factors in certain populations for certain types of abuse, but a true longitudinal approach to understanding and preventing injuries from child victimization will await the results of LONGSCAN, a longitudinal, multi-site study of maltreatment incidence and risk factors originally sponsored by the National Center on Child Abuse and Neglect (National Research Council, 1993b). For example, risk factors for infant deaths and abusive head trauma are being assessed in retrospective studies, but a prospective incidence study of shaken baby syndrome with adequate sample size has yet to be reported (Brewster et al., 1998; Brown et al., 1998; Kotch, Browne, Dufort, Winsor, & Catellier, 1999). We are only beginning to use methods derived from economics to understand the medical and nonmedical costs of victimization (Jaffe, Massagli, & Martin, 1993), and medical professionals are beginning to study the characteristics of perpetrators of abuse in addition to their victims (Starling, Holden, & Jenny, 1995).

An emerging area of research involves designing and evaluating health services for victimized children. Such "health services research" offers the opportunity to study objectively the types of such services, their accessibility, costs, and ability to provide specialized services for child victims. This type of research can evaluate the effectiveness of certain types of services and compare different settings such as inpatient hospitalization, emergency departments, offices, and child advocacy centers. For example, little is known about the recurrence of abuse after hospitalization, and it is suspected that many children with abusive injuries, such as abusive head trauma, are not identified by health care professionals (Jenny, Hymel, Ritzen, Reinert, & Hay, 1999; Levy, Markovic, Chaudry, Ahart, & Torres, 1995). Further questions exist regarding the appropriate level of services for victimized children, whether their treatment is best provided by primary care physicians or specialists, and the long-term outcomes from different levels of specialists at those services (Leventhal, Pugh, Berg, & Garber, 1996; Makoroff, Brauley, Brandner, Meyers, & Shapiro, 2002). Do subspecialists, for example, offer better care or promise better outcomes after examination, as compared to generalists, or is there really no difference in outcome for the child? While various programs have been designed to integrate medical services into the child welfare system, no evaluations of their effectiveness have been reported (Socolar et al., 2001). Few prospective studies have reported outcomes after child welfare interventions such as foster care and mandated child abuse reporting systems through child protective services agencies, and the opportunity exists for medical professionals to make important contributions in this non-traditional area of medical research (Takayama et al., 1998).

CONCLUSIONS

Health care practitioners play a vital role in the assessment, care, and treatment of child victims of abuse and neglect. Physicians, nurses, and other health professionals have historically identified physical injuries after victimization and have developed increasingly sophisticated techniques for diagnosing abusive head trauma, Shaken Baby Syndrome, fractures, abdominal and skin injuries, anogenital trauma, and STDs. They have integrated such diagnostic findings with improved techniques in interviewing children, and their assessments have been increasingly used in child welfare and legal settings to improve outcomes for children and families.

Heath care professionals have a responsibility to report their suspicions of maltreatment as required by law. Beyond this, they also have the responsibility to receive appropriate training in the identification, reporting, and treatment of child abuse and neglect if they provide care for children. Of prime importance for all health care providers is the need for an understanding of their important roles in the legal and child welfare systems. Physicians and nurses should not shy away from participating in multidisciplinary settings or court for the benefit of the child victim. Multidisciplinary teams offer physicians and nurses a unique opportunity to advocate for their patients and to improve the lives of all children within their communities. Specialists in forensic medicine and pediatrics have unique responsibilities to teach students and other trainees about victimization, to lead biomedical research efforts to enhance our understanding of the pathophysiology of maltreatment, and to design and evaluate systems providing medical care in the child welfare and foster care systems. Our response to the needs of children requires the earnest dedication and skill of all medical professionals in clinical care, training, research, and advocacy to identify, treat, and prevent the devastating physical and emotional consequences of child victimization.

REFERENCES

Adams, J. A., Harper, K., Knudson, S., & Revilla, J. (1994). Examination findings in legally-confirmed child sexual abuse: It's normal to be normal. *Pediatrics, 94,* 310-317.

Adams, J. A., & Knudson, S. (1996). Genital findings in adolescent girls referred for suspected sexual abuse. *Archives of Pediatric Adolescent Medicine, 150,* 850-857.

Administration for Children, Youth and Families, U.S. Department of Health and Human Services. (1992). *Child abuse and neglect: A shared community concern* (pp. 3-14). Washington, DC: Department of Health and Human Services (ACF).

American Academy of Pediatrics. (1966). Maltreatment of children: The physically abused child. *Pediatrics, 37,* 377-381.

American Academy of Pediatrics. (1992). The child as witness. *Pediatrics, 89*, 513-515.

American Academy of Pediatrics. (1994). Sexual assault in the adolescent. *Journal of Pediatrics, 94*, 761-765.

American Academy of Pediatrics. (1996). Adolescent assault victim needs: A review of issues in a model protocol. *Pediatrics, 98*, 991-1001.

American Academy of Pediatrics. (2001a). American pediatrics: Milestones at the millennium. *Pediatrics, 107*, 1482-1491.

American Academy of Pediatrics. (2001b). Health care for children and adolescents in the juvenile correctional care system. *Pediatrics, 107*, 799-803.

American Academy of Pediatrics, Committee on Child Abuse and Neglect. (1993a). Shaken baby syndrome: Inflicted cerebral trauma. *Pediatrics, 92*, 872-875.

American Academy of Pediatrics, Committee on Child Abuse and Neglect. (1993b). Investigation and review of unexpected infant and child deaths. *Pediatrics, 92*, 734-735.

American Academy of Pediatrics, Committee on Child Abuse and Neglect. (1998a). Gonorrhea in prepubertal children. *Pediatrics, 101*, 134-135.

American Academy of Pediatrics, Committee on Child Abuse and Neglect. (1998b). The role of the pediatrician in recognizing and intervening on behalf of abused women. *Pediatrics, 101*, 1091-1092.

American Academy of Pediatrics, Committee on Child Abuse and Neglect. (1999a). Guidelines for the evaluation of sexual abuse in children: Subject review. *Pediatrics, 103*, 186-191.

American Academy of Pediatrics, Committee on Children With Disabilities. (1999b). Care coordination: Integrating health and related systems of care for children with special health care needs. *Pediatrics, 104*, 978-981.

American Academy of Pediatrics, Committee on Community Health Services. (1999c). The pediatrician's role in community pediatrics. *Pediatrics, 103*, 1304-1306.

American Academy of Pediatrics, Task Force on Violence. (1999d). The role of the pediatrician in youth violence prevention in clinical practice and at the community level. *Pediatrics, 103*, 173-181.

American Academy of Pediatrics, Committee on Child Health Financing. (2000). Guiding principles for managed care arrangements for the health care of newborns, infants, children, adolescents, and young adults. *Pediatrics, 105*, 132-135.

American Academy of Pediatrics, Section on Radiology. (1991). Diagnostic imaging of child abuse. *Pediatrics, 87*, 262-264.

American Medical Association Council on Scientific Affairs. (1985). AMA diagnostic and treatment guidelines concerning child abuse and neglect. *Journal of the American Medical Association, 254*, 796-800.

American Professional Society on the Abuse of Children. (1996). *Descriptive terminology in child sexual abuse medical evaluations.* Chicago, IL: Author.

American Professional Society on the Abuse of Children. (2001). *About APSAC.* Retrieved June 1, 2001, from http://www.apsac.org.

Anne E. Casey Foundation. (2001). *Kids count data book: State profiles of child well being, 2000.* Baltimore, MD: Author.

Ards, S., & Harrell, A. (1993). Reporting of child maltreatment: A secondary analysis of the national incidence surveys. *Child Abuse & Neglect, 17*, 337-344.

Arizona Child Fatality Review Program. (2001). *AZ Citizen Review Panel Third Annual Report*. Retrieved September 14, 2001, from http://www.hs.state.az.us/cfhs/azcf/index.htm.

Bays, J., & Chadwick, D. (1993). Medical diagnosis of the sexually abused child. *Child Abuse & Neglect, 17*, 91-110.

Bearup, R. S., & Palusci, V. J. (1999). Improving child welfare through a children's ombudsman. *Child Abuse & Neglect, 23*, 449-457.

Bell, L. (2001). Patterns of interaction in multidisciplinary child protection teams in New Jersey. *Child Abuse & Neglect, 25*, 65-80.

Berenson, A. B., Chacko, M. R., Wiemann, C. M., Mishaw, C. O., Friedrich, W. N., & Grady, J. J. (2000). A case-control study of anatomic changes resulting from sexual abuse. *American Journal of Obstetrics & Gynecology, 182*, 820-834.

Berson, N. L., Herman-Giddens, M. E., & Frothingham, T. E. (1993). Children's perception of genital examinations during sexual abuse evaluations. *Child Welfare, 71*, 41-49.

Blythe, M. J., & Orr, D. P. (1995). Childhood sexual abuse: Guidelines for evaluation. *Indiana Medicine, 88*, 11-18.

Brewster, A. L., Nelson, J. P., Hymel, K. P., Colby, D. R., Lucas, D. R., McCanne, T. R., & Milner, J. S. (1998). Victim, perpetrator, family and incident characteristics of 32 infant maltreatment deaths in the United States Air Force. *Child Abuse & Neglect, 22*, 91-101.

Briere, J., Berliner, L., Bulkley, J. A., Jenny, C., & Reid, T. (Eds.). (1996). *The APSAC handbook on child maltreatment*. Thousand Oaks, CA: Sage.

Britton, H. (1998). Emotional impact of the medical examination for child sexual abuse. *Child Abuse & Neglect, 22*, 573-579.

Bross, D., Chadwick, D., Philip, J., & Newberger, E. (1993). Why your hospital needs a child abuse team. *Headlines*, p. 22.

Bross, D. C., Krugman, R. D., Lenherr, M. R., Rosenburg, D. A., & Schmitt, B. D. (Eds.). (1988). *The new child protection team handbook*. New York, NY: Garland Publishing.

Brown, J., Cohen, P., Johnson, J. G., & Salzinger, S. (1998). A longitudinal analysis of risk factors for child maltreatment: Findings of a 17-year prospective study of officially recorded and self-reported child abuse and neglect. *Child Abuse & Neglect, 22*, 1065-1078.

Bruhn, C. M. (2003). Children with disabilities: Abuse, neglect, and the child welfare system. *Journal of Aggression, Maltreatment, & Trauma, 8*(1/2), 173-203.

Bureau of Communicable Disease Epidemiology. (1989). *Canadian guidelines for health care providers for the examination of children suspected to have been sexually abused*. Ottawa, Canada: Minister of the National Health & Welfare.

Burke, E. C. (1998). Abraham Jacobi: The man and his legacy. *Pediatrics, 101*, 309-312.

Byard, R. W., & Cohle, S. D. (Eds.). (1994). *Sudden death in infancy, childhood and adolescence*. Cambridge, England: Cambridge University Press.

Caffey, J. (1946). Multiple fractures of the long bones of infants suffering from chronic subdural hematoma. *American Journal of Roentgenology, 56*, 163-173.

Caffey, J. (1972). On the theory and practice of shaking infants. Its potential residual effects of permanent brain damage and mental retardation. *American Journal of Diseases in Children, 124*, 161-169.

Caffey, J. (1974). The Whiplash Shaken Baby Syndrome: A manual shaking by the extremities with whiplash-induced intracranial and intraocular bleeding, linked with residual permanent brain damage and mental retardation. *Pediatrics, 54,* 396-403.

Ceci, S. J., & Hembrooke, H. (1998). *Expert witnesses in child abuse cases: What can and should be said in court.* Washington DC: American Psychological Association.

Centers for Disease Control and Prevention. (1998). Sexually transmitted diseases treatment guidelines. *Morbidity and Mortality Weekly Report, 47*(RR-1), 1-118.

Chadwick, D., & Krous, H. F. (1997). Irresponsible medical testimony by medical experts in cases involving the physical abuse and neglect of children. *Child Maltreatment, 2*(4), 313-321.

Child Abuse Prevention and Treatment Act (CAPTA), P.L. 93-247, U.S. Code title 42, chapter 67 (1974).

Cohn, F., Salmon, M. E., & Stobo, J. D. (Eds.). (2002). Committee on the Training Needs of Health Professionals to Respond to Family Violence, Institute of Medicine Board on Children, Youth, and Families. *Confronting chronic neglect: The education and training of health professionals on family violence* (pp. 81-102). Washington, DC: National Academy Press.

Council of the American Academy of Child and Adolescent Psychiatry. (1997). Statement: Practice parameters for the forensic evaluation of children and adolescents who may have been physically or sexually abused. *Journal of the American Academy of Child and Adolescent Psychiatry, 36,* 423-442.

Cupoli, J. M., & Sewell, P. M. (1988). One thousand fifty-nine children with a chief complaint of sexual abuse. *Child Abuse & Neglect, 12,* 151-162.

Daubert v. Merrell Dow Pharmaceuticals, Inc., 509 U.S. 579, 113 S.Ct. 2786, 125 L.Ed.2d 469 (1993).

De San Lazaro, C. (1995). Making paediatric assessment in suspected sexual abuse a therapeutic experience. *Archives of Diseases in Children, 73,* 174-176.

DeJong, A. R., & Rose, M. (1989). Frequency and significance of physical evidence in legally proven cases of child sexual abuse. *Pediatrics, 84,* 1022-1026.

DiPietro, E. K., Runyan, D. K., & Fredrickson, D. D. (1997). Predictors of disclosure during medical evaluation for suspected sexual abuse. *Journal of Child Sexual Abuse, 6,* 133-142.

Dorland, W. A. (Ed.). (1974). *Dorland's Illustrated Medical Dictionary* (25th ed.). Philadelphia, PA: W.B. Saunders & Co.

Dube, R., & Hebert, M. (1988). Sexual abuse of children under 12 years of age: A review of 511 cases. *Child Abuse & Neglect, 12,* 321-330.

Dubowitz, H. (1998). Children's response to the medical evaluation for child sexual abuse. *Child Abuse & Neglect, 22,* 581-584.

Dubowitz, H. (Ed.). (1999). *Neglected children: Research, practice and policy.* Thousand Oaks, CA: Sage.

Dubowitz, H., & Black, M. (1991). Teaching pediatric residents about child maltreatment. *Developmental & Behavioral Pediatrics, 12,* 305-307.

Dubowitz, H., Black, M., & Harrington, D. (1992). The diagnosis of child sexual abuse. *American Journal of Diseases of Children, 146,* 688-693.

Duhaime, A. C., Alario, A. J., & Lewander, M. D. (1992). Head injury in very young children: Mechanisms, injury types, and ophthalmologic findings in 100 hospitalized patients younger than 2 years of age. *Pediatrics, 90*, 179-185.

Duhaime, A. C., Christian, C., Moss, E., & Seidl, T. (1996). Long-term outcome in infants with the shaking impact syndrome. *Pediatric Neurosurgery, 24*, 292-298.

Duhaime, A. C., Gennarelli, T. A., Thibault, L. E., Bruce, D. A., Marguiles, S. S., & Wiser, R. (1987). The shaken baby syndrome: A clinical, pathological and biomechanical study. *Journal of Neurosurgery, 66*, 409-415.

Durfee, M., Durfee, D. T., & West, M. P. (2002). Child fatality review: An international movement. *Child Abuse & Neglect, 26*, 619-636.

Eckenrode, J., Ganzel, B., Henderson, C. R., Smith, E., & Olds, D. L. (2000). Preventing child abuse and neglect with a program of nurse home visitation: The limiting effects of domestic violence. *Journal of the American Medical Association, 284*, 1385-1391.

Emans, S. J., Woods, E. R., Flatt, N. T., & Freeman, A. (1987). Genital findings in sexually abused, symptomatic and asymptomatic girls. *Pediatrics, 79*, 778-785.

Ewigman, B., Kivlahan, C., & Land, G. (1993). The Missouri child fatality study: Under-reporting of maltreatment fatalities among children younger than 5 years of age, 1983 through 1986. *Pediatrics, 91*, 330-337.

Ewing-Cobbs, L., Kramer, L., Prasad, M., Canales, D. N., Louis, P. T., Fletcher, J. M., Vollero, H., Landry, S. H., & Cheung, K. (1998). Neuroimaging, physical and developmental findings after inflicted and non-inflicted brain injury in young children. *Pediatrics, 102*, 300-307.

Faller, K. C., & Henry, J. (2000). Child sexual abuse: A case study and community collaboration. *Child Abuse & Neglect, 24*, 1215-1225.

Fingerhut, L. A. (1989). *Trends and current status in childhood mortality, U.S. 1900-85* (pp. 6-10). Washington, DC: Department of Health and Human Services (PHS).

Finkelhor, D. (1979). *Sexually victimized children*. New York, NY: The Free Press.

Finkelhor, D. (1999). The science: Working toward the elimination of child maltreatment. *Child Abuse & Neglect, 23*, 969-974.

Flaherty, E. G., & Weiss, H. (1990). Medical evaluation of abused & neglected children. *American Journal of Diseases in Children, 144*, 330-334.

Fluke, J. D., Yuan, Y. Y. T., & Edwards, M. (1999). Recurrence of maltreatment: An application of the national child abuse and neglect data system (NCANDS). *Child Abuse and Neglect, 23*, 633-650.

Fontana, V. J. (1989). Child abuse: The physician's responsibility. *New York State Journal of Medicine, 89*, 152-155.

Friedrich, W. N., Grambsch, P., Broghton, D., Kuiper, J., & Beilke, R. L. (1991). Normative sexual behavior in children. *Pediatrics, 88*, 456-464.

Frye v. United States. 54 App. D.C. 46, 293 F. 1013 (1923).

Gallmeier, T. M., & Bonner, B. L. (1992). University-based interdisciplinary training in child abuse & neglect. *Child Abuse & Neglect, 16*, 513-521.

Giedinghagen, D. H., Hoff, G. L., & Biery, R. M. (1992). Gonorrhea in children: Epidemiologic unit analysis. *Pediatric Infectious Disease Journal, 11*, 973-974.

Goodwin, S. R., Friedman, W., & Bellefleur, M. (1991). Is it time to use evoked potentials to predict outcome in comatose children and adults? *Critical Care Medicine, 19*, 518-524.

Gordon, M., & Palusci, V. J. (1991a). Physician training in the recognition and reporting of child abuse, maltreatment and neglect (Commentary). *New York State Journal of Medicine, 91*, 1.

Gordon, M., & Palusci, V. J. (1991b). *Medical investigation in child sexual abuse.* Columbus, OH: Ross Laboratories.

Hager, A., Emans, S. J., & Muram, D. (Eds.). (2000). *Evaluation of the sexually abused child* (2nd ed.). Oxford, England: Oxford University Press.

Hammerschlag, M. R. (1998). The transmissibility of sexually transmitted diseases in sexually abused children. *Child Abuse & Neglect, 22*, 623-635.

Hanes, M., & McAuliff, T. (1997). Preparation for child abuse litigation: Perspective of the prosecutor and pediatrician. *Pediatric Annals, 26*, 288-295.

Health Insurance Portability and Accountability Act, P.L. 104-191 (1996).

Helfer, M. E., Kemp, R. S., & Krugman, R. D. (1997). *The battered child* (5th ed.). Chicago, IL: University of Chicago Press.

Helfer, R. E. (1984). *Childhood comes first: A crash course in childhood for adults* (2nd ed.). East Lansing, MI: Author.

Helfer, R. E., Slovis, T. L., & Black, M. (1977). Injuries resulting when small children fall out of bed. *Pediatrics, 60*, 533-535.

Heger, A., Ticson, L., Velasquez, O., & Bernier, R. (2002). Children referred for possible sexual abuse: Medical findings in 2,384 children. *Child Abuse and Neglect, 26*, 546-659.

Hennes, H., Kini, N., & Palusci, V. J. (2001). The epidemiology, clinical characteristics and public health implications of Shaken Baby Syndrome. *Journal of Aggression, Maltreatment & Trauma, 5*(1), 19-40.

Herman-Giddens, M. E., Brown, G., Verbiest, S., Carlson, P. J., Hooten, E. G., Howell, E., & Butts, J. D. (1999). Underascertainment of child abuse mortality in the United States. *Journal of the American Medical Association, 282*, 463-467.

Hibbard, R. A., Serwint, J., & Connolly, M. (1987). Educational program on evaluation of alleged sexual abuse victims. *Child Abuse & Neglect, 11*, 513-519.

Hicks, R. A., & Gaughan, D. C. (1995). Understanding fatal abuse. *Child Abuse & Neglect, 19*, 855-863.

Higgins, M. (1998). Docking doctors? AMA eyes discipline for physicians giving false testimony. *American Bar Association Journal, 84*, 20.

Hobbs, C. J., & Wynne, J. M. (1996). *Physical signs of child abuse: A colour atlas.* London, England: W.B. Saunders Co., Ltd.

Hymel, K. P., Bandak, F. A., Partington, M. D., & Winston, K. R. (1998). Abusive head trauma? A biomechanical approach. *Child Maltreatment, 3*, 116-128.

Ingram, D. L., Everett, V. D., Flick, L. A. R., Russell, T. A., & White-Sims, S. T. (1997). Vaginal gonococcal cultures in sexual abuse evaluations: Evaluation of selective criteria for preteenaged girls. *Pediatrics, 99*, e8.

Ingram, D. L., Everett, V. D., Lyna, P. R., White, S. W., & Rockwell, L. A. (1992). Epidemiology of adult sexually transmitted disease agents in children being evaluated for sexual abuse. *Pediatric Infectious Disease Journal, 11*, 945-950.

Ison, C. A. (1990). Laboratory methods in genitourinary medicine: Methods of diagnosing gonorrhoea. *Genitourinary Medicine, 66*, 453-459.

Jaffe, K. M., Massagli, T. L., & Martin, K. M. (1993). Pediatric traumatic brain injury: Acute and rehabilitation costs. *Archives of Physical Medicine and Rehabilitation, 74*, 681-686.

Jason, J. (1983). Fatal child abuse in Georgia: The epidemiology of severe physical child abuse. *Child Abuse & Neglect, 7*, 1-9.

Jason, J., Gilliland, J. C., & Tyler, C. W. (1983). Homicide as a cause of pediatric mortality in the United States. *Pediatrics, 72*, 191-197.

Jenny, C. (1996). *Medical evaluation of physically and sexually abused children: The APSAC study guide III.* Thousand Oaks, CA: Sage.

Jenny, C. (1999). *Application to the American Board of Pediatrics from the American Academy of Pediatrics Section on Child Abuse and Neglect for establishment of subspecialty boards in child abuse and forensic pediatrics.* Chicago, IL: American Academy of Pediatrics.

Jenny, C., Hymel, K., Ritzen, A., Reinert, S., & Hay, S. (1999). Analysis of missed cases of abusive head trauma. *Journal of the American Medical Association, 281*, 621-626.

Jenny, C., Taylor, R. J., & Cooper, M. (1996). *Diagnostic imaging and child abuse: Technologies, practices and guidelines.* Washington, DC: Medical Technologies and Practice Patterns Institute.

Johnson, C. F. (1993a). Physicians and medical neglect: Variables that affect reporting. *Child Abuse & Neglect, 17*, 605-615.

Johnson, C. F. (1993b). Use of MD-social worker team in the evaluation of child sexual abuse: A response. *Journal of Child Sexual Abuse, 2*, 99-101.

Johnson, C. F. (1999). Medical evaluation of child abuse. *Children's Health Care, 28*, 91-108.

Kadish, H. A. (1998). Pediatric male rectal and genital trauma: Accidental and nonaccidental injuries. *Pediatric Emergency Care, 14*, 95.

Kanda, M., Thomas, J., & Lloyd, D. (1985). The role of forensic evidence in child abuse and neglect. *American Journal of Forensic Medicine and Pathology, 6*, 7-15.

Kempe, C. H., Silverman, F. N., Steele, B. F., Droegemueller, W., & Silver, H. K. (1962). The battered child syndrome. *Journal of the American Medical Association, 181*, 17-24.

Kendall-Tackett, K. (2001). Chronic pain: The next frontier in child maltreatment research. *Child Abuse & Neglect, 25*, 997-1000.

Kerns, D. L. (1998). Establishing a medical research agenda for child sexual abuse: Historical perspective and executive summary. *Child Abuse & Neglect, 22*, 453-465.

Kienberger Jaudes, P., & Martone, M. (1992). Interdisciplinary evaluations of alleged sexual abuse cases. *Pediatrics, 89*, 1164-1168.

Kini, N., & Lazoritz, S. (1998). Evaluation for possible physical or sexual abuse. *Pediatric Clinics of North America, 45*, 205-219.

Kirschner, R. H. (1998). The pathology of child abuse. In M. E. Helfer, R. S. Kempe, & R. D. Krugman (Eds.), *The battered child* (5th ed.) (pp. 248-295). Chicago, IL: University of Chicago Press.

Kirschner, R. H., & Wilson, H. L. (1994). Fatal child abuse: The pathologist's perspective. In R. Reece (Ed.), *Child abuse: Medical diagnosis and management* (pp. 325-357). Philadelphia, PA: Lea & Febiger.

Kleinman, P. K. (1989). Radiologic contributions to the investigation and prosecution of cases of fatal infant abuse. *New England Journal of Medicine, 320*, 507-511.

Kleinman, P. K. (1998). *Diagnostic imaging of child abuse* (2nd ed.). St. Louis, MO: Mosby.

Kleinman, P. K., Marks, S., & Blackbourne, B. (1986). The metaphyseal lesion in abused infants: A radiologic-histopathologic study. *American Journal of Radiology, 146*, 895-905.

Kolbo, J. R., & Strong, E. (1997). Multidisciplinary team approaches to the investigation and resolution of child abuse and neglect: A national survey. *Child Maltreatment, 2*, 61-72.

Kotch, J. B., Browne, C. B., Dufort, V., Winsor, J., & Catellier, D. (1999). Predicting child maltreatment in the first 4 years of life from characteristics assessed in the neonatal period. *Child Abuse & Neglect, 23*, 22-32.

Krugman, R. D. (1984). The multidisciplinary treatment of abusive and neglectful families. *Pediatric Annals, 13*, 761-764.

Krugman, R. D. (1985). Fatal child abuse: Analysis of 24 cases. *Pediatrician, 12*, 68-72.

Ladson, S., Johnson, C. F., & Doty, R. E. (1997). Do physicians recognize sexual abuse? *American Journal of Diseases of Children, 144*, 411-415.

Lamb, M. E. (1994). The investigation of child sexual abuse: An interdisciplinary consensus statement. *Child Abuse & Neglect, 18*, 1021-1028.

Lazoritz, S. (1990). Whatever happened to Mary Ellen? *Child Abuse & Neglect, 14*, 143-150.

Lazoritz, S. (1997). Four hundred years of the shaken infant: From Henry II to John Caffey. *APSAC Advisor, 10*, 15-6.

Lazoritz, S., Baldwin, S., & Kini, N. (1997). The whiplash shaken infant syndrome: Has Caffey's syndrome changed or have we changed his syndrome? *Child Abuse & Neglect, 21*, 1009-1014.

Lazoritz, S., & Palusci, V. J. (Eds.). (2001). *The multidisciplinary approach to the shaken baby.* Binghamton, NY: The Haworth Press, Inc.

Leventhal, J., Thomas, S., & Rosenfield, N. (1993). Fractures in young children: Distinguishing child abuse from unintentional injuries. *American Journal of Diseases of Children, 147*, 87-92.

Leventhal, J. M., Pugh, M. C., Berg, A. T., & Garber, R. B. (1996). The use of health services by children who are identified during the postpartum period as being at high risk of child abuse and neglect. *Pediatrics, 97*, 331-335.

Levin, A. V. (1990). Ocular manifestations of child abuse. *Ophthalmology Clinics of North America, 3*, 249-263.

Levitt, C. J., Smith, W. L., & Alexander, R. C. (1994). Abusive head trauma. In R. M. Reece (Ed.), *Child abuse: Medical diagnosis and management* (pp. 1-22). Philadelphia, PA: Lea & Ferbiger.

Levy, H. B., Markovic, J., Chaudry, U., Ahart, S., & Torres, H. (1995). Reabuse rates in a sample of children followed for 5 years after discharge from a child abuse hospital assessment program. *Child Abuse and Neglect, 19*, 1363-1377.

Little, K. (2001). *Sexual assault nurse examiner (SANE) programs: Improving the community response to sexual assault victims* (NCJ 186366). Washington, DC: U.S. Department of Justice, Office of Justice Programs.

Ludwig, S., & Kornberg, A. E. (1992). *Child abuse: A medical reference* (2nd ed.). New York: Churchill & Livingstone.

Lyon, T. D., Gilles, E. E., & Cory, L. (1996). Medical evidence of physical abuse in infants and young children. *Pacific Law Journal, 28,* 93-167.

Makoroff, K. L., Brauley, J. L., Brandner, A. M., Meyers, P. A., & Shapiro, R. A. (2002). Genital examinations for alleged sexual abuse of prepubertal girls: Findings by pediatric emergency medicine physicians compared with child abuse trained physicians. *Child Abuse and Neglect, 26,* 1235-1242.

Marshall, W. N. (1997). Hospitalization of abused and neglected children. *Archives of Pediatric and Adolescent Medicine, 151,* 273-275.

McCann, J. (1990). The use of the colposcope in childhood sexual abuse examinations. *Pediatric Clinics of North America, 37,* 863-880.

McClain, P. W., Sacks, J. J., Froehlke, R. G., & Ewigman, B. G. (1993). Estimates of fatal child abuse and neglect, United States, 1979 through 1988. *Pediatrics, 91,* 338-343.

McClay, W. D. S. (Ed.). (1996). *Clinical forensic medicine* (2nd ed.). London, England: Greenwich Medical Media.

McDonald, A. E., & Reece, R. M. (1979). Child abuse: Problems in reporting. *Pediatric Clinics of North America, 26,* 785-791.

Mears, C. J., Helfin, A. H., & Finkel, M. (1997). Adolescents' responses to videocolposcopy and educational information provided during a sexual abuse evaluation. *Journal of Adolescent Health, 20,* 128.

Michigan Child Death State Advisory Team. (2001). *Child deaths in Michigan: Second annual report.* Okemos, MI: Michigan Public Health Institute.

Michigan Public Health Institute. (2001). *Keeping kids alive: Michigan Child Death Review Program.* Retrieved September 14, 2001, from http://www.michilddeath.com.

Migley, G., Wiese, D., & Salmon-Cox, S. (1996). *World perspectives on child abuse: The second international resource book.* Chicago, IL: International Society for Prevention of Child Abuse and Neglect.

Missouri Department of Social Services, State Technical Assistance Team (STAT). (1998). *The death scene checklist.* Jefferson City, MO: Missouri Department of Social Services.

Mohn, J. C. (2000). American medical malpractice litigation in historical perspective. *Journal of the American Medical Association, 283,* 1731-1737.

Morris, J. L., Johnson, C. F., & Clasen, M. (1985). To report or not to report: Physicians' attitudes toward discipline and child abuse. *American Journal of Diseases of Children, 139,* 194-197.

Muram, D., & Jones, C. E. (1993). The use of videocolposcopy in the gynecologic examination of infants, children and young adolescents. *Adolescent & Pediatric Gynecology, 6,* 154-156.

Myers, J. E. B. (1997). *Evidence in child abuse and neglect cases* (3rd ed.). Somerset, NJ: John Wiley & Sons.

Nashelsky, M. B., & Dix, J. D. (1995). The time interval between lethal infant shaking and onset of symptoms: A review of the shaken baby syndrome literature. *American Journal of Forensic Medicine and Pathology, 16*, 154-7.

National Association of Children's Hospitals and Related Institutions. (2001). *About NACHRI.* Retrieved September 14, 2001, from http://www.childrenshospitals.net/nachri/aboutn/index.html.

National Call to Action. (2001). *Home.* Retrieved September 14, 2001, from http://www.nationalcalltoaction.com.

National Center for Child Fatality Review. (2001). *About us.* Retrieved September 14, 2001, from http://ican-ncfr.org.

National Children's Alliance. (2001). *About us.* Retrieved September 14, 2001, from http://www.nca-online.org/welcome.html.

National Committee to Prevent Child Abuse. (1998). *Child abuse and neglect statistics.* Chicago, IL: Author.

National Fetal-Infant Mortality Review Program (NFIMR). (1999). *When an infant dies: Cross-cultural expressions of grief and loss.* Washington, DC: Health Resources and Services Administration.

National Institutes of Health. (1999). NIH Consensus Development Panel on Rehabilitation of Persons with Traumatic Brain Injury. Rehabilitation of persons with traumatic brain injury. *Journal of the American Medical Association, 282*, 974-983.

National Research Council. (1993a). Consequences of child abuse and neglect. In *Understanding child abuse and neglect, Volume 40* (pp. 208-252). Washington, DC: National Academy of Sciences Press.

National Research Council. (1993b). Interventions and treatment. In *Understanding child abuse and neglect, Volume 40* (pp. 253-291). Washington, DC: National Academy of Sciences Press.

New York City Health & Hospitals Corporation. (1991). *Suspected child abuse and neglect: Protocol for identification, reporting and treatment.* New York: Author.

New York State Department of Social Services. (1985). *Child sexual abuse.* New York: Goldner Press.

Olds, D. L. (1992). Home visitation for pregnant women and parents of young children. *American Journal of Diseases in Children, 146*, 704-708.

Ommaya, A. K., Fass, F., & Yarnell, P. (1968). Whiplash injury and brain damage: An experimental study. *Journal of the American Medical Association, 204*, 285-289.

Overpeck, M., Brenner, R., Trumple, A., Trifiletti, L., & Berendes, H. (1998). Risk factors for infant homicide in the United States. *New England Journal of Medicine, 339*, 1211-1216.

Palusci, V. J. (2002). *Occurrence and recurrence of physical abuse in young children: A secondary analysis of NCANDS.* Unpublished master's thesis. East Lansing, MI: Michigan State University.

Palusci, V. J., Cox, E. O., Cyrus, T. A., Heartwell, S. W., Vandervort, F. E., & Pott, E. S. (1999). Medical assessment and legal outcome in child sexual abuse. *Archives of Pediatric & Adolescent Medicine, 153*, 388-392.

Palusci, V. J., & Cyrus, T. A. (2001). Reaction to videocolposcopy in the assessment of child sexual abuse. *Child Abuse & Neglect, 25*, 1535-1546.

Palusci, V. J., Hicks, R. A., & Vandervort, F. E. (2001). You are hereby commanded to appear: Pediatrician subpoena and court appearance in child maltreatment. *Pediatrics, 107*, 1427-1431.

Palusci, V. J., & McHugh, M. T. (1995). Interdisciplinary training in the evaluation of child sexual abuse. *Child Abuse & Neglect, 19*, 1031-1038.

Palusci, V. J., & Stoiko, M. A. (2001). End of life decisions in children with concerns of child maltreatment. *Michigan Child Welfare Law Journal, 5*, 25-27.

Pollak, J., & Levy, S. (1989). Counter-transference and failure to report child abuse and neglect. *Child Abuse & Neglect, 13*, 515-522.

Pounder, D. J. (1997). Shaken adult syndrome. *American Journal of Forensic Medicine, 18*, 321-324.

Reece, R. M. (1993). Fatal child abuse and sudden infant death syndrome: A critical diagnostic decision. *Pediatrics, 91*, 423-429.

Reece, R. M., & Ludwig, S. (Eds.). (2001). *Child abuse: Medical diagnosis and management* (2nd ed.). Philadelphia, PA: Lippincott, Williams & Wilkins.

Reiniger, A., Robison, E., & McHugh, M. T. (1995). Mandated training of professionals: A means for improving reporting of suspected child abuse. *Child Abuse & Neglect, 19*, 63-69.

Rhodes, K. V., & Levinson, W. (2003). Interventions for intimate partner violence against women: Clinical applications. *Journal of the American Medical Association, 289*, 601-605.

Ricci, L. R. (1986). Child sexual abuse: The emergency department response. *Annals of Emergency Medicine, 15*, 711-716.

Ricci, L. R. (1988). Medical forensic photography of the sexually abused child. *Child Abuse & Neglect, 12*, 305-310.

Ricci, L. R. (2001). Photodocumentation of the abused child. In R. M. Reese, & S. Ludwig (Eds.), *Child abuse medical diagnosis and management* (2nd ed.) (pp. 385-404). Philadelphia, PA: Lipincott, Williams & Wilkins.

Rimsza, M. E., & Niggermann, E. H. (1982). Medical evaluation of sexually abused children: A review of 311 cases. *Pediatrics, 69*, 8-14.

Robinson, A. J., Watkeys, J. E., & Ridgway, G. L. (1998). Sexually transmitted organisms in sexually abused children. *Archives of Diseases in Childhood, 79*, 356-358.

Runyan, D. K. (2001). Formation of the Ray E. Helfer Society (letter). *Child Abuse & Neglect, 25*, 199-201.

San Lazaro, C., Steele, A. M., & Donaldson, L. J. (1996). Outcome of criminal investigation into allegations of sexual abuse. *Archives of Diseases in Childhood, 75*, 149-152.

Sattler, J. M. (1998). *Clinical and forensic interviewing of children and families.* San Diego, CA: Author.

Saulsbury, F. T., & Campbell, R. E. (1985). Evaluation of child abuse reporting by physicians. *American Journal of Diseases in Children, 139*, 393-395.

Schmidt, B. D. (1980). The child with non-accidental trauma. In C. H. Kempe, & R. E. Helfer (Eds.), *The battered child* (3rd ed.) (pp. 134-146). Chicago, IL: University of Chicago Press.

Sedlak, A. J., & Broadhurst, D. D. (1996). *The Third National Incidence Study of Child Abuse and Neglect (NIS-3).* Washington, DC: US Department of Health and Human Services.

Shapiro, R. A. (2000). *Ohio pediatric sexual abuse protocol.* Cincinnati, OH: Ohio Chapter of the American Academy of Pediatrics.

Shapiro, R. A., Schubert, C. J., & Siegel, R. M. (1999). Neisseria gonorrhea infections in girls younger than 12 years of age evaluated for vaginitis. *Pediatrics, 104,* e72.

Shelman, E. A., & Lazoritz, S. (1998). *Out of the darkness: The story of Mary Ellen Wilson* (pp. 326-332). Lake Forest, CA: Dolphin Moon Publishing.

Showers, J. (1992). Don't shake the baby: Effectiveness of a prevention program. *Child Abuse & Neglect, 16,* 11-18.

Sicoli, R. A., Losek, J. D., Hudlett, J. M., & Smith, D. (1995). Indications for Neisseria gonorrhoeae cultures in children with suspected sexual abuse. *Archives of Pediatric and Adolescent Medicine, 149,* 86-89.

Siegel, R. M., Schubert, C. J., Myers, P. A., & Shapiro, R. A. (1995). The prevalence of sexually transmitted diseases in children and adolescents evaluated for sexual abuse in Cincinnati: Rationale for limited STD testing in prepubertal girls. *Pediatrics, 96,* 1090-1094.

Silverman, F. M. (1953). The roentgen manifestations of unrecognized skeletal trauma in infants. *American Journal of Radiology, 69,* 413-426.

Silverman, F. M. (1972). Unrecognized trauma in infants, the battered child syndrome, and the syndrome of Ambroise Tardieu. *Radiology, 104,* 347-353.

Socolar, R. R. S., Fredrickson, D. D., Block, R., Moore, J. K., Tropez-Sims, S., & Whitworth, J. M. (2001). State programs for a medical diagnosis of child abuse and neglect: Case studies of five established or fledgling programs. *Child Abuse and Neglect, 25,* 441-455.

Spivak, B. S. (1992). Biomechanics of nonaccidental trauma. In S. Ludwig, & A. E. Kornberg (Eds.), *Child abuse: A medical reference* (2nd ed.) (pp. 61-84). New York: Churchill Livingstone.

Starling, S. P., Holden, J. R., & Jenny, C. (1995). Abusive head trauma: The relationship of perpetrators to their victims. *Pediatrics, 95,* 259-262.

Starling, S. P., Sirotnak, A. P., & Jenny, C. (2000). Child abuse and forensic pediatric medicine fellowship curriculum statement. *Child Maltreatment, 5,* 58-62.

Steward, M. S., Schmitz, M., Steward, D. S., Joye, N. R., & Reinhart, M. (1995). Children's anticipation of and response to colposcopic examination. *Child Abuse & Neglect, 19,* 997-1005.

Swenson, C. C., & Spratt, E. G. (1999). Identification and treatment of child physical abuse for medical and mental health collaborations. *Children's Health Care, 28,* 123-139.

Takayama, J. I., Wolfe, E., & Coulter, K. P. (1998). Relationship between reason for placement and medical findings among children in foster care. *Pediatrics, 101,* 201-207.

Theodore, A. D., & Runyan, D. K. (1999). A medical research agenda for child maltreatment: Negotiating the next steps. *Pediatrics, 104,* 168-177.

Thomas, D. E., Leventhal, J. M., & Friedlander, E. (2001). Referrals to a hospital-based child abuse committee: A comparison of the 1960's and 1990's. *Child Abuse and Neglect, 25,* 203-213.

Tilelli, J. A., Turek, D., & Jaffe, A. C. (1980). Sexual abuse of children: Clinical findings and implications for management. *New England Journal of Medicine, 302,* 319-323.

Tjaden, P. G., & Anhalt, J. (1994). *The impact of joint law enforcement-Child Protection Services evaluations in child maltreatment cases*. Denver, CO: Center for Policy Research.

United States Advisory Board on Child Abuse and Neglect. (1995). *A nation's shame: Fatal child abuse and neglect in the United States*. Washington, DC: Author.

United States Department of Health and Human Services, Centers for Disease Control and Prevention, & National Center for Health Statistics. (1998). *ICD-10: International statistical classification of diseases and related health problems, tenth revision*. Washington, DC: US Government Printing Office.

United States Department of Health and Human Services, Children's Bureau. (2001). *Child maltreatment 1999: Reports from the states to the national child abuse and neglect data system*. Washington, DC: US Government Printing Office.

Walker, A. G. (1994). *Handbook on questioning children: A linguistic perspective* (pp. 1-19). Washington, DC: American Bar Association.

Wang, C. T., & Daro, D. (1998). *Current trends in child abuse reporting and fatalities: The results of the 1997 annual fifty states survey*. Chicago, IL: National Committee to Prevent Child Abuse.

Warner, J. E., & Hansen, D. J. (1994). The identification and reporting of physical abuse by physicians: A review and implications for research. *Child Abuse & Neglect, 18*, 11-25.

Wathen, C. N., & MacMillan, H. L. (2003). Interventions for violence against women: Scientific review. *Journal of the American Medical Association, 289*, 589-600.

Woodling, B. A., & Heger, A. (1986). The use of the colposcope in the diagnosis of sexual abuse in the pediatric age group. *Child Abuse & Neglect, 10*, 111-114.

World Health Organization. (1999). *Report of the consultation on child abuse prevention*. Geneva, Switzerland: World Health Organization.

Zitelli, B. J., & Davis, H. W. (Eds.). (1987). *Atlas of pediatric physical diagnosis*. St. Louis, MO: CV Mosby Company.

Children with Disabilities:
Abuse, Neglect, and the Child Welfare System

Christina M. Bruhn

SUMMARY. Children in out-of-home care due to abuse and neglect are at disproportionately high risk for disabling conditions. The reasons for the over-representation of children with disabilities in the child welfare system are reviewed and discussed in this chapter. Factors discussed include impact of abuse and neglect, the impact risk factors such as exposure to community and domestic violence and poverty, risk of abuse or neglect associated with disability, and child welfare system factors. In addition, the need for greater efficacy in identification of disability, identification of service needs, and linkage with and delivery of services to serve the needs of children with disabilities in out-of-home care is addressed. Recommendations for policy review at State and Federal levels are offered along with direction for future research. *[Article copies available for a fee from The Haworth Document Delivery Service: 1-800-HAWORTH. E-mail address: <docdelivery@ haworthpress.com> Website: <http://www.HaworthPress.com> © 2003 by The Haworth Press, Inc. All rights reserved.]*

KEYWORDS. Children with disabilities, child welfare, foster care, abuse and neglect

Address correspondence to: Christina M. Bruhn, Children and Family Research Center, University of Illinois at Urbana-Champaign, 2 North LaSalle Street, Suite 1700, Chicago, IL 60602 (E-mail: bruhn@uiuc.edu).

[Haworth co-indexing entry note]: "Children with Disabilities: Abuse, Neglect, and the Child Welfare System." Bruhn, Christina M. Co-published simultaneously in *Journal of Aggression, Maltreatment & Trauma* (The Haworth Maltreatment & Trauma Press, an imprint of The Haworth Press, Inc.) Vol. 8, No. 1/2 (#15/16), 2003, pp. 173-203; and: *The Victimization of Children: Emerging Issues* (ed: Janet L. Mullings, James W. Marquart, and Deborah J. Hartley) The Haworth Maltreatment & Trauma Press, an imprint of The Haworth Press, Inc., 2003, pp. 173-203. Single or multiple copies of this article are available for a fee from The Haworth Document Delivery Service [1-800-HAWORTH, 9:00 a.m. - 5:00 p.m. (EST). E-mail address: docdelivery@haworthpress.com].

Children with disabilities are a vulnerable population in many ways and are over-represented in child welfare systems in relation to the general population (Crosse, Kaye, & Ratnofsky, n.d.). These children have generally been subject to abuse and neglect but may be victimized in a host of other ways as well. Abuse and neglect certainly have the potential to impede children's optimal physical, emotional, and cognitive development. Disability may also impede optimal development, not only as a result of physical, emotional, or cognitive characteristics but also as a result of the social repercussions of having those characteristics. Treatment within the child welfare system may do little or nothing to address the affronts to development posed by children's histories and current circumstances and can even cause harm to children. Most child welfare workers have the best interests of children at heart and work diligently on their behalf but may never have received training in identifying and responding to disability. The consequences of inappropriate response can be very serious for children. One might, for example, consider the case of Jonathan:

> *Jonathan, a seven-year-old, has severe autism. He was removed from the care of his mother and father when they left him alone with his younger brothers in an apartment with the oven on as they visited a public assistance office. He was placed in a foster home with foster parents who immediately took steps to educate themselves regarding understanding of and response to autism. The foster parents received no reimbursement for their educational expenses; for the extensive damage done to their home by the child during aggressive outbursts; or for the time, travel, and expense of a specialized evaluation that they arranged for the child. One day, an agency worker witnessed the foster mother executing a controlled physical restraint of the child to prevent him from injuring himself during an aggressive outburst. Despite the fact that the foster mother had been taught this technique by a professional, the agency worker called the hotline, and the child was removed from the home and placed in a hospital setting.[1]*

Although this example represents a single, isolated incident, it can lead the reader to consider the systemic nature of the problem. Child welfare workers who are untrained in disability related topics and have no resources available to them to assist in decision-making for children with disabilities may take inappropriate actions with regards to placement and services for these children. Children with disabilities and histories of abuse and neglect have faced and will certainly continue to face discrimination and oppression in the world at large; the systems designed to protect them must be continually re-assessed in the effort to ensure that these systems do not exacerbate the very harms they seek to ameliorate.

This discussion, a product of the author's experience in working with children with disabilities in out-of-home care, will cover some of the many aspects of the intersection between disability and child welfare. The first section will cover the prevalence of disability in children in out-of-home care and the reasons why children with disabilities are so disproportionately represented. These reasons include increased likelihood of abuse and neglect for children with disabilities, the fact that abuse and neglect can cause disability, and systemic factors. The second section will address the treatment of these children by the child welfare system. This section will consider child welfare outcomes, including safety, permanency, and well-being as they pertain to children with disabilities.

PREVALENCE OF CHILDREN WITH DISABILITIES IN OUT-OF-HOME CARE

How Many Children Have Disabilities?

A disability is defined in the Americans with Disabilities Act of 1990 as a "physical or mental impairment that substantially limits one or more of the major life activities." The findings of the 2001 U.S. Census Supplementary Survey (U.S. Census Bureau, 2001) indicate that 4,185,627 children between the ages of five and twenty in the United States have disabilities. This figure, representing 6.62% of all children in the country, excludes children in institutional settings.

How Many Children Are Abused or Neglected? How Many Are in Out-of-Home Care?

These numbers are more difficult to report than one might think. A number of factors contribute to the uncertainty. The first and foremost is that different states define and measure abuse and neglect differently. Moreover, the definitions have changed drastically over time, primarily in response to pressure generated by rising censuses of children in out-of-home care. For example, truant children were, in times past, considered to be victims of educational neglect. This is no longer the case in most states. Public Law 100-294, the Child Abuse Prevention, Adoption, and Family Services Act of 1987, was passed in part to address the issue of interstate diversity and to establish a means for tracking the extent of child abuse and neglect on a national level. One of the provisions of the law was for the establishment of the National Child Abuse and Neglect Data System (NCANDS). States are required to report certain elements of their data collection concerning child abuse and neglect to NCANDS administrators yearly. The most recent report from the data system, issued in 1999, states that child protective services agencies received 2,659,000 reports of abuse and neglect in the previous year (U.S. Department of Health and Human Services, 2001a). Of these, 67.3% were accepted for investigation based on the information reported. Of those investigations, 27.5% were substantiated or indicated, and 59.2% were not substantiated. Others were classified according to state systems under such headings as "In Need of Services." According to NCANDS data, the best estimate is that close to 492,000 children were maltreated nationally in 2001.

A second source of information concerning the extent of child abuse and neglect nationally is the National Incidence Study of Child Abuse and Neglect (NIS). The difference between the NIS and the NCANDS data is that the NIS also represents children who were seen by community professionals but whose cases were either not reported to child protective services or not accepted for investigation. The survey relied upon the use of "sentinels" as data collectors. These sentinels were professional staff likely to come into contact with maltreated children. Westat, Inc. and James Bell Associates, under contract with the U.S. Department of Health and Human Services, conducted the most recent of these studies, the NIS-3 (Sedlak & Broadhurst, 1996); this study was also mandated by Public Law 100-294. The data on which the 1996 NIS-3 report is based were collected in 1993 and 1994, with a total of 5,600 sentinels reporting from 842 agencies. The study also involved examination of a sample of cases reported to local child protection agencies and a reporting of the demographic features of cases of all children reported to child protection as having been abused or neglected in the three-month study period. The findings of the most recent survey indicated that abuse or neglect harmed 1,553,800 children nationally, and 2,815,600 were considered to be endangered. These findings represented a substantial increase over the previous set of findings, which were derived from data collected in 1986 and 1987 and were published in 1988.

Critics have raised concerns about the sentinel methodology employed in this study and have suggested that perhaps, in future studies, finding a way to represent the unreported observations of non-professionals in surveyed communities would increase the representativeness of the findings. However, the NIS in its present form provides compelling evidence that relying only on reports of abuse or neglect made to child protective agencies results in a considerable underestimation of the problem.

The number of children in out-of-home care is best estimated by reports from the Adoption and Foster Care Analysis and Reporting System (AFCARS), also established and maintained by the Federal government. States are required to report annually the number of children in foster care and certain information about those children. The most recent report concerning this data set, published in March 2003, provides preliminary estimates indicating that 542,000 children were in out-of-home care at some point during the 2001 fiscal year. The report also provides a wealth of data concerning the case specifics of children in out-of-home care at that time but does not report on the number of children with disabilities in foster care (U.S. Department of Health and Human Services, 2003).

How Many Children with Disabilities Are in Out-of-Home Care?

The short answer is that no one really knows. A number of factors contribute to this problem. The first factor is a chronic under-recognition of disability in the child welfare system. Schilling, Kirkham, and Schinke (1986) conducted a survey of caseworkers in which they asked about the number of children with "handicapping conditions" on each caseload. Of fifty-one caseworkers, forty-three could not recall any children with handicapping conditions on their caseloads, which averaged thirty cases each. Based on an estimate of 10% as a rate of children with disabilities in the general population, caseworkers should have identified at least 153 children with disabilities. In another study, West, Richardson, LeConte, Crimi, and Stuart (1992) examined child welfare case records in order to evaluate the availability of health and developmental information contained therein. They found that 11% of children receiving services from a county child welfare agency had been identified as having developmental delays. However, based on information in the records, an additional 23% were found to be likely to be "identified as such with further evaluation" (p. 224).

In addition to the two aforementioned studies, indications of chronic under-representation can be found in state reports concerning children with disabilities in foster care to the Federal government. Disability is one of the characteristics of children in foster care that states are required to report to the AFCARS system annually. The reporting format requests information indicating the presence or absence of a clinically diagnosed disability and the type of disability or disabilities. These types include mental retardation, visual or hearing impairment, physical disability, emotional disturbance, and other diagnosed conditions. With regard to presence or absence of a clinically diagnosed disability, states can report "yes" "no" or "not yet determined" for a given child. Many states do not utilize the third category. In the 1999 AFCARS data set, thirty-nine states and Puerto Rico are identified as having reported data concerning disabilities. Some of the data reported are not usable; for instance, Washington reported that none of the children in foster care in that state had disabilities, and Florida reported clinically diagnosed disabilities for only 21 of 34,254 children who were in foster care in that state. The great variability observed in states reporting higher numbers brings into question the means by which disability is identified and tracked at the state level. Kansas, for instance, reported that 0.7 percent of children in foster care had disabilities, while North Dakota reported 46.7 percent. While these numbers are not definitive in answering the question of how many children in foster care have disabilities, they do suggest that many states do not place a priority on accurate tracking of these conditions.

Another factor influencing a total "count" of children with disabilities in out-of-home care has to do with the fact that not all children in out-of-home care entered by way of the child welfare system, nor have they been abused or neglected. A large number of children in the past were placed voluntarily through state agencies for mental retardation and developmental disabilities. This number decreased from 91,000 in 1977 to 48,500 in 1986 (Taylor, Lakin, & Hill, 1989). Blacher and Bromley (1990) suggest that the decrease was, in part, due to cultural awareness, philosophical changes, and policy changes, including implementation of Public Law 94-142, the Education for All Handicapped Children Act of 1975. Children with disabilities placed voluntarily may be at greater risk of abuse or neglect than children in the general population as a result of their disabling conditions, and they could also be at greater risk as a result of type of placement. Dick Sobsey (1994) offers a detailed history of severe and pervasive institutional abuse since the 1700s. The term "institutional," in this context, refers to any out-of-home placement; however, the most egregious abuses reported occurred in large, congregate settings. Historically, these types of settings have been the most common living arrangements for voluntarily placed children with disabilities. He also reviewed work suggesting a serious under-reporting of abuse of children in out-of-home settings. The discussions to follow will relate only to children reported to child welfare systems as having been abused or neglected, but one can consider that these topics may relate to children who have not been reported as well.

A final factor influencing assessment of prevalence of disability in abused or neglected children placed in out-of-home care relates to nomenclature. In the literature, the terms "health problems" and "disabilities" are often referred to as if they were interchangeable constructs. This circumstance is understandable, as health problems may have the potential to result in limitations in one or more domains of life activity, and disabilities may bring with them attendant health problems. Furthermore, the determination of what degree of impairment actually constitutes a "disability" has not been conclusively arrived at. Harbin, Danaher, and Derrick (1994) reviewed eligibility criteria of all fifty states for early intervention programs for children aged zero to two and children aged three to five. Their work documents diversity across states in modes of assessment of children and criteria for eligibility for services. Moreover, their work demonstrates the potential for children receiving early intervention services (from ages zero to two) to lose eligibility for special education preschool services upon their third birthdays as a result of policy discontinuities. Given these considerations and the fact that studies concerning abuse and disability vary in their use of terminology and instrumentation, a clear accounting of abused or neglected children with disabilities has not yet been achieved.

What, then, is known of how many children placed out-of-home as a result of abuse or neglect have disabilities? Although answers vary somewhat, they can offer a general impression regarding prevalence of disability in this population. The most common strategy for making this determination is to derive a sample of children in the custody of child welfare systems and evaluate them for presence of disabilities. As related, disabilities and health problems are often reported in congregate. To the extent that specific problems are identified in the existing literature, those problems seem best classified as psychosocial, cognitive, and/or physical. The percentages of children in out-of-home care experiencing each of these types of problems reported in the literature are presented below.

Psychosocial Problems. Estimates of the prevalence of psychosocial problems vary but consistently indicate that children in out-of-home care suffer these problems at higher rates than children in the general population. While rates of psychological or psychiatric impairment in the general population are estimated at around 10% (U.S. Department of Health and Human Services, 2001b), an early study by Swire and Kavaler (1977) reported that 35% of children in out-of-home care suffered moderate impairment, and 35% suffered marked-to-severe impairment. Only 4% of children evaluated were found to be unaffected. Later studies produced findings that were largely consistent with these figures. Findings suggest that 29% of children studied have a psychosocial diagnosis (Schor, 1982), 35% have "emotional problems" (Moffatt, Peddie, Stulginskas, Pless, & Steinmetz, 1985), and 56.9% have probable psychological treatment needs (Hochstadt, Jaudes, Zimo, & Schacter, 1987). The variation in instruments used in these studies may account, in part, for inconsistency in reporting.

Cognitive Delays. Several researchers utilized the Denver Developmental Screening Test (DDST; Frankenberg, Dodds, & Fandal, 1970) to assess development in children under the age of five years. Use of the DDST allowed assessors to characterize development as "normal," "suspect (questionable)," or "abnormal." Swire and Kavaler (1977) found 10% of children to have "abnormal" development and 19% to have "questionable" development. Chernoff, Combs-Orme, Risley-Curtis, and Heisler (1994) found 23% of children to have "abnormal" or "suspect" development. Hochstadt et al. (1987) noted developmental problems in 53% of children ranging in age from one to seven. Of these, 49% experienced problems in one or two functional domains, 26% experienced problems in three or four, and 25% experienced problems in five or more. Children in this study ranged in age from one to seven. Hill, Hayden, Lakin, Menke, and Amado (1990) conducted a study in an attempt to identify the number of children in state custody by state, the types of placements in which children were residing (foster homes, group homes, and so forth), and the numbers of children identified as having specific "handicaps." This study was hampered by lack of specificity in state responses (for example, states indicated the presence of "special need" but did not identify specific disabilities in some circumstances) and variations in classification schema. Of those identified in this study as having specific disabilities, 33% were identified as having mental retardation.

Physical Conditions. Physical conditions are difficult to characterize well, given the great diversity in factors such as type, severity, frequency, duration, amenability to treatment, and outcome. Studies generally report only the presence of chronic conditions and report a wide variety of conditions under aggregate headings such as "well" or "other than well." A great deal of specificity is lost in this type of reporting, and the extent to which these conditions are disabling is unknown. However, reports useful in giving a gross indication of the level of service need of children being served by child welfare systems. Swire and Kavaler (1977) found that 26% of children examined were "other than well," and 45% had at least one chronic condition. Chronic conditions included musculoskeletal, congenital, speech, and cardiovascular conditions among others. A later study by Horowitz, Simms, and Farrington (1994) produced similar findings, suggesting that 26% of children examined at a clinic had at least one significant medical problem. Medical problems cited in this study were similar to those cited by Swire and Kavaler. Moffatt et al. (1985), on the high end of the scale, found 86% of children to have health problems, including mental retardation or learning problems, psychiatric disorders, and cerebral palsy or muscular dystrophy. The reporting of physical, cognitive, and mental health issues in aggregate accounts for the high percentage of problems identified in this study.

The issue of whether these rates of occurrence are similar to those that would be experienced by children who are living in poverty but have no exposure to the child welfare system was raised by several authors. Swire and Kavaler (1977) contrasted their findings to those of the Health Examination Survey, a national survey they identified as being representative of the general population. That survey produced findings indicating that only 11% of children in the general population were classified as other than well. However, the authors reported that their findings indicated that the incidence of psychosocial, developmental, and physical problems in children in their sample was similar to that experienced by other "disadvantaged populations." In contrast, Blatt and Simms (1997) found the rate of chronic health conditions in foster children to be three to seven times higher than that of other children living in poverty.

Reasons for Disproportionate Numbers of Children with Disabilities in Out-of-Home Care: Why So Many?

A number of different factors can be thought to have some bearing on the issue of disproportionate representation of children with disabilities in the child welfare system. Several of these factors will be discussed in turn. The first to be covered relates to relationships between race, disability, and socioeconomic status. The second relates to the impact of disability on the likelihood of both entry into and exit from the child welfare system. The third is really a constellation of factors having to do with the relationship between disability and abuse and neglect. This discussion will consider the possibility that disability may bring with it an increased vulnerability to abuse or neglect, while abuse and neglect have the potential to cause disabilities. While these factors have not been quantified in any study, their combined impact is likely to account substantially for the levels of over-representation of psychosocial, cognitive, and physical problems faced by children in out-of-home care discussed above.

Race, Disability, Socioeconomic Condition, and Child Welfare System Exposure

While relationships among socioeconomic condition, race, disability, and child welfare system involvement have not been fully explored, relationships among subsets of these factors suggest that some interactions could be expected. First, socioeconomic status and race are associated such that average socioeconomic status varies by racial group. Moreover, both socioeconomic status and race have been demonstrated historically to have an association with likelihood of diagnosis of a developmental disability. People living in poverty are more likely to have such a diagnosis. In analyses that did not factor in the effects of poverty, African-Americans were also found to be more likely to have such a diagnosis (Larson, 1999). In studies taking factors such as age, economic status, and family structure into consideration, the effect of race was attenuated for groups above the low-income threshold, although it was still measurable (Fujiura, Yamaki, & Czechowicz, 1998).

Living in poverty and having minority racial group status are both associated with a greater likelihood of entry into out-of-home care (Massat, Gleason, & Weagant, 1993). This is true, even with the understanding that African-American children have been found in the context of a national study *not* to be at greater risk of abuse or neglect than White children (Sedlak & Schultz, in press). Disability also is associated with a greater likelihood of entry into out-of-home care, as will be discussed shortly. How the associations between socioeconomic status, race, and disability relate to entry into out-of-home care is not well understood. In addition to impacting likelihood of entry into care, these factors also play a role in perpetuating child welfare system involvement. These characteristics could be considered factors in some larger construct driving the observed dynamics of child welfare system involvement, and further research and exploration are warranted.

Child Welfare System Trajectories: Entry into and Exit from Out-of-Home Care

Children with disabilities are over-represented in child welfare systems, in part because they are more likely to enter out-of-home care than children without disabilities and less likely to leave. Over time, these functions result in what could be considered an "accumulation" of children with disabilities in the system. Robert Hill (in press) recently explored findings from the National Study of Protective, Preventive, and Reunification Services to Children and Their Families to identify factors that predict placement in foster care. He found that child disability makes an independent contribution to likelihood of being placed. He also found an association between disability and race in these data.

"Health problems" have also been identified as having a relationship with the likelihood of reunification, or the return of children to the homes of their biological parents (Barth, Courtney, Berrick, & Albert, 1994). This finding did not hold true for children who were originally placed with relatives for foster care (children entering state custody in large urban settings are often placed with relatives such as grandparents because of both shortages of qualified foster parents and the primacy of family relationships). Children with health problems who were placed with non-relatives were found to have about half the chance of returning home that children without health problems living in similar placements had. "Health problems," in this case, included easily identifiable physical, mental, or emotional problems.

Coyne (1997), studying a sample of children in state custody in Nebraska in 1988, found that 36% of the children had physical, mental, and/or emotional disabilities, had Individualized Education Plans in school, and received special education services. The children with physical disabilities or mental retardation were found to have spent a much longer time in care, an average of 5.6 years, than children without such conditions, who had spent an average of 4.4 years in out-of-home care. Moreover, children with disabilities were less likely to be in pre-adoptive homes. Of children with behavioral impairments, only 21% were in adoptive placements, while 31% of children with mental retardation and 40% of non-disabled children were in such placements. Horowitz et al. (1994) also found increased lengths of stay in out-of-home care without permanent resolution (such as return home or adoption) for children with disabilities. They found that being non-White, being over two years of age at first placement, and having developmental problems were all related to increased lengths of stay in care. Moreover, they found these factors to interact such that a child with all three factors was 1.93 more times likely to remain in foster care than a child with none.

The findings reviewed here suggest a variety of mechanisms at work producing a situation of social inequity for children with disabilities who come into contact with child welfare systems. These factors are likely not the only ones producing an over-representation of children with disabilities in the system, however. A preponderance of evidence suggests that children with disabilities are more likely to experience abuse and neglect and therefore to come to the attention of child welfare systems. Moreover, abuse and neglect themselves can cause disabilities. This complex set of factors will be discussed next.

ABUSE AND NEGLECT OF PERSONS WITH DISABILITIES

As related above, one strategy for examining the relationship between disability and abuse or neglect has been to assess children known to have been abused or neglected for incidence of disability. The opposite strategy is to assess children known to have disabilities to evaluate the incidence of abuse; a number of studies carried out since 1967 have utilized this approach (Sobsey, 1994). Most of the studies concerning abuse or neglect histories of children with disabilities have produced findings indicating that children with disabilities are more likely to experience abuse or neglect than persons in the general population would be. These include studies by Verdugo, Bermejo, and Fuertes (1995); Ammerman, Herson, and Van Hasselt (1994); Benedict, White, Wulff, and Hall (1990); Jaudes and Diamond (1985); Souther (1984); Frisch and Rhoades (1982); and Buchanan and Oliver (1977). The percentages of persons with disabilities identified as having experienced abuse or neglect depends upon the exact nature of the population studied. For example, Verdugo et al. (1995) found that 11.5% of intellectually impaired children in a particular region had suffered abuse or neglect, with physical neglect being the most common form of maltreatment. However, a study of developmentally delayed children with psychiatric disorders in hospital settings indicated that 61% had experienced severe maltreatment (Ammerman, Herson, & Van Hasselt, 1994).

The most compelling study design undertaken to date involves an examination of the general population to determine incidences of disability, abuse or neglect, and co-occurrence. Sullivan and Knutson (1998, 2000) have carried out two such studies. These studies, conducted in school and hospital settings, involved neither a population of children known to have disabilities nor one known to have experienced abuse or neglect. In their most recent study, Sullivan and Knutson arrive at an array of troubling conclusions. They find that children with disabilities are 3.76 times more likely than children without disabilities to experience neglect, 3.79 times more likely to experience physical abuse, 3.14 times more likely to experience sexual abuse, and 3.88 times more likely to experience emotional abuse. Children with disabilities were also found to be more likely to experience multiple types and episodes of maltreatment.

Regardless of study design, the association between disability and abuse or neglect has been found to be such that children with one condition are more likely to experience the other. Some attempts have been made to understand the underlying dynamics of this association.

The Relationship Between Disability and Abuse or Neglect: Which Came First?

Both high proportions of children with disabilities in state custody as a result of having been abused and neglected and high percentages of persons with disabilities reporting having been abused or neglected suggest that there is a relationship between disability and abuse or neglect. However, the direction of causality–that is, whether disability makes one more vulnerable to abuse and neglect or is caused by abuse and neglect–is not well understood. The efforts that have been made in this direction suggest that both circumstances are true and can even be at work simultaneously. One particularly affecting story comes to mind.

Billy lives in a nursing home in the Midwest. He is sixteen years old. Neglected and unsupervised as a young child, he came into contact with lead-based paint, which he consumed. He experienced severe developmental delays as a result. His mother, reportedly because of feelings of guilt, attempted to kill the child but only succeeded in further injuring him. Billy lost most of the use of all of his limbs and does not have the ability to speak or perform basic self-care functions. His primary means of communication at this time is the use of sign language within the severely limited range of motion of his hands and of guttural utterances. This makes communication slow and difficult. Those who make the effort will learn that Billy's dream is to learn to drive a car and possibly to become a race car driver.

The example demonstrates a situation where neglect led to an injury that resulted in a disability, and the disability was likely a factor in a subsequent incident of physical abuse. A discussion regarding the contribution of disability to risk for abuse and neglect and the contribution of abuse or neglect to risk for disability follows.

Child and Family Characteristics as Contributors to Risk for Abuse or Neglect

Suggestions have been made that the type and degree of disability an individual has may have an association with whether or not he or she is likely to suffer abuse or neglect (Goldson, 1997). Empirical evidence concerning child disability as a risk factor for abuse or neglect is somewhat mixed. Verdugo et al. (1995) found that children with less obvious disabilities are more likely to be mistreated. The hypothesis as to why this might be the case is that parents have higher expectations of children with less apparent disabilities, and when those expectations cannot be met, the resultant disharmony creates elevated stress. Verdugo et al. did find some exceptions to this finding. For example, children with more impaired speech or language capabilities and children with more severe behavior problems were more likely to suffer maltreatment than other children were. Ammennan and his colleagues (1994) found a very complex set of interactions in their evaluations of abuse potential of parents of children with disabilities. Like Verdugo et al., they found that children with higher independent functioning scores were more likely to be exposed to severe discipline (that is, discipline resulting in injury). In addition, they found a number of interactions between the characteristics of the mother and those of the child in predicting disciplinary response. For example, they found that higher functioning children with mothers with fewer resources for social support were more likely to experience severe discipline, as were more rebellious children of mothers with increased anger reactivity. Ammerman and Patz (1996) conducted a follow-up study to assess the relationship between child and parent characteristics in predicting child abuse potential. They found that child characteristics made an independent contribution to prediction of abuse potential once other factors, including socioeconomic status, mother's IQ, mother's psychopathology, and social support, were taken into consideration. They did not find that disability made an independent contribution once the other child characteristics (for example, adaptability and hyperactivity) had been entered. A final study, conducted by Burrell, Thompson, and Sexton (1994), found that mothers of children with disabilities had higher abuse potential than did mothers of children without disabilities. These findings are not necessarily inconsistent with those of Ammerman and Patz, however. Burrell et al. also reported that parenting stress, perceived adequacy of resources, and social support had the same relationship to abuse potential for parents of children with disabilities as they did for parents of children without disabilities. They did not examine specific child characteristics, as Ammerman and Patz did. However, their report indicates that parents of children with disabilities experienced considerably higher stress associated with child factors than parents of children without disabilities did. One can discern from these collected findings that disability in itself may not cause abuse or neglect but that certain factors associated with disability can interact with familial factors to result in a heightened risk.

HOW ABUSE AND NEGLECT CAN CAUSE DISABILITIES

This topic is compelling on a number of different levels. First, it speaks to the issue of why so many children served by child welfare systems have disabilities. More importantly, though, it speaks to the consequences of abuse or neglect for children. All children experiencing abuse or neglect will experience threats to normal, healthy development. However, when the abuse or neglect is severe enough to result in a disabling condition, those threats are amplified considerably. Children experiencing severe impairments as a result of abuse and neglect are likely to be placed in out-of-home care, resulting in a change that further disrupts their normal development. They may experience multiple placements and extended stays in foster or group care, which can result in further impacts. Consider the following case study:

> *Winston is fourteen years old. He has experienced severe and chronic neglect over the course of his entire lifetime. His IQ testing indicated he is functioning at the level of borderline mental retardation, and he has major depression. He was initially placed in out-of-home care as a result of running away from home. He finally presented himself at a police station, stating his wish to commit suicide. At that time, his mother indicated that she was unable to resume caring for Winston. His father, who has maintained only*

minimal involvement in Winston's upbringing, also indicated that he was not in a position to care for Winston. The child was placed in a group home situation and later moved to a foster home where a number of other teenagers were also living. At the school he was moved to, he obtained a firearm. He threatened to kill both his foster mother and himself. He was moved to a secure hospital setting and remains there at this time. His prospects for future placement are extremely limited.

The case example illustrates the idea that the injuries of parental abuse or neglect can be exacerbated by experiences within the child welfare system when children are placed and moved in this manner. Children with emotional or behavioral disturbances are far more likely to experience multiple moves (Hartneft, Falconnier, Leathers, & Testa, 1999). While it is believed that the moves are primarily a result of child behavior, multiple moves can be expected to have a profound impact on a child's social and psychological development. Children who move frequently and live in congregate settings never have the opportunity to connect with an involved and potentially permanent caregiver, and this situation probably amplifies the problems they face.

The ways in which abuse or neglect can cause disabilities are varied. A brief discussion of factors related to biological risk for development of disabilities or delays as well as risks associated with physical abuse and neglect follows.

Biological Risk. Biological risk is created any time that conditions necessary for healthy physical development are disrupted. Prenatally, this can be the result of such factors as exposure of a fetus to drugs or alcohol, domestic violence, and maternal malnutrition. These factors may not be considered legally to constitute abuse or neglect, but at the very least, the types of insults to prenatal development discussed here are related, directly or indirectly, to increased risk for abuse or neglect. Exposure to drugs and alcohol has received particular attention in the professional literature. A number of studies (e.g., Barth & Needell, 1996; Franck, 1996) have suggested that initial predictions concerning child developmental outcomes as a result of exposure to crack cocaine overstated the consequences. Ongoing studies conducted over a period of years have indicated that early impacts on factors such as growth and neurobehavioral functioning are diminished over time in some respects. However, some impacts do remain. Cognitive deficits are not noted in children exposed prenatally to cocaine or other drugs except in that such deficits are mediated by poor quality in the home environment. Children exposed to cocaine and other drugs are impacted behaviorally, however, particularly in terms of ability to self-regulate. This finding is not mediated by the quality of the home environment (Chasnoff, Anson, Hatcher, Stenson, Iaukea, & Randolph, 1998).

Studies concerning alcohol are clear in indicating that prenatal exposure has initial impacts on size and neurobehavioral functioning and results in attention difficulties, slower information processing, and learning problems (Streissguth, Barr, Sampson, & Bookstein, 1994). Even moderate drinking can result in growth deficits and intellectual and behavioral problems (Jacobsen & Jacobsen, 1999). The effects can vary by type and quantity of drugs or alcohol used, timing, and duration, as well as other factors, and poor outcomes are by no means universal. However, it remains the case that these types of biological risk factors have the potential to impact children in extremely negative ways, and such impacts may prove to be lifelong. Even exposure to violence prenatally has the potential to produce measurable physical impacts. Women exposed to physical or sexual abuse during their pregnancies have been found to be significantly more likely to have pre-term, low-birth-weight infants (Parker, McFarlane, & Soeken, 1994).

Impacts of Abuse and Neglect. The difference between abuse and neglect is that abuse involves an action taken that results in harm to the child (commission), and neglect involves harm to the child that results from inaction (omission). Clearly both have the potential to produce very immediate and serious physical and emotional consequences for children. The ways in which abuse or neglect can cause physical injuries or illnesses and have detrimental effects on physical, cognitive, and emotional development and the types of effects seen are numerous and complex. This topic, which is quite involved and has been studied at length, cannot be reported fully here. However, a few notes will be made on some of the ways in which abuse or neglect can and do lead to disabilities in some circumstances.

Jaudes and Shapiro (1999) offer a comprehensive discussion of sequelae of physical abuse. They relate the findings of a 1985 study by Billmire and Myers indicating that most incidents of brain damage in children under the age of one are a result of child abuse. While the most immediate and apparent effect of physical abuse is physical injury, short- and long-term consequences can include impacts to cognitive, physical, and psychological development.

Susan is a large-eyed, petite four-year old. She became the subject of a child abuse investigation after her parents presented with her at a large, urban hospital stating that another child had hit her head with a heavy object, resulting in a concussion. She was two years old at that time. She had been the subject of a previous investigation within the past year, subsequent to having been brought to a different hospital with a similar complaint. Detailed radiographic studies indicated she had also suffered several untreated fractures. Susan is a silent child, never having spoken readily, and seems almost frozen in her interactions with others.

The force of their abuse experiences can significantly disrupt development of children like Susan; neglect also has the potential to result in damage to the cognitive, physical, and psychosocial development of children in a number of ways. Failure to supervise or protect a child can result in harm to the child, as can failure to provide such necessities as adequate food, clothing, shelter, and medical treatment. Apart from the risks to physical and cognitive development and physical health, however, are the risks to mental health. Morrison, Frank, Holland, and Kates (1999) discuss the various means by which maltreatment can lead to disrupted or "derailed" development. They detail work demonstrating that maltreatment can lead to insecure attachments, which can, in turn, lead to a range of problems having to do with social relatedness. The authors also identified a number of specific disorders or classes of disorders for which abuse or neglect can place children at heightened risk. These disorders include post-traumatic stress disorder, disturbances in self-regulation, disorders of attachment, depressive disorders, and anxiety disorders. Post-traumatic stress disorder, in particular, has received increasing attention. Research suggests that prolonged exposure to stress can lead to an enduring "alarm reaction" that influences catecholamine activity, which in turn can alter the development of the central nervous system. Altered functioning of the central nervous system can result in a number of enduring physiological and psychological effects (Perry, 1994).

Other studies offer supporting evidence regarding long-term impacts of neglect. For example, neglected children have been found to have different educational experiences than nonmaltreated children. Kendall-Tackett and Eckenrode (1996) found that neglected children had lower grades, more grade repetitions, and more school suspensions and disciplinary referrals. In most circumstances, these problems were exacerbated for children who had been both abused and neglected. Such children were found to have more suspensions and more disciplinary referrals. Elementary and junior high school students who had been abused and neglected also demonstrated lower average grades and more grade repetitions.

A final important factor to keep in mind when evaluating the impact of abuse or neglect on children and their physical, cognitive, and emotional development is that studies have repeatedly demonstrated that children are likely to experience more than one kind of maltreatment. This appears to be particularly true of children with disabilities. Sullivan and Knutson (2000) succinctly pointed out that "children with disabilities tended to be maltreated multiple times and in multiple ways" (p. 1262). Hence, in anticipating the consequences of abuse and neglect, one must consider that they may not evolve along a single trajectory.

One of the difficulties in demonstrating that abuse or neglect does in fact cause a substantial proportion of the disabilities observed in children in out-of-home care has to do with timing. Given that the children have already experienced abuse or neglect and have already developed disabilities, there are few means by which to establish which came first. In fact, situations can be more complex than a simple causal explanation would suggest–abuse and neglect could cause disabilities that render a child more difficult to care for, thereby elevating stress and increasing the likelihood of abuse or neglect. Alternatively, a single factor could be at work to increase risks for both maltreatment and disability (for example, parental substance use) (Sobsey, 2002). The best way to establish a clear line of causation is not with a retrospective study, one that involves a group of people for whom an occurrence has already taken place. Instead, a prospective study–that is, one involving a group of people for whom that occurrence might or might not take place–is preferable because the likelihood that the occurrence will take place can be established, and occurrence can be correlated with other factors. Very few attempts at this have been made.

A recent study (Strathearn, Gray, O'Callaghan, & Wood, 2001) produced compelling findings with regard to the topic of causal link between neglect and development. The authors of the study followed a total of 352 infants with low birth weight for four years. Those children who were referred to child protective services for child maltreatment, specifically neglect, were found to differ from those not so referred. The development of children referred for neglect was significantly delayed in comparison to children not referred. A finding of even greater gravity is that the children referred for neglect experienced a significant *decline* in cognitive ability over time. Those children with substantiated findings were more likely to be identified as having an "intellectual disability" than children not referred. Head circumference was also found to be reduced in referred children at two and four years, despite the fact that initial measurements did not differ between the two groups.

The Sullivan and Knutson (1998) study involved a carefully planned analysis of records, including hospital, foster care, law enforcement and Central Registry (recording reports of abuse or neglect) records. This study and the follow-up study (Sullivan & Knutson, 2000) offer the best quantification of the relationship between maltreatment and disabilities. As part of this study, the authors made an attempt to identify which children had been seen at the hospital and identified as having a disability prior to the reporting of maltreatment and which children were seen and identified subsequent to the report. Children without disabilities and children with speech or language problems, mental retardation, hearing impairments, health impairments, and other disabilities were more likely to be seen at the hospital before the maltreatment report. Children with behavioral disorders, learning disorders, or attention deficit disorders were more likely to be seen and identified as having these problems subsequent to the maltreatment report. The results are open to interpretation, but with additional research they could provide supporting evidence for the hypothesis that different types of problems might relate differently to risk of maltreatment.

Other studies have produced results that vary somewhat with regard to quantification of the problem; however, these studies are consistent in their conclusions that abuse and neglect can and do cause disabilities. Jaudes and Shapiro (1999) reported the work of Diamond and Jaudes in identifying the number of impairments resulting from maltreatment. They found that, among children with cerebral palsy, the disorder was attributable to physical abuse in 9% of cases. In a retrospective study they found that 3-16% of neurological problems resulted from maltreatment. Finally, in a national study conducted by Westat, Inc., in 1993 (Cosse, Kaye, & Ratnofsky, n.d.), workers from thirty-five representative child welfare agencies were asked about their judgements concerning whether disabilities amongst children on their caseloads had resulted from abuse or neglect, or vice versa. In 47.2% of cases, workers reported that disabilities were suspected to have led to maltreatment, and in 36.6% of cases workers reported that maltreatment definitely caused or was likely to have caused disabilities.

Socioeconomic Risks. Outside the realm of discrete injury resulting from the actions or inaction of parents in relation to their children is the topic of risk. This topic relates to the social and economic circumstances into which children are born, and these circumstances can have a profound effect on risk to optimal development. In a 1987 study, Sameroff, Seifer, Barocas, Zax, and Greenspan examined cumulative risk and its impact on child cognition. They found that in children four years of age, an accumulation of two identified risk factors had relatively little impact on child cognition. However, children with a total of any four of the identified risk factors experienced an average diminishment in IQ of a total of nineteen points. Risk factors included poverty, absence of father, low parental education, rigid and punitive childrearing style, minority group status, parental substance abuse, maternal mental illness, and large family size. Clearly, many of these factors correlate highly with poverty, and their mechanisms of action are not yet understood and need to be explored further.

One must be careful in discussing such factors in the context of a discussion of abuse and neglect. The factors identified by Sameroff and colleagues (1987) as contributing to cumulative risk to developmental status are not the same as abuse or neglect. In some cases, an association with abuse or neglect has been identified, and in others, such an association has been ruled out. In the context of this conversation, however, the important focus is not on the relationship between identified risk factors and abuse or neglect, but on the impact of these factors on children who have experienced abuse or neglect. Most children in out-of-home care in urban settings come from situations of poverty, absence of father, low parental education, minority group status, and parental substance abuse. Based on Sameroff et al.'s findings, these children are likely to demonstrate substantially diminished IQ scores. These socially mediated consequences of these risk factors are likely to have a profound impact on the development of children in out-of-home care.

CHILDREN WITH DISABILITIES IN THE CHILD WELFARE SYSTEM: RESPONSES

A considerable degree of effort has been expended by the research community in the evaluation of the prevalence of abuse and neglect among persons with disabilities, the incidence of disability among children victimized by abuse or neglect, and the correlates and outcomes of disability. However, relatively little attention has been paid to what happens to children with disabilities placed in out-of-home care in response to maltreatment. Outcomes in child welfare settings are generally thought of in terms of safety, permanency, and well-being. To the extent that such information is available for children with disabilities, some indications suggest that they have the potential to experience worse outcomes, and on that basis an increased focus on their needs is warranted.

Safety. The safety of children in out-of-home care is periodically a focus of community concern, primarily as a result of media response to cases of child fatalities. However, repeated evaluations have shown that foster care is safe for most children. Careful assessments done in Illinois, the state with the third-highest foster care population in the mid-to late-nineties, demonstrate that incidence of substantiated reports of abuse or neglect of foster children has hovered for several years at around 2% (averaged across different types of placements). This figure may overestimate the actual rate of occurrence somewhat, however, as it includes reports children make while they are in foster care of abuse that transpired prior to their placement in foster care (Poertner & Gamier, 2001). These reports may be entered into administrative data systems as if they occurred while children were in care, which would cause the number of instances of abuse or neglect to children in care to be falsely elevated. No evaluation conducted to date has specifically examined the issue of abuse in foster care or after return home of children with disabilities. Based on the studies suggesting that disability or factors associated with disability might place children at greater risk for maltreatment, one might expect that the children with disabilities in foster care are at greater risk for re-abuse.

Permanency. A discussion regarding permanency for children with disabilities in state custody was presented previously, in the context of a discussion of over-representation of children with disabilities in out-of-home care. The research reviewed suggests that children with disabilities are less likely to be reunified with their birth parents and more likely to experience extended lengths of stay in care. However, very little is known as to why this might be the case. Studies have suggested that children with disabilities are adoptable (Brown, 1988; Wirnmer & Richardson, 1990) but that a variety of barriers to the initiation, processing, and finalization of adoptions for these children exist. Barriers can take the form of a lack of public awareness about the types of children available for adoption, about adoption processes, and about particular disabilities. In addition, barriers can exist at a systemic level because system failures and lack of coordination among service agencies can lead to mistrust on the part of families (Brown, 1988).

One element of the mistrust some families allude to in discussions of adoption relates to the provision of adoption subsidies. Adoption subsidies are intended to and do support families "adopting children who, because of a variety of specific factors or conditions, could not be adopted without assistance" (Public Law 96-272, the Adoption Assistance and Child Welfare Act of 1980). In one evaluation, 40% of children needing adoption assistance had disabilities (Barth, 1993). Other conditions associated with eligibility can include age, ethnic background, sibling group status, or a combination of factors. The problems related to subsidies can also be considered systems-level barriers to permanence for children. First, variation exists from state to state regarding determination of eligibility for subsidies. As Rosemary Avery (1998) states in her thorough policy analysis of these issues, "children with essentially identical characteristics but living in different states have differential access to adoption support under the same law" (p. 22). Second, the rate of support offered can vary from state to state and even, in some circumstances, from county to county (Avery, 1998). Finally, there have been instances in which states have attempted to reduce adoption subsidies. These attempts erode the confidence of adoptive parents and potential adoptive parents in the state's commitment to support adoptive families of children with special needs. Such attempts are not in the public interest given that: (1) nearly one in three adoptive parents receiving subsidies in one study stated that they would not have adopted without the subsidy; (2) subsidies at present levels have been found to be insufficient in compensating parents for their costs in raising children with special needs; and (3) subsidized adoptions offer enormous cost savings in comparison to long-term foster care (Barth, 1993).

Barriers to adoption are also found at the level of individual agencies and workers. Findings in the literature repeatedly indicate that caseworkers may determine which children are offered to which families for adoption (Coyne, 1997; Wimmer & Richardson, 1990). This can act as a barrier to adoption in that caseworkers may not recruit potential adoptive parents who do not fit the "profile" of a family likely to adopt a child with a disability. Similarly, Brown (1988) indicated that, in some circumstances, foster parents were not even made aware that adoption and medical subsidies could be made available to them if they elected to adopt their foster children with special needs. When decision-making is made unilaterally by caseworkers and information is not shared with all the parties to a decision-making process, opportunities for children could be lost.

Barriers to permanence can also occur at the level of individual children and families. One can think of permanence in broader terms than those constrained by legal relationships of adoption or guardianship. To families and children, permanence is not about a legal definition, but about a commitment to remain together. Hence, those factors that threaten the stability of a child's placement in a family are threats to permanence. Findings repeatedly demonstrate that the primary reason for a child's removal from a foster home has to do with problems with the child's behavior (Hartnett et al., 1999; James Bell and Associates, Inc., 1990). In the most recent study reviewed, 45% of foster parents and 39% of caseworkers indicated that inability to meet a child's behavioral needs was the first or second most important contributor to the decision to request that the child be placed elsewhere. This figure is consistent with those reported earlier. Children with behavioral needs were, consequently, found to experience a substantially greater number of placements and a reduced likelihood of timely permanency outcomes than those without such needs. Other findings of this study indicated that children with medical needs but *without* behavioral needs actually experienced fewer placements. This phenomenon highlights the need to avoid consideration of children with disabilities as a monolithic group.

Despite the problems that often arise in achieving permanency for children, one should not imagine that the many children with disabilities who do find loving, stable homes with their families of origin or with new families by way of adoption or guardianship experience poor long-term outcomes. The studies conducted by Rosenthal and Groze (1994) clearly indicate, in fact, that the vast majority of outcomes of adoption of children with special needs are positive. While the researchers measured more problems as children in their study aged into adolescents, many of these problems would be expected in families *not* formed by adoption. The authors state in conclusion, "special needs adoption continues to work well for most children and their families" (p. 703).

Well-Being. Little is known about the well-being of children with disabilities in the child welfare system. Children in out-of-home care have been demonstrated to have more health, mental health, and educational problems than children in the general population do. To the extent that disability correlates with the likelihood of experiencing such problems, children with disabilities would be expected to have more problems than children without disabilities. Of greater concern to child welfare professionals at this time is whether or not the responses of the child welfare system to those problems are appropriate and sufficient. The system has a responsibility to ensure that children in its care receive needed services to address the negative impacts of abuse and neglect and to provide children with the greatest opportunities possible for success (for an in-depth discussion of health care for victimized children, see Palusci, this volume).

Some indications that the system fails to meet this responsibility for some children are clearly evident. In 1995, for example, the United States General Accounting Office released a report stating that "a significant portion of young foster children do not receive critical health-related services . . . an estimated twelve percent of young foster children received no routine health care, thirty-four percent received no immunizations, and thirty-two percent had at least some identified health needs that were not met" (p. 2). The same report indicated that young children in foster care are unlikely to receive early intervention services. This area of service delivery is particularly critical for a substantial proportion of children in foster care. The number of children entering foster care under the age of six years has risen over the past decade; recent figures indicate that over 60% of children entering foster care in 2000 were in this age group (Poertner & Gamier, 2001).

Children with developmental delays or physical or mental conditions with a high probability of resulting in developmental delays, and the families of these children are eligible for a wide variety of services provided for by the Early Intervention Program mandated by the Individuals with Disabilities Education Act (IDEA), as reauthorized in 1997. These services can enhance opportunities for immediate and long-term child development, improving outcomes for both children and families. Some experts have suggested that this individualized program designed to address the needs of parents in providing appropriately for their children could even enhance permanency outcomes. However, fewer than 10% of children are reported as receiving such services, and only a very small proportion of these are placed with relatives (GAO, 1995). This 10% includes all children receiving Head Start services, for which all children in families living below the poverty line are eligible. Low levels of service delivery persist despite the fact that 52% of children in foster care age three and under were judged in one study as being in need of early intervention (Hochstadt et al., 1987).

The barriers to service delivery to young children in foster care are not known, but some authors have pointed out a variety of issues that pose a potential risk to proper service delivery. One of these was identi-fied by Dicker and Gordon (2001) who, after careful policy analysis, concluded that the IDEA does not allow for the provision of early inter-vention service in the absence of consent of the biological parent, ex-cept in very narrowly defined circumstances. This is the case, despite the facts that biological parents often cannot be located and that those who can be located may decline to consent. In this instance, the value of family involvement in service planning and delivery conflicts with the critical importance of providing services to young children in foster care who need them.

These issues of safety, permanency, and well-being of children with disabilities in foster care are vital to policy planning and case practice in child welfare but have not, in many instances, been systematically ex-plored. They add to the list of questions for future research. Among those questions would be those concerning, to a finer degree than has been thus explored, the relationship between disability and abuse. Such examinations could lead to a greater understanding of which children in which conditions are at the greatest risk, allowing for strategic direction of prevention efforts. In addition, attention to the child welfare dynam-ics affecting permanent placement of children with disabilities could re-duce placement disruptions and decrease lengths of stay for this vulnerable group. Finally, attention to the service needs of and service delivery to children with disabilities could result in the elimination of barriers to access to existing services and the creation of new services where necessary.

Children with disabilities in foster care can and often do experience improved growth and development as the problems that led to child welfare system involvement are resolved, and as their needs are ad-dressed.

Sharmica is now four years old, was nearly three when she was placed in foster care. At that time, she appeared to have autistic features. She was averse to physical touch, some fabric textures, and various foods based on their consistency. She was almost en-tirely nonverbal. Her biological mother had a twenty-year heroin use history and was transient in terms of housing and employment. Sharmica's case came to the attention of the Department of Hu-man Services when her mother's employer called to report that she had been left in a car parked at the place of employment in be-low-freezing temperatures for an entire day while her mother worked a shift. When Sharmica was initially placed in the foster home, her foster mother noted that she repeatedly attempted to eat dog food from the bowl on the floor in the kitchen and that she did not know how to use toilet paper. Since that time, she has made tremendous gains in all domains. Sharmica no longer appears to have any features of autism or problems with sensory integration and is demonstrating only minor speech and language delays. She is well integrated into her new family, school, and community. The foster family plans to adopt her, and the adoption should be finalized within the next month.

Learning more about how to improve chances for success for children like Sharmica can positively affect the everyday experiences and futures of many, many children and families. Case workers, program managers, administrators, and policy makers all need information for planning and delivery of programs and services. Increased awareness of and attention to the problems and needs of children with disabilities in out-of-home care can begin to provide that information and will benefit both child welfare professionals and the families that they serve.

NOTE

1. Identifying characteristics altered to protect confidentiality. Some vignettes represent amalgamations of case specifics.

REFERENCES

Adoption Assistance and Child Welfare Act of 1980, 42 U.S.C.S. §608, et seq. (Lexis Nexis, 2003).
Americans with Disabilities Act of 1990, as amended 42 U.S.C.S. §12101, et seq. (Lexis Nexis, 2003).
Ammerman, R. T., Herson, M., & Van Hasselt, V. B. (1994). Maltreatment of psychiatrically hospitalized children and adolescents with developmental disabilities: Prevalence and correlates. *Journal of the American Academy of Child and Adolescent Psychiatry, 33*(4), 567-576.
Ammerman, R. T., & Patz, R. J. (1996). Determinants of child abuse potential: Contribution of parent and child factors. *Journal of Clinical Child Psychiatry, 25*, 300-307.
Avery, R. J. (1998). Adoption assistance under P.L. 96-272: A policy analysis. *Children and Youth Services Review, 20*(112), 29-55.
Barth, R. P. (1993). Fiscal issues and stability in special-needs adoptions. *Public Welfare, 51*, 21-28.

Barth, R. P., Courtney, M., Berrick, J. D., & Albert, V. (1994). *From child abuse to permanency planning: Child welfare service pathways and placements.* New York: Aldine De Gruyter.

Barth, R. P., & Needell, B. (1996). Outcomes for drug-exposed children four years post-adoption. *Children and Youth Services Review, 18*(1/2), 37-56.

Benedict, M. I., White, R. B., Wulff, L. M., & Hall, B. J. (1990). Reported maltreatment in children with multiple disabilities. *Child Abuse & Neglect, 14,* 207-217.

Blacher, J., & Bromley, B. E. (1990). Correlates of out-of-home placement of handicapped children: Who places and why? In L. E. Glidden (Ed.), *Formed families: Adoption of children with handicaps* (pp. 3-40). Binghamton, NY: The Haworth Press, Inc.

Blatt, S. D., & Simms, M. (1997). Foster care: Special children, special needs. *Contemporary Pediatrics, 14*(4), 109-129.

Brown, E. (1988). Recruiting adoptive parents for children with developmental disabilities. *Child Welfare, 67*(2), 123-135.

Buchanan, A., & Oliver, J. E. (1977). Abuse and neglect as a cause of mental retardation. *British Journal of Psychiatry, 131,* 458-467.

Burrell, B., Thompson, B., & Sexton, D. (1994). Predicting child abuse potential across family types. *Child Abuse and Neglect, 18,* 1039-1049.

Chasnoff, I. J., Anson, A., Hatcher, R., Stenson, H., Jaukea, K., & Randolph, L. A. (1998). Prenatal exposure to cocaine and other drugs: Outcomes at four to six years. *Annals of the New York Academy of Sciences, 846*(21), 314-328.

Chernoff, R., Combs-Orme, R., Risley-Curtis, C., & Heisler, A. (1994). Assessing the health status of children entering foster care. *Pediatrics, 93*(4), 594-601.

Child Abuse Prevention, Adoption, and Family Services Act of 1987, 42 U.S.C.S. §5104 et seq. (Lexis Nexis, 2003).

Coyne, A. (1997). Disabled children and adoption. In R. Avery (Ed.), *Adoption policy and special needs children* (pp. 61-76). Westport, CT: Auburn House.

Crosse, S. B., Kaye, E., & Ratnofsky, A. C. (n.d.). *A report on the maltreatment of children with disabilities.* Washington, DC: National Center on Child Abuse and Neglect, DHHS.

Dicker, S., & Gordon, E. (2001). Early intervention and early intervention programs: Essential tools for child welfare advocacy. *Clearinghouse Review: Journal of Poverty Law and Policy, 34*(11-12), 727-743.

Education for All Handicapped Children Act of 1975, 20 U.S.C.S. §1400 et seq. (Lexis Nexis, 2003).

Franck, E. J. (1996). Prenatally drug-exposed children in out-of-home care: Are we looking at the whole picture? *Child Welfare, 75*(1), 19-34.

Frankenburg, W. K., Dodds, J. B., & Fandal, A. W. (1970). Denver Developmental Screening Test, American Guidance Service, Circle Pines, MN.

Frisch, L. E., & Rhoades, F. A. (1982). Child abuse and neglect in children referred for learning evaluation. *Journal of Learning Disabilities, 15,* 583-586.

Fujiura, G. T., Yamaki, K., & Czechowicz, S. (1998). Disability among ethnic and racial minorities in the United States. *Journal of Disability Policy Studies, 9,* 111-130.

Goldson, E. J. (1997). Commentary: Gender, disability, and abuse. *Child Abuse & Neglect, 21,* 903-905.

Harbin, G., Danaher, J., & Derrick, T. (1994). Comparison of eligibility policies for infant/toddler programs and preschool special education programs. *Topics in Early Childhood Special Education, 14*(4), 455-471.

Hartnett, M. A., Falconnier, L., Leathers, S., & Testa, M. (1999). *Placement stability study. Final report* (Available from the Children and Family Research Center, University of Illinois at Urbana-Champaign, 1203 W. Oregon Street, Urbana, IL 61801).

Hill, B. K., Hayden, M. F., Lakin, K. C., Menke, J., & Amado, A. R. N. (1990). State-by-state data on children with handicaps in foster care. *Child Welfare, 69*(5), 447-462.

Hill, R. B. (in press). The role of race in foster care placements. In D. M. Derezotes, & J. Poertner (Eds.), *Factors contributing to the overrepresentation of African American children in the child welfare system: What we know and don't know.* Washington, DC: Child Welfare League of America.

Hochstadt, N. J., Jaudes, P. K., Zimo, D. A., & Schacter, J. (1987). The medical and psychosocial needs of children entering foster care. *Child Abuse & Neglect, 11*, 53-62.

Horowitz, S. M., Simms, M. D., & Farrington, R. (1994). Impact of developmental problems on young children's exits from foster care. *Developmental and Behavioral Pediatrics, 15*(2), 105-110.

Individuals with Disabilities Education Act as reauthorized in 1997, 20 U.S.C.S. §1400 et seq. (Lexis Nexis, 2003).

Jacobsen, J. L., & Jacobsen, S. W. (1999). Drinking moderately and pregnancy: Effects on child development. *Alcohol Research and Health, 23*(1), 25-30.

James Bell Associates, Inc., & Westat, Inc. (1990). *The National Survey of Current and Former Foster Parents.* Washington, DC: United States Department of Health and Human Services, Administration on Children, Youth, and Families.

Jaudes, P. K., & Diamond, L. J. (1985). The handicapped child and child abuse. *Child Abuse & Neglect: The International Journal, 9*, 341-347.

Jaudes, P. K., & Shapiro, L. D. (1999). Child abuse and developmental disabilities. In J. A. Silver, B. J. Amster, & T. Haecker (Eds.), *Young children and foster care* (pp. 213-234). Baltimore, MD: Paul H. Brookes Publishing Co.

Kendall-Tackett, K. A., & Eckenrode, J. (1996). The effects of neglect on academic achievement and disciplinary problems: A developmental perspective. *Child Abuse & Neglect, 20*(3), 161-169.

Larson, S. (1999, January). *Disability trends and issues.* Presented at the Changing Universe of Disability Conference, sponsored by the Institute for Disability and Human Development, University of Illinois at Chicago. Chicago, Illinois.

Massat, C., Gleason, J., & Weagant R. (1993). Children, poverty, and child welfare in Illinois. In R. Weagant, & S. Dubey (Eds.), *Policies and programs for children and families in poverty: The Illinois experience* (pp. 10-48). Chicago, IL: The Jane Addams Center for Social Policy and Research.

Moffatt, M. E. K., Peddie, M., Stulginskas, J., Pless, I. B., & Steinmetz, N. (1985). Health care delivery to foster children: A study. *Health and Social Work, 10*, 129-137.

Morrison, J. A., Frank, S. J., Holland, C. C., & Kates, W. R. (1999). Emotional development and disorders in young children in the child welfare system. In J. A. Silver, B. J. Amster, & T. Haecker (Eds.), *Young children and foster care* (pp. 33-64). Baltimore, MD: Paul H. Brookes Publishing Co.

National Center for Health Statistics (1973). Examination and health history findings among children and youth, 6-17 years–United States. *Vital and Health Statistics, 11* (129).

Palusci, V. J. (2003). The role of health care professionals in the response to child victimization. *Journal of Aggression, Maltreatment, & Trauma, 8*(1/2), 133-171.

Parker, B., McFarlane, J., & Soeken, L. (1994). Abuse during pregnancy: Effects on maternal complications and birth weight in adult and teenage women. *Obstetrics and Gynecology, 84*, 323-328.

Perry, B. D. (1994). Neurobiological sequelae of childhood trauma: Post traumatic stress disorders in children. In M. Murburg (Ed.), *Catecholamine function in post traumatic stress disorder. Emerging concepts* (pp. 253-276). Washington, DC: American Psychiatric Press.

Poertner, J., & Gamier, P. (2001). *Report on child safety and permanency in Illinois for fiscal year 2000.* Urbana, IL: Children and Family Research Center.

Rosenthal, J. A., & Groze, V. K. (1994). A longitudinal study of special-needs adoptive families. *Child Welfare, 73*(6), 689-706.

Sameroff, A., Seifer, R., Barocas, R., Zax, M., & Greenspan, S. (1987). Intelligence quotient scores of 4-year-old children: Social-environmental risk factors. *Pediatrics, 30*, 343-350.

Schilling, R. F., Kirkham, M. A., & Schinke, S. P. (1986). Do child protection services neglect developmentally disabled children? *Education and Training of the Mentally Retarded, 21*(1), 21-26.

Schor, E. L. (1982). The foster care system and health status of foster children. *Pediatrics, 69*(5), 521-528.

Sedlak, A., & Schultz, D. (in press). Race differences in risk of maltreatment in the general population. In D. M. Derezotes, & J. Poertner (Eds.), *Factors contributing to the overrepresentation of African American children in the child welfare system: What we know and don't know.* Washington, D.C.: Child Welfare League of America.

Sedlak, A. J., & Broadhurst, D. D. (1996). *Executive summary of the Third National Incidence Study of Child Abuse and Neglect.* Retrieved April 23, 2003, from http://www.calib.com/nccanch/pubs/statinfo/nis3.cfm.

Sobsey, D. (1994). *Violence and abuse in the lives of people with disabilities: The end of silent acceptance?* Baltimore, MD: Paul H. Brooks Publishing Co.

Sobsey, D. (2002). Exceptionality, education, and maltreatment. *Exceptionality, 10*, 29-46.

Souther, M. (1984). Developmentally disabled abused and neglected children: A high risk/high need population. In National Center on Child Abuse and Neglect (Ed.), *Perspectives on child maltreatment in the mid '80's.* (DHHS Publication No. [ODHS] 84-30338). Washington, DC: U.S. Department of Health and Human Services.

Strathearn, L., Gray, P. H., O'Callaghan, M. J., & Wood, D. O. (2001). Childhood neglect and cognitive development in extremely low birth weight infants: A prospective study. *Pediatrics, 108*(1), 142-151.

Streissguth, A. P., Barr, H. M., Sampson, P. D., & Bookstein, F. L. (1994). Prenatal alcohol and offspring development: The first 14 years. *Drug and Alcohol Dependence, 36*(2), 89-99.

Sullivan, P. M., & Knutson, J. F. (1998). The association between child maltreatment and disabilities in a hospital-based epidemiological study. *Child Abuse & Neglect*, *22*(4), 271-288.

Sullivan, P. M., & Knutson, J. F. (2000). Maltreatment and disabilities: A population-based epidemiological study. *Child Abuse & Neglect*, *24*(10), 1257-1273.

Swire, M. R., & Kavaler, F. (1977). The health status of foster children. *Child Welfare*, *61*(10), 635-653.

Taylor, S. J., Lakin, K. C., & Hill, B. K. (1989). Permanency planning for children and youth: Out-of-home placement decisions. *Exceptional Children*, *55*(6), 541-549.

U.S. Census Bureau. (2001). *2001 Supplementary Survey profile*. Retrieved April 23, 2003, from http://www.census.gov/acs/www/Products/Profiles/Single/2001/5501/Tabular/010/01000US2.htm.

U.S. Department of Health and Human Services, Administration for Children and Families, Administration on Children, Youth and Families, Children's Bureau. (2001a). *Child maltreatment*. Retrieved April 23, 2003, from http://www.acf.hhs.gov/programs/cb/publications/cmreports.htm.

U.S. Department of Health and Human Services. (2001b). *Report of the Surgeon General's Conference on Children's Mental Health: A national action agenda*. Retrieved April 23, 2003, from http://www.surgeongeneral.gov/topics/cmh/.

U.S. Department of Health and Human Services, Administration for Children and Families, Administration on Children, Youth and Families, Children's Bureau. (2003). *The AFCARS Report*. Retrieved April 23, 2003, from http://www.acf.hhs.gov/prorams/cb/publications/afcars/report8.html.

United States General Accounting Office. (1995). *Services for young foster children*. (GAO/HEHS-95-114). Washington, DC: General Accounting Office.

Verdugo, M. A., Bermejo, B. G., & Fuertes, J. (1995). The maltreatment of intellectually handicapped children and adolescents. *Child Abuse & Neglect*, *19*, 205-215.

West, M. A., Richardson, M., LeConte, J., Crimi, C., & Stuart, S. (1992). Identification of developmental disabilities and health problems among individuals under child protective services. *Mental Retardation*, *30*(4), 221-225.

Wimmer, J. S., & Richardson, S. (1990). Adoption of children with developmental disabilities. *Child Welfare*, *69*(6), 563-569.

EMERGING LEGAL ISSUES PERTAINING TO CHILD VICTIMIZATION

Fetal Homicide: Emerging Statutory and Judicial Regulation of Third-Party Assaults Against the Fetus

Jeff Maahs

SUMMARY. Under common law, a crime resulting in the death of a fetus that was viable but not "born alive" was viewed as a transgression less serious than murder. Accordingly, courts did not allow parents to bring wrongful death suits for the death of a fetus. In the past decade, however, several states have amended their criminal or civil statutes to include the specific crime of "feticide" or "fetal homicide," and the Federal government is considering similar legislation. This paper ex-

Address correspondence to: Jeff Maahs, Department of Sociology-Anthropology, University of Minnesota Duluth, Duluth, MN 55812-2496 (E-mail: jmaahs@ d.umn.edu).

[Haworth co-indexing entry note]: "Fetal Homicide: Emerging Statutory and Judicial Regulation of Third-Party Assaults Against the Fetus." Maahs, Jeff. Co-published simultaneously in *Journal of Aggression, Maltreatment & Trauma* (The Haworth Maltreatment & Trauma Press, an imprint of The Haworth Press, Inc.) Vol. 8, No. 3 (#17), 2003, pp. 205-231; and: *The Victimization of Children: Emerging Issues* (ed: Janet L. Mullings, James W. Marquart, and Deborah J. Hartley) The Haworth Maltreatment & Trauma Press, an imprint of The Haworth Press, Inc., 2003, pp. 205-231. Single or multiple copies of this article are available for a fee from The Haworth Document Delivery Service [1-800-HAWORTH, 9:00 a.m. - 5:00 p.m. (EST). E-mail address: docdelivery@haworthpress.com].

amines the history and current status of criminal and civil law regarding the third-party killing of a fetus. *[Article copies available for a fee from The Haworth Document Delivery Service: 1-800-HAWORTH. E-mail address: <docdelivery@haworthpress.com> Website: <http://www.HaworthPress.com> © 2003 by The Haworth Press, Inc. All rights reserved.]*

KEYWORDS. Feticide, fetal homicide, fetal rights, wrongful death

Imagine the following scenario: The driver of a car is seven months pregnant. The intoxicated driver of a different vehicle strikes her car, and the resulting accident causes serious injury (but not death) to the pregnant mother. At the hospital, the fetus, removed by cesarean section, shows no signs of life.

Can the intoxicated driver in this situation be prosecuted for the death of the fetus? Can a wrongful death suit be filed on behalf of the fetus? The answers to these questions depend largely upon the legal jurisdiction in which the accident occurred. Changing aspects of this scenario add even more complexity. For example, what if the female driver were only eight weeks pregnant, and the fetus not yet "viable"? In Minnesota, the driver could be charged with vehicular homicide, regardless of whether the fetus was viable. In Georgia, on the other hand, a charge of vehicular "feticide" would stand only if the fetus were viable. In yet other states, no charge at all would be possible because a fetus is not included in the legal definition of a "person." A similar state of affairs exists for wrongful death suits.

The injury or death of a fetus caused by a third party raises complex philosophical, social, and legal issues. Accordingly, recent legislative and judicial action related to this issue, including the Unborn Victims of Violence Act (2001) recently passed by the House of Representatives, has evoked heated responses from many interest groups (Mitchell, 2001). This article seeks to make clear some of those responses (in particular, arguments related to the overlap between "fetal rights" and the abortion debate) and to outline the current legal status regarding third-party assaults on a fetus. After a brief survey of the history of this legal issue, this paper addresses its current judicial and legislative treatment in both civil and criminal actions.

HISTORICAL CONTEXT

The history of the legal debate regarding fetal homicide (and wrongful death actions) is important for at least two reasons. First, the legal and social issues surrounding the debate have not changed. Second, many states are still guided in their interpretation of fetal homicide cases by the specific principles outlined in English common law.

English Common Law and the Born Alive Rule

English common law defined homicide as the killing of one human being by another human being. However, a fetus was not viewed as a "human being" prior to birth, and in cases in which a fetus had died, the crime of homicide was therefore not possible under common law definition, unless the fetus were "born alive." Sir Edward Coke, the great seventeenth-century legal scholar, summarized the born-alive rule in the following manner:

> If a woman be quick with childe, and by a potion or otherwise killeth it in her womb, or if a man beat her, whereby the childe dyeth in her body, and she is delivered of a dead childe, this is a great misdemeanor, and no murder; but if the childe be born alive and dyeth of the potion, battery, or other cause, this is murder; for in law it is accounted a reasonable creature, in *rerum natura*, when it is born alive. (cited in Obasi, 1998, p. 211)

Given the medical technology of Coke's day, it was extraordinarily difficult to determine whether the fetus was alive when a third party (defendant) committed the alleged act and whether the defendant's conduct, in fact, caused the death of the fetus. The born-alive rule allowed doctors and prosecutors to establish with a modicum of certainty the life of the fetus before a third-party assault, as well as the cause of death (Schroedel, 2000).

Also noteworthy in this oft-cited passage is Coke's distinction between a fetus that is born alive, and a fetus that is killed in utero after "quickening." Quickening is defined as the first recognizable fetal movement, which typically occurs during the fourth month of pregnancy. Under English common law, informed by theological and philosophical consensus, quickening was the point at which a fetus was furnished a soul, and thus became a "person." The death of a fetus prior to quickening (through abortion, negligence, or assault from a third party) was not a crime, but became a "great misdemeanor" after quickening.

American Jurisprudence and the Born-Alive Rule

American courts uniformly adopted the born-alive rule and the concept of "quickening" by the middle of the nineteenth century (Schroedel,

2000). That is, a fetus was not considered a "person" in the legal sense, unless born alive. The 1884 case of *Dietrich v. Inhabitants of Northampton* is often cited as a leading case for wrongful death suits. In *Dietrich*, a woman miscarried because of a fall caused by a defect in a public road and subsequently filed a wrongful death suit on behalf of her fetus. Writing for the majority, Justice Oliver Wendell Holmes argued that the fetus is "so intimately united with its mother as to be a 'part' of her and as a consequence is not to be regarded as a separate, distinct, and individual entity" (at 17). In other words, Holmes reasoned that the fetus had no independent right of recovery, separate from the mother. Even in cases in which the baby was born alive, connecting the third party to the death of the fetus was difficult. The limited technology of Holmes' day made it difficult to prove that an outside force caused fetal injuries (Schroedel, 2000).

Since the 1800s, medical knowledge and technology have improved dramatically. Physicians can establish fetal health and viability through heart monitoring, sonography, and other techniques, and medical experts can usually establish the link between a defendant's acts and the death of a fetus (Kime, 1995). Despite these advances, the born-alive-rule is still the controlling standard for civil and criminal law in many jurisdictions. Courts that retain the born alive rule generally do so on the grounds that legislators are aware of common law and that if legislators want fetuses included in the homicide statute, they should revise the criminal statutes accordingly. Courts have also reasoned that charging a defendant with the homicide of a fetus would violate due process rights, specifically the right to a fair warning that a particular act is illegal (Wasserstrom, 1998).

A classic case that illustrates this type of legal reasoning is *Keeler v. Superior Court of Amador County* (1970). In this case, a husband, whose wife was thirty-five weeks pregnant with another man's child, confronted her saying, "I'm going to stomp it out of you," and kneed his wife in the abdomen. An emergency cesarean procedure yielded a stillborn child with a fractured skull. Keeler, the husband, was charged with murder under common law definition: "Murder is the unlawful killing of a human being, with malice aforethought." In this case, however, the California Supreme Court held that the term "human being" did not apply to a fetus unless it was born alive. Writing the majority opinion, Justice Mosk stated, "We conclude that the Legislature did not intend such a meaning, and that for us to construe the statute to the contrary and apply it to this petitioner would exceed our judicial power and deny petitioner due process of law" (at 617).

In response to the *Keeler* decision, the California legislature revised the murder statute to include a fetus, and other states have since followed suit (Schroedel, 2000). In yet other states, the courts have overturned the born alive rule for civil law, criminal law, or both (Smith, 2000; Snow, 1997). At present, then, there are great inconsistencies across the states in the treatment of third party assaults on a fetus. Further, states that proscribe fetal homicide vary widely in statutory coverage, gestational age of the fetus, and sentencing options.

THIRD-PARTY HARM TO A FETUS AND THE CRIMINAL LAW

Criminal law changes through either legislative or judicial efforts. Legislators change the law by either amending or adding to the criminal statutes, while judicial interpretation of the statutes creates common (or case) law. The first part of this section addresses common law developments in fetal homicide cases, while the second section treats fetal homicide legislation.

Judicial Assessment of the Born-Alive Rule

As noted above, the courts in some states retain the born alive rule despite advances in medical technology that allow pathologists to establish fetal cause of death. In these states, the statutes leave the definition of *person*, *human being*, or *individual* to the discretion of the judicial system. In turn, courts are resistant (as evident in the *Keeler* decision) to creating "new law" by interpreting the word "person" or "human being" (within the homicide statutes) to include a fetus. Currently, sixteen states require that a fetus be born alive before allowing prosecution under homicide statutes (Smith, 2000). In eight of these states, the criminal statutes explicitly define *person* or *human being* as one that is born alive, precluding judicial treatment of the issue. These states are considered in the next section. Table 1 displays the statute that defines homicide and the controlling case that affirms the born-alive rule for each of the remaining eight states.[1] These are states in which legislators have not defined "person" or "human being" and the courts have explicitly ruled that such terms exclude a fetus unless born alive.[2]

The Courts in these eight jurisdictions have upheld the born-alive rule despite the grisly facts and obviously culpable defendants associated with some cases. In *Hollis v. Commonwealth*, for example, the de-

TABLE 1. Statute citations and the controlling case in states where the courts interpret "person" or "human being" to exclude a fetus

State and Statute Defining the Victim[a]	Controlling Case
Connecticut Conn. Gen. Stat. Ann. § 53a-3(1)	*State v. Anonymous,* 516 A.2d 156 (1986)
Kentucky Ky. Rev. Stat. Ann. § 507.020	*Hollis v. Commonwealth,* 652 S.W.2d 61 (1983)
Maryland Md. Ann. Code, art. 27, § 407	*Williams v. State,* 550 A.2d 722 (1988)
New Jersey N.J. Stat. Ann. § 2C: 1-14	*In re A.W.S.,* 440 A.2d 1144 (1981)
New York N.Y. Penal Law § 125.00, 125.05	*People v. Vercelletto,* 514 N.Y.S.2d 177 (1987); *People v. Joseph,* 469 N.Y.S. 2d 328 (1985)
North Carolina N.C. Gen. Stat. § 14-17	*State v. Beale,* 376 S.E.2d 1 (1989)
Vermont Vt. Stat. Ann. tit. 13, § 5301(4)	*State v. Oliver,* 563 A.2d 1002 (1989)
West Virginia W.Va. Code § 61-2-1	*State ex rel. Atkinson v. Wilson,* 332 S.E.2d 807 (1984)

[a] All statutes cited were located through an electronic search of the Lexis-Nexis database (http://web.lexis-nexis.com/universe) which at the time, contained codes updated through 2002. Thus, the date for all code editions cited is 2002.

fendant took his estranged wife from inside her parents' house out into a barn. There, he told her he did not want the baby and forced his hand inside her vagina, causing damage to her vagina and uterus and killing the fetus. The court concluded that Hollis could not be charged with "the death of another person." Despite the obvious culpability in this case, the court adhered to the legal definition of the born-alive rule.

The legal thread that ties the eight states shown in Table 1 to the born-alive rule appears to be judicial reluctance to create new law. Justice Frye, writing the opinion in *State v. Beale,* summarized this position:

> The creation and expansion of criminal offenses is the prerogative of the legislative branch of the government. The legislature has considered the question of intentionally destroying a fetus and determined the punishment therefore . . . It has adopted legislation dealing generally with the crimes of abortion and kindred offenses . . . It has also created the new offenses of felony and misdemeanor death by vehicle . . . Nothing in any of the statutes or amendments shows a clear legislative intent to change the common law rule that the killing of a viable but unborn child is not murder . . . We do not discern any legislative intent to include the act of killing a viable fetus within the murder statute. (p. 4)

Despite such judicial reluctance, courts in three states have over-turned the born alive rule. Table 2 outlines the precedent-setting cases from Massachusetts, Oklahoma, and South Carolina. In each of these states, the courts interpreted the word "person" or "human being" contained in the general homicide statutes to include a viable fetus. In departing from common law, the decisions rested upon one or more of the following conclusions: (a) medical science is sufficient to establish the cause of death for prenatally inflicted injuries; (b) third-party assaults that result in the death of the fetus should not go unpunished; (c) it would be inconsistent and unjust to impose civil liability, but not criminal liability; and/or (d) it is the court's duty and right to develop the common law (Wasserstrom, 1998).

In *Hughes v. State*, the appellant was originally convicted of manslaughter when she drove her vehicle, while intoxicated, into oncoming traffic and collided with another vehicle. The driver of the other vehicle was nine months pregnant, and the impact of the steering wheel on her abdomen was sufficient to break the steering wheel. The baby was delivered via cesarean section and died, despite the detection of a faint heartbeat and subsequent resuscitation efforts. The appellate court found that, despite the heartbeat, the fetus was not born alive because it was brain dead. However, the court rejected the born-alive rule, and upheld the original conviction, based on the following two conclusions: (a) the medical and scientific evidence established that the fetus was alive and viable before the crash and that it died from placental abruption caused by the collision, and (b) the court would not want the

TABLE 2. Statute citations and the controlling case in states where the courts interpret "person" or "human being" to include a fetus

State and Statute[a]	Controlling Case	Holding
Massachusetts Mass. Gen. Law Ann ch. 90 § 24 G(b)	*Commonwealth v. Cass* 467 N.E.2d 1324 (1984)	A viable fetus is a "person" under the Massachusetts vehicular homicide statute.
Oklahoma Okla. Stat. tit. 21, 691	*Hughes v. State* 868 P.2d 730 (1994)	A viable fetus is a "human being" that may be the subject of a homicide under Oklahoma law. The common law "born alive rule" is abandoned.
South Carolina S.C. Code § 16-3-10	*State v. Horne* 319 S.E.2d 703 (1984)	The general murder statutes of South Carolina apply to a viable fetus.

[a] All statutes cited were located through an electronic search of the Lexis-Nexis database (http://web.lexis-nexis.com/universe) which at the time, contained codes updated through 2002. Thus, the date for all code editions cited is 2002.

infliction of prenatal injuries that caused the death of a viable fetus to go unpunished.

In *Commonwealth v. Cass*, the Supreme Court of Massachusetts rejected the argument that the legislature intended the word "person" within the vehicular homicide statute to limit the application of this law to its common law definition. Affirming the court's right to create common law, the court stated, "We think that the better rule is that infliction of prenatal injuries resulting in the death of a viable fetus, before or after it is born, is homicide" (p. 1329).

Thus, adherence to or rejection of the born-alive rule turns on the presence or absence of judicial activism in a particular jurisdiction. Courts that shy from judicial activism force the legislators to address this issue. Indeed, a majority of states now have some form of legislation that proscribes third-party violence towards an embryo or fetus.

Legislative Regulation of Third-Party Harm to a Fetus

Legislation criminalizing third-party harm to a fetus is a recent phenomenon. As early as 1835, Missouri revised its manslaughter statute to include third-party killing of a fetus, and Michigan, Mississippi, Iowa, and New Hampshire followed suit prior to the Civil War (Schroedel, 2000). Over the last twenty years, however, states have passed more (and more comprehensive) statutes targeting third-party harm towards unborn children.

Currently, a majority of states have some type of legislation designed to prevent third-party assaults on a fetus. In the survey that follows, fetal homicide legislation is organized into the following three segments: (a) statutes that exclude a fetus via legislation; (b) statutes that treat the fetus as a victim; and (c) statutes that treat the pregnant woman as a victim.

Exclusion of the Fetus Through Legislation. As noted above, eight states codified the common law born-alive requirement in their criminal statutes. Table 3 contains the statutes and specific language for each of these eight states. The statutes in these states explicitly define the terms *person, human being,* or *individual* to mean one who is born alive. In some of the states, these definitions apply specifically to cases of homicide, while in others they apply to all criminal statutes.

Legislation Defining the Fetus as Victim. As of 1999, twenty-three states had statutes prohibiting a third party (aside from legal abortions) from killing or harming a fetus. Each of these statutes specifically identifies the fetus, as opposed to the pregnant female, as the victim. Table 4 illustrates the specific statutes and lists the crimes covered by the legis-

TABLE 3. State statutes that define a homicide victim as a person who is born alive

State	Statute Citation[a]	Statutory Language
Alabama	Ala. Code § 13A-6-1(2)	Such term, ["person"] when referring to the victim of a criminal homicide, means a human being who had been born and was alive at the time of the homicidal act.
Alaska	Alaska Stat. § 11.41.140	"Person," when referring to the victim of a crime, means a human being who has been born and was alive at the time of the criminal act. A person is "alive" if there is spontaneous respiratory or cardiac function.
Colorado	Colo. Rev. Stat. Ann. § 18-3-101	"Person," when referring to the victim of a homicide, means a human being who had been born and was alive at the time of the homicidal act.
Hawaii	Haw. Rev. Stat. Ann. § 707-700	"Person" means a human being who has been born and is alive.
Montana	Mont. Code Ann. § 45-2-101(28)	"Human being" means a person who has been born and is alive.
Nebraska	Neb. Rev. Stat. Ann. § 28-302(2)	"Person," when referring to the victim of a homicide, shall mean a human being who had been born and was alive at the time of the homicidal act.
Oregon	Or. Rev. Stat. § 163.005(3)	"Human being" means a person who has been born and was alive at the time of the criminal act.
Texas	Tex. Penal Code Ann. § 1.07(26)	"Individual" means a human being who has been born and is alive.

[a] All statutes cited were located through an electronic search of the Lexis-Nexis database (http://web.lexis-nexis.com/universe) which at the time, contained codes updated through 2002. Thus, the date for all code editions cited is 2002.

lation. This table is organized according to the threshold gestational age of the fetus necessary to prosecute an individual under the criminal statutes.

Inspection of Table 4 reveals that statutes in eleven states allow prosecution regardless of the gestational age of the fetus. The specific statutory schemes and language vary by state. Wisconsin, for example, amended many of its personal offense crimes to include an unborn child as a possible victim. The term "unborn child" is subsequently defined as "any individual of the human species from fertilization until birth that is gestating inside a woman."[3] In Missouri, "unborn child" is defined as "all unborn children or children or the offspring of human beings from the moment of conception until birth at every stage of biological development."[4]

TABLE 4. State legislation prohibiting third-party assaults against a fetus, based on the gestational development of the fetus

State	Statute[a]	Crimes Addressed
Any Gestational Age		
Arizona	Ariz. Rev. Stat. § 13-1103(A)5	manslaughter
Illinois	Ill. Comp Stat. ch. 720, §§ 5/9-1.2, 5/9-2.1, 5/9-3.2, 5/12-3.1	intentional homicide, voluntary and involuntary manslaughter, and battery of an unborn child
Louisiana	La. Rev. Stat. Ann. §§ 14:32.5 to 14.32.8	1st, 2nd, or 3rd degree feticide
Minnesota	Minn. Stat. Ann. §§ 609.266, 609.2661 to 609.2665, 609.268(1), 609.21(3)	murder (1st, 2nd, 3rd degree), manslaughter (1st and 2nd degree), and assault (1st, 2nd, 3rd degree) of an unborn child, criminal vehicular homicide of an unborn child
Missouri	Mo. Stat. Ann. § 1.205	all criminal laws
North Dakota	N.D. Cent. Code §§ 12.1-17.1-01 to 12.1-17.1-08	murder, manslaughter, negligent homicide, aggravated assault, and assault of an unborn child
Ohio	Ohio Rev. Code Ann. §§ 2903.08, 2303.11, 2903.14	aggravated vehicular assault, felonious and negligent assault
Pennsylvania	Pa. Const. Stat. 18 §§ 2601 to 2609	murder (1st, 2nd, 3rd degree), voluntary manslaughter, and aggravated assault of an unborn child
South Dakota	S.D. Cod. Laws. Ann. §§ 22-16-1, 22-16-1.1, 22-16-15(5), 22-16-20, 22-16-41	fetal homicide, manslaughter, vehicular homicide
Utah	Utah Code Ann. § 76-5-201	all forms of criminal homicide
Wisconsin	Wis. Stat. Ann. §§ 939.75, 939.24, 939.25, 940.01, 940.02, 940.05, 940.06, 940.08 to 940.10, 940.195, 940.25	all homicide offenses, battery to an unborn child, injury by intoxicated use of vehicle
Embryonic Stage		
California	Cal. Pen. Code § 187(a)	murder
Twelve Weeks		
Arkansas	Ark. Code Ann. 5-1-102(13)(B)	capital murder, 1st and 2nd degree murder, manslaughter, negligent homicide
Quickening		
Florida	Fla. Stat. Ann. § 782.09	manslaughter
Georgia	Ga. Code Ann. §§ 16-5-80, 40-6-393.1, 52-7-12.3	feticide, vehicular feticide, feticide by vessel
Michigan	Mich. Comp. Laws § 750.322	manslaughter
Mississippi	Miss. Code Ann. § 97-3-37	manslaughter, aggravated assault, assault
Nevada	Nev. Rev. Stat. §200.210	manslaughter
Oklahoma	Okla. Stat. Ann. tit. 21, § 713	manslaughter
Washington	Wash. Rev. Code Ann. §9A.32.060(1)(b)	manslaughter

TABLE 4 (continued)

State	Statute[a]	Crimes Addressed
Twenty-Four Weeks		
New York	N.Y. Pen. Law § 125.00, but see N.Y. Pen law § 125.05	homicide
Viability		
Florida	Fla. Stat. Ann. § 782.071	vehicular homicide
Indiana	Ind. Code Ann. §§ 35-42-1-1, 35-42-1-3, 35-42-1-4, 35-42-2-1.5	murder, voluntary and involuntary manslaughter, aggravated battery
Rhode Island[b]	R.I. Gen. Laws § 11-23-5	manslaughter
Tennessee	Tenn. Code Ann. §§ 39-13-107, 39-13-214	all homicide and offenses and assault offenses

a All statutes cited were located through an electronic search of the Lexis-Nexis database (http://web.lexis-nexis.com/universe) which at the time, contained codes updated through 2002. Thus, the date for all code editions cited is 2002.
b This statute is titled as "willful killing of an unborn quick child," but is subsequently defined as "an unborn child whose heart is beating, who is experiencing electronically measurable brain waves, who is discernibly moving, and who is so far developed and matured as to be capable of surviving the trauma of birth with the aid of usual medical care and facilities available in this state."

California and Arkansas set unique gestational age thresholds. The California statutes define murder as "the unlawful killing of a human being, or a fetus, with malice aforethought." Thus, the legislature left the term fetus undefined. In *People v. Davis* (1994), however, the California Supreme Court established that prosecutions may proceed as long as "the state can show that the fetus has progressed beyond the embryonic stage of seven to eight weeks" (at 602). In Arkansas, a section of the penal code identifies "unborn children in utero at any stage of development" as victims for purposes of the homicide statutes. In the next subsection, "unborn child" is defined as "a living fetus of twelve weeks or greater gestation."[5]

Despite advances in medical technology, seven states retain the common law concept of "quickening" to define the parameters of their feticide legislation. As noted above, quickening refers to the first fetal movement, which typically occurs between the sixteenth and twentieth weeks of pregnancy. Admittedly, the majority of these laws were enacted in the nineteenth century. However, as recently as 1982, the Georgia Legislature enacted a statute defining feticide as the "willful killing of an unborn child so far developed as to be ordinarily called quick."[6] The Georgia Supreme Court subsequently defined quickening as the time at which a fetus is able to move in the womb (regardless of whether it does move), generally sixteen weeks, but as early as ten weeks (*Brinkley v. State*, 1984, at 51).

The final gestational age used to define fetal assault legislation is viability. In the medical and scientific sense, viability refers to the point at which a fetus has reasonable odds of survival if removed from the uterus, usually between twenty and twenty-four weeks (Barlow, 1995). In *Roe v. Wade* (1973), the Supreme Court defined viability as the period at the end of the second trimester when there is potential for meaningful life outside of the womb. In a later case (*Colautti v. Franklin*, 1979), however, the Court ruled that viability is a judgment appropriate for the medical profession and should therefore not be set (on the grounds of standardized fetal weight or age) by the legislature (Barlow, 1995). These issues in mind, examination of Table 4 reveals that four states criminalize third-party assaults against a viable fetus. Indiana's murder statute, for example, states that a person who "knowingly or intentionally kills a fetus that has attained viability . . . commits murder, a felony."[7]

In addition to fetal gestational age, Table 4 reveals that the state statutes also vary widely in terms of the type and number of offenses proscribed. Most states simply amend the statutes for crimes already on the books. Thus, a crime such as "vehicular manslaughter" is amended to include specifically an "unborn child" as a possible victim. Seven states include only manslaughter; this list partially reflects the states that amended their statutes in the nineteenth century, when amending the manslaughter statute was the status quo method of enacting fetal homicide legislation (Schroedel, 2000). Florida's statute, enacted prior to 1900, reads, "The willful killing of an unborn quick child, by any injury to the mother of such child which would be murder if it resulted in the death of such mother, shall be deemed manslaughter, a felony of the second degree."[8] Additionally, two states include the fetus as a victim for multiple types of homicide. The Arkansas criminal code contains a section in the general provisions chapter that defines "person," in the context of capital murder, first-degree and second-degree murder, manslaughter, and negligent homicide, as including an unborn child developed beyond twelve weeks. In Utah's criminal code, an "unborn child" is similarly recognized as a victim for purposes of all forms of criminal homicide.

Four states (Missouri, Ohio, Pennsylvania, and Mississippi) include a fetus as a victim for offenses other than homicide. Missouri has a very broad statute:

Effective January 1, 1988, the laws of this state shall be interpreted and construed to acknowledge on behalf of the unborn child at every stage of development, all the rights, privileges, and immunities available to other persons, citizens, and residents of this state, subject only to the Constitution of the United States, and decisional interpretations thereof by the United States Supreme Court and specific provisions to the contrary in the statutes and constitution of this state.[9]

A statute this broad certainly leaves room for judicial interpretation. In *State v. Holcomb* (1997), however, the court held that an unborn child is a "person," for the purposes of the first-degree-murder statute, specifically noting that the unborn-child statute and the general murder statute were passed at the same legislative session. The remaining three states include the fetus as a victim of either assault or aggravated assault, in addition to homicide offenses.

Table 4 reveals that, in contrast to the states that add "unborn children" as possible victims for traditional criminal offenses, six states (Georgia, Illinois, Louisiana, Minnesota, North Dakota, and Wisconsin) have created new criminal offenses to define third-party harm against the fetus. Reacting to a decision by their state Supreme Court in 1985, Minnesota legislators added the "Crimes Against Unborn Children" chapter to the penal code.[10] This chapter creates offenses ranging from "murder of an unborn child" to "assault of an unborn child." Similarly, Georgia created the crimes of "feticide, vehicular feticide, and feticide by vessel." The difference between creating a "new" offense and adding the fetus as a victim to previously defined offenses appears to be a stylistic preference–the penalties for "new" offenses are nearly identical to the analogous offenses in the criminal statutes.

Legislation Specifying Crimes Against Pregnant Women. Rather than specify the fetus as a victim and thereby enter the realm of "fetal rights" and the abortion debate (see below), some states have enacted legislation that specifies the pregnant woman as the victim. Table 5 contains the statutory citation and type of crime proscribed for the ten states that have such provisions. A word of caution is warranted regarding the "crimes" column: For some states the name of the crime does not accurately reflect the description of the offense, and for others the actual offense is unnamed. Interested readers are therefore encouraged to review the individual statutes. Most (but not all) of the statutes hinge on whether or not the pregnant woman loses the baby through miscarriage or stillbirth as a result of the alleged crime.

TABLE 5. States that penalize against pregnant women

State	Statute[a]	Crime
Arkansas	Ark. Code Ann. 5-13-201(5)	miscarriage-producing injury to pregnant woman is 1st degree battery
Delaware	Del. Code Ann. tit. 11 §§ 222(22), 605-06, 612(a)	1st and 2nd degree abuse of a pregnant female (felony), unlawful termination is "serious bodily injury"
Iowa	Iowa Code Ann. § 707.8	nonconsensual termination–serious injury to a human pregnancy (intentional and non-intentional)
Kansas	Kan. Stat. Ann. §§ 21-3440, 21-3441	injury to a pregnant woman, injury to a pregnant woman by vehicle
Michigan	Mich. Comp. Laws 750.90a	felony crime to commit assault or robbery against a pregnant woman
New Hampshire	N.H. Rev. Stat. Ann. §§ 631:1 to 631:2	miscarriage-producing injury to a pregnant victim satisfies conditions for 1st or 2nd degree assault
New Mexico	N.M. Sat. Ann. §§ 30-3-7, 66-8-101.1	injury to a pregnant woman, injury to a pregnant woman by vehicle
North Carolina	N.C. Gen. Stat. § 14-18.2	injury to a pregnant woman
Ohio	Ohio Rev. Code Ann. §§ 2903.01 to 2903.07, 2903.09	aggravated murder, murder, manslaughter, negligent homicide, aggravated vehicular homicide
Virginia	Va. Code Ann. §§ 18.2-31, 18.2-32.1, 18.2-51.2	murder of a pregnant woman, pregnant victim satisfies statutory requirement for aggravated malicious wounding and capital murder charges
Wyoming	Wyo. Stat. Ann. §§ 6-2-502(a)(iv), 31-5-233(h)	aggravated assault and battery, miscarriage-producing injury to a pregnant woman is "serious bodily injury" for purposes of driving under the influence of alcohol

[a] All statutes cited were located through an electronic search of the Lexis-Nexis database (http://web.lexis-nexis.com/universe) which at the time, contained codes updated through 2002. Thus, the date for all code editions cited is 2002.

The majority of the crimes listed in Table 5 are analogous to "felony murder" crimes, in which a homicide committed during a separate felony (e.g., burglary) offense is treated as murder. Within the context of fetal protection, states charge a defendant with a separate offense when the victim of the initial crime (e.g., assault, robbery, homicide) is a pregnant woman. Six states (Delaware, Iowa, Kansas, Michigan, New Mexico, and North Carolina) adopt this strategy. The Delaware criminal statutes, for example, hold that a person is guilty of "abuse of a pregnant female in the first degree" when, "in the course of or in furtherance of the commission or attempted commission of third degree assault or any violent felony against or upon a pregnant female, or while in immediate flight therefrom, the person recklessly and without her consent causes the unlawful termination of her pregnancy."[11] Similarly, the Michigan Penal Code[12] specifies that

> [i]f a person intentionally commits conduct proscribed under sections 81 to 89 [assaults and robbery] against a pregnant individual, the person is guilty of a felony punishable by imprisonment if all of the following apply: (a) The person intended to cause a miscarriage or stillbirth by that individual or death or great bodily harm to the embryo or fetus, or acted in wanton or willful disregard of the likelihood that the natural tendency of the person's conduct to cause a miscarriage or stillbirth or death or great bodily harm to the embryo or fetus.

Three states (New Hampshire, Virginia, and Wyoming) include a "pregnant victim" or the "unwanted termination of a pregnancy" as a circumstance that allows the defendant to be charged with a particular (more serious) offense. The Virginia penal code, for example, specifies that "the willful, deliberate and premeditated killing of a pregnant woman" where the defendant knows of the pregnancy and has intent to cause an "involuntary termination" of the pregnancy is capital murder. Similarly, a person can be charged under Wyoming's aggravated assault and battery statute if he or she "intentionally, knowingly or recklessly causes bodily injury to a woman whom he knows is pregnant."

It is worth noting that fetus-as-victim laws and pregnant woman-as-victim laws are not mutually exclusive. Ohio, for example, specifies "another's unborn child" as a victim (see Table 4) for three types of assault. For homicide offenses, however, the relevant statutes (presented in Table 5) refer to the "unlawful termination of another's pregnancy."[13] Similarly, Michigan statutes identify the fetus as the victim for manslaughter, but identify the pregnant woman as the victim if she is harmed during a separate felony offense.

Scope of Legislation: Vehicular Homicide as an Example. As noted above, there is wide variation in the breadth of crimes covered by fetal homicide (or assault) legislation, regardless of who is identified as the victim. While some states have enacted broad legislation covering most forms of homicide and assaults, legislation in others may cover only one or two types of offenses. In jurisdictions with limited coverage, the courts may or may not extend coverage to a fetus for crimes not explicitly dealt with by the legislature. Accordingly, those interested in affecting public policy regarding specific offenses should be aware of the coverage in their state.

The case of *Commonwealth v. Booth* (2001), decided by the Pennsylvania Supreme Court in February of 2001, illustrates this point in the context of vehicular homicide. The defendant Booth, while intoxicated, struck another car and caused serious injury to the pregnant driver of the vehicle; the driver's thirty-two week old fetus died as a result, and the defendant was charged with homicide by vehicle while driving under the influence. As noted in Table 4, Pennsylvania has fetal homicide laws governing first, second, and third degree murder, voluntary manslaughter, and aggravated assault of an unborn child. The Pennsylvania General Assembly also enacted a statute directing the courts to "extend to the unborn the equal protection of the laws" in "every relevant civil or criminal proceeding in which it is possible to do so without violating the Federal Constitution."[14]

Despite these facts, the Court held that Booth could not be charged with vehicular homicide because the legislature did not create the crime of "vehicular homicide of an unborn child," and for purposes of the Pennsylvania vehicular homicide statute, the term "person" includes only persons born alive. Indeed, given the laws for other types of fetal homicides, the Court reasoned that the legislature had considered the issue and had chosen not to include vehicular homicide within the "Crimes Against Unborn" chapter of the criminal code.

Currently, through either legislation or judicial interpretation, nineteen states provide penalties for individuals that cause miscarriages or stillbirths through drunk driving incidents (Smith, 2000).[15] It is worth noting that many of these states lack a specific "vehicular homicide" statute, but instead prosecute intoxicated driving incidents under the general manslaughter, involuntary manslaughter, or reckless homicide statutes.[16] In these states, fetal homicide legislation that covers manslaughter or reckless homicide is applicable to drunk drivers.

Judicial Scrutiny of Fetal Homicide Legislation. Legislation targeting third-party fetal assaults has been upheld against a variety of legal challenges, including (a) violation of equal protection, (b) violation of the Establishment Clause of the First Amendment, (c) unconstitutional vagueness, and (d) violation of the double jeopardy clause (Barlow, 1995).[17] Challenges under the Equal Protection Clause of the Fourteenth Amendment are most common. Equal protection challenges have generally focused on the discrepancy between the treatment of a non-viable fetus in legal abortions (as interpreted in *Roe v. Wade*, 1973) and the treatment of a non-viable fetus in feticide legislation. In essence, defendants argue that it is unfair to be prosecuted for the same action (terminating a non-viable fetus) that is legal under current abortion laws.

Courts from several jurisdictions have invalidated this argument.[18] These courts held that a person who assaults a pregnant woman and causes the death of the fetus she is carrying destroys the fetus *without the consent* of the woman. In the case of abortion, the woman's choice and the doctor's actions are based on the woman's constitutionally protected right to privacy. Thus, there is no conflict between the right to privacy and the state's interest in protection of potential human life (as with abortion). In other words, the state's interest in protecting potential life is confined to a viable fetus only when it conflicts with a woman's right to privacy (Barlow, 1995).

Socio-Legal Issues: Fetal Personhood, Abortion, and Maternal Fetal Abuse. Despite the constitutionality of fetal homicide legislation in the context of legal abortions, civil rights activists and pro-choice advocates are leery of feticide legislation for at least two reasons. First, they make a "slippery slope" argument: Granting "fetal rights" to unborn children at all stages of conception in one policy area (fetal homicide legislation) will lead to similar fetal rights in other policy arenas, including abortion (American Civil Liberties Union, 1996). Indeed, pro-life organizations such as the National Right to Life Committee (NRLC) and Americans United for Life have drafted model legislation for states and the federal government and are at the forefront of the push to enact feticide legislation. As Douglas Johnson, a spokesman for the NRLC, states, "The unborn babies that are killed in these assaults are just as dead as the ones killed in abortion clinics" (cited in Welch, 2001, p. A4).

A related point made by civil rights activists is that granting "fetal rights" pits the fetus against the pregnant mother and may lead to the "policing" of pregnancy (Janssen, 2000; Paltrow, 1999; Richer, 2000). In essence, fetal homicide and assault laws (and granting rights to a fetus generally) might allow states to prosecute women who use illicit drugs or ignore a doctor's advice to be prosecuted for assaulting or murdering the fetus. To alleviate the friction between fetal rights and fetal protection from third-party assaults, policymakers might consider several legislative options.

Woman-as-victim statutes, because they avoid vesting a fetus with rights, nullify concerns over the erosion of abortion rights and the policing of pregnancy.[19] Pro-life groups and some victims' advocates, however, typically oppose such legislation on the grounds that it does not count the fetus as a true victim.[20] Second, most current feticide legislation includes exemptions to the statute. In most cases, the statute explicitly states that "legal abortions" are exempt. Some states also exempt the pregnant mother from prosecution under the statute, easing concern over the "pregnancy police" issue. Regardless of statutory construction, interest groups should be aware of the ideological minefield associated with fetal homicide legislation. Although many of these same issues are germane to fetal status under civil law, this legal issue has garnered less attention.

CIVIL LIABILITY:
WRONGFUL DEATH SUITS ON BEHALF OF A FETUS

Wrongful death suits are tort[21] actions that allow a deceased person's relative (typically a spouse) to recover damages from the party who is responsible, either through overt actions or omission, for the death (Siano, 1998). Unlike homicide offenses, which stem from common law, wrongful death actions have no common law roots.[22] The Fatal Accidents Act of 1846 (or "Lord Campbell's Act") established this civil redress in England, and American jurisdictions quickly followed suit. Currently, every state has a statutory remedy for wrongful death (Hartsoe, 1995).

The legal question addressed in this section is whether the parents of a fetus who dies in utero can bring a wrongful death suit on behalf of their unborn child.[23] Early American courts were reluctant to allow civil recovery for fetal injuries. The fetus was considered part of the mother, and establishing the link between a third party assault (or malpractice) and fetal death or disfigurement was difficult. It was not until 1946 that a court allowed recovery for fetal injury, and then only when the fetus was later born alive (Klasing, 1995). Currently, all states allow recovery for fetal injuries where the child is subsequently born alive. The controlling case for each state regarding wrongful death suits brought on behalf of a fetus is illustrated in Table 6. Inspection of Table 6 reveals that ten states deny recovery unless the fetus is subsequently born alive,[24] thirty-five states allow recovery for a stillborn but viable fetus, and four states allow recovery for the wrongful death of a non-viable fetus.[25]

The minority of courts that require live birth justify their position on several grounds (Shapero, 1997; Siano, 1998; Snow, 1997). First, the courts reason that because the mother can recover damages for a

TABLE 6. State differences in whether a wrongful death suit can be brought on behalf of a fetus killed in utero

	Live Birth	Viable Fetus	Pre-Viable Fetus
	N = 10	*N* = 35	*N* = 4
AL		*Eich V. Town of Gulf Shores*, 300 So.2d 354 (1974)	
AK		*Mace v. Jung*, 210 F. Supp. 706 (1962)	
AZ		*Summerfield v. Superior Court*, 698 P.2d 712 (1985)	
AR		*AKA v. Jefferson Hosp. Ass'n Inc.*, 42 S.W.3d 508 (2001)	
CA	*Justus v. Atchison*, 565 P.2d 122 (1977)		
CO		*Espadero v. Feld*, 649 F. Supp. 1480 (1986)	
CT		*Gorke v. LeClerke*, 181 A.2d 448 (1962)	
DE		*Worgan v. Greggo & Ferrara, Inc.*, 128 A.2d 557 (1956)	
FL	*Duncan v. Flynn*, 342 So.2d 123 (1977)		
GA			*Porter v. Lassiter*, 87 S.E.2d 100 (1955)
HI		*Wade v. United States*, 745 F. Supp. 1573 (1990)	
ID		*Santana v. Zilog, Inc.*, 878 F. Supp. 1373 (1995)	
IL		*Chrisafogeorgis v. Brandenburg*, 304 N.E.2d 88 (1973)	
IN		*Britt v. Sears*, 277 N.E.2d 20 (1971)	
IA	*Weitl v. Moes*, 311 N.W.2d 259 (1981)		
KS		*Hale v. Manion*, 368 P.2d 1 (1962)	
KY		*Mitchell v. Couch*, 285 S.W.2d 901 (1955)	
LA		*Danos v. St. Pierre*, 402 So.2d 633 (1981)	
ME	*Milton V. Cary Med. Ctr.*, 538 A.2d 252 (1988)		
MD		*State v. Sherman*, 198 A.2d 71 (1964)	

	Live Birth	Viable Fetus	Pre-Viable Fetus
	N = 10	*N* = 35	*N* = 4
MA		*Mone v. Greyhound Lines, Inc.*, 331 N.E.2d 916 (1975)	
MI		*O'Neill v. Morse*, 188 N.W.2d 785 (1971)	
MN		*Verkennes v. Corniea*, 38 N.W.2d 838 (1949)	
MS		*Rainey v. Horn*, 72 So.2d 434 (1954)	
MO			*Connor v. Monkem Co.*, 898 S.W.2d 89 (1995)
MT		*Strzelczyk v. Jett*, 870 P.2d 730 (1994)	
NE	*Smith v. Columbus Community Hosp. Inc.*, 387 N.W.2d 490 (1986)		
NV		*White v. Yup*, 458 P.2d 617 (1969)	
NH		*Poliquin v. Macdonald*, 135 A.2d 249 (1957)	
NJ	*Graf v. Taggert*, 204 A.2d 140 (1964)		
NM		*Salazar v. St. Vincent Hospital*, 619 P.2d 826 (1980)	
NY	*Endresz v. Friedberg*, 248 N.E.2d 901 (1969)		
NC		*DiDonato v. Wortman*, 358 S.E.2d 489 (1987)	
ND		*Hopkins v. McBane*, 359 N.W.2d 862 (1984)	
OH		*Stidam v. Ashmore*, 167 N.E.2d 106 (1959)	
OK		*Evans v. Olson*, 550 P.2d 924 (1976)	
OR		*Libbee v. Permanente Clinic*, 518 P.2d 636 (1974)	
PA		*Amadio v. Levin*, 501 A.2d 1085 (1985)	
RI		*Presley v. Newport Hosp.*, 365 A.2d 748	
SC		*Fowler v. Woodward*, 138 S.E.2d 42 (1976)	
SD			*Wiersma v. Maple Leaf Farms*, 543 N.W.2d 787 (1996)
TN		Tenn. Code Ann. § 20-5-106(c) (2001)	
TX	*Witty v. American Gen. Capital Distrib.*, 727 S.W.2d 503 (1987)		

TABLE 6 (continued)

	Live Birth	Viable Fetus	Pre-Viable Fetus
	N = 10	*N* = 35	*N* = 4
UT	*Webb v. Snow,* 132 P.2d 114 (1942)		
VT		*Vaillancourt v. Medical Ctr. Hosp.,* 425 A.2d 92 (1980)	
VI	*Lawrence v. Craven Tire Co.,* 169 S.E.2d 440 (1969)		
WA		*Moen v. Hanson,* 537 P.2d 266 (1975)	
WV			*Farley v. Sartin,* 466 S.E.2d 522 (1995)
WI		*Kwaterski v. State Farm Mut. Auto. Ins. CO.,* 148 N.W.2d 107 (1967)	

stillbirth, allowing recovery on behalf of the fetus amounts to double jeopardy. Second, some courts cite the difficulty of proving causation and the speculative nature of assessing damages (e.g., loss of companionship, earnings) in cases involving the death of a fetus. Finally, because the right to recovery for wrongful death is purely statutory, some courts refuse to interpret wrongful death statutes beyond their plain meaning. The controversial overlap between fetal rights, wrongful death suits, and abortion may hinder such judicial activism.

Case law from the minority jurisdictions that require live birth illustrates the courts' reasoning. In *Graf v. Taggert* (see Table 6, New Jersey), the defendant collided with Mrs. Graf's vehicle, causing the stillbirth of her seven-month old fetus. The Supreme Court of New Jersey interpreted the word "person" within the wrongful death statute to exclude unborn children. The court's main objection to allowing recovery was the speculative nature of damages:

> But not even these scant proofs can be offered when the child is stillborn. It is virtually impossible to predict whether the unborn child, but for its death, would have been capable of giving pecuniary benefit to its survivors. We recognize that the damages in any wrongful death action are to some extent uncertain and speculative.

But our liberality in allowing substantial damages where the proofs are relatively speculative should not preclude us from drawing a line where the speculation becomes unreasonable. (p. 11)

In *Weitl v. Moes* (see Table 6, Iowa), the Supreme Court of Iowa, noting that the legislature had already enacted criminal legislation (feticide statutes) dealing with an unborn child, argued that

an unborn fetus was not generally considered a "person" at common law. . . . If the legislature intended to abrogate that rule for the purpose of wrongful death actions under the survival statute, it presumably would have made that intention clear by a specific reference to the unborn in the statute. (p. 271)

The vast majority of courts, however, have come to the opposite conclusion, ruling that wrongful death suits brought on behalf of a stillborn fetus are permissible. Courts in these jurisdictions note that assessing damages for a stillborn baby is no more speculative than assessing damages for prenatal injuries where the death occurs shortly after birth. Further, they point out that wrongful death statutes are remedial[26] in nature and therefore should be liberally construed to accomplish their objective (Snow, 1997). Courts have also looked to other areas of the law, noting that unborn children may inherit property and have a guardian *ad litem* appointed to care for their interests (Snow, 1997).

The most recent state to abrogate the live birth requirement in civil cases is Arkansas. In 2001, in *AKA v. Jefferson Hospital Association Inc.* (see Table 6), the Supreme Court of Arkansas overruled a precedent set six years prior in *Chatelain v. Kelly* (1995). In *Chatelain*, the Court held that judicial expansion of the wrongful death statute to include a fetus was a "legislative prerogative," and it would be inconsistent with both probate and criminal law. Subsequently, the Arkansas legislature enacted fetal homicide legislation, treating a twelve-week old fetus as a "person" within the criminal law. The *Chatelain* court also recognized an amendment to the Arkansas constitution that stated, "The policy of Arkansas is to protect the life of every unborn child from conception until birth, to the extent permitted by the Federal Constitution" (p. 219). Accordingly, the court reversed the *Chatelain* decision to bring the status of a fetus in line with legislative intent and the criminal law.[27]

The Arkansas Court, like the vast majority of jurisdictions, limited this ruling to a viable fetus (see Table 6). The argument for the viability threshold made by most courts is that a "separate existence" is required for a separate cause of action. The Massachusetts Supreme Court, for example, states,

> The purpose of the wrongful death statute is to compensate a decedent's survivors for the loss of the decedent's life. . . . The statute allows recovery if the decedent had, or was capable of having an independent life. There is recovery for the death of a fetus that was viable at the time of injury because it could have survived and lived apart from its mother. . . . Because the fetus could maintain a separate existence, it is entitled to a separate cause of action. (p. 1026)[28]

Other courts have cited a lack of legislative intent and a lack of precedent from other jurisdictions as justifications for the viability standard. Indeed, only four (Georgia, Missouri, South Dakota, and West Virginia) state courts allow wrongful death suits on behalf of a non-viable fetus. Georgia permits recovery if the unborn child is "quick," and the remaining states specify no point at which recovery is denied. In *Connor v. Monkem Co.* (see Table 6), the Missouri Supreme Court based its ruling on a general statute instructing the courts to act in accordance with the view that life begins at conception. Similarly, the Supreme Court of South Dakota interpreted the phrase "unborn child" within the wrongful death statute to include a fetus at all stages of prenatal development. Finally, in *Farley v. Sartin* (see Table 6), the West Virginia Supreme Court of Appeals couched their decision to allow wrongful death suits not within legislative intent, but rather in terms of equity and justice:

> Our concern reflects the fundamental value determination of our society that life–old, young, and prospective–should not be wrongfully taken away. In the absence of legislative direction, the overriding importance of the interest that we have identified merits judicial recognition and protection by imposing the most liberal means of recovery that our law permits. (p. 533)

CONCLUSIONS

Treatment of third-party fetus assault under the civil and criminal law is moving in the direction of increased fetal rights. Currently, about half of all states have some form of fetus-as-victim criminal legislation, and the vast majority of states allow wrongful death recovery for the parents of a viable fetus. Still, there is a great deal of variation in the type and comprehensiveness of criminal legislation.

The implications of this evolution for policymakers and other interested parties are twofold. First, the tension between abortion, maternal privacy issues, and increased fetal rights remains an important factor in the success of proposed legislation in this area. Accordingly, the variety of statutory language and strategy present in current law may help guide compromises between advocates with varying interests in the abortion debate. Second, policymakers or interest groups interested in specific crimes (e.g., manslaughter, or vehicular homicide) should be aware of whether the statutes and case law governing third party fetal-assaults in their state apply to their issue or crime of interest. For example, a law that prohibits "fetal homicide" may or may not (depending upon judicial interpretation) apply to a fetus killed in a drunk driving accident. If the state has specific "vehicular homicide" statutes, the courts might also require a specific "vehicular fetal homicide statue."

The law governing third-party fetal harm is more settled with regard to wrongful death suits brought on behalf of the fetus. Only ten states maintain a live birth requirement for this type of suit, and the vast majority of states allow the recovery for the death of a viable fetus.

NOTES

1. In Idaho and Maine, the statutes do not define "person," but the courts have not considered the issue.
2. Table 1 shows only those states that do not have any form of feticide legislation. Several states enacted fetal homicide statutes in response to judicial adherence to the born alive rule. Thus, while the judicial system upheld the born alive rule, the legislators subsequently amended their statutes to remove the issue from judicial oversight. The case law from these states is therefore not presented in Table 1.
3. Wis. Stat. Ann. § 939.75 (2001).
4. M. Stat. Ann. § 1.205 (2001).
5. Ark Code Ann. § 5-1-102(13)(b)(i)(a); 5-1-102(13)(b)(i)(b) (2001).
6. O.C.G.A. § 16-5-80 (2001).
7. Ind. Code Ann. § 35-42-1-1 (2001).
8. Fla. Sat. Ann. § 782.09 (2001).

9. Mo. Rev. Stat. § 1.205.3 (2001).
10. Minn. Stat. § 609 (2001).
11. Del. Code Ann. § 605 (2001).
12. Mich. Comp. Laws 750.90a (2001).
13. In Ohio, this difference is more apparent than real. Virtually all forms of homicide identified in the statutes include a section that designates the "unlawful termination of another's pregnancy" as a form of that particular homicide. The murder statute (Ohio Rev. Code Ann. § 2903.02), for example, reads, "No person shall purposely cause the death of another or the unlawful termination of another's pregnancy." Therefore, while the language ("unlawful termination") suggests a crime against the pregnant mother, the specific crime (murder) implies that the fetus is the real victim.
14. 18 Pa.C.S. §3202(c) (2001).
15. In three states (Massachusetts, Oklahoma, South Carolina), the courts overturned the born alive rule and now treat a viable fetus as a person for all forms of homicide. Of the twenty-five states that have fetus-as-victim legislation, eleven states include statutes that may be used to prosecute drunk drivers. These states are Arkansas, Florida, Georgia, Illinois, Indiana, Tennessee, Louisiana, Minnesota, Missouri, North Dakota, Ohio, South Dakota, Utah, and Wisconsin. Of the ten states that have woman-as-victim legislation, five have statutes that may be used to prosecute drunk drivers. These states are Iowa, Kansas, New Mexico, Ohio, and Wyoming.
16. For example, the Illinois statute (Ill. Comp. Stat. Ann. 5/9-3.2) reads, "A person who unintentionally kills an individual without lawful justification commits involuntary manslaughter if his acts whether lawful or unlawful which cause the death are such as are likely to cause death or great bodily harm to some individual, and he performs them recklessly, except in cases in which the cause of the death consists of the driving of a motor vehicle or operating a snowmobile, all-terrain vehicle, or watercraft, in which case the person commits reckless homicide."
17. See *State v. Bauer*, 471 N.W.2d 363 (establishment clause); *State v. Black*, 526 N.W.2d (vagueness); *State v. Smith*, 676 So.2d 1068 (double jeopardy).
18. See *State v. Black*, 526 N.W.2d; *State v. Merrill*, 450 N.W.2d 318; *People v. Ford*, 581 N.E.2d 1189, *People v. Davis*, 872 P.2d 591.
19. To be sure, some might argue that even statutes that give women a "special status" due to pregnancy would allow activists to "chip away" at abortion rights. Nevertheless, women-as-victim statues do not vest the fetus with any legal status, and are therefore less threatening to those who are advocates of abortion rights.
20. In support of the federal "Unborn Victims of Violence Act," the NRLC distributed a flyer entitled "One Victim or Two?" that features assault victim Tracy Marciniak holding her dead child at a funeral (National Right to Life Committee, 2001). A letter from the NRLC to House Representatives is even more blunt, stating that the "one-victim substitute amendment is a callous and irrational ideological statement that would gravely trivialize the worth of unborn members of the human family. In NRLC's scorecard of significant congressional votes for 2001, a vote in favor of a one-victim substitute amendment to H.R. 503 will be accurately described as a vote to declare that when a criminal assaults a mother and kills her unborn child, nobody has really died" (Johnson, 2001).

21. Tort law is similar in intent and form to criminal law, but tort cases are tried in civil (as opposed to criminal) court. Thus, in tort actions, the victim brings the case forward (rather than the state), and a finding in favor of the victim results in monetary awards rather than state sanctioned punishment such as jail time. For a more detailed explanation of these differences, see Siegel (2003, p. 33).

22. Common law refers to early English law developed by judges that incorporated tribal customs and feudal rules into a standardized set of laws. It can be distinguished from "statutory law," which is the body of law created by legislators.

23. All states allow some form of recovery for the death of a fetus. In some states, however, the parents cannot bring a wrongful death suit on behalf of the fetus, but instead must sue for the pain and suffering caused by the death of their unborn child.

24. Although this is counterintuitive, these are wrongful death suits that require the fetus to be born alive and subsequently die. The fetus must be "born alive" to meet the requirement of a "person."

25. Wyoming has no case law regarding wrongful death suits brought on behalf of a fetus, and is therefore not included in Table 6.

26. This means simply that the statutes are designed to remedy a wrong rather than punish an individual.

27. While this case was under review, the Arkansas legislature amended the wrongful death statute (Act 1265 of 2001, April 4, 2001) to include a fetus.

28. *Thibert v. Milka*, 646 N.E.2d 1025 (1995).

REFERENCES

American Civil Liberties Union. (1996). *What's wrong with fetal rights: A look at fetal protection statues and wrongful death actions on behalf of fetuses.* Retrieved July, 2002, from http://www.aclu.org/issues/reproduct/fetal.html.

Barlow, B. A. (1995). Severe penalties for the destruction of 'potential life'–Cruel and unusual punishment? *University of San Francisco Law Review, 29,* 463-507.

Brinkley v. State, 322 S.E.2d 49 (1984).

Chatelain v. Kelly, 910 S.W.2d 215 (1995).

Colautti v. Franklin, 439 U.S. 379 (1979).

Commonwealth v. Booth, 766A.2d 843 (2001).

Dietrich v. Inhabitants of Northampton, 138 Mass. 14 (1884).

Fatal Accidents Act (U.K.), 9 & 10 Vict., c. 93 (1846).

Hartsoe, T. (1995). Person or thing–In search of the legal status of a fetus: A survey of North Carolina law. *Campbell Law Review, 17,* 169-242.

Janssen, N. D. (2000). Fetal rights and the prosecution of women for using drugs during pregnancy. *Drake Law Review, 48,* 741-768.

Johnson, D. (2001). *NRLC Letter to U.S. Senators in support of Unborn Victims of Violence Act.* Retrieved August 24, 2001, from http://www.nrlc.org/Unborn_Victims/NRLlettertosenate.html.

Keeler v. Superior Court of Amador County, 470 P.2d 617 (1970).

Kime, M. L. (1995). Hughes v. State: The 'Born Alive' Rule dies a timely death. *Tulsa Law Journal, 30,* 539-558.

Klasing, M. S. (1995). The death of an unborn child: Jurisprudential inconsistencies in wrongful death, criminal homicide, and abortion cases. *Pepperdine Law Review, 22*, 933-979.

Mitchell, A. (2001, April 27). House approves bill criminalizing violence to fetus. *New York Times*, p. A4.

National Right to Life Committed. (2001). *One victim . . . Or two?* Retrieved August 24, 2001, from http://www.nrlc.org/Unborn_Victims/Zachariahad.pdf.

Obasi, A. R. (1998). Protecting our vital organs: The case for fetal homicide law in Texas. *Texas Wesleyan Law Review, 4*, 207-230.

Paltrow, L. M. (1999). Pregnant drug users, fetal persons, and the threat to Roe v. Wade. *Albany Law Review, 62*, 999-1054.

People v. Davis, 872 P.2d 574 (1994).

Richer, C. J. (2000). Fetal abuse law: Punitive approach and the honorable status of motherhood. *Syracuse Law Review, 50*, 1127-1150.

Roe v. Wade, 410 U.S. 113 (1973).

Schroedel, J. R. (2000). *Is the fetus a person? Comparison of policies across the fifty states*. Ithaca: Cornell University Press.

Shapero, W. C. (1997). Does a nonviable fetus's right to bring a wrongful death action endanger a woman's right to choose? *Southwestern University Law Review, 27*, 325-351.

Siano, R. R. (1998). A woman's right to choose: Wrongful death statutes and abortion rights–Consistent at last. *Women's Rights Law Reporter, 19*, 279-292.

Siegel, L. (2003). *Criminology* (8th ed.). Belmont, CA: Wadsworth.

Smith, S. L. (2000). Fetal homicide: Woman or fetus as victim? A survey of current state approaches and recommendations for future state application. *William and Mary Law Review, 41*, 1845-1884.

Snow, B. D. (1997). Wrongful death: A viable fetus is not a 'person' under the Arkansas Wrongful Death Statute. Chatelain v. Kelly. *University of Arkansas at Little Rock Law Journal, 19*, 307-325.

State v. Holcomb, 956 S.W.2d 286 (1997).

Unborn Victims of Violence Act of 2001, H.R. 503, 107th Cong. (2001).

Wasserstrom, A. S. (1998). Homicide based on killing of unborn child. *American Law Reports, 64*, 671-730.

Welch, W. M. (2001, April 26). Bill would make it a Federal crime to harm a fetus. *USA Today*, p. A4.

Legal and Social Issues Surrounding Closed-Circuit Television Testimony of Child Victims and Witnesses

Katherine J. Bennett

SUMMARY. Prosecution of crimes involving child victims and witnesses is particularly difficult because of the age of the children involved. Facing the alleged offender in court and the experience itself of testifying in an open court with dozens of onlookers are acutely difficult. The effect on children may be traumatic, with the potential to produce substantial psychological and emotional harm. Various court procedures have been implemented in the United States in an effort to minimize these effects. Court procedures can include erecting screens to shield the child victim or witness, presenting videotaped testimony, or testifying via one-way or two-way closed-circuit television. Closed-circuit television (CCTV) testimony, which is especially controversial, involves both legal issues surrounding the constitutionality of such testimony and social issues regarding the effectiveness of closed-circuit television testimony. Substantial variation across states in provisions for closed-circuit

Address correspondence to: Katherine J. Bennett, Department of Criminal Justice, Social and Political Science, Armstrong Atlantic State University, 11935 Abercorn Street, Savannah, GA 31419-1997 (E-mail: bennetka@mail.armstrong.edu).

The author acknowledges and appreciates the substantive criticisms of two anonymous reviewers and incorporated their suggestions where possible.

[Haworth co-indexing entry note]: "Legal and Social Issues Surrounding Closed-Circuit Television Testimony of Child Victims and Witnesses." Bennett, Katherine J. Co-published simultaneously in *Journal of Aggression, Maltreatment & Trauma* (The Haworth Maltreatment & Trauma Press, an imprint of The Haworth Press, Inc.) Vol. 8, No. 3 (#17), 2003, pp. 233-271; and: *The Victimization of Children: Emerging Issues* (ed: Janet L. Mullings, James W. Marquart, and Deborah J. Hartley) The Haworth Maltreatment & Trauma Press, an imprint of The Haworth Press, Inc., 2003, pp. 233-271. Single or multiple copies of this article are available for a fee from The Haworth Document Delivery Service [1-800-HAWORTH, 9:00 a.m. - 5:00 p.m. (EST). E-mail address: docdelivery@haworthpress.com].

233

television testimony for child witnesses is problematic. Consideration is given to how social science research directly influenced the Supreme Court's decision in *Maryland v. Craig* (1990), and the current state of research regarding use of CCTV and court outcomes. Some research suggests a pro-defense bias when CCTV is used. *[Article copies available for a fee from The Haworth Document Delivery Service: 1-800-HAWORTH. E-mail address: <docdelivery@haworthpress.com> Website: <http://www.HaworthPress.com> © 2003 by The Haworth Press, Inc. All rights reserved.]*

KEYWORDS. Closed-circuit television testimony, CCTV, child victims, child witnesses, *Maryland v. Craig*

INTRODUCTION

Every day children are victims or witnesses of violent crimes. In 1996, over 969,000 reported cases of violent crimes were committed against children (American Academy of Child and Adolescent Psychiatry, 1999). The child victims are often very young. For example, one-third of sexual assault victims are under the age of twelve (Children as Victims, 2000) (for an in-depth discussion of child maltreatment, see Paulsen, this volume). A majority of violent crimes against children may go unreported, and in many cases of reported crimes, the alleged perpetrator may be arrested but not prosecuted. When cases do go forward, both adult and child victims often report feeling victimized a second time by the judicial system. Prosecution of crimes involving child victims and witnesses is all the more difficult because of the age of the children involved. The effect on children is traumatic, with the potential to produce substantial psychological and emotional harm. Facing the alleged offender in court and the experience itself of testifying in an open court with dozens of onlookers, which are particularly difficult, can result in the child's inability to communicate and complete his or her testimony. Various alternatives have been legislated, ranging from screens placed between the child and defendant to recorded videotaped depositions to one-way or two-way closed-circuit television (CCTV) testimony.

One-way CCTV testimony usually means that the child testifies in another place outside the courtroom while the jury and defendant view him or her on a television monitor. Two-way CCTV means that the child is also able to see the courtroom and defendant on a monitor as he or she is testifying. Governmental support for the use of CCTV is positive. Since 2000, the U.S. Department of Justice has assisted states and local jurisdictions with obtaining closed-circuit television equipment and conducting training (Catalog of Federal Domestic Assistance 16.611, 2001).

Under the Bureau of Justice Assistance Closed-Circuit Televising of Testimony of Children Who Are Victims of Abuse Grant Program, over thirty-eight federal grants have been issued to states to provide equipment and personnel training, technical assistance, and evaluation. The program is authorized under the Victims of Child Abuse Act of 1990, Public Law 90-351 (as amended, 42 U.S.C. 3796aa, Catalog of Federal Domestic Assistance, 2001). One of the most important uses of these grants is in obtaining closed-circuit television equipment for televising the testimony of child victims at Children's Advocacy Centers. The testimony is transmitted via links to courtrooms (Bureau of Justice Assistance, 2001).

More than 350 jurisdictions in the United States have Children's Advocacy Centers (National Center for Victims of Crime, 1999). Also authorized under the Victims of Child Abuse Act, Children's Advocacy Centers have been in existence since 1995. These centers use teams of professionals that include law enforcement officers, child protection workers, prosecutors, therapists, and victim advocates (Delany-Shabazz, 1995). Child victims' involvement in the justice system is limited as much as possible. Parties work together in order to support children while, at the same time, cases are investigated and prosecuted.

Closed-circuit television testimony instead of in-court testimony is an alternative utilized in both state and federal judicial systems and by the military justice system. However, this alternative is not without controversy. The purpose of this chapter is to address these controversies and discuss both the legal issues surrounding the constitutionality of closed-circuit television testimony and social issues regarding its effectiveness. It also explores federal legislation and military rules providing for closed-circuit television testimony, as well as the variation in statutes at the state level. The chapter gives additional consideration to the role of social science research in the judicial systems and how this research has directly impacted court testimony of children.

LEGAL ISSUES:
THE CONSTITUTIONALITY OF CLOSED-CIRCUIT
TELEVISION TESTIMONY

Legal challenges to the constitutionality of alternative modes of testimony have generally come in the form of alleged violations of the Confrontation Clause of the Sixth Amendment. *Maryland v. Craig*, the landmark Supreme Court case directly addressing closed-circuit television testimony of children, was decided in 1990. However, two prior Supreme Court decisions merit discussion in order to illustrate the path of judicial reasoning. In 1987, the Supreme Court ruled in a 6-3 decision that the right to confront witnesses was not violated when the defendant in a child sexual abuse case was excluded from the competency hearing for the child victim (*Kentucky v. Stincer*). The attorney for the defendant was not excluded, and the Court noted that the nature of the competency hearing did not address questions of substantive testimony.

The American Psychological Association submitted an amicus curiae brief in this case, noting that an important question raised by *Stincer* was the potential harm to children who have to confront defendants in court. In 1987, however, few studies existed which showed that face-to-face confrontation had more negative effects on child victims than it had on adult victims (Underwager & Wakefield, 1992).

In a 6-2 decision the following year, in *Coy v. Iowa* (1988),[1] the Supreme Court had occasion to address protective measures for children testifying in court. The defendant had been convicted of sexually assaulting two thirteen-year-old girls. A 1985 Iowa statute allowed a child witness to be shielded behind a screen or mirror. In the case at hand, a large screen had been placed between the defendant and the two child witnesses during their testimony. The witnesses could not see the defendant, although he could see them dimly. Upon appeal, Coy claimed that his Sixth Amendment rights had been violated, as well as his right to due process. The use of the screen in the courtroom, reasoned Coy, made him appear guilty and thus violated the presumption of innocence.

The Supreme Court reversed the decision of the lower court on the basis that the procedures used violated the Confrontation Clause of the Sixth Amendment, thus not needing to address the due process claim. Writing for the Majority, Justice Scalia stated that the Confrontation Clause of the Sixth Amendment guarantees the right to a face-to-face confrontation. Justice Scalia noted "that there is something deep in human nature that regards face-to-face confrontation between accused and accuser as 'essential to a fair trial in a criminal prosecution,'"[2] and "[t]he phrase still persists, 'Look me in the eye and say that.'"[3] The Majority further stated, "We leave for another day, however, the question whether any exceptions exist. Whatever they may be, they would surely be allowed only when necessary to further an important public policy."[4]

In a concurring opinion, Justice O'Connor cautioned that rights under the Confrontation Clause are not absolute. Certain procedures designed to shield children from the trauma of testifying in court could be permitted in an appropriate case. She noted that while Iowa was the only state that authorized the protective screen shield, half of the states permitted one- or two-way closed-circuit television testimony. She emphasized that the decision in *Coy* in no way jeopardized the use of alternative modes of testimony. Further, the Confrontation Clause challenge would not be applicable to state statutes such as Alaska's and Georgia's, because they provided for one-way closed circuit television testimony in the presence of the defendant.

California and New York provided for two-way CCTV, thus permitting the child witness to see the courtroom and defendant. Justice O'Connor further added " . . . even if a particular state procedure runs afoul of the Confrontation Clause's general requirements, it may come within an exception that permits its use."[5] She noted that the Confrontation Clause reflected only a "preference" for meeting one's accusers face-to-face, and in light of compelling public policy and a case-specific finding of necessity, that preference could be overcome.

In the dissenting opinion, Justice Blackmun observed that the use of the screen did not violate the Confrontation Clause because the "important public policy in protecting child witnesses from the fear and trauma" of testifying in court in front of the defendant prevailed over the Confrontation Clause's preference for face-to-face confrontation. He also disagreed with the case-specific finding of necessity.

That "appropriate case" to which Justice O'Connor referred was not long in coming before the Court. Two years later, in a 5-4 decision, Justice O'Connor wrote the Majority opinion in *Maryland v. Craig* (1990). *Craig* opened the door for closed-circuit television testimony of child victims and witnesses (Beckett, 1994) and adopted the public policy exception to the Confrontation Clause that was not reached in *Coy*.

Craig required that the Court decide whether a six-year-old child abuse victim could testify against the defendant by one-way CCTV. Unlike the court in the *Coy* decision, the trial court in *Craig* had made a specific finding that the child victim, as well as three other children who were allegedly abused by Craig, would be traumatized by Craig's presence.

Attesting to the important public policy of protecting child witnesses in child abuse cases was the fact that by 1990, twenty-four states had passed statutes providing for one-way CCTV, and eight states provided for two-way CCTV. However, the Majority noted that the use of a special procedure such as CCTV must be case-specific:

> The trial court must hear evidence and determine whether use of the one-way closed circuit television procedure is necessary to protect the welfare of the particular child witness who seeks to testify.... The trial court must also find that the child witness would be traumatized, not by the courtroom generally, but by the presence of the defendant.... Finally, the trial court must find that the emotional distress suffered by the child witness in the presence of the defendant is more than *de minimis*, i.e., more than 'mere nervousness or excitement or some reluctance to testify.' ... We need not decide the minimum showing of emotional trauma required ... because the Maryland statute, which requires a determination ... [of] 'serious emotional distress such that the child cannot reasonably communicate' ... suffices to meet constitutional standards.[6]

The Court further noted that the Maryland appellate court had interpreted the decision in *Coy v. Iowa* to impose two requirements. The first would mandate that, instead of relying solely on expert testimony on the ability of the child to communicate, the child first had to be questioned in the presence of the defendant so that the judge could observe the child's behavior on the witness stand and could question the child. The second requirement would mandate that the judge determine whether or not the child could testify by two-way CCTV without trauma before utilizing the one-way closed-circuit system. While acknowledging that these two requirements would strengthen the basis for using protective measures, the Court declined to establish any such "categorical evidentiary prerequisites"[7] for the use of one-way closed-circuit television.

In the dissent, Justice Scalia wrote, "Seldom has this Court failed so conspicuously to sustain a categorical guarantee of the Constitution against the tide of prevailing current opinion."[8] He reiterated his opinion in *Coy* and other cases that the Confrontation Clause explicitly provides for a "face-to-face confrontation" and criticized the Majority for incorrectly relying on past decisions that regarded admissibility of hearsay evidence for support of their claim that the confrontation clause suggests a "preference" for a face-to-face meeting. Other legal scholars have noted that with the decision in *Craig*, the Supreme Court "found a way to assure that the child victim would not suffer further harm, but this assurance is clearly at the defendant's expense" (Beckett, 1994, p. 1627).

The Supreme Court has stood firmly by its decision in *Maryland v. Craig* to allow closed-circuit television procedures for the testimony of child victims, while Justice Scalia has stood just as firmly by his position. In 1998, the Supreme Court denied a petition for a writ of certiorari in a Kentucky case in which the trial court allowed the use of CCTV even though the judge could not define the compelling factors for such use (*Danner v. Kentucky*, 1998).

Danner was charged and subsequently convicted of repeatedly raping and sodomizing his daughter when she was between five and ten years old. At the time of the trial, she was fifteen. When the judge questioned the daughter pursuant to allowing CCTV, she stated that she was not afraid of the defendant but just could not be near him. When the judge asked if she would be able to testify if they allowed her to take breaks, she replied that she did not know. The trial court then allowed her to testify via CCTV. Danner was convicted and appealed, claiming his constitutional right to face his accuser had been violated. The defendant argued that the relevant state statute allowing CCTV applied to victims under the age of twelve. The Kentucky Supreme Court agreed with the lower court that the statute's age provisions applied to children at the time the offense was committed. Danner petitioned for a writ of certiorari, but the United States Supreme Court declined to review the case. Justices Scalia and Thomas dissented.

In his dissent, Justice Scalia noted that although he still believed *Craig* was wrongly decided, the case at hand did not fit within the limited exceptions provided by *Craig*. Scalia questioned whether *Craig* applies to fifteen-year-olds and noted that he would have liked to have seen this case heard by the Court and reversed in order to make clear that the exception to the Confrontation Clause of the Sixth Amendment is a narrow one. "It is a dangerous business to water down the confrontation right so dramatically merely because society finds the charged crime particularly reprehensible. Indeed, the more reprehensible the charge the more the defendant is in need of all constitutionally guaranteed protection for his defense."[9]

The Supreme Court denied another petition for a writ of certiorari in a case involving CCTV in 1999 (*Marx v. Texas*, 1999). Marx was charged with sexual abuse of two girls, one thirteen years old and the other six years old. The six-year-old testified via CCTV as a witness to the abuse of the thirteen-year-old. At a hearing to determine whether the child witness should testify by CCTV, both the mother and a doctor who had examined her seemed to believe that she could testify in open court. The doctor, who stated that the child said that she wanted to testify, believed that she would suffer no additional trauma as a result of testifying. The mother also acknowledged that she thought the child was ready for in-court testimony. However, the prosecutor moved to allow CCTV. Thus, the Supreme Court's denial of certiorari in effect expands *Craig* to allow alternative modes of testimony such as CCTV for child witnesses whose abuse is not the subject of prosecution or of the testimony. Further, in this case there was no showing of trauma that would render the child unable to reasonably communicate. As in *Danner*, Justices Scalia and Thomas dissented from the denial of certiorari, and Justice Scalia observed, "If the decision here is correct, the right to confrontation of allegedly abused child witnesses has not simply been . . . watered down, it has been washed away."[10]

Constitutional Challenges at the State Level

The constitutionality of CCTV varies across states. Legal challenges after *Craig* have generally centered on whether or not state constitutions have afforded defendants more rights than the Federal Constitution. Most state challenges have arisen as a result of confrontation clauses in state constitutions that explicitly afford the defendant the right to face-to-face confrontation of witnesses. Before 1994, for example, the confrontation clause of the Illinois state constitution stated that in criminal prosecutions, the accused shall have the right to meet witnesses face-to-face (Small, 1994). In February of 1994, in *People v. Fitzpatrick*, the Illinois State Supreme Court ruled that CCTV, as provided for by Illinois' Child Shield Act, violated the state constitution. The state supreme court ruled that *Craig* did not apply because the Sixth Amendment Federal Confrontation Clause did not expressly contain the face-to-face provision contained in the Illinois constitution.

By November 8, 1994, a proposed amendment to the state constitution was on the election ballot. This amendment, removing the "face-to-face" phrase of the Illinois Confrontation Clause and simply permitting a defendant the right to be confronted with witnesses against him or her, passed with sixty-three percent of voters being in favor of the change (Small, 1994). The state legislature then repealed the Child Shield Act and passed new legislation allowing closed-circuit television testimony in child witness/abuse cases (Bowman, 1998).

A recent case in Illinois shows that physical barriers in the courtroom *instead of* one-way CCTV violate a defendant's right to confront witnesses. In November 2000, the Illinois Supreme Court overturned a conviction for two counts of predatory criminal sexual assault of a child because the trial court did not use one-way CCTV as permitted by the legislation. In *People v. Lofton*, the Supreme Court found that using podiums to prevent the child witness and the defendant from viewing one another violated the Confrontation Clause of both the United States and Illinois Constitutions (*People of the State of Illinois*, 2000). At Lofton's trial, the court could not find that the five-year-old child victim would experience any adverse effect from testifying in front of the jury, although she would experience such an effect if she saw the defendant. Therefore, the court moved two podiums behind the child, positioning her in a chair in front of the jury and with her back to the defendant. The judge noted that he wanted to try this setup before moving to the CCTV system. Lofton, who was found guilty, appealed the conviction, in part on the grounds that his due process rights had been violated as well as his right to confront witnesses against him. The Illinois appellate court agreed with Lofton that his right to confrontation had been violated, and the State appealed to the Illinois Supreme Court. The Illinois Supreme Court agreed with the lower court, noting that the physical barrier in the courtroom "improperly expanded the narrow exception to the right to face-to-face confrontation created by the Court in *Craig* for the taking of testimony of a child witness in a child abuse case by the use of one-way closed-circuit television" (at 11). One-way CCTV would not have prevented the defendant from observing the child witness.

Like Illinois, Pennsylvania has experienced a similar situation with respect to needing to amend its constitution, although voters have yet to amend the constitution successfully. The Pennsylvania Constitution guarantees to the defendant the right to meet witnesses face-to-face (Small, 1994). In *Commonwealth v. Ludwig* (1991), the Pennsylvania Supreme Court held that CCTV violated the state constitution because of this "face-to-face" requirement. In November 1995, a majority of Pennsylvania voters voted to amend the requirement and to allow the General Assembly to pass laws providing for closed-circuit television testimony and videotaped depositions of children. However, the amendment subsequently was found to be in violation of Article XI, Section 1, of the Constitution because the two propositions were presented as one amendment instead of two separate questions (*Bergdoll v. Kane*, 1997/1999). In June of 2001, the Senate approved Senate Bill 211, a new constitutional amendment sponsored by Senator Stewart Greenleaf, which would provide for closed-circuit television testimony for child victims. The primary election of 2003 is the earliest that the proposed amendment can appear on a ballot referendum (*Senate approves Greenleaf child witness measure*, 2001).

Challenges to CCTV testimony in other states have generally been unsuccessful, with state courts ruling that the confrontation clauses in state constitutions are to be interpreted in accordance with the U.S. Constitution's Confrontation Clause (Small, 1994).[11] Even when state constitutions have contained the explicit "face-to-face" language similar to Pennsylvania's constitution, the use of CCTV can survive constitutional challenges, depending on whether or not the closed-circuit system is a one-way or two-way system. The Indiana Supreme Court stated in *State v. Brady* (1991) that two-way CCTV in effect is a face-to-face encounter, although one-way testimony where the child cannot hear or see the defendant would violate the defendant's rights under Indiana's Constitution. The Kentucky Supreme Court held in *Commonwealth v. Willis* (1986) that the words "face-to-face" do not constitute the right of "eyeball to eyeball" confrontation, noting that use of the words "face-to-face" may have reflected an inability on the part of the legislature to "foresee technological advances that permit cross-examination and confrontation without physical presences" (Small, 1994, p. 375).

Public support for child witness protection legislation such as the use of CCTV is strong. The people of more than one state have demonstrated their willingness to amend confrontation clauses in state constitutions in order to assure the constitutionality of such legislation. The next arena for challenging the constitutionality of CCTV may be alleged violations of the defendant's right to due process, although state courts have so far been generally unsympathetic to such claims (Small, 1994), and such cases are likely to be unsuccessful. Some critics of CCTV still maintain, despite court rulings to the contrary, that "emotional" implementation of rules of procedure such as the use of CCTV allows for courts "too often [to] straddle the line between a fair trial and an unconstitutional trial" (Bowman, 1998, p. 1-2).

The next sections of this chapter look at federal, military, and state legislation specifically providing for closed-circuit television testimony. They also consider legal challenges to the federal legislation.

FEDERAL LEGISLATION
AND CLOSED-CIRCUIT TELEVISION TESTIMONY

Federal legislation pertaining to alternatives to in-court testimony for child victims and child witnesses under the age of eighteen is provided for in the United States Criminal Code, Title 18, Section 3509, Child Victims' and Child Witnesses' Rights. This legislation was enacted by Congress as the Victims of Child Abuse Act (18 U.S.C. §§403, 2258, 3509), part of the Crime Control Act of 1990, after the Supreme Court decision in *Maryland v. Craig.*

As this legislation states, testimony by two-way closed-circuit television may be permitted upon a court finding that the child victim or witness is "unable to testify in open court in the presence of the defendant," for any one of the following four reasons: fear, substantial likelihood that the child would suffer emotional trauma from testifying, the knowledge that the victim suffers a mental or other infirmity, or conduct by the defendant or defense counsel that causes the child to be unable to continue testifying.[12] If the second reason applies, expert testimony is required to establish the substantial likelihood of trauma. If CCTV is allowed, the persons who are permitted to be in the room with the child during the testimony are the child's attorney or guardian ad litem, the attorney for the Government, the defense attorney unless the defendant is pro se, closed-circuit television equipment operators, a court-appointed judicial officer, and any other persons whose presence is determined by the court to be necessary to the welfare and well-being of the child. During transmission of the child's testimony into the courtroom, the defendant is able to communicate privately with his or her attorney. The defendant's image and the judge's voice are transmitted into the room in which the child is testifying. The statute allows for CCTV testimony for any alleged offense against a child.

Another alternative provided in federal legislation is videotaping the deposition upon a court finding that the child is unlikely to be able to testify in the presence of the defendant, jury, judge, and public for the same four reasons that CCTV may be allowed.[13] The judge presides at the videotaping. Other persons allowed to be present include the same individuals allowed during CCTV, with the addition of the defendant. The defendant may be excluded if his or her conduct causes the child to be unable to testify. If the defendant is excluded from the videotaping proceeding, then the defendant, by way of two-way CCTV, will view the proceeding from another room. The defendant's image will be transmitted into the room where the videotaping is taking place, and the defendant will be able to communicate privately with his or her attorney during the deposition.

As a third alternative to testifying in open court, the judge can order the courtroom to be closed. This alternative is based upon a court finding that testifying in open court would cause substantial psychological harm to the child or would result in the child's inability to communicate effectively. "Such an order shall be narrowly tailored to serve the Government's specific compelling interest."[14]

Legal Challenges to the Federal Legislation

Constitutional challenges to the federal statute have generally been unsuccessful. In 1993, a Navajo Indian appealed his conviction of four counts of aggravated sexual abuse partly on the grounds that the district court violated his constitutional right to confront his accusers (*United States v. Garcia*, 1993). The defendant was living on a reservation in Arizona when he was convicted of four counts of aggravated sexual abuse of his eleven-year-old niece. The victim testified by two-way CCTV. Prior to the testimony, the district court held hearings to determine whether the victim should be permitted to testify in this manner.

At the hearings, a mental health specialist who had counseled the victim testified that the child would be emotionally traumatized by the presence of the defendant in the courtroom and advocated using CCTV to decrease the trauma. A child psychiatrist testified as an expert witness to possible trauma of testifying in court and agreed that testifying by CCTV would not be as stressful. The defendant argued that the district court did not make sufficient findings authorizing use of two-way CCTV. Garcia asserted that the federal statute did not make clear how much emotional trauma the child must suffer. However, the Ninth Circuit Court of Appeals found the language in the federal statute to be similar to the Maryland statute at issue in *Craig*.

Garcia further argued that the psychiatrist had not met with the victim so his testimony was not specific to the case at hand, and that the mental health counselor was not a qualified expert. The appellate court disagreed, noting that the psychiatrist only provided background information and that the testimony of the mental health specialist, together with that background information, was sufficient for the trial court to conclude that it was likely that the victim would not be able to communicate reasonably in court in Garcia's presence. The court upheld the district court's use of closed-circuit television testimony.

In 1998, in another federal case challenging the use of CCTV testimony, the defendant prevailed (*United States v. Moses*). Moses, a Chippewa Indian, was charged with sexually abusing his infant niece. The abuse was witnessed by another niece, then four years old. After testimony by the social worker and the defense counsel's investigative assistant, the district court examined the child witness. Concluding that the child was fearful and would be traumatized by testifying, the judge ordered that she be permitted to testify by one-way CCTV. Moses was convicted and subsequently appealed on the basis of an alleged violation of his right to confront his accusers because the child witness was allowed to testify by CCTV.

The Sixth Circuit Court of Appeals noted that several courts of appeals have reviewed the federal statute in terms of *Craig* and have held that "a general fear of the courtroom" is not enough reason to employ CCTV: The child witness must be unable to reasonably communicate in court due to the "physical presence of the defendant" (at 898). In the case at hand, the child witness emphatically stated that she was not afraid of the defendant. The Sixth Circuit court ruled that the district court focused upon the child's statement that she did not want to see the defendant again instead of her statements that she was not afraid of him.

The circuit court also ruled that the social worker who testified as to the likelihood of the witness's trauma was not a proper expert. The court stated that expert testimony provided by a "psychiatrist, psychologist, or other mental health specialist" (at 898) is required by the federal statute in order to establish trauma. After ruling that the district court erred in allowing testimony by CCTV, the circuit court considered whether or not the error was harmless. Because the court could not rule that the CCTV testimony was a harmless error, the court reversed Moses' conviction and remanded a new trial.

Many cases of child abuse and other crimes involving child victims or witnesses are heard in military courts. Therefore, legislation permitting the use of CCTV in the military justice system is discussed in the next section.

MILITARY RULES PERTAINING TO CCTV

Despite the federal legislation in place since 1990, the military justice system was slower to incorporate procedures for CCTV of children. Explicit applicability to military courts was not stated in the Crime Control Act of 1990, and requests to use CCTV for victim testimony in courts-martial for child abuse have not always been granted.

In 1996, the Court of Appeals for the Armed Forces had an opportunity in *United States v. Longstreath* to decide whether the federal legislation addressing rights of child victims and witnesses applied to the military justice system and specifically to children who refuse to testify in courts-martial (Berger, 1999).[15] Longstreath, charged with rape, carnal knowledge, sodomy, and committing indecent acts with his step-daughter and two natural daughters, had been tried by a military judge between December 1990 and June 1991.[16] One daughter was two years old at the time of the trial so did not testify. At the Government's request, the other natural daughter, who was ten years old, was allowed to testify by CCTV after an expert witness testified that requiring the ten-year-old to testify in the presence of the defendant would pose serious psychological harm.

During the trial, the Government also requested that the sixteen-year-old stepdaughter be allowed to testify via CCTV. The Government had initially attempted to have her testify in open court; however, she began to cry during the initial direct examination and became unresponsive. The Government then requested that she be allowed to continue testimony by CCTV. This request was denied by the military judge, and the sixteen-year-old was recalled to the stand. She was able to complete her testimony during direct examination by trial counsel, but during the cross-examination, and after several recesses, she would break down crying and become unresponsive. The military judge reconsidered his earlier ruling and allowed testimony to be taken by CCTV. Longstreath was found guilty of three indecent acts, involving his step-daughter and one of his two natural daughters.

On appeal, the Navy-Marine Corps Court of Criminal Appeals was asked to consider, among other issues, whether the defendant's Sixth Amendment rights had been violated by the use of CCTV for both the natural daughter and the stepdaughter. The defense counsel claimed that use of televised testimony in a court-martial was not an option available to the Government. However, the appellate court noted the passage of the Victims of Child Abuse Act of 1990 and acknowledged that, while Congress did not expressly provide for application of this provision at courts-martial, preventing further trauma to "victims of child abuse testifying at courts-martial is an important public policy and . . . the provisions of the 1990 Act . . . are applicable and provide guidance for us."[17]

Longstreath appealed this decision to the Court of Appeals for the Armed Forces in 1996, now claiming that the use of one-way CCTV instead of two-way television violated the federal legislation (*United States v. Longstreath*, 1996). The Court of Appeals for the Armed Forces observed that "[w]hether Congress intended the Act to apply to courts-martial or only to cases in federal district courts arising from federal enclaves, is not clear" (at 372). This court addressed the lower court's ruling that the federal legislation applied to the military justice system, but noted that "[w]e need not and do not decide if 18 USC § 3509 applies to courts-martial." The higher court went on to rule that even if the statute did apply, the use of one-way CCTV instead of two-way CCTV did not violate statutory provisions. Since the federal legislation used the word "may," as in the court "may" allow the use of two-way CCTV, then the Act means that two-way CCTV is authorized but not mandated. Further, one-way television was upheld in *Maryland v. Craig.*

In order to bring military practice into closer compliance with the federal statute, the Joint Services Committee on Military Justice proposed changes relating to closed-circuit television testimony to the military manual for courts-martial. By executive order on October 6, 1999, amendments to Rules of Courts-martial and Military Rules of Evidence[18] were passed and were made applicable to arraigned cases after November 1, 1999.

Military Rule of Evidence 611(d) was amended to provide for remote live testimony of a child victim or witness in child abuse or domestic violence cases. In such cases, the child must be under sixteen years of age at the time of the trial. Criteria for admissibility of remote live testimony include a finding by the military judge that the child is unable to testify for any of the same four criteria in the federal legislation: fear, substantial likelihood established by expert testimony that the child would suffer emotional trauma from testifying, knowledge that the victim suffers a mental or other infirmity, or conduct by the defendant or defense counsel that causes the child to be unable to continue testifying.[19]

Rules of Courts-martial 914A is a new rule that specifies general procedures for remote testimony. Persons allowed in the room with the child are the counsel for each side (excluding a defendant pro se), equipment operators, an attendant for the child, and other persons as deemed necessary by the judge. The military judge remains in the courtroom with the accused. Procedures will normally be determined by the military judge, although the rule states that testimony should normally be taken by two-way CCTV. However, an amended rule states that a "one-way closed circuit television system may be used if deemed necessary by the military judge."[20] This rule further states that if the accused elects to absent himself or herself voluntarily from the courtroom, then remote live testimony is not permitted.

This amendment gives the accused a greater role in determining how testimony by CCTV may be used (Berger, 1999). The defense has a "tactical choice" of forcing a child to testify on the stand in the absence of the accused or of allowing the accused to remain in the courtroom while the child testifies via CCTV. Berger (1999) suggests that the new legislation, while a good start to complying with the existing federal legislation, does not go far enough. Two alternatives omitted in the new military policies that are allowed for by the federal law are the use of videotaped depositions and closing of the courtroom under specific circumstances when a child victim or witness is testifying.

Three cases tried in military courts show how the military has accommodated child victims without using CCTV or by employing it in a different manner than that required by the new rules. For example, in 1988, Thompson, an Air Force sergeant, was convicted of repeatedly sodomizing his two stepsons, ages seven and ten. After testimony by the boys' psychologist regarding their fear and possible inability to communicate if they had to face the defendant, they testified in the courtroom but with their backs to their stepfather. The military judge, trial, and defense counsel could see the boys, but the defendant could not see them nor could they see him.

This case was tried before *Coy* or *Craig* had been decided by the Supreme Court. However, both of these cases had been decided by the time *United States v. Thompson* (1990) reached the Court of Military Appeals and provided guidance. In a concurring opinion, one judge noted that the Uniform Code of Military Justice and the Manual for Courts-Martial did not at this time provide for alternatives to face-to-face confrontation of child witnesses, as did Maryland's state statute. However, even without such a provision, "a military judge has inherent authority to dispense with face-to-face confrontation of a child-witness who otherwise will suffer emotional distress that will prevent the child from testifying meaningfully" (at 173-174).

The military appellate court also noted in a footnote that a question could be raised as to whether the particular procedure used in this instance violated the defendant's right to due process. As this was a general court-martial tried before a military judge alone, the court stated that they were confident that the judge would not have inferred guilt. However, a concurring opinion noted that judges in trials by court members should be careful to give appropriate instructions to those members in order to avoid inferences of guilt. In this instance, not using CCTV could be said to have benefited the accused because the children remained in the courtroom, where the judge and counsel could observe them as they testified.

In a second case, in 1996, the Court of Appeals for the Armed Forces reversed a decision of the Air Force Court of Criminal Appeals. In *United States v. Daulton* (1996), the lower court affirmed a decision in a military court-martial of an Air Force sergeant. CCTV was used, but in a different manner than that utilized in *Craig*. In this case, the alleged victims were the defendant's daughters, who were eleven and nine years old at the time of trial. The prosecutor requested that the nine-year-old be allowed to testify by one-way CCTV, and a therapist testified as to the emotional trauma that would likely occur and the inability to communicate if the child had to testify in the accused's presence. The defense wanted the child to testify from a chair in the courtroom with her back to the accused, similar to arrangements used in the *Thompson* case. However, this arrangement was seen as being more frightening for this child because she would know that the accused was behind her and there would be no screen blocking her. Instead of allowing the victim to testify via CCTV, the military judge ordered that the accused go to a nearby room where he would observe the proceedings by closed-circuit. Thus the child testified in the courtroom, and the defendant watched the proceedings in another room with a court bailiff. Subsequently, the defendant claimed that this procedure violated his Sixth Amendment right to confront his accusers.

By 1996, Congress had passed the federal legislation permitting CCTV of child victims and witnesses. The appellate court noted, however, that whether the statute applied to courts-martial had not been decided. Even so, the procedure used in this case was exactly opposite to the procedure in *Craig*. Excluded from the courtroom, the defendant was prevented from observing reactions of the court members and the judge, and they could not observe him. Further, the only way that he could communicate with his counsel was to send messages by the bailiff. The Court of Appeals for the Armed Forces agreed with the defendant that the procedure in this case violated the Sixth Amendment as well as military rules and that *Craig* did not authorize excluding the accused from the courtroom or restricting communication with counsel. Upon subjecting the procedural error to harmless-error analysis, the court could not find the error to be harmless beyond a reasonable doubt and reversed the lower criminal appellate court's decision, setting aside the finding of guilt and noting that a rehearing could be ordered.

In the third case, in 1999, the Court of Appeals for the Armed Forces heard a 1994 case involving another Air Force sergeant (*United States v. Anderson*). In this case, the female child victims were eleven and nine years old at the time of the trial. A licensed psychologist, selected by the prosecution, interviewed the alleged victims and testified to their emotional trauma and ability to testify. During her testimony, the nine-year-old faced the trial counsel with a screen positioned along the side of the witness box. The military judge ordered the older child to testify facing away from the accused and directly facing the court members. A closed-circuit television camera projected the images of both girls to a television for the military judge, defense counsel, accused, and court reporter to see. The judge instructed the court not to draw any inferences from the arrangements. When the eleven-year-old came in, she could not take the witness stand and left the court, saying "under her breath, 'I can't do this'" (at 149). The judge asked the accused to leave the room and the screen and television equipment were repositioned. The eleven-year-old was brought back in and seated behind the screen. Once she was seated, Anderson returned to the courtroom. The judge gave another instruction to the court not to draw inferences from the procedures being used. The defense appealed these procedures as due process violations. However, the Court of Appeals ruled that the television and screens allowed all parties to see each child as she testified. Additionally, the arrangement allowed the defense team to cross-examine each witness while communicating fully with the defendant; therefore, there was no denial of due process or the right to face-to-face confrontation.

One judge for the appellate court dissented, observing that the courtroom was "modified in a manner that identified appellant before the members of the court-martial as a person to be feared, a person whose impact on the witness was so traumatizing that extraordinary measures were warranted. . . . [W]ithout an adequate showing of necessity, . . . [such measures] are unconstitutional" (at 157). It is important to note that this case was denied certiorari by the Supreme Court on November 29, 1999.[21] Apparently, the High Court does not share the opinion of the dissenting judge. This denial of certiorari also reinforces the earlier observation in this chapter that alleged due process violations regarding CCTV are likely to be unsuccessful.

Statutory provisions for closed-circuit television testimony of children at the state level are similar to the federal statute previously discussed, although there are numerous variations across states. The following section addresses state legislation.

STATE LEGISLATION REGARDING
CLOSED-CIRCUIT TELEVISION TESTIMONY

By the end of 1999, thirty-seven states had statutes permitting the use of CCTV. The majority of these statutes have either been found to be constitutional or have not been challenged in court. As discussed in an earlier section, Pennsylvania's statute has been held unconstitutional. The elements of state statutes contrast widely in terms of alleged criminal acts for which CCTV may be allowed; whether use of CCTV applies to victims only or both victims and witnesses; the age of the person who may be allowed to testify by CCTV; criteria for admissibility of CCTV; and specific individuals who may be in the room in which CCTV is being conducted.[22] Each of these characteristics is explored in detail.

CCTV Testimony and Alleged Crimes

States vary markedly in terms of alleged crimes for which CCTV may be used. While almost all thirty-seven state statutes permit CCTV testimony for sexual offenses, they differ as to types of listed sexual offenses. For example, Arkansas and Kentucky statutes explicitly include indecent exposure. Seven statutes provide for sexual offenses only: Colorado, Florida, Illinois, Mississippi, New York, Rhode Island, and Vermont. New York bills that would have extended CCTV testimony for children in some murder cases, criminal assault, and endangering the welfare of a child died in Assembly in January of 2002. Conversely, Arizona, Arkansas, Kansas, and Wisconsin will permit televised testimony for any crime, while other states permit such testimony for any crime involving children. Iowa's statute permitting testimony by CCTV does not specify the applicable crimes. In March 2001, murder was added to the list of applicable offenses in Virginia's statute.[23] Table 1 displays state statute citations providing for CCTV and the alleged crimes for which CCTV may be utilized.

Applicability of CCTV and Age

Whether or not use of CCTV applies to child victims only or may also apply to witnesses varies widely according to state legislation. Victims only may testify via CCTV in sixteen states: California, Colorado, Connecticut, Georgia, Hawaii, Idaho, Illinois, Kansas, Louisiana, Maryland, Ohio, Oregon, Rhode Island, Texas, Vermont, and Washington. Either victims or witnesses may testify via CCTV for applicable crimes in the other

TABLE 1. State, statute citations and crimes for which CCTV is allowed

State	Statute Citation	Crimes
Alabama	Ala. Code § 15-25-3	Sexual offense, sexual exploitation, physical offense
Alaska	Alaska Stat. § 12.45.046	Sexual assault, sexual abuse of minor, incest, indecent exposure, unlawful exploitation of minor
Arizona	Ariz. Rev. Stat. Ann. § 13-4251 Ariz. Rev. Stat. Ann. § 13-4253	Any crime
Arkansas	Ark. Code Ann. § 16-43-1001	Any crime
California	Cal. Penal Code § 1347	Sexual offenses, violent felony
Colorado	Colo. Rev. Stat. § 18-3-413.5	Unlawful sexual offense
Connecticut	Conn. Gen. Stat. Ann. § 54-86g	Assault, sexual assault, child abuse
Delaware	Del. Code Ann. Tit. 11, § 3514	Sexual abuse, physical injury, death, abuse or neglect
Florida	Fla. Stat. Ann. Ch. 92.54	Unlawful sexual act, contact, intrusion, penetration, or other sexual offense
Georgia	Ga. Code Ann. § 17-8-55	Cruelty to children, rape, sodomy, child molestation, sexual assault against persons in custody
Hawaii	Haw. R. Evid. 616	Abuse or sexual offense
Idaho	Idaho Code § 19-3024A	Injury to children, ritualized abuse of child, disseminating harmful materials to minors, crime against nature
Illinois	725 Ill. Comp. Stat. Ann. § 5/106B-5	Criminal or agg. criminal sexual assault, predatory criminal sexual assault against child, criminal or agg. criminal sexual abuse
Indiana	Ind. Code § 35-37-4-8	Sex crimes, battery upon child, kidnapping & confinement, incest, neglect, attempt of applicable felonies
Iowa	Iowa Code § 915.38(1)	Not specified
Kansas	Kan. Stat. Ann. § 22-3434	Any crime
Kentucky	Ky. Rev. Stat. Ann. § 421.350	Rape, indecent exposure, permitting prostitution, incest, use of minor in sexual performance, promoting sexual performance by minor, endangering welfare of minor, inducing, assisting, causing minor to engage in illegal sexual activity
Louisiana	La. Rev. Stat. Ann. § 15.283 La. Children's Code art. 329	Physical or sexual abuse
Maryland	Md. Ann. Code, art. 27 § 774	Abuse of a child
Massachusetts	Mass. Gen. Laws Ann. Ch. 278, § 16D	Indecent assault & battery, rape, child abuse, assault w/intent to rape, lascivious cohabitation & lewdness, incest, exhibition of deformities, sodomy, unnatural & lascivious acts, child pornography, prostitution related offenses
Minnesota	Minn. Stat. Ann. § 595.02(4)	Physical abuse or sexual contact or penetration, crime of violence

State	Statute Citation	Crimes
Mississippi	Miss. Code Ann. § 13-1-401 et. seq. Miss. R. Evid. 617	Unlawful sexual act, contact, intrusion, penetration/other sexual offense
New Jersey	N.J. Stat. Ann. § 2A:84A-32.4	Sexual or agg. sexual assault, criminal or agg. criminal sexual contact, child abuse or any action alleging child abuse or neglect
New York	N.Y. Crim. Proc. Law § 65.00 et seq. N. Y. Exec. Law § 642-a	Incest, sexual misconduct, rape, sodomy, sexual or agg. sexual abuse
Ohio	Ohio Rev. Code Ann. § 2907.41 Ohio Rev. Code Ann. § 2937.11(B)	Rape, sexual battery, corruption of minor, sexual or gross sexual imposition, compelling prostitution, disseminating material harmful to juveniles, pandering, endangering children, illegal use of minor in nudity-oriented material or performance, felonious sexual penetration
Oklahoma	Okla. Stat. tit. 22, § 753	Any offense against child
Oregon	Or. Rev. Stat. § 40.460(24)	Abuse or sexual conduct
Pennsylvania	42 Pa. Cons. Stat. Ann. § 5982 42 Pa. Cons. Stat. Ann. § 5985	Any prosecution or adjudication involving child victim/witness
Rhode Island	R.I. Gen. Laws § 11-37-13.2	Sexual assault
South Dakota	S.D. Codified Laws § 26-8A-30 S.D. Codified Laws § 26-8A-31	Sexual contact, rape, physical abuse, neglect, crime of violence
Tennessee	Tenn. Code Ann. § 24-7-120	Agg. sexual battery, rape of child, incest, agg. child abuse, kidnapping, esp. agg. kidnapping, criminal attempt of any crimes in this subsection
Texas	Tex. Code Crim. P. Ann. § 38.071	Indecency with child, sexual or agg. sexual assault, agg. assault, injury to child, prohibited sexual conduct, sexual performance by child
Utah	Utah R. Crim. Proc. 15.5(2)	Child abuse, sexual offense against child
Vermont	Vt. R. Evid. 807	Sexual or agg. sexual assault, lewd or lascivious conduct with child, incest
Virginia	Va. Code Ann. § 18.2-67.9	Kidnapping, criminal sexual assault, family offenses, alleged murder
Washington	Wash. Rev. Code Ann. § 9A.44.150	Sexual contact, physical abuse
Wisconsin	Wis. Stat. Ann. § 972.11(2m)	Any criminal prosecution

twenty-one states with such statutes: Alabama, Alaska, Arizona, Arkansas, Delaware, Florida, Indiana, Iowa, Kentucky, Massachusetts, Minnesota, Mississippi, New Jersey, New York, Oklahoma, Pennsylvania, South Dakota, Tennessee, Utah, Virginia, and Wisconsin. In March 2001, Virginia's statute was expanded to include child witnesses as well as child victims.[24]

The average age of the victim or witness for which CCTV is permitted is thirteen years and younger and ranges from nine years old in the state of Washington to under eighteen in Hawaii, Illinois, Iowa, Maryland, and Rhode Island. In Iowa and South Dakota, if the court finds it necessary, testimony by CCTV may be allowed regardless of age in cases of victims or witnesses with mental illness, mental retardation, or other developmental disabilities. Table 2 delineates applicability of each state's CCTV legislation and the ages at which CCTV may be used.

Criteria for Admissibility of CCTV

Because the Supreme Court held that the state's interest in protecting children from trauma can justify altering traditional methods of confronting witnesses in court, state statutes specify the degree of trauma to the child that must be shown before CCTV testimony may be used. The criteria for admissibility of testimony by CCTV ranges from good cause in several states to clear and convincing evidence or a preponderance of the evidence in other states. Kentucky's statute requires a showing of compelling need, defined as "substantial probability that the child would be unable to reasonably communicate because of serious emotional distress produced by the defendant's presence."[25] Other statutes require clear and convincing evidence that courtroom testimony would be harmful to the child, resulting in serious emotional or mental distress. Most state statutes focus on the serious mental or emotional harm on the child, thus rendering the child unable to communicate reasonably in court, while states such as California and Idaho focus singularly on the unavailability of the child as a witness if CCTV is not used. States also differ according to persons required to make the determination of trauma or unavailability as a witness. While some states allow the judge to make this determination, still others require expert testimony by a psychiatrist, physician, or psychologist. Table 3 shows admissibility criteria by state.

Persons Allowed in Room During CCTV

Laws in almost all thirty-seven states allow defense and prosecuting or district attorneys to be in the room with the child while the CCTV testimony is taking place. Idaho's statute is the only one that does not specifically provide for the presence of defense and prosecuting attorneys in the room, instead requiring that the CCTV equipment "accurately communicate the image and demeanor of the minor to the judge, jury, defendant or defendants and attorneys."[26]

Most state statutes also provide for the actual CCTV operators to be in the room. Only the statutes for Hawaii, Idaho, and Washington omit mentioning the presence of persons required to operate the equipment.

TABLE 2. Applicability of closed-circuit television testimony and age by state

State	Applicability	Age
Alabama	Victim/Witness	15 or younger
Alaska	Victim/Witness	15 or younger
Arizona	Victim/Witness	14 or younger
Arkansas	Victim/Witness	12 or younger
California	Victim	13 or younger
Colorado	Victim	11 or younger
Connecticut	Victim	12 or younger
Delaware	Victim/Witness	10 or younger
Florida	Victim/Witness	15 or younger
Georgia	Victim	10 or younger
Hawaii	Victim	Under 18 at time of testimony or trial
Idaho	Victim	15 or younger
Illinois	Victim	17 or younger
Indiana	Victim/Witness	13 or younger
Iowa	Victim/Witness	17 or younger
Kansas	Victim	12 or younger
Kentucky	Victim/Witness	12 or younger
Louisiana	Victim	13 or younger
Maryland	Victim	17 or younger
Massachusetts	Victim/Witness	14 or younger
Minnesota	Victim/Witness	11 or younger
Mississippi	Victim/Witness	15 or younger
New Jersey	Victim/Witness	16 or younger
New York	Victim/Witness	12 or younger
Ohio	Victim	Under 13 when complaint, indictment, or information filed
Oklahoma	Victim/Witness	12 or younger
Oregon	Victim	Under 12 at time of testimony or trial
Pennsylvania	Victim/Material witness	15 or younger
Rhode Island	Victim	17 or younger[a]
South Dakota	Victim/Witness	11 or younger
Tennessee	Victim/Witness	13 or younger
Texas	Victim	12 or younger

TABLE 2 (continued)

State	Applicability	Age
Utah	Victim/Witness	13 or younger
Vermont	Victim	12 or younger
Virginia	Victim/Witness	14 or younger[b]
Washington	Victim	9 or younger
Wisconsin	Victim/Witness	11 or younger[c]

[a] If child under 14, a rebuttable presumption exists that child is unable to testify without suffering unreasonable/unnecessary mental or emotional harm.
[b] at time of alleged offense; under 17 at time of trial for victim.
[c] at time of trial/under 16 if court finds interests of justice warrant child's testimony by CCTV and simultaneously televised in courtroom.

More importantly for the victim or witness in terms of who is allowed in the room, at least three states explicitly allow for the presence of the defendant: Alabama, Connecticut, and Florida. In Massachusetts, Minnesota, and New York, the defendant may be excluded upon a court finding that the child is likely to suffer psychological damage in the defendant's presence. In New York, if the defendant remains in the courtroom, both the defense attorney and district attorney also must remain in the courtroom unless there is a determination that their presence in the room with the child will not prejudice a jury against the defendant and will not hinder communication between the defendant and the defense attorney. South Dakota's statute provides for the exclusion of the defendant at the discretion of the court. Table 4 delineates, by state, persons who may be in the room with the child during CCTV.

Uniform Child Witness Testimony by Alternative Methods Act

In August 2002, the National Conference of Commissioners on Uniform State Laws, recognizing the wide variation across states in legislative provisions for alternative modes of testimony by children, drafted the Uniform Child Witness Testimony by Alternative Methods Act. "Alternative methods" include CCTV and would apply to both criminal and non-criminal proceedings instead of just criminal proceedings involving physical or sexual abuse. Further, the Act applies to child witnesses and not just child victims, as is presently the case in many states. The criterion for admissibility of testimony by alternative methods in criminal proceedings is clear and convincing evidence that "the child witness would suffer serious emotional trauma that would substantially

TABLE 3. Admissibility criteria for closed-circuit television testimony by state

State	Criteria for Admissibility
Alabama	Good cause
Alaska	Inability to communicate effectively
Arizona	Not specified
Arkansas	Clear and convincing evidence that testifying in court would be harmful or detrimental
California	Clear and convincing evidence that the child would be unavailable as witness unless CCTV is used
Colorado	Testimony is taken during proceeding, judge determines that child would be unable to communicate reasonably in court and in presence of defendant, availability of CCTV equipment
Connecticut	Not specified
Delaware	Judge determines that child would be unable to communicate reasonably in court
Florida	Court determines that child would suffer at least moderate or mental harm or be otherwise unavailable to testify
Georgia	Judge determines that child would suffer serious emotional distress and thus cannot communicate reasonably
Hawaii	Court determines that child's ability to communicate would be substantially impaired and that child would likely suffer serious emotional distress in presence of defendant
Idaho	Clear and convincing evidence that child would be unavailable as witness
Illinois	Testimony taken during proceeding, judge determines that child would suffer serious emotional distress rendering inability to communicate reasonably or would suffer severe adverse effects
Indiana	Testimony by psychiatrist, physician, or psychologist that child would suffer serious emotional harm and court finds that child could not reasonably communicate in presence of defendant
Iowa	Specific finding of necessity to protect child from trauma
Kansas	Clear and convincing evidence of trauma rendering child unable to communicate reasonably or otherwise be unavailable to testify
Kentucky	Compelling need
Louisiana	Expert testimony of serious emotional distress and inability to communicate reasonably without CCTV
Maryland	Judicial determination of serious emotional distress rendering inability to communicate reasonably
Massachusetts	Preponderance of evidence of psychological or emotional trauma if testifying in open court or in defendant's presence
Minnesota	Not specified
Mississippi	Expert testimony of substantial likelihood of traumatic emotional or mental distress if child testifies in open court
New Jersey	Court finding of substantial likelihood of severe emotional or mental distress if child testifies in open court
New York	Defendant's presence would contribute to child's suffering severe mental or emotional harm or clear and convincing evidence as result of extraordinary circumstances that child will suffer severe mental or emotional harm if required to testify

TABLE 3 (continued)

State	Criteria for Admissibility
Ohio	Judicial determination of unavailability
Oklahoma	Court determination of serious emotional distress rendering child unable to communicate reasonably
Oregon	Expert testimony to substantial likelihood of severe emotional or psychological harm if child is required to testify in open court
Pennsylvania	Court determination of serious emotional distress rendering child unable to communicate reasonably
Rhode Island	Showing of unreasonable and unnecessary mental or emotional harm rendering child unable to testify in court
South Dakota	Court finding of more than de minimis emotional distress and that CCTV testimony is necessary to protect child's welfare
Tennessee	Court finding of trauma due to defendant's presence and more than de minimis emotional distress rendering inability to communicate reasonably
Texas	Good cause
Utah	Good cause
Vermont	Court finding of substantial risk of trauma which substantially impairs ability to testify
Virginia	Court finding of unavailability to testify in open court
Washington	Court finding of substantial evidence of serious emotional or mental distress due to defendant's presence rendering inability to communicate reasonably [a]
Wisconsin	Court finding of serious emotional distress due to defendant's presence rendering inability to communicate reasonably and making CCTV testimony necessary to minimize trauma due to open court testimony and to secure better uninhibited, truthful testimony

[a] If the court finds that testifying in front of the jury will cause child to suffer serious emotional distress preventing child from reasonably communicating, the defendant will remain in the room. The court finds that the prosecutor has made all reasonable efforts to prepare child for testifying. Court balances strength of state's case without child's testimony against defendant's constitutional rights and degree of infringement of closed-circuit procedure on those rights. Court finds that no less restrictive method of obtaining testimony exists that can adequately protect child from serious emotional or mental distress.

impair the child's ability to communicate with the finder of fact" if the child were required to testify in an open forum or to be "confronted face-to-face by the defendant" (National Conference of Commissioners on Uniform State Laws, 2002, p. 5). Using alternative modes of testimony in non-criminal proceedings requires a preponderance of the evidence that the alternative method is "necessary to serve the best interests of the child or enable the child to communicate with the finder of fact" (p. 3-4). The first reading of the act was presented at the national conference the year before (National Conference of Commissioners on Uniform State Laws, 2001) and initially defined "child witness" as un-

TABLE 4. Persons allowed in room during CCTV testimony

State	Persons allowed in room other than defense and prosecuting or district attorneys and CCTV operators
Alabama	Defendant, others permitted by court considering child's welfare/well-being
Alaska	Person who contributes to child's well-being as determined by court
Arizona	Any person who contributes to welfare/well-being of minor
Arkansas	Judge or court-appointed judicial officer, defense attorney except pro se defendant, child's attorney, any person who contributes to welfare/well-being of child as determined by court
California	Support person, non-uniformed bailiff, court-appointed representative
Colorado	Guardian ad litem, person who contributes to welfare/well-being of child as determined by court, unless defendant objects
Connecticut	Judge, defendant unless excluded by court, any person who contributes to welfare/well-being of child
Delaware	Defense unless defendant is pro se, any person who contributes to well-being of child in court's opinion
Florida	Judge, defendant, interpreter, any person who contributes to well-being of child in court's opinion and who is not witness
Georgia	Judge, any person who contributes to well-being of child
Hawaii	Statute only provides for presence of defense and state's attorneys
Idaho	Non-uniformed bailiff, court-appointed representative after consultation with prosecution and defense[a]
Illinois	Judge, any person(s) who contributes to well-being of child, parent or guardian, court security personnel, defense attorney unless defendant is pro se
Indiana	Defense attorney unless defendant is pro se, persons who contribute to well-being of protected person as determined by court, court bailiff or representative[b]
Iowa	Judge, any person who contributes to welfare and well-being of child in court's opinion
Kansas	Any person who contributes to welfare and well-being of child
Kentucky	Any person who contributes to welfare and well-being of child
Louisiana	Judge, any person other than relative who is necessary to welfare and well-being of child
Maryland	Child's attorney, any person who contributes to well-being of child in court's opinion, unless defendant objects
Massachusetts	Judge, such persons as court allows, defendant unless court order based on finding that child is likely to suffer trauma in defendant's presence
Minnesota	Judge, any person who contributes to welfare and well-being of child, defendant unless court finds child likely to suffer psychological trauma in defendant's presence rendering child unavailable to testify
Mississippi	Not specified who may be present in room
New Jersey	Specific order as to who will be excluded based on specific findings regarding impact of each person excluded
New York	CCTV operators, defendant unless court finds likelihood child will suffer severe emotional or mental harm in defendant's presence

TABLE 4 (continued)

State	Persons allowed in room other than defense and prosecuting or district attorneys and CCTV operators
Ohio	Judge, interpreter(s), one person chosen by child who is not a witness, person who contributes to welfare and well-being of child
Oklahoma	Person who contributes to welfare and well-being of child
Oregon	Judge, person who contributes to welfare and well-being of child
Pennsylvania	Court reporter, judge, person who contributes to welfare and well-being of child
Rhode Island	Judge, person who contributes to welfare and well-being of child
South Dakota	Person who contributes to welfare and well-being of child, discretion of court regarding exclusion of defendant
Tennessee	Interpreter, court security personnel, parent, counselor, or therapist, person who contributes to well-being of child[c]
Texas	Judge, court reporter, person who contributes to welfare and well-being of child
Utah	Judge, counselor or therapist whose presence contributes to welfare and well-being of child, defendant[d]
Vermont	Person not a witness who contributes to welfare and well-being of child[e]
Virginia	Person who contributes to welfare and well-being of child
Washington	Neutral and trained victim's advocate, does not specifically provide for presence of CCTV operators
Wisconsin	Parents, guardian, legal custodian, or other person who contributes to welfare and well-being of child, person designated by state attorney and approved by court and person designated by defendant or defense and approved by court

[a] Statute does not provide for defense and prosecuting attorneys being present or for presence of CCTV operators.
[b] Defendant may question the child witness if not represented by an attorney.
[c] Defendant may be present if acting as attorney pro se.
[d] Unless defendant consents to be hidden from child's view. Upon court determination of serious emotional or mental strain or unreliable testimony on part of child if required to testify in defendant's presence; if defendant is not excluded, court shall ensure that child cannot hear or see defendant.
[e] Defendant's image shall be transmitted to witness unless court finds that hearing and seeing defendant presents substantial risk of trauma substantially impairing ability to testify.

der the age of eighteen. However, the final act was amended to define child witness as an individual under the age of thirteen. The act was presented for adoption at the American Bar Association meeting in February 2003.

While the previous discussion illustrates how far the federal government, the military justice system, and states have come in protecting child victims in criminal court proceedings, this discussion also portrays the serious weaknesses in current legislation. State laws that limit CCTV only to child victims of sexual offenses force children who witness violent crimes to face alleged offenders in court. For example, in most states, a child who witnesses one parent murdered by another parent will have to testify in court, facing that parent. The emotional impact is great, and the potential for trauma is still present. It has been seen how firm public support is for CCTV for child victims and witnesses. In spite of this support, one critical problem is that we know little about how using CCTV affects court outcomes. Further, the research regarding the harm suffered by child victims when facing defendants in court that was relied upon by the Supreme Court in *Maryland v. Craig* (1990) has been criticized by some scholars as being of questionable validity. The next section of this chapter discuss the role that social science research played in the *Craig* opinion, followed by a review of more recent research on the use of CCTV in court outcomes.

THE ROLE OF SOCIAL SCIENCE RESEARCH IN MARYLAND V. CRAIG

In 1990, the American Psychology-Law Society (AP-LS) collaborated with the American Psychological Association in submitting a pro bono brief in *Maryland v. Craig* (1990). The brief writers took a direct role in bringing research on the effects on child victims of testifying in court in front of defendants to the attention of the Court. This brief played a substantial role in influencing the majority opinion (Roesch, Golding, Hans, & Reppucci, 1991; Goodman, Levine, Melton, & Ogden, 1991). The APA brief stated:

> The . . . body of research supports the proposition that children as a class may be especially likely to be emotionally distressed by courtroom confrontation with their alleged abusers (p. 17). . . . Sexually abused children frequently suffer serious emotional trauma and may be particularly vulnerable to further distress through the legal process (p. 18). . . . Child victims may be more likely than adult victims to suffer substantial distress as a result of testifying in the physical presence of the defendant (p. 20). (as cited in Underwager & Wakefield, 1992, p. 235)

The Supreme Court opinion noted the "growing body of academic literature documenting psychological trauma suffered by child abuse victims who must testify in court,"[27] citing the APA brief twice and referencing authorities cited in the brief. An APA executive associate said,

"The court adopted our entire argument. It's very clear the court listened to what we had to say" (Underwager & Wakefield, 1992, p. 235).

However, some scholars have observed that the brief was "poor psychology" and produced "poor law" in the *Maryland v. Craig* decision. At the time the brief was written, there were few empirical studies examining the effects of testifying on children, and those that did exist were of "low and doubtful validity" (Underwager & Wakefield, 1992, p. 234). According to Underwager and Wakefield, the APA brief presented speculations, overstated data, and generally misrepresented the state of scientific research regarding the effects of in-court testimony on child victims.

Underwager and Wakefield (1992) note that the assumption of the brief that the child is afraid of facing the defendant because of having been abused by this individual "already assumes guilt and violates the presumption of innocence. This assumption ignores the possibility that a child witness, in the interim between accusation and testimony, may have been taught by adults to fear the accused" (p. 237). The authors emphasized that only information of "high and clear validity" should be presented in a legal brief that is "considering the question of a state interest compelling limitation of an individual constitution right" (p. 239). They further surmised that the ruling in *Maryland v. Craig* would only complicate and confuse "the attempt to deal fairly and accurately with allegations of child sexual abuse" (p. 242). While it is clear now that support for CCTV and other alternative modes of child witness testimony is strong, it is not so clear just how the use of CCTV affects court outcomes. The final section of this chapter addresses this issue.

IMPACT OF THE USE OF CCTV ON THE COURT PROCESS

Crucial issues central to the use of CCTV are how it affects children's testimony, jurors' perceptions in general, and more specifically, jurors' ability to detect deception. In *Coy v. Iowa* (1988), Justice Scalia wrote that it is always more difficult to tell a lie "to a person's face."[28] Given this reasoning, allowing child victims and witnesses to testify by CCTV would make jurors less able to detect deception. Therefore, opponents of CCTV uphold face-to-face confrontation for at least three reasons:

(a) witnesses on the stand will more readily emit signs and cues that will assist jurors in assessing credibility; (b) placing witnesses under a certain amount of stress will improve the quality and accuracy of their evidence, and as a result (c) the decision-making function of the jury will be more effectively accomplished. (Davies, 1999, p. 244)

These three suppositions lack empirical evidence, however. In fact, early research examining the impact of videotaped testimony by adult witnesses showed that observers concentrated more on what the witnesses were saying rather than on their nonverbal behavior. More recent laboratory research with children shows this same trend, suggesting "the use of CCTV might be expected to improve rather than impair the decision-making powers of the jury" (Davies, 1999, p. 245).

The argument that stress improves the substance of testimony is also unsupported by research. Research shows that signs of stress exhibited by witnesses are often interpreted by observers to indicate deception. Further, there is no support for the argument that stress aids recall. In fact, at least three experimental studies with children support the view that a more relaxed witness has better recall. In one court simulation study, six-year-olds made more errors of omission when they testified in the defendant's presence and were more influenced by leading questions than those testifying via CCTV (Davies, 1999).

While the above findings support the use of CCTV, there is also experimental research showing that jurors may prefer live testimony to CCTV and may rate witnesses more positively in terms of attractiveness, reliability, intelligence, and other characteristics. However, these trial simulation studies also show that the mode of testimony has no effect on jury verdicts, suggesting that while jurors might prefer live testimony, they do not allow that preference to influence decision-making (Davies, 1999).

The evidence for the above research relies on court simulations and experimental research in the laboratory, thus posing methodological concerns of external validity. In order to reach better conclusions, observational studies of actual child witness trials conducted with and without CCTV testimony must be considered. Three major evaluations of televised testimony in countries other than the United States have resulted in mixed findings. One evaluation of the use of CCTV in England and Wales surveyed judges, barristers, and court administrators, finding that the majority of court personnel had favorable opinions toward televised testimony. The most frequently mentioned negative feature was the loss of immediacy and a lesser impact on the jury. This study also rated children's evidence via CCTV in a hundred trials and compared ratings with child testimony in open court in Scotland. The English children were rated as less unhappy, and their testimony was judged to be more forthcoming and audible.

An evaluation in Australia, comparing child testimony by CCTV with testimony in open court, found that children who testified by CCTV were less anxious. Court officials, parents, and child witnesses gave favorable opinions of the televised testimony mode. A final evaluation comparing the two modes of testimony in Scottish courts found open-court testimony to contain more detail, with children appearing more audible and more resistant to leading questions. However, CCTV testimony of children who were under stress was more consistent on timing of events and on the defendant's main actions, and an overwhelming majority of children who testified by CCTV reported that they "were glad they had testified in this way" (Davies, 1999, p. 251).

Research examining the type of shot used in television testimony finds that close-up shots may enhance the facial features of the child, but they prevent jurors from noting the height and size of the child. Consequently, jurors may overestimate the witness' maturity and build. Since age and apparent maturity are linked with how jurors evaluate testimony in terms of accuracy, amount of detail recalled, and plausibility, the court should allow jurors to observe the child's size before testimony, perhaps by taking the child to the door of the courtroom (Davies, 1999).

Various types of CCTV technologies and arrangements currently are in place, and research comparing these types is needed. The typical British system involves counsel remaining in the courtroom and interviewing the child by a television link. As shown in the previous discussion of state statutes, the usual arrangement in the United States is for the attorneys to question the child in another room with testimony being relayed into the courtroom. Some observers have argued that the two-way link is more distracting because of the equipment and poses potential for communication problems. Two studies looking at the British system have found no differences between the two-way link and face-to-face testimony in terms of accuracy, completeness, or credibility (Davies, 1999).

To date, at least two experimental studies in the United States have tested the effects of CCTV on children's eyewitness testimony, perceptions of jurors toward child testimony via CCTV, and adults' abilities to distinguish deceptive testimony by CCTV versus deceptive testimony in open court (Goodman et al., 1998; Orcutt, Goodman, Tobey, Batterman-Faunce, & Thomas, 2001).

The sample in the 1998 study consisted of 85 five- to six-year olds and 101 eight- to nine-year-olds. In this experiment, the defendant videotaped individual children in one of two scenarios. In the "guilty" scenario, the defendant told the boys and girls to place stickers on their bare arms, toes, and navels. He then instructed the boys and girls to display their bare arms, toes, and navels to the video camera. In the "innocent" scenario, children placed the stickers on their shirt sleeves, belt buckles, and shoes, which they displayed to the camera. The defendant was "charged" with making a video of children exposing bare body parts. In this way, the "crime" mimicked a child-pornography situation (Orcutt et al., 2001). Two weeks later, the children came to a courthouse and testified individually in mock jury trials about what had happened, either in open court or by CCTV.

Testimony by CCTV took place in a witness room. The parent was in the room with the child. Each child sat on a couch in full view of the video camera, while parents sat off camera and out of direct line of sight. A large television monitor was in the courtroom, allowing jurors, the defendant, attorneys, and judge to view the child's testimony. Attorneys entered the witness room individually to question the child witness. After the questioning was over, the monitor was turned off, and the trials proceeded in the same format as the open court trials. However, in the CCTV trial conditions, the judge noted in his final instructions that "no implications should be drawn from use of CCTV, that it is not evidence in itself, and that it should not be considered during deliberations" (Goodman et al., 1998, pp. 180-181).

Children's responses to free recall, directive, and misleading questions were analyzed for significant differences with respect to age, guilt, and trial conditions. Comparing the responses of eight-year-olds who testified in regular court to those who testified via CCTV revealed no significant differences. Significant differences did emerge with respect to trial condition and six-year-olds' errors of omission in response to misleading questions, one indicator of suggestibility. Specifically, six-year-olds made more omission errors to misleading questions in open court than did the six-year-olds in the CCTV trial condition.

For the total sample, anxiety was higher for children who expected to testify in open court compared to anxiety levels of children who expected to testify via CCTV. When the defendant was guilty, eight-year-olds testifying in regular court expressed significantly more anxiety than either six- or eight-year-olds who testified via CCTV. However, six-year-olds testifying in regular court when the defendant was guilty did not display more anxiety than six- or eight-year-olds testifying via CCTV. Legal knowledge was found to alleviate anxiety for the total sample. "Children with a better understanding of the legal system expressed the least anxiety about taking the stand" (Goodman et al., 1998, p. 188), thus illustrating the importance of educating potential child witnesses about what happens in courtrooms, regardless of the trial condition.

Children asked to testify in the regular court condition were more likely to refuse to testify than were the children asked to testify via CCTV. However, the difference in refusal to testify compared by trial conditions only approached significance at a .08 level of significance.

Differences in perceptions of jurors by trial condition also were analyzed. Women were significantly more likely to view the CCTV trial condition as fairer to the child than women who were part of the regular trial proceedings; however, the mean difference was small (5.58 compared to 5.44, $p < .05$).

Jurors in the regular court condition were not able to recognize accuracy of children's testimony better than jurors viewing testimony by CCTV. The researchers examined twenty-four correlations between measures of children's overall accuracy and jurors' judgment of accuracy. There was no significant relationship between twenty-two of these correlations. The only significant relationships occurred with jurors' judgments of accuracy when eight-year-olds were testifying via CCTV and six-year-olds were testifying in open court. In short, jurors overall did a poor job in detecting accuracy of children's testimony.

Subsequent path analyses indicated a small but significant relationship between trial condition and accurate testimony, with children testifying via CCTV being slightly more accurate in answering direct questions (path coefficient = .04, $p = .01$). Conversely, jurors in the regular trial condition viewed children as more accurate or believable than did jurors who viewed children's testimony by CCTV (path coefficient = −.09, $p = .001$). However, the relationship between accurate testimony and accuracy/believability was greater (path coefficient = .18, $p = .0001$). The researchers noted that while "[t]he direct effect of CCTV was to lower children's credibility in the eyes of the jurors, . . . an indirect effect of trial condition was that when children provided more accurate testimony, it led jurors to believe the children more" (Goodman et al., 1998, p. 196). Trial condition did not affect post-deliberation verdicts.

The above research results do not offer compelling reasons for wholesale acceptance of CCTV over in-court testimony. The authors suggest that attorneys may decide to rely on CCTV only in "extreme circumstances such as when children have been severely injured or threatened and refuse to testify unless they can do so via CCTV" (Goodman et al., 1998, p. 199).

The sample in the 2001 study consisted of 70 seven- to nine-year-old children. This experiment followed the same scenario and procedures as the previous one published in 1998, with one difference. A number of children in the "innocent" scenario were asked to give a false testimony that matched the guilty condition so that there were three experimental conditions: guilt, innocence, and deception on the part of the child witness.[29] Half of the children testified in open court, and half testified by CCTV. Procedures for testimony by CCTV followed the same format as the 1998 study previously discussed.

Research findings revealed that CCTV was associated with more negative ratings of child witnesses than was testimony in open court. Children testifying in open court were seen as significantly more honest, more attractive, and more intelligent than children testifying by CCTV. Children testifying in open court also were perceived as more consistent, confident, and believable and significantly less likely to have been making up a story. In addition, before deliberations began, jurors were significantly more likely to convict the defendant after hearing the testimony of children in open court than were jurors who heard testimony by CCTV. However, verdicts after deliberation were not affected significantly by the mode of testimony (Orcutt et al., 2001).

This research study supports previous findings that CCTV is associated with bias toward the defense rather than a pro-prosecution bias. After deliberation, jurors were no more likely to convict the defendant in the true "guilty condition" than when the child was lying about the defendant's guilt, regardless of mode of testimony. Thus, in this sense, researchers note that CCTV does not impede jurors' fact-finding abilities, nor does CCTV appear to bias jurors against the defendant. However, given that jurors were more likely to perceive the child witnesses in a negative light, CCTV "may not always be in the best interests of justice or the truth-telling child" (Orcutt et al., 2001, p. 370).

Results from these studies are inconclusive when it comes to the impact on quality of evidence. Adding to the inconclusiveness regarding the efficacy of CCTV are researchers who believe that it helps child abuse victims in terms of esteem and feelings of personal safety to face their abusers, particularly when they see abusers assume responsibility for their acts (American Academy of Pediatrics, 1999). Yet there is no doubt that CCTV is viewed as a valuable and permanent addition to the justice system, as evidenced by the issuance of federal grants for obtaining CCTV equipment and the recent move toward standardizing statutes allowing for alternative modes of testimony, such as CCTV, for child witnesses.

CONCLUSION

This chapter has explored myriad issues surrounding the use of CCTV for child victims and witnesses. It has discussed constitutional challenges to CCTV at federal and state levels, as well as challenges in military courts. It has also noted that CCTV testimony can generally survive Sixth Amendment challenges, as well as allegations of due process violations. This chapter has presented the current status of federal and state legislation providing for alternatives to courtroom testimony, including a detailed look at the diversity among states in their CCTV statutes. States were seen to vary in terms of alleged crimes for which CCTV may be allowed, applicability to victims only or both victims and witnesses, age, admissibility criteria, and allowed persons in the room in which CCTV takes place. This chapter examined the role that social science research, however questionable, played in paving the way for acceptance of CCTV legislation. The state of social science research in the area of CCTV testimony has also been discussed. While it appears that use of CCTV is becoming more and more acceptable, its use should still be the exception rather than the norm. CCTV testimony is not necessary for all children. More research in the area of how CCTV affects juror perceptions and court outcomes is crucial. Initial findings from research are certainly inconclusive at best. Further, uniform standards in states' child witness protection statutes are recommended. The implementation of innovations such as Children's Advocacy Centers suggests that we are making some progress in the area of victims' rights. However, protecting the rights of accused persons while guarding against the potential of the criminal justice system to do more harm to child victims of crimes continues to be a balancing act.

NOTES

1. Justice Kennedy did not participate in this decision.
2. *Coy v. Iowa*, 487 U.S. 1012 at 1017, citing *Pointer v. Texas*, 380 U.S. 400, 404 (1965).
3. *Coy v. Iowa*, 487 U.S. 1012 at 1018.

4. *Id.* at 1021.
5. *Id.* at 1024.
6. *Maryland v. Craig*, 110 S.Ct. 3157 at 3169.
7. *Id.* at 3171.
8. *Id.* at 3171.
9. *Danner v. Kentucky*, 119 S.Ct. 529 at 530.
10. *Marx v. Texas*, 120 S.Ct. at 577.
11. *Carmona v. State*, 880 S.W. 2d 227 (Tex. App.-Austin 1994); *Gonzales v. State*, 818 S.W.2d 756 (Tex.Crim.App. 1991).
12. 18 U.S.C.§3509(b)(1).
13. 18 U.S.C.§3509(b)(2).
14. 18 U.S.C.§3509(e).
15. Berger noted that legislative intent that the Act applies to military courts was clearly evident during congressional debates. Representative Michael DeWine (R-Ohio), one of the drafters of the provisions protecting victims of crime, stated during floor debates that "While there are a limited but rising number of child abuse cases tried in the Federal courts, many states have adopted innovative procedures that have far outpaced Federal law, leaving those children who do enter the system through military bases, Indian reservations, and other Federal lands and facilities inadequately protected" (Berger, 1999, citing 136 Cong. Rec. H13288 (daily ed. Oct. 27, 1990)).
16. See *United States v. Longstreath* 42 M.J. 806 (1995).
17. *Id.* at 815.
18. R.C.M. 804, 914A, and M.R.E. 611(d).
19. Mil.R.Evid. 611 (d)(3).
20. R.C. M. 804(c)(2).
21. 1999 U.S. LEXIS 7832.
22. Information regarding elements of state law is from "The use of closed-circuit television testimony," Number 20 in Child abuse and neglect state statutes elements: Child witnesses. National Clearinghouse on Child Abuse and Neglect Information. URL: http://www.calib.com/nccanch/pubs/stats00/cctv.pdf. The report is current through December 31, 1999. Updated information since 1999 is so noted by specific state statutes.
23. §18.2-67.9 Code of Virginia.
24. §18.2-67.9 Code of Virginia.
25. KRS 421.350(5).
26. Idaho Code 19-3024A.2(c).
27. *Maryland v. Craig*, 110 S.Ct. 3157 at 3168.
28. 487 U.S. 1012 at 1019.
29. See Orcutt et al. (2001) for a full discussion of the study and the high ethical standards that were maintained, in addition to the protective measures that were taken to ensure that children were not harmed.

REFERENCES

American Academy of Child and Adolescent Psychiatry. (1999). *1999 violence fact sheet*. Retrieved January 30, 2002, from http://www.aacap.org/info_families/ National Facts/99ViolFctSh.htm.
American Academy of Pediatrics. (1999). The child in court: A subject review. *Pediatrics, 104*(5), 1145-1148.

Beckett, J. M. (1994). The true value of the confrontation clause: A study of child sex abuse trials. *Georgetown Law Journal, 82*, 1605-1642.

Bergdoll v. Kane, 694 A.2d 1155 (Pa. Cmwlth. 1997), affmd 731 A.2d 1261 (Pa. 1999).

Berger, D.A. (1999, June). Proposed changes to Rules for Courts-Martial 804, 914A and Military Rule of Evidence 611(d)(2): A partial step towards compliance with the Child Victims' and Child Witnesses' Rights Statute. *Army Lawyer*, 19-31.

Bowman, J. J. Hon. (1998). Balancing the emotional needs of a child and the due process rights of a defendant in sexual abuse cases. *DuPage County Bar Association Brief, January*. Retrieved January 31, 2002, from http://www.dcba.org/brief/janissue/1998/art10198.html.

Bureau of Justice Assistance. (2001). *Annual report to Congress: Creating a safer America: Fiscal year 2000.* Retrieved November 30, 2001, from http://www.ncjrs.org/txtfiles1/bja/187302.txt.

Catalog of Federal Domestic Assistance. (2001). *16.611: Closed-circuit televising of child victims of abuse (CCTV).* Retrieved November 30, 2001, from http://www.cfda.gov/public/viewprog.asp?progid=554.

Children as Victims. (2000, May). *1999 National Report Series Juvenile Justice Bulletin* (NCJ 180753). Washington, D.C.: U.S. Department of Justice, OJJDP Bulletin.

Commonwealth v. Ludwig, 527 Pa. 472, 594 A.2d 281 (1991).

Commonwealth v. Willis, 716 S.W.2d 224 (Ky. 1986).

Coy v. Iowa, 487 U.S. 1012; 108 S.Ct. 2798; 101 L.Ed. 2d 857 (1988).

Crime Control Act, Pub. L. No. 101-647 (1990).

Danner v. Kentucky, 525 U.S. 1010, 119 S.Ct. 529; 142 L.Ed. 2d 439 (1998).

Davies, G. (1999). The impact of television on the presentation and reception of children's testimony. *International Journal of Law and Psychiatry, 22*, 242-256.

Delany-Shabazz, R. (1995). *VOCA: Helping victims of child abuse, FS9526.* Retrieved November 30, 2001, from http://www.ncjrs.org/txtfiles/voca.txt.

Goodman, G. S., Levine, M., Melton, G. B., & Ogden, D. W. (1991). Child witnesses and the confrontation clause: The American Psychological Association brief in *Maryland v. Craig. Law and Human Behavior, 15*, 13-29.

Goodman, G. S., Tobey, A. E., Batterman-Faunce, J. M., Orcutt, H., Thomas, S., Shapiro, C., & Sachsenmaier, T. (1998). Face-to-face confrontation: Effects of closed-circuit technology on children's eyewitness testimony and jurors' decisions. *Law and Human Behavior, 22*, 165-203.

Kentucky v. Stincer, 482 U.S. 730; 107 S.Ct. 2658; 96 L.Ed.2d 631 (1987).

Marx v. Texas, 528 U.S. 1034; 120 S.Ct. (1999).

Maryland v. Craig, 497 U.S. 836; 110 S.Ct. 3157; 111 L.Ed.2d 666 (1990).

National Center for Victims of Crime. (1999). *FYI: Special provisions for children in the criminal justice system.* Retrieved November 30, 2001, from http://www.ncvc.org/Infolink/Info58.htm.

National Conference of Commissioners on Uniform State Laws. (2001). *Uniform child witness testimony by alternative methods act.* Retrieved February 3, 2002, from http://www.law.upenn.edu/bll/ulc/ucwtbama/child601.htm.

National Conference of Commissioners on Uniform State Laws. (2002). *Uniform child witness testimony by alternative methods act.* Retrieved January 3, 2003, from http://www.law.upenn.edu/bll/ulc/ucwtbama/2002act.pdf.

Orcutt, H. K., Goodman, G. S., Tobey, A. E., Batterman-Faunce, J. M., & Thomas, S. (2001). Detecting deception in children's testimony: Factfinders' abilities to reach the truth in open court and closed-circuit trials. *Law and Human Behavior, 25,* 339-372.

Paulsen, D. J. (2003). No safe place: Assessing spatial patterns of child maltreatment victimization. *Journal of Aggression, Maltreatment & Trauma, 8*(1/2), 63-85.

People v. Fitzpatrick, 158 Ill. 2d 360 (1994).

People of the State Of Illinois, Appellant, v. Anthony W. Lofton, Appellee. (2000). Retrieved May 6, 2003, from http://www.state.il.us/court/Opinions/SupremeCourt/2000/November/Opinions/Html/87382.htm.

Roesch, R., Golding, S. L., Hans, V. P., & Reppucci, N. D. (1991). Social sciences and the courts: The role of amicus curiae briefs. *Law and Human Behavior, 15,* 1-11.

Senate approves Greenleaf child witness measure. (2001, June 12). News release retrieved on February 1, 2002, from http://greenleaf.pasenategop.com/sb211.html.

Small, M. (1994). Constitutional challenges to child witness protection legislation: An update. *Violence and Victims, 9,* 369-377.

State v. Brady, 575 N.E.2d 981 (Ind. 1991).

Underwager, R., & Wakefield, H. (1992). Poor psychology produces poor law. *Law and Human Behavior, 16,* 233-243.

United States v. Anderson, 51 M.J. 145 (1999).

United States v. Daulton, 45 M.J. 212 (1996).

United States v. Garcia, 7 F.3d 885 (9th Cir. 1993).

United States v. Longstreath, 45 M.J. 366 (1996).

United States v. Moses, 137 F.3d 894 (6th Cir. 1998).

United States v. Thompson, 31 M.J. 168 (1990).

Victims of Child Abuse Act, 18 U.S.C. §§403, 2258, 3509 (1990).

Addressing Family Violence Within Juvenile Courts: Promising Practices to Improve Intervention Outcomes

Sarah M. Buel

SUMMARY. Whether as overt or underlying issues, family violence is prevalent within juvenile court caseloads, yet often is not identified within intake and disposition. Focusing on juvenile victimization of parents, and to a lesser extent teen dating partners, this article discusses model programs emerging in juvenile courts specifically addressing these issues. A comparative analysis of the drug court trend is explored in the context of its applicability for specialized family violence applications in the Juvenile Court. An overview of the King County (Washington) Juvenile Court's Step-Up Program and the Santa Clara County (California) Juvenile Court's Family Violence program is offered, followed by the process by which the Travis County (Texas) Juvenile Court has implemented a program similar to these models. Effective interventions with violent families must be informed by the domestic violence

Address correspondence to: Sarah M. Buel, University of Texas School of Law, 727 East Dean Keeton Street, Austin, TX 78705 (E-mail: sbuel@mail.law.utexas.edu).

The author wishes to thank David Bain, Emily Fry, Chike Okpara, Nina Marie Olivo, and Monica Valdez for their invaluable research assistance.

[Haworth co-indexing entry note]: "Addressing Family Violence Within Juvenile Courts: Promising Practices to Improve Intervention Outcomes." Buel, Sarah M. Co-published simultaneously in *Journal of Aggression, Maltreatment & Trauma* (The Haworth Maltreatment & Trauma Press, an imprint of The Haworth Press, Inc.) Vol. 8, No. 3 (#17), 2003, pp. 273-307; and: *The Victimization of Children: Emerging Issues* (ed: Janet L. Mullings, James W. Marquart, and Deborah J. Hartley) The Haworth Maltreatment & Trauma Press, an imprint of The Haworth Press, Inc., 2003, pp. 273-307. Single or multiple copies of this article are available for a fee from The Haworth Document Delivery Service [1-800-HAWORTH, 9:00 a.m. - 5:00 p.m. (EST). E-mail address: docdelivery@haworthpress.com].

http://www.haworthpress.com/web/JAMT
Digital Object Identifier: 10.1300/J146v08n01_03

community's treatment expertise, building on the paradigm of youth resilience. *[Article copies available for a fee from The Haworth Document Delivery Service: 1-800-HAWORTH. E-mail address: <docdelivery@haworth press.com> Website: <http://www.HaworthPress.com> © 2003 by The Haworth Press, Inc. All rights reserved.]*

KEYWORDS. Family violence, domestic abuse, juvenile delinquency, parental victimization, teen dating violence

INTRODUCTION

While media attention consistently focuses on youth violence in schools, it is rare to see coverage regarding the widespread problem of teen perpetrated domestic violence[1] (E. Hyman, personal communication, March 22, 2001; Valente, 1996). Indeed, the violence perpetrated against teachers has reached such levels that many U.S. schools are offering safety planning information to teachers regarding protecting themselves from students, and the National Education Association has provided every teacher with a free life insurance policy valued at $150,000 (Sierra, 2001). Yet there appears to be a dearth of assistance for parents victimized by their own children, though battered women often report this phenomenon as accompanying the abuse from an adult partner (Bancroft, 2002). Occasionally afternoon talk shows will present desperate parents confronting abusive adolescents or a tearful teen lamenting that she cannot leave her violent boyfriend, but sorely lacking is any practical guidance for dealing with the devastating impact of youth-perpetrated physical and psychological abuse. As it is unrealistic to expect talk shows to provide remedial guidance, juvenile justice professionals must fill the void. However, most juvenile justice systems have few resources to offer either intimate partners or family members being battered by a youth. Scant attention has been paid to the issue, in part, because of the reluctance of parents, siblings, and partners to involve the aggressor in the juvenile court system, particularly with the specter of adult prison or a secure youth facility. For families of color, dramatically disproportionate confinement of their children only serves to further alienate them from the justice system: In 1995, while youth of color constituted just 32% of the juvenile population in the United States, they comprised 68% of the youth in secure detention (Office of Juvenile Justice and Delinquency Prevention, 1998).

While in no way minimizing the gravity of teen dating violence, this article will focus primarily on the victimization of parents by juveniles and the model programs emerging in juvenile courts to address this phenomenon. Part I will provide a brief overview of the problem: Family violence is prevalent in the juvenile court caseloads, but is neither identified nor seriously considered in most dispositions. Part II begins with a cursory, comparative analysis of the drug court trend and its applicability for specialized family violence applications in the Juvenile Court. Part II also introduces the King County (WA) Juvenile Court's Step-Up Program, which directly addresses family violence with intervention programs for the perpetrating youth *and* abused parents.

Part III presents the outstanding Santa Clara County (CA) Juvenile Court's Family Violence program, highlighting its primary components as a model worthy of replication. In Part IV, the process by which the Travis County (TX) Juvenile Court is implementing a program similar to the above-referenced models is detailed. This chapter concludes that juvenile courts must address the family violence presenting as an overt or underlying issue in so many of their cases and asserts that it is imperative for the rich expertise of the family violence community to inform the intervention services.

Part I: An Overview of the Problem

Domestic violence presents in juvenile court cases primarily in three forms. The first may not be readily apparent as it may be the underlying cause of the youth's delinquent behavior rather that the presenting offense. Here, the youth is charged with what appears to be an unrelated offense (e.g., theft or drug possession), but directed inquiry reveals that the juvenile's mother and/or his siblings and himself are being abused. In the second, the youth is charged with battering a parent, caretaker, or sibling, while in the third form, s/he is charged with abusing an intimate partner, usually in the context of a dating relationship (Levy, 1993). Often the domestic violence goes undetected and untreated because most juvenile courts do not screen for it, and if found, do not have specialized resources to which they can refer the parties.

Effects of Violence Exposure on Youth

Children who grow up in a violent family are more likely to abuse others or to be victims of abuse as adolescents and adults (Bowker, Arbitell, &

McFerron, 1988; Gondolf, 2002; Jaffe, Wolfe, & Wilson, 1990; Lehrman, 1996; Pagelow, 1990; Rabin, 1995; Rhea, Chafey, Dohner, & Terragno, 1996; Shichor & Tibbetts, 2002). Those children who do not replicate the abuse generally have had at least one adult protecting them or clearly speaking out against the violence. Children need not be directly beaten in order to take on violent and delinquent behavior: It is enough for them to witness their mother's[2] abuse (Dutton, 1995).

The Massachusetts' Department of Youth Services (Guarino, 1985) found that children growing up in violent homes had a six times higher likelihood of attempting suicide, a 24% greater chance of committing sexual assault crimes, a 74% increased incidence of crimes committed against persons, and a 50% higher chance of abusing drugs and/or alcohol. Another study comparing youth who were delinquent with those who were non-offending found that a history of family abuse was the primary distinction between the two groups (Miller, 1989). Such youth are in pain, and they are too often self-medicating in response to an adult community disregarding the violence within their families (Dutton, 1995).

Arguing that juveniles who assault a parent often are not entirely to blame, Director of the Travis County (TX) Juvenile Court Services Brian Snyder (in Fry, 2000) suggests that the abused parent may have been the perpetrator of violence against the child or another family member in the past. While prior victimization does not justify the juvenile's present actions, it certainly helps explain why some youth have adopted an abusive mode of conflict resolution (Jacobson & Gottman, 1998).

Dating Violence Among Youth

Twenty percent of female high school students report being sexually or physically abused by a dating partner, but due to underreporting, the actual number is no doubt higher (Rennison & Wilchans, 2001). Such violence adversely impacts the safety and health of teenage girls as it strongly correlates with pregnancy, substance abuse, harmful weight control, suicide attempts, and dangerous sexual behavior. In 1997 and again in 1999, the Massachusetts Youth Risk Behavior Survey (YRBS) was the first to ask teens if they had "ever been hurt physically or sexually by a date or someone they were going out with. This would include being shoved, slapped, hit, or forced into any sexual activity." Of the 4,163 teen girls surveyed, approximately 6% reported both physical and sexual victimization. The researchers report that, with regard to racial and ethnic differences in reporting dating violence, their findings are inconclusive (Silverman, Raj, Mucci, & Hathaway, 2001). The victimized teens were more likely to use alcohol, tobacco, and cocaine, and were less apt to use condoms when engaging in sexual activity. Such behaviors increase the likelihood of the teen dating violence victims contracting sexually transmitted diseases and becoming pregnant (Silverman et al., 2001). Not only does teen pregnancy increase the likelihood of high school non-completion and concomitant poverty, but also of prenatal violence. In one study, over 16% of teens reported prenatal abuse, with 9.4% describing severe violence, including kicking and stabbing (Covington, Justason, & Wright, 2001). Far more likely to deliver pre-term and abuse alcohol, 56% of the abused, pregnant teens indicated abdominal trauma (Covington et al., 2001). Teen dating violence can be an early predictor of victim and offender patterns that may continue without effective early intervention programs.

Although one in three teenagers will suffer physical abuse in a dating relationship (Harrison, 1997), most schools and courts do not address the issue at all. Barrie Levy, a psychotherapist who has written three books on teen dating violence, cautions that the signs of abuse may not be easy to detect. Some warning signs include the batterer's controlling behavior and extreme jealousy, and the victim's withdrawal from friends and hypervigilence toward obeying the abusive partner's rules.

PROMISING PRACTICES TO ADDRESS THE PROBLEM

Part II: Drug Courts and the King County, WA, Juvenile Courts Step-Up Program

Routine screening, suitable referrals, and judicial oversight for both victims and offenders should become institutionalized practices within our juvenile courts. As the *Journal of the American Medical Association* (e.g., Silverman et al., 2001) and numerous researchers (e.g., Rodriguez, Bauer, McLoughlin, & Grumbach, 1999) suggest that health care professionals should address dating violence among their patients, juvenile courts should do the same. The opportunities for effective interventions are numerous, as juvenile courts can fashion case dispositions that include an appropriate balance of rehabilitation and punishment for the offender, while affording victims access to safety as well as counseling and other services.

Lessons from Drug Courts Applied to Family Violence Juvenile Courts

While there exist several key distinctions between drug courts and Family Violence Juvenile Courts, closer examination is essential to engender replication of the successful models. A National Institute of Justice study of the Dade County Drug Court–the first in the country–reported a 33% decrease in recidivism for drug court graduates than for those chemically dependent defendants in the control group. Similar results are being seen in other drug courts, with reports that 50-65% of their graduates actually cease substance abuse. With well over 200 bona fide drug courts (National Association of Drug Court Professionals [NADCP], 1997)[3] operating across the country as of 1997, and a substantial body of literature evaluating their efficacy, ten key components can be identified for adaptation in the emerging Family Violence Juvenile Courts.

Key component #1: With drug courts, the justice system integrates substance abuse treatment services into case processing (NADCP, 1997). Given that the purpose of the Family Violence Juvenile Court is cessation of all youth-perpetrated violence and related criminal behavior, teen battering intervention services must be utilized in all cases in which abusive youth are present. With substance abuse treatment, it has been found that those ordered to participate have comparable success rates as those who volunteer (Hubbard, Marsden, Rachal, Harwood, Cavanaugh, & Gnizburg, 1989). Likewise, batterer's treatment providers have long reported that *most* abusers have a lower recidivism rate when coerced into treatment (Adams, 1989). Thus, all professionals must be united in their insistence that the youth successfully complete the batterer's intervention program, save for extremely rare and extenuating circumstances. Benchmarks of program effectiveness would include the on-going collaboration of all related service providers and the juvenile court judges retaining the practice of monitoring the youth's compliance.

Key component #2: The prosecutor and defense attorney adopt a non-adversarial stance with the goal of protecting the parties' due process rights while advancing public safety. The long-established practice of defense attorneys has focused not only on denying any criminal behavior, but also resisting any attempts at rehabilitative services (NADCP, 1997). Without compromising the defense attorney's role as advocate for the accused, she can provide guidance on the benefits of seeking counseling to deal with his violence. Based on this author's experience after 25 years of working with domestic violence and juvenile justice cases in the courts of five states, with seven years as a prosecutor, prosecutors often felt so overwhelmed by high caseloads that they were willing make plea agreements that lacked treatment mandates. In the drug court model on which the Family Violence Juvenile Court should be predicated, the prosecutor and defense counsel collaborate as a team. The team's goal is ensuring that the juvenile ceases all violence with the pending court case a secondary concern. One performance benchmark reflects the close participation of defense and prosecution in the planning and implementation process to negotiate through the challenges inherent in the changing of roles while adjusting to a new program. Another is insisting upon an experienced, designated judge, prosecutor, defense attorney, and probation officer to ensure consistency and stability in the Family Violence Juvenile Court.

Key component #3: The early identification of substance abusers means the drug court can quickly immerse them in treatment programs. Making denial more difficult, arrest brings the offense to light and creates a significant opportunity for expeditious treatment (NADCP, 1997). Similarly, with Family Violence Juvenile Courts' one goal is to expedite the time between arrest and case disposition. Performance benchmarks include the use of a written screening tool establishing the criteria on which referrals will be made. The youth must also be quickly notified of all program requirements as well as the benefits of successful completion, and then enrolled immediately in the mandated programs.

Key component #4: Through drug courts defendants can gain access to a gamut of chemical dependency and other rehabilitation services (NADCP, 1997). It is understood that the causes of juvenile family violence are complex and varied, shaped by the cumulative cultural and social experiences of that youth. If the court's interventions are to prove effective, the primary and mental health, substance abuse, education, and other social services resources must be utilized as indicated. Co-occurring problems may include depression, sexually-transmitted diseases and HIV, homelessness, learning disabilities, domestic violence being perpetrated by the mother's partner, and attempting to cope with the trauma of childhood physical and/or sexual abuse (for in-depth discussions of childhood physical and sexual abuse, see Bottoms, Nielsen, Murray, & Filipas, this volume; Bruhn, this volume; McGlone, this volume). Age, race, gender, ethnicity, culture, sexual orientation, and other youth characteristics must also be considered in fashioning *individualized* intervention plans. If the community lacks appropriate treatment options, the Family Violence Juvenile Court can serve as the impetus for the establishment of needed programs. Performance benchmarks must cover periodic assessment of the youth to address changing needs, ensuring that treatment services are accessible and comprehensive, as well as accountable to the court and the participants (NADCP, 1997).

Key component #5: Frequent drug and alcohol testing monitor the user's abstinence and serve as an accurate, objective, and efficient means to establish accountability. Chemical abuse testing should be random, with urine or hair samples collected in the presence of staff and the judge immediately notified of any failed tests (NADCP, 1997). The corollary for Family Violence Juvenile Courts is to establish a mechanism by which the youth appears regularly before the judge to report on his progress, but also that staff maintain contact with the victims as a check on the accuracy of the defendant's statements. Performance benchmarks should incorporate safety planning with victims as they are being consulted regarding the perpetrator's current behavior.

Additionally, the youth and all victims should be made aware of possible outcomes as the offender goes through the intervention programs. For example, batterer's treatment experts explain that batterers will frequently stop the physical violence in the aftermath of arrest, but may intensify the psychological abuse (Adams, 1989; Dutton, 1995; Gondolf, 2002; Jacobson & Gottman, 1998). At this juncture the victim support groups are helpful in teaching the abused parents how to set limits, what behavior should be reported to the court, and on-going safety planning. Since juveniles being treated for chemical dependency may seek alternative substances when deprived of their drug of choice (Cooper, 1995), safety planning must include education regarding the indicators and patterns of new, unlawful behavior.

Key component #6: The drug court professionals closely coordinate their responses to litigants' level of compliance. A continuum of responses will be necessary to address incremental successes as well as likely relapses. Planned, complementary strategies must be the hallmark of all involved professionals (NADCP, 1997). Particularly with juvenile offenders, the court should reward their progress based on a realistic evaluation of their abilities. The youth's punctual arrival at court and treatment programs, active engagement in the services, school attendance, cessation of the violence, and similar positive steps should be acknowledged by the court. Depending on the degree of compliance, the judge could offer praise and encouragement, decrease supervision, reduce the number of court appearances, eliminate or decrease the fines and fees, shorten the duration of probation, suspend or decrease time in detention, and, ultimately, close the case. Noncompliance should result in punitive responses, perhaps in the reverse direction of those listed above (NADCP, 1997).

Key component #7: Continuing judicial involvement with each defendant is critical. As the court team's leader, the judge is usually knowledgeable about treatment options and prepared to insist upon compliance. Performance benchmarks should include regular status hearings to increase the likelihood of improved behavior, not only on the part of the youth but also with all of the system professionals. Just as effective drug courts entail judges reaching beyond the traditional parameters of independent practice (NADCP, 1997), so too must those presiding over Family Violence Juvenile Courts. Judges taking an active, supervisory role with abusive youth will more often be rewarded with violence cessation than those wed to maintaining the status quo.

Key component #8: To gauge the program's effectiveness, careful monitoring and evaluation must be integral to daily court functioning. Concretely formulated goals, defined in measurable terms, will assist in achieving program accountability. Constructive evaluation involves the process of the court's on-going collection and analysis of program data to measure its efficacy. Such studies can then be utilized to adjust court procedures, modify therapeutic interventions (NADCP, 1997), and make whatever other changes are so indicated. With Family Violence Juvenile Courts, much new ground is being broken as we gain expertise regarding the similarities and distinctions between adult and youth offenders, victims, and treatment providers. Thus, flexibility in implementation, as well as program monitoring and evaluation, are essential to achieving the goals of victim safety and offender accountability.

Key component #9: On-going interdisciplinary training and education encourage effectual planning and implementation of drug court operations (NADCP, 1997). All court personnel should be mandated to attend these sessions to enhance the stakeholders' understanding of program goals and be exposed to cutting edge practices to improve the programs. National and regional conferences can augment local trainings, with each proving invaluable in maintaining high staff morale and enthusiasm for tackling these tough cases. It is essential to select motivational trainers who can present realistic, practical recommendations for program enhancement, ensuring that the speakers are also culturally competent and reflect the rich diversity of the community being served. The goal is to ensure that juvenile court staff and stakeholders maintain a high level of commitment to the provision of optimal services.

Key component #10: The drug court's efficacy is augmented by building partnerships among community-based programs, public entities, and every facet of the court. Functioning as a conduit of information to the public and related agencies, the court should take on a leadership role in facilitating such linkages (NADCP, 1997). Without the foundation of such partnerships, the court will find its mission overwhelming–to the detriment of the distressed juveniles and their families. From faith community leaders, nurses, and teachers to sports coaches, police officers, and counselors, there exist many stakeholders who can be instrumental in turning around violent youth *if* courts routinely involve them in the intervention plans. Community-based providers can also assist the court in identifying those practices leading to differential treatment of minority youth.

Adapting the model of adult drug courts to include children was taken a step further by Santa Clara County (CA) Judge Leonard Edwards in establishing a Juvenile Dependency Drug Treatment Court, designed to treat chemically dependent parents who wish to retain custody of their children. Judge Edwards was determined to improve the assessment process, increase the number of in-patient beds for addicted mothers and their children, and designate a weekly court session to this population. Beginning in October of 1998, the Juvenile Dependency Drug Treatment Court has convened on Wednesdays and has had 75 participants and 32 graduates as of 2001. Judge Edwards believes that the parents (95% of whom are mothers) are more motivated to cease their substance abuse when the court is clear that reunification with their children is contingent upon staying clean. An innovative component of the program developed when two graduates were hired to be "Mentor Moms" to those clients undergoing treatment (Edwards, 2001).

The importance of such models cannot be underestimated; if the substance abusing parent receives immediate, intensive treatment under the scrutiny of a court that is strict but caring, the youth are far less likely to become involved in unlawful activities. Reno's (NV) Judge Charles McGee found that by pairing foster grandparents with drug court families, the chemically dependent parents were exposed to modeling of healthy parenting styles to which many of the clients had never been exposed. Additionally, Judge McGee stresses that since courts should end their intervention as soon as is feasible, the foster grandparents can maintain on-going contact–sometimes still on a daily or weekly basis. Such guidance appears to greatly help the clients maintain sobriety, indicating that courts must be open minded about integrating creative components that benefit all involved (McGee, 2001).

The Step-Up Program in King County, Washington

In King County, Washington, the Department of Judicial Administration and Prosecuting Attorney's Office established the Step-Up Program in their Juvenile Court (Step-Up, 1999).[4] Step-Up is essentially a domestic violence and sexual assault unit, prioritizing the protection of victims while offering specific services to hold juvenile perpetrators accountable. As part of accomplishing the latter, Step-Up developed a batterer's intervention program targeting 13-17 year olds who batter their parents or dating partners. Separately, Step-Up offers a support group for the abused parents. Unlike the youth who are court ordered to attend the Step-Up batterer's intervention program, the parents' participation in their support group is voluntary (Step-Up, 1999).

Understanding that anger management programs are often ineffective in dealing with domestic violence perpetrators, the Step-Up Program modeled its juvenile batterer's intervention program after the Duluth Domestic Abuse Intervention Project (DAIP) for adult male perpetrators. The DAIP is clear that its primary objective is victim safety, achieved in part by insisting that the batterers acknowledge their choice to be abusive, then teaching them models of healthy relationships (Pence, 1999). Believing that youth who batter dating partners need different intervention that those who abuse their parents, the Step-Up Program's group facilitator Greg Routt has developed separate curricula. While the dating violence course teaches the youth to consider the victim as his equal, in the family violence curriculum he is taught that the adult parent is in charge and must be respected (G. Routt, personal communication, March 14, 2001).

Employing a Cognitive Behavioral Treatment Model, the Step-Up Program begins from the standpoint that the youth's sense of entitlement to be abusive is predictive of such behavior. The Step-Up sessions last for 1.5 hours, meeting once a week for six months (Step-Up, 1999). Prior to admission to the program, a comprehensive intake session is scheduled with both parent and child. In order to increase the likelihood of more truthful parental and youth disclosures, as well as safety for any victimized parties, each is interviewed separately. The interviewer screens for a history of family violence, as well as any medical, substance abuse, mental health, or school problems impacting the juvenile. Upon admission to the Step-Up Program, the youth, mothers, and fathers are each assigned to different groups. Separating the mothers and fathers was found to be necessary as 35% of the juveniles reported witnessing domestic violence between their parents, with 88% identifying their father as the abuser (Step-Up, 1999).

Juvenile Group. The Step-Up Group facilitators list six primary goals they seek to achieve during the six-month program. First, while it may sound obvious, it is essential that the juveniles understand what behavior is considered abusive. Those who have witnessed violence as the preferred method of conflict resolution within their homes may have no concept of non-abusive alternatives. Adapted from the Duluth *Power and Control Wheel*, an *Abuse of Family Members Wheel* and a *Mutual Respect Wheel*[5] are used to provide practical guidance to engender changed behaviors. Second, the facilitators work with each youth batterer to identify the rationale used to excuse the violence. The group format lends itself well to discussions on violence in the lives of each juvenile, the media images of intimate relationships, and societal gender stereotypes. By isolating the situations that trigger their violent behavior, then assuming non-abusive alternatives, the youth will satisfy goals three and four. The fifth goal requires that the juvenile acknowledge responsibility for his abuse and be clear that the victim is not to blame for the violence. Finally, the Step-Up Program seeks to help the abusive youth learn to empathize with their victims (Step-Up, 1999).

In addition to mandatory attendance at every week's session, the youth must complete six requirements in furtherance of the above goals. Each participant must maintain a "Time-Out Log" in order to document what s/he was thinking and all actions taken when tempted to use violence against a family member or dating partner. This exercise is designed to help the youth recognize when he is choosing violence over a peaceful resolution. In the group sessions, each participant shares the time-out log entries from the week. The teen perpetrator is also required to write a *Responsibility Letter* to the victim, describing an abusive incident and taking full responsibility for his/her actions. The intent of the letter is not to be sent to the victim, but rather to be shared in the weekly batterer's group. Another responsibility is completion of an *Abuse Journal* and an *Empathy Letter*, in which the youth acknowledges the physical and mental trauma suffered by his victim.

Utilizing the *Abuse of Family Members Wheel* and the *Mutual Respect Wheel*, the juvenile reports to the group his positive and negative behaviors toward family members during the week. Finally, the parent and youth engage in a role-play in front of the group, giving the offender practice in respectfully interacting with his parent and allowing the group to offer suggestions (Step-Up, 1999).

Parent Group. The Step-Up Program's Parent Group focuses on teaching safety planning and response tactics that increase the chances of resolving the conflicts without violence. Parents are advised to call the police when their child becomes dangerous. Due to parental guilt, shame, and a myriad of other valid reasons, they may need "permission" to involve law enforcement officials (Buel, 1999).[6] By clarifying how to avoid or leave the abusive confrontation with her child, the parent can develop a safety plan. Given the chaos inherent in a violent incident, it is essential for the parent to have a prepared action plan–including utilizing any support network the family has. Just as with the juvenile perpetrators, the parents must learn that the abuse is most often not based in anger, but rather as a means of exerting control within the family. Step-Up also has an excellent brochure, explaining its program and dynamics of domestic violence, as well as community resources to which the parents can turn (Step-Up, 1999).[7]

Facilitators also remind the parents that they are role models, and if their children learn that violence is an appropriate means of resolving conflict, they are more likely to model such conduct (Lehrman, 1996) and adopt other delinquent and harmful behaviors (Guarino, 1995). For example, the Massachusetts' Department of Youth Services found that children growing up in violent homes had a six times higher likelihood of attempting suicide, a 24% greater chance of committing sexual assault crimes, a 74% increased incidence of crimes committed against the person, and a 50% higher chance of abusing drugs and/or alcohol (Guarino, 1995).[8] Another study comparing youth who were delinquent versus those who were non-offending found that a history of family abuse was the primary distinction between the two groups (Miller, 1989). Believing that children tend to emulate the interaction model of the adults in their home, social learning theorists offer that youth witnessing violence between their parents will likely internalize the assumption that this represents acceptable behavior (Kratcoski, 1985). As parents may be unaware of the degree to which their abusive conduct impacts their children, this group is an ideal starting point.

Finally, parents in the support group are encouraged to identify the support mechanisms to which they can turn upon completion of the program. Facilitators continue to urge parents to call on law enforcement, the youth's probation officer, and other community resources to address any on-going abuse. An attempt is made to individualize the long-term safety plan, utilizing assistance from youth ministers, school counselors, etc., depending on the juvenile's interests and contacts.

Part III: The Santa Clara County, CA, Juvenile Court's Family Violence Program

In April of 1999, a Juvenile Delinquency Domestic/Family Violence Court (hereinafter Juvenile FV Court) was established in San Jose, under the leadership of Judge Eugene Hyman, who previously had presided over the Santa Clara County Domestic Violence Court. With one assistant district attorney and two probation officers assigned to it, the Juvenile FV Court is in session each Wednesday afternoon. The specialized probation officers attend at least eight hours of training on domestic/family violence issues. Court support for the effort is derived in part from an understanding that addressing family violence in younger defendants has a higher likelihood of success. For example, Judge Jerome Brock, of the adult domestic violence court in Santa Clara County, said, "When I heard about it, my first thought was, 'What a stroke of genius.' I'm dealing with adults, trying to break that cycle, and it's a lot more difficult when they're thirty, forty or fifty" (Guido, 2000).

Currently, youth convicted of domestic violence-related crimes can continue on probation until they are 21 years of age. If they are still on probation but recidivate after turning 18, the District Attorney's Office will turn over the case to the juvenile division. The Deputy Probation Officers handles most of the juvenile family violence cases, with an average of 35 active cases all involving the clients, victims, and their respective parents. These youth remain on a "maximum level supervision," meaning that office and home visits are combined with a once monthly appearance in court to report to Judge Hyman on their progress. "That's what changes a batterer's behavior," Deputy Probation Officer Karen Berlin notes. "It's everyone–police, judges, probation, the community–giving the perpetrator the same message so he knows there's no way out for him. That we, as a community, won't tolerate domestic violence" (Guido, 2000, p. 1).

Through the adoption of a written protocol, the Santa Clara County Juvenile Probation Department (1999) has standardized its procedures for handling family violence cases. The protocol was established with two goals in mind, the first being the protection of abuse victims from further harm. To that end, probation officers provide parents with educational materials, describing how to obtain a protective order and file a police report, should the abuse recur. Based on each family's needs, the parents are also given an extensive list of community resources, emphasizing those assisting with emergency support (Santa Clara County Probation Department, 1999).

The Probation Department's second goal is to ensure that the juvenile batterer takes total responsibility for his abusive behavior. Successful completion of their Juvenile Batterer's Intervention Program is thus a requirement, in addition to any substance abuse, mental health, or other counseling indicated as necessary. Juvenile probation officers view their role as being both supportive to the youth in furtherance of behavior modification, as well as punitive to engender adherence to social norms of nonviolence. Of particular importance is the probation officer's investigation of all violence occurring within the youth's family, not only that perpetrated by or against the youth. They recognize that if the mother is currently being battered by an adult partner, the youth is likely modeling that behavior and will not cease unless all violence within the home is addressed (Santa Clara County Probation Department, 1999). In Santa Clara County, when a law enforcement officer brings a juvenile domestic violence perpetrator to their detention facility, the DV/FV Unit immediately receives the referral for review. If the Supervising Probation Officer decides that the case warrants specialized attention, the DV/FV Unit will retain it. The factors considered in making this determination include evaluating the severity of the incident, studying the history of abuse within this family, reading any Child Protective Services reports, and as a priority, assessing the parent's level of safety (Santa Clara County Probation Department, 1999).

As in most other juvenile court jurisdictions, Santa Clara County affords each youthful offender the right to a detention hearing to determine whether s/he should be released pending the next court date. If the judge decides that the parent's safety will be jeopardized by the juvenile's release, s/he will be held. While most juvenile courts premise the youth's freedom upon his agreeing to "conditions of release,"[9] the Santa Clara County Court usually issues a *Juvenile Delinquency Protection Order*. Very similar to most states' adult domestic violence protective orders, this one specifically mandates that the youth "Shall not annoy, harass, strike, threaten, sexually assault, batter, or otherwise disturb the peace of the protected persons named below." However, unlike the adult protective orders, the juvenile order clearly precludes any witness tampering: "Shall not attempt to or actually prevent or dissuade any victim or witness from attending a hearing, testifying or making a report to any law enforcement agency or person" (Santa Clara County Probation Department, 1999). Upon issuance, the Santa Clara County Court clerk's office sends the sheriff's department a fax of the order, and the sheriff enters the protection order into the California Statewide Domestic Violence Registry.

Subsequent to the detention hearing, the probation officer commences an in-depth investigation of the juvenile's home situation, regardless of whether the youth is held or released. The probation officer obtains copies of all law enforcement and child protection reports, in addition to collecting the criminal histories of all household members. Of particular interest to the court will be any evidence of past or current family violence that may be contributing to the current crisis. Concurrent with the investigation, the probation officer also informs the parents of the Victim Witness Assistance Program within the District Attorney's Office of their right to offer a *Victim Impact Statement* at the juvenile's sentencing, and notice of all upcoming court dates (Santa Clara County Probation Department, 1999). Given that most parents lack even basic knowledge of the juvenile justice system and are quite intimidated by the process, the probation officers attempt to quell some of their unease by the provision of on-going guidance.

The full report is then presented to the court at the disposition hearing, with the probation officer including recommendations for the youth's rehabilitation plan. Those cases involving family violence most often include the following four suggestions. The first involves mandatory attendance at the twenty-six-week juvenile batterer intervention program at the Center for Human Development of San Jose (Santa Clara County Probation Department, 1999). Judge Hyman orders the juvenile batterers into the program as a condition of their probation. This option is available only to males as the groups are gender-specific and none currently exist for females. Part of the basis for this deficiency is founded in the belief that the vast majority of juvenile female offenders are better suited for group counseling geared to victims, as they are often responding in self-defense or as a result of childhood trauma, such as sexual and/or physical abuse (Hoyt & Scherer, 1998). While not offered as an excuse for their behavior, it is nonetheless essential to screen for prior abuse in order to provide the most effective rehabilitative services.

If a Juvenile Delinquency Protective Order was not issued at the detention hearing, the probation officer will usually request one at the disposition hearing. Based on the Full Faith and Credit provisions of the U.S. Constitution,[10] the Juvenile Delinquency Protective Order is enforceable throughout the country. Furthermore, violation of the order constitutes a criminal offense for which the youth will be immediately arrested.[11]

There are three probation officers assigned to this court, with two of them focusing on teen dating violence and the other on family violence (parent, sibling, or other family member) cases. In their family violence caseload, the court currently has slightly more females than males. Judge Hyman and his staff are able to identify the presence of mental health issues among this juvenile population, with females also presenting more often with mental health issues (as defined in the *Diagnostic and Statistical Manual of Mental Disorders*, 4th edition [American Psychiatric Association, 1994]). Perpetrating females are also required to attend an intervention class, but it is not yet as specialized as the one for males as their numbers are still too small to justify. Judge Hyman laments that the youth batterer intervention program also does not have the cultural specificity that their adult programs have achieved (E. Hyman, personal communication, March 22, 2001). He also reports being surprised that, thus far, their research suggests that those youth who batter family members do not necessarily cross over to also batter partners. Certainly, they have seen some youth being violent with both family members and dating partners, but not to the extent they had expected.

Another unique component of the Santa Clara County Juvenile Court's program is the focus not only on the youth's violent behavior, but an in-depth evaluation of that child's home and school life, especially any exposure to violence. Many juvenile courts pay scant attention to the defendant's concurrent victimization, choosing what appears expeditious by limiting the scope of its investigations. The illusion of expediency is quickly dispelled when juvenile justice policymakers understand the correlation between domestic violence and juvenile delinquency.[12] Recognizing the folly of ignoring what may be the source of the juvenile's abusive behavior, Santa Clara County devotes reasonable efforts to identifying and treating any violence being modeled for the youth. As soon as possible in the investigation process, the probation officer tries to determine if the juvenile has been abused by his parent. If so, the officer recommends that the parent attend a *Parenting Without Violence* course. It is hoped that the abusive parents can learn a non-violent interactional style and thereby decrease their own victimization in the process. After the disposition hearing, the probation officer remains involved in the cases to ensure the youth's compliance with all conditions of release. In addition to supervising the juvenile's attendance at the Batterer Intervention Program, the probation officer also maintains contact with the abused parent, ensuring at least a once monthly check-in (Santa Clara County Probation Department, 1999). Probation officers are also sure to fully explain all conditions of release with the juvenile as well as the parents. As part of the parent's safety planning, the probation officer explains that participation in the Juvenile Batterer's Intervention Program and the existence of the Juvenile Delinquency Protection Order provide no guarantee of security from harm. Parents are also referred to victim advocates for assistance with formulating a long-term safety plan (Santa Clara County Probation Department, 1999).

Even in the face of success with a number of the juvenile perpetrators, challenges remain. "People have tried to differentiate teen violence from adult violence, but now that I've had some of the young survivors in front of me, I've seen that they are exactly like adult victims," Judge Hyman observed. "The recantation, the denial. You're seeing sixteen-year-old women acting the same as thirty-year-old victims" (Guido, 2000, p. 1). Judge Hyman and Ms. Berlin stress that Santa Clara County's commitment to a coordinated community response to domestic violence greatly facilitates the work of their program. Presiding over the County's juvenile dependency court, Superior Court Judge Len Edwards says, "Frankly, this is the smartest thing we've done. In order to have a successful prosecution where the offender 'gets it' and ultimately changes his behavior, you have to have good police work, good judicial work, good probation work and good follow-up on the law enforcement side. We're getting more and more sophisticated in this county" (Guido, 2000, p. 1).

Part IV: Travis County, TX, Juvenile Court Replication Efforts

Subsequent to observing the success of the King County and Santa Clara County Juvenile Court's Domestic Violence Programs, the Youth Issues Committee[13] of the Travis County Domestic Violence Task Force[14] decided to replicate their innovations. Additionally, several members of the Committee had worked with both adult and youth domestic violence victims as well as offenders and believed that since Travis County already had an adult Domestic Violence Court, it was worth the effort to bring the innovations to juvenile court. The momentum was spurred by a 1999 Youth Issues Committee Report on juvenile batterers in Travis County, and a compelling paper written by Emily Fry, a University of Texas law student. Ms. Fry had worked as a public defender in the Travis County Juvenile Court and believed that family violence issues could be more adequately addressed as part of intake, referral, and disposition (Frey, 2001). By highlighting the unmet therapeutic and safety needs of Travis County juveniles, Ms. Fry made an eloquent argument for implementing reforms. She also identified potential funding sources for a domestic violence unit within the Travis County Juvenile Court (hereinafter TCJC) (Frey, 2001; Office of the Governor, 1999b).

Highlighting the need for improved data collection, screening, and counseling services for the victims and offenders, the 1999 Youth Issues Committee Report on current practices with juvenile batterers elucidated the need for action (Travis County Family Violence Task Force, 1999). With the full support of District Attorney Ronnie Earle and the Juvenile Court Judges Jeanne Meurer, Bill King, and Allison Benesch, the Committee began its planning in earnest. The King and Santa Clara Counties' Courts generously shared information regarding the funding of their programs, as well as reports, protocols, and other relevant documents that would facilitate replication.

On the Youth Issues Committee (hereinafter the Committee), TCJC Judges King and Benesch joined with probation, prosecution, defense, mental health, law enforcement, social work, and school district staff, as well as domestic violence attorneys, advocates, and survivors to determine how to weave family violence-oriented services into the on-going planning process. The Committee is co-chaired by attorney Vicki McFadden and Cisco Garcia, Director of the Safeplace Shelter's Expect Respect Program, which is administered in Travis County elementary, middle, and high schools. Covering dating violence, sexual harassment, and bullying, the nationally recognized Expect Respect program includes counseling for survivors, support groups on healthy dating relationships, prevention education, and staff and parent trainings.[15] The Expect Respect program provides a model for the type of court-based intervention most appropriate for violent youth; thus, the involvement of Mr. Garcia has been critical to designing effective programming. Fortunately, the TCJS was already in the process of establishing an Assessment Center, geared to identifying the mental health, substance abuse, education, and other needs with which the youth present. Psychological evaluations are prioritized for those juveniles being held in detention, but could also be available for out-of-custody family violence cases, if needed (S. Moore, oral report to Youth Issues Committee at Travis County Juvenile Court, July 16, 2001).

Cultural Competence in Addressing Juvenile Family Violence

Nationwide, juveniles of color comprise just 32% of the youth population, yet constitute 68% of the juveniles in secure detention facilities (Office of Juvenile Justice and Delinquency Prevention, 1998). Federal and state studies indicate that youth of color experience a "cumulative disadvantage" as a result of being unfairly treated at every juncture in the system. In comparing white and minority youth who are before the court for the same offenses, African American juveniles with no prior admission to a secure facility had a six times greater likelihood of being incarcerated than did the white youth; in addition, Hispanic juveniles had a three times greater chance of being incarcerated than the white youth (National Council of Juvenile and Family Court Judges, 2001). In Texas, juvenile referrals to probation for misdemeanor and felony offenses also reflect a disheartening disparity based on race. Although African American youth are just 13% of the juvenile population, they reflect 23% of the juvenile referrals. Fifty-one percent of Texas youth are white, yet represent only 38% of the youth adjudicated in the juvenile court system. Hispanic youth account for 39% of the referrals, and are 36% of the juvenile population (Fabelo, 2001).

While unequal access to legal representation may account for some of the disparity, it is widely believed that race bias is the predominant driving force, just as with adult cases. For example, Milwaukee County reports that although African-Americans constitute just 24% of the population, they represent 66% of the domestic violence arrests that find their way to the district attorney's office. In contrast, whites are 62% of the populace, but surface in just 32% of the domestic violence cases reviewed by prosecutors (National Council of Juvenile and Family Court Judges, 2001). To its credit, Milwaukee County has established a Judicial Oversight Initiative Committee (JOIC) to address the disparity, in part by studying the city versus suburban police responses. In the more white suburbs, the Committee found batterers were often issued municipal citations and paid fines, while those of color in the City of Milwaukee tended to be arrested, charged with state crimes, and prosecuted. The JOIC Report states, "The problem lies in the fact that it appears that some people in our community, depending on where they live, their race, ethnicity, income or occupation, are not being held to the same standard of accountability" (Doege, 2001, p. 5B).

The Texas Criminal Justice Policy Council reports that in Travis County, African-American youth are 13% of the juvenile population, but represent 29% of those referred to juvenile probation. Hispanic juveniles reflect 34% of the youth population, yet constitute 44% of the cases within juvenile probation. Fifty-three percent of the youth are white, but they comprise just 27% of the referrals (Fabelo, 2001). In Travis County, our statistics reflect the need to further examine the correlation between race and case dispositions. The Committee seeks to analyze how decisions are made at critical points in the justice system, from arrests and detention to adjudication and disposition, with particular regard to youth of color. We want to ensure that there is direct advocacy on the issues that disproportionately impact minority youth, including conditions of confinement in juvenile facilities, prisons, and jails; adequacy of representation; school discipline; and family violence matters. A priority is building on existing partnerships with community-based stakeholders of color to determine the most effective strategies for helping our youth.

Viewed through the lens of cultural values, the Committee seeks also to address the complex ethical dilemmas presented to the Juvenile Court when American law conflicts with cultural beliefs. How should the Court intervene when parents, guided by their cultural ideology, force their twelve- and thirteen-year-old girls to have sexual relations with and marry adult men? Can courts become involved when adolescent girls' and boys' genital excision is directed by parents following centuries-old cultural practices? Is it proper for the Court to intercede if parents, following legitimate cultural principles, refuse to allow their children access to medical care or will utilize only herbal or alternative medicines (Levesque, 2001)? What response is appropriate with families whose traditions include allowing nine- and ten-year-old children to provide long term childcare for younger siblings, perhaps resulting in missed school? How can the Court gain the cooperation of parents whose church is insisting that it, rather than the legal system, handle a sexual assault or family violence case? While cultural evidence should not exonerate the perpetrators in the above examples, it is certainly conceivable that sanctions could take into consideration the offender's genuine belief that he or she was acting in the children's best interest. Those courts desiring to be *respectfully* responsive to our diverse communities are grappling with these fundamental issues, both urgent and controversial.

Changes in U.S. immigration laws and patterns of re-settlement have substantially impacted the numbers of those foreign born interacting with the legal system. For instance, upwards of 60% of Asian Americans were not born in America, a rate ten times that of the U.S. population (Wang, 1996, as cited in Levesque, 2001, p. 198). Thus, in some communities, many of the victims and offenders may not be familiar with the American justice system and are understandably suspicious of any governmental involvement in family affairs. Compounded by the backlash against immigrants and general attitude of intolerance toward "difference," efforts to improve interventions with families of color may be sabotaged by local bigotry (Pierce-Baker, 1998). The increasingly punitive approach to juvenile offenders serves only to further marginalize minority youth, whether foreign or American born (Levesque, 2001). The challenge for progressive juvenile courts is to balance the cultural influences with legal doctrine designed to protect victims, while holding the perpetrators responsible.

Collaboration with Law Enforcement

Although some officers view juvenile family violence as crime worthy of their involvement, others voice skepticism at interceding in what they believe to be simply family disputes. However, Santa Clara County Judge Hyman advises against the Committee drafting a law enforcement protocol on this issue. Rather, he suggests, garnering police cooperation must be premised on respecting their expertise by encouraging that they develop a protocol, perhaps with the Committee's assistance. Judge Hyman explains that when Santa Clara County was developing its specialized court, they engaged the support of the Santa Clara County Police Chief's Association (E. Hyman, personal communication, March 22, 2001). The Association's Chair, Palo Alto Chief Pat Dwyer, then ensured that the Domestic Violence Protocol of Law Enforcement was amended to include interventions with juvenile offenders (P. Dwyer, personal communication, March 26, 2001). The Protocol states that officers must employ Santa Clara County's mandatory arrest policy when responding to family violence cases, whether the accused is an adult or juvenile. Particularly heartening is the policy statement now included in the Protocol: "The Police Chief's Association of Santa Clara County recognizes that acts of domestic violence are a serious problem among juveniles, and therefore has included juveniles in this protocol" (Police Chief's Association, 2001, p. 12).

Both the Austin Police Department and the Travis County Sheriff's Department follow state law presuming that arrest is the appropriate response when the officer has probable cause to believe a domestic violence crime has occurred.[16] As yet, neither department's written policies specifically require equal treatment of adult and juvenile batterers; however, both maintain that officers should arrest a domestic violence offender without consideration of age (A. LeBlanc, personal communication, April 21, 2001).

Intake and Screening for Abuse

Recognizing that courts must utilize a comprehensive screening mechanism[17] to identify abuse victims and offenders as early as possible, the Committee adopted a plan for *all* juvenile offenders to be screened for domestic violence as part of the present intake process. The

Travis County Juvenile Court had already planned to open the Travis County Juvenile Probation Assessment Center (hereinafter Assessment Center) in January of 2002, under the direction of Dr. Eric Frey. One of the goals is to expedite case handling in order to get the youth in the prescribed treatment programs as quickly as possible. The primary objectives of the Assessment Center are to:

1. Assess social and academic functioning, mental health, and substance use for all youth detained by TCJPD within 10 days of being detained;
2. Apply assessment and research data to provide rehabilitation and treatment recommendations that promote positive behavioral and emotional change, decrease risk of re-offending, and protect the youth and community; and
3. Identify available resources and match them to recommendations so that youth receive appropriate rehabilitation and/or treatment services. (Frey, 2001)

Judge King has worked with the intake staff to ensure that the screening for family violence will occur as part of the social history assessment. However, beginning in September of 2001, the Juvenile Court will be using the Massachusetts Youth Screening Instrument (hereinafter MAYSI-2; National Youth Screening Assistance Project, 2001) to conduct a mental health assessment, as mandated by recent Texas law.[18] MAYSI-2 consists of a 52-item questionnaire designed to identify possible mental disturbance or distress. Interestingly, this assessment tool makes no inquiry specific to family violence, but does ask about violence the youth may have witnessed.[19] Assisting with this effort, law student David Bain (2000) drafted a *Travis County Juvenile Court Domestic Violence Policy & Protocol Manual*, working closely with Judge King and the Juvenile Court staff. The Committee will assist Judge King and his staff with selecting several questions, specific to family violence, which will be incorporated into the assessments of all incoming youth.

When interviewing parents, Ms. Levy, of the King County Step-Up Program, suggests that each partner should be approached separately if abuse is suspected, though neither partner may be willing to acknowledge the problem. Rather than trying to stop all contact, Levy cautions adults to focus on safety. For example, a teacher, probation officer, judge, or advocate might say, "I understand that you love him, but I can see you're being hurt." Professionals stepping out of their usual roles can often reach a youth, as evidenced by Boston Juvenile Court Judge

Leslie Harris' practice of speaking honestly with adolescent offenders and victims about an array of dangerous choices they are making. A critical next step is providing information and referrals for where the teen can get help (Harrison, 1997; Silverman et al., 2001).

Specialized Family Violence Session

On Thursday afternoons, Judge Benesch hears the "CPS cross-over docket," a special session begun in April of 2000. It is designed to handle the criminal cases involving juveniles who are also involved with Child Protective Services. Should the Juvenile Court decide to fully replicate the Santa Clara County model, a similar specialized family violence docket could be designated.

Rethinking Dispositions and Services

Scrutiny of the caseload revealed that many juveniles before the Court are charged with offenses unrelated to family violence, yet its presence in their lives all but ensures continued delinquent behavior. Thus, Judge King suggested that youth being adjudicated in such cases should also be referred to the specialized batterer's intervention program. He explained that a juvenile adjudicated delinquent for theft crimes could be ordered to attend drug treatment if a substance abuse problem is indicated. As the probation officers will be screening for family violence, their findings will be reported to the Juvenile Court judge, who should then ensure the youth's attendance at the juvenile batterer's intervention program regardless of the nature of the underlying offense (Youth Issues Committee, 2001). Judge King's proposal is significant for its potential to dramatically increase the juvenile perpetrators' access to the particular services that will likely prove most helpful in decreasing recidivism.

In relevant part, the Texas Juvenile Justice Code construes its purpose as " . . . consistent with the protection of the public and public safety: (C) to provide treatment, training, and rehabilitation that emphasizes the accountability and responsibility of both the parent and child for the child's conduct."[20] Such mandate provides the Juvenile Court with the means to order the combination of services that have the greatest probability of helping violent families empower themselves toward healthy relationships. As keeping parents involved in remedial services is often a frustrating challenge, the Committee is interested in developing a support group for the abused parents, similar to that offered as part of King County's Step-Up Program. Just as King County found that parents actively participated if the support groups were geared to their unique issues, so it is hoped that Travis County's abused parents will follow suit.

School based dating violence intervention programs should be implemented in collaboration with domestic violence advocates. Austin's Safeplace shelter began a Teen Dating Violence Project (TDVP) in 1988, offering twenty-four-week therapeutic peer support groups to victims in their public schools, and expanding the program to include perpetrators in 1991. Barri Rosenbluth, who directs the Safeplace School-based Intervention Programs, has used the *Expect Respect* curriculum, which teaches the warning signs of batterers, including excessive use of power and control (Harrison, 1997). Ms. Rosenbluth explains that early on she surveyed a number of teen victims who reported on-going, increasingly violent behavior by their partners but an unwillingness to break off the relationships. When asked to raise their hands if they thought all men were violent, every girl responded affirmatively. It was then that the focus shifted from simply warning the victims about abusive behaviors to teaching them how to set limits, protect themselves, and expect respect and equality in their relationships (Harrison, 1997). Cisco Garcia, who now heads the *Expect Respect Project*, includes gender, race, and culture as part of the revised curriculum also covering dating violence, harassment, and bullying.[21]

Juvenile Delinquency Protective Orders

Judge Hyman (personal communication, March 22, 2001) is a strong proponent of his court's utilizing specific orders, stating:

> Juvenile Protection Orders, like their adult counterpart, are an essential tool to help provide additional victim safety. It is important that the victim be informed that an Order cannot guarantee safety and that a safety plan must be prepared and followed. However, the Order sends a strong message to the batterer (orally at the hearing as well as in writing) that there will be no contact, and other prohibited behavior, during the duration of the order. The Order also allows the victim time away from the batterer to receive victim services, including the assistance of advocates. Finally, the Order allows law enforcement to make arrests for violations of orders even if not committed in their presence.

Travis County Juvenile Court will want to either adopt the Santa Clara County concept of a protective order designed specifically for juvenile batterers or to adopt a policy of tailoring Texas Protective Orders to the same end. In Texas, as in every other state, protective orders can be procured against a family or household member.[22] Additionally, as of September 1, 2001, victims of dating violence in Texas can now also obtain protective orders and are now able to avail themselves of the full panoply of legal remedies previously only available to those who were related by blood, marriage, or had a child in common.[23]

In fact, the Texas Protective Order statute delineates that any " . . . district court, court of domestic relations, juvenile court having the jurisdiction of a district court, statutory county court, constitutional county court, or other court expressly given jurisdiction under this title"[24] may issue a protective order upon making a finding that " . . . family violence has occurred and is likely to occur in the future."[25] If the youth is returning home to live with a parent he has been victimizing, the Protective Order could simply prohibit the juvenile from committing family violence[26] and require that he " . . . complete a battering intervention and prevention program . . . "[27] as the law provides. It would thus appear that the Court could commence issuing Protective Orders in juvenile family violence cases under current provisions of the Texas law. Other states need only conduct the same statutory analysis to determine if they are now permitted to issue juvenile protective orders or if legislative amendments are necessary to achieve this end.

Juvenile Anger Management vs. Batterer's Intervention Programs

Committee members expressed concern that while in Travis County, adult domestic violence perpetrators were precluded from attending short-term anger management classes due to their proven ineffectiveness (Adams, 1989; Kivel, 1992), juvenile family violence offenders were routinely being ordered into just such courses.[28] Rather than having poor impulse control, many of the violent youth use anger to manipulate and control their parents and dating partners. As Paul Kivel, the co-founder of the Oakland Men's Project, says, "Anger is not the problem" (p. 100). By listening to perpetrators *and* examining their behavior, counselors have learned that the violent behavior is most often deliberate; that is, the batterers *choose* to be violent. While there are some batterers who exhibit generalized violence, most will not assault the teacher who punishes them for being tardy to school or the Constable who charges them with truancy. Indeed, most adult abusers with a criminal record have either assaulted other intimate partners or been convicted of drunk driving or substance abuse offenses (Isaac, Cochran, Brown, & Adams, 1994).

Given that long-term batterer's intervention programs are more successful at reducing recidivism,[29] it is important for stakeholders planning a program not to be seduced by those offering short-term, quick-fixes. Additionally, cultural competence must be prioritized in determining whom to hire as program facilitators and therapists. More often discussed than practiced, the staff of service providers and juvenile courts rarely represent the rich diversity of the communities they serve, to the detriment of our youth. While there is a dearth of research on abusers of color and of culturally specific intervention programs, they are generally over-represented in batterer's intervention programs (Ritchie, 1998; see also Williams, 1994a). Not surprisingly, batterer's treatment programs have proven to be more effective when culturally competent[30] *and* behaviorally-based.[31] Researchers have documented that men of color do have a greater likelihood of completing the programs if the staff reflect similar ethnicity (Williams, 1994b). As most of the literature is based on studies of adult perpetrator interventions, it is hoped that the expansion of *specific* juvenile batterer's intervention programs will ultimately produce data on this population.

In spite of the high correlation between substance abuse and domestic violence (Williams, 1994b), batterers experts report that while the alcohol or drugs might act as a disinhibitor, they do not *cause* the batterers to be violent. Therefore, it is imperative that abusers who exhibit both violence and substance abuse are recognized to have two separate problems for which they must be held accountable and get help (Williams, 1994b). There must also be community support to provide sanctions for new incidents[32] and on-going partner contacts.[33]

The Committee has prioritized cultural competence in the process of designing the Travis County Juvenile Court Domestic Violence Program. When deemed appropriate, presently Travis County can send its adjudicated youth to a two-session anger management course. The Committee has been gathering data from adult and youth batterer's intervention programs in order to devise a dramatically improved program, similar to those offered in King and Santa Clara Counties.

Mediation

Many juvenile courts focus their intervention on mediation between the abusive youth and the victimized parent(s) in spite of consistent findings that juveniles, particularly those in custody, will agree to virtually any conditions that bring short-term freedom (Fischer, Vidmar, & Ellis, 1993). Given that juvenile batterers, like their adult counterparts, will rarely negotiate in good faith (Adams, 1989), it behooves juvenile courts to seek alternative models of case resolution. Especially because many of the assaultive youth will return home, effective programs focus on Safety Planning with the parents and other victims. It is noteworthy that Duluth's DAIP, the King County Step-Up Program, and the Santa Clara County Family Violence Court do not utilize mediation in their youth family violence programs.

Travis County youth counselors and probation officers reported to the Committee that many juveniles are sent to mediate conditions of release with the parents against whom they have offended. Acknowledging that the concept might appear logical on paper, the professionals confirmed results similar to those in national studies: that most abusive youth were not negotiating in good faith. Rather, they voiced agreement with whatever stipulations were necessary to facilitate their release. It is thus not surprising that the counselors and probation officers reported a high recidivism rate among the mediated cases. Compounding the problem, most mediators are not familiar with the complex dynamics of family violence and thus cannot be expected to effect safe resolutions (Fischer et al., 1993; Gondolf, 2002; Rhea et al., 1996; Shichor & Tibbetts, 2002).

Parent and child victims report fear of retaliation for revealing the extent of abuse; thus the mediators' attempts to negotiate a peaceful resolution can only be viewed as disingenuous. The power imbalance between victim and offender is too great, effectively forcing the victim to minimize or deny the danger (Bancroft, 2002; Hart, 1990). Such practices place the victim in the untenable position of having to assert, in the perpetrator's presence, her trepidation regarding his propensity for further violence. While mediation may be appropriate in other types of juvenile offenses, such as truancy or theft, it appears to sabotage the two goals of victim safety and offender accountability. Just as with adult domestic violence cases, mediation is contraindicated in most youth family abuse cases.

CONCLUSIONS

The campaign to only punish and no longer attempt rehabilitation with juvenile offenders is ill-advised. Bowing to political expediency by just peripherally treating juvenile batterers constitutes an abdication of our responsibility to these high-risk children and their families. As the King County and Santa Clara County Programs make clear, we must not only focus on the deed but on the doer as well. Juvenile batterers and their victims enjoy neither political power nor a constituency, leaving their fate in the hands of the professionals with whom they interact in the justice system. These children's unique treatment needs must be prioritized, leaving egos, turf battles, and sorry excuses in the dust. In Travis County, we have taken on the challenge of improving our interventions with juvenile batterers and their families, with a tremendous debt of gratitude to the innovators in King and Santa Clara Counties who have been more than generous in sharing their expertise. For youth or parents with no safe purchase in a violent family, juvenile court may be the only refuge, the sole source of safety and hope. Every juvenile court should be challenged to enter the fray; to replicate the exemplary models that King and Santa Clara Counties have provided. Our troubled children deserve no less from those of us paid to protect and rehabilitate them.

NOTES

1. "Domestic violence" occurs when one intimate partner or family member uses physical violence, threats, stalking, harassment, or emotional or financial abuse to control, manipulate, coerce, or intimidate the other partner. *See, e.g.,* Texas Family Code (2001), Title 4, Ch. 71. Definitions, § 71.004 "Family Violence means: (1) an act by a member of a family or household against another member of the family or household that is intended to result in physical harm, bodily injury, assault, or sexual assault or that is a threat that reasonably places the member in fear of imminent physical harm, bodily injury, assault, or sexual assault, but does not include defensive measures to protect oneself; or (2) abuse . . . toward a child of that family or household."

2. Females are overwhelmingly the victims of domestic violence at the hands of male partners. The feminine pronoun in no way denies that there are male victims, rather it recognizes that the vast majority are females. See Bureau of Justice Statistics (2001): "During 1999 females experienced 671,110 (85%) such violent victimizations" (p. 2) by intimate partners.

3. Those drug courts that "coordinate treatment delivery with judicial oversight" are considered bona fide drug courts.

4. The Washington State Governor's Juvenile Justice Advisory Committee provided a $102,187 grant to the King County Judicial Administration, utilizing federal grants.

5. The Duluth "Wheels" offer specific examples of negative and positive behaviors associated with partner abuse. For example, the "Power and Control Wheel" includes "using coercion and threats, using intimidation, using emotional abuse, using isolation, and minimizing, denying and blaming," within the context of physical and sexual abuse. The "Equality Wheel" includes options such as honesty and accountability, non-threatening behavior and respect, within the context of nonviolent behavior.

The Wheels can be obtained from the Duluth Domestic Violence Intervention Project's web site: www.duluth-model.org/daippce.htm.

6. An abused parent may also be dependent on the teen for assistance with younger siblings, fear deportation by INS, hope for change based on the perpetrator's promises, or desperately want to keep her family together. For further explanation, see Buel (1999).

7. The brochure's front cover says, "Do you have a son or daughter that scares you sometimes? Do they yell at you, call you names, put you down, demand that you do things for them? Do they shove, push, kick or threaten you? Are you afraid to tell them 'NO'? There is HELP available . . ." Step-Up Program brochure provided to the author in May of 1998 and again on August 15, 2001.

8. Note: The Texas Youth Commission has also conducted an unpublished study documenting the high correlation between domestic violence and juvenile delinquency.

9. For example, this is the practice in Travis County (TX) Juvenile Court.

10. U.S. CONST., art. IV, § 1.

11. California Penal Code Sections 273.6 and 166 Contempt of Court. See also 136.1 and 136.2.

12. See infra Section II.

13. Revised on March 26, 2001, the Committee's mission is to coordinate a whole community approach for youth experiencing family/relationship violence and to create positive change by promoting safe, healthy relationships.

14. Founded in 1989, the Travis County Domestic Violence Task Force is comprised of myriad professionals handling domestic violence matters, including judges, prosecutors, advocates, batterer's intervention specialists, law enforcement and probation officers, pre-trial services and child protection staff, defense attorneys, mental health providers, and the clergy. The group meets monthly to tackle the challenges facing the community, with sub-committees taking an action-oriented approach to problem solving. The author has been an active member of the Task Force since 1996, and of the Youth Issues Committee since 1999.

15. For additional information on the Expect Respect Program and to order their free information packet or the Expect Respect Program Curriculum for Preventing Teenage Dating Violence and Promoting Healthy Relationships for $35, call 512/385-5181 or on the internet at www.austin-safeplace.org.

16. Texas Code of Criminal Procedure, Art. 5.04(a) (2000-2001) "Duties of Peace Officers (a) The primary duties of a peace officer who investigates a family violence allegation or who responds to a disturbance call that may involve family violence are to protect any potential victim of family violence, enforce the law of this state, enforce a protective order from another jurisdiction as provided by Chapter 88, Family Code, and make lawful arrests of violators."

17. Contact the Battered Women's Justice Project, phone 1-800-903-0111, for further information regarding screening tools.

18. Texas Human Resource Code, Section 141.042(e) amended to read "Juvenile probation departments shall use the mental health screening instrument selected by the commission for the initial screening of children under the jurisdiction of probation departments who have been formally referred to the department." The Texas Juvenile Probation Commission selected the MAYSI-2. Presentation by Dr. Eric Frey.

19. Id.

20. Texas Family Code, Title 3. Juvenile Justice Code, Sec. 51.01(2)(C) (2000-2001).

21. In 1998 Safeplace received a Centers for Disease Control grant for more than $500,000 to expand the program to elementary, middle and high schools in the Austin

area. For further information on their program, including a copy of the *Expect Respect* curriculum ($35), contact Safeplace at (512) 385-5181 or www.austin-safeplace.org.

22. Texas Family Code, Title 4. Protective Orders and Family Violence, Sec. 81.01. See also Finn and Colson (1990).

23. Texas Family Code, Sec. 71.0021: "(a) 'Dating Violence' means an act by an individual that is against another individual with whom that person has or has had a dating relationship and that is intended to result in physical harm, bodily injury, assault, or sexual assault or that is a threat that reasonably places the individual in fear of imminent physical harm, bodily injury, assault, sexual assault, but does not include defensive measures to protect oneself."

24. Texas Family Code, Id. at Sec. 71.002.

25. Id. at Sec. 81.001.

26. Id. at Sec. 85.022 (b) (1).

27. Id. at Sec. 85.022 (a) (1).

28. The Travis County Family Violence Task Force's Batterer's Intervention Program Committee has negotiated an agreement with the Travis County Courts not to refer domestic violence offenders to short-term, anger management classes. As of February of 2001, Lifeworks counseling program was working with approximately one hundred youth referred by the TCJC. Julie Speer and David Jenkins, counselors at Lifeworks, reporting to the Youth Issues Committee on Feb. 5, 2001, at TCJC.

29. Experts suggest that a minimum of one year is essential since many batterers do not even emerge from the denial phase for about six months. One of the most successful programs is directed by Hamish Sinclair, a former batterer, and runs for three years, and called "Man Alive" in Marin County, California. Similarly, at the Pivot Project in Houston, the Men's Education Network in Tyler (TX) and Family Services of Beaumont (TX), Inc., batterers are encouraged to continue attending sessions after completing the standard program. As with Man Alive, some of these "graduates" are then able to confront the new batterers entering the program with myriad excuses. At the Family Diversion Network in Austin (TX) and the Women's Haven of Tarrant County, batterers who have finished their program can attend a weekly support group.

30. The LifeWorks batterer's intervention programs in Austin (TX) have been particularly conscientious about ensuring a diverse and well-trained staff. See also Williams and Becker (1994).

31. See above discussion as to the contraindication of "Anger Management" programs since domestic violence is not about the inability to control anger, but rather is based on the abuse of power and control with violence. Thus, Dr. David Adams asserts, batterers need to be taught that they will be held responsible for their actions, just as everyone else is.

32. The Quincy (MA) Court Probation Department's Domestic Violence Unit (Chief Andy Klein and Deputy Chief Bruce Carr) takes a tough, no-nonsense approach to batterers who violate the terms and conditions of their pre-trial release or sentences. By establishing a "revocation session" every Tuesday morning, Presiding Judge Charles Black further reinforces the message that there will be sanctions for the violation of protective or any other court orders.

33. Beth Ledoux, a survivor and veteran legal advocate, also served as the post-conviction liaison with victims at the Quincy (MA) Court Probation Department. As a result of her on-going contacts and safety planning, the Court was able to dramatically increase the number of victims reporting violations and seeking the help they needed to escape.

REFERENCES

Adams, D. (1989). Identifying the assaultive husband in court: You be the judge. *Boston Bar Journal, 29,* 24-27.

American Psychiatric Association. (1994). *Diagnostic and statistical manual of mental disorders* (4th ed.). Washington, DC: Author.

Bancroft, L. (2002). *Why does he do that? Inside the minds of angry and controlling men.* New York: G.P. Putnam's Sons.

Bottoms, B. L., Nielsen, M., Murray, R., & Filipas, H. (2003). Religion-related child physical abuse: Characteristics and psychological outcomes. *Journal of Aggression, Maltreatment & Trauma, 8*(1/2), 87-114.

Bowker, L. H., Arbitell, M., & McFerron, J. R. (1988). *On the relationship between wife beating and child abuse.* In K. Yllo, & M. Bograd (Eds.), *Feminist perspectives on wife abuse* (pp. 158-174). Newbury Park, CA: Sage.

Bruhn, C.M. (2003). Children with disabilities: Abuse, neglect, and the child welfare system. *Journal of Aggression, Maltreatment, & Trauma, 8*(1/2), 173-203.

Buel, S. (1999). Fifty obstacles to leaving a.k.a. why abuse victims stay. *Colorado Bar Journal, 28,* 19-24.

Bureau of Justice Statistics. (2001, October). *Intimate partner violence and age of victim, 1993-99* (NCJ-178247). Washington, DC: US Department of Justice.

Cooper, C. (Ed.). (1995). *Applying drug court concepts in the juvenile and family court environments, a primer for judges, 22.* Washington, DC: American University Justice Programs Office.

Covington, D., Justason, B., & Wright, L. (2001). Severity, manifestations, and consequences of violence among pregnant adolescents. *Journal of Adolescent Health, 28,* 55-61.

Doege, D. (2001, August 20). Police practices are behind racial disparities, panel suspects. *Milwaukee Journal Sentinel,* WL 9374110, p. 5B.

Dutton, D. G. (1995). *The batterer: A psychological profile.* New York: Basic Books.

Edwards, L. P. (2001). The Juvenile Dependency Drug Treatment Court of Santa Clara County, California. *Juvenile and Family Justice Today, 10,* 16.

Fabelo, T. (2001). *Profiles of referrals to selected juvenile probation departments in Texas,* Criminal Justice Policy Council Report prepared for the 77th Texas Legislature.

Finn, P., & Colson, S. (1990, March). *Civil protection orders: Legislation, current court practice, and enforcement.* Washington, DC: U.S. Dept. of Justice, Office of Justice Programs, National Institute of Justice.

Fischer, K., Vidmar, N., & Ellis, R. (1993). The culture of battering and the role of mediation in domestic violence cases. *SMU Law Review, 46,* 2117, 2131-2132.

Frey, E. (2001, August 20). *Summary of Travis County Juvenile Probation Assessment Center.* Presented at the Youth Issues Committee meeting at the Travis County Juvenile Court.

Fry, E. (2000). *Breaking the 5th: The juvenile batterer, a juvenile batterer intervention program proposal for the Travis County Juvenile Justice System.* Unpublished manuscript.

Gondolf, E. W. (2002). *Batterer intervention systems: Issues, outcomes and recommendations.* Thousand Oaks, CA: Sage.

Guarino, S. (1985). *Delinquent youth and family violence: A study of abuse and neglect in the homes of serious juvenile offenders.* Unpublished report. Massachusetts Department of Youth Services: Boston.

Guido, M. (2000, March 25). County tries to break cycle of domestic violence early, pioneering justice system gives special attention to juveniles who batter. *San Jose Mercury News*, p. 1.

Harrison, M. (1997). Equal partners. *Teaching Tolerance, 8,* 41-44. Available from www.splcenter.org/teachingtolerance/tt-articles.html.

Hart, B. (1990). Gentle jeopardy: The further endangerment of battered women and children in custody mediation. *Mediation Quarterly, 7,* 317-322.

Hoyt, S., & Scherer, D. G. (1998). Female juvenile delinquency: Misunderstood by the juvenile justice system, neglected by social science. *Law and Human Behavior, 22,* 81-107.

Hubbard, R., Marsden, M., Rachal, J., Harwood, H., Cavanaugh, E., & Gnizburg, H. (1989). *Drug abuse treatment: A national study of effectiveness.* Chapel Hill, NC: University of North Carolina Press.

Isaac, N., Cochran, D., Brown, M., & Adams, S. (1994). Men who batter, profile from a restraining order database. *Archives of Family Medicine, 3,* 50-54.

Jacobson, N., & Gottman, J. (1998). *When men batter women: New insights into ending abusive relationships.* New York: Simon & Schuster.

Jaffe, P., Wolfe, D., & Wilson, S. (1990). *Children of battered women: Issues in child development and intervention planning.* Newbury Park, CA: Sage.

Kivel, P. (1992). Unlearning violence: A breakthrough book for violent men and all those who love them: How to replace domestic abuse with new rules and new roles, real power and responsible action. New York: Fine Communications.

Kratcoski, P. (1985). Youth violence directed towards significant others. *Journal of Adolescence, 8*(2), 145-157.

Lehrman, F. L. (1996). *Domestic violence practice and procedure.* Eagan, MN: West Group.

Levesque, R. (2001). Cultural life, family violence and U.S. law. In R. Levesque, *Culture and family violence: Fostering change through human rights law* (pp. 197-232). Washington, DC: American Psychological Association.

Levy, B. (1993). *In love and in danger: A teen's guide to breaking free of abuse relationships.* Seattle, WA: Seal Press.

McGee, C. M. (2001). The Washoe County (Reno) Family Drug Court. *Juvenile and Family Justice Today, 10,* 21-22.

McGlone, G. J. (2003). The pedophile and the pious: Towards a new understanding of sexually offending and non-offending Roman Catholic priests. *Journal of Aggression, Maltreatment & Trauma, 8*(1/2), 115-131.

Miller, G. (1989). Violence by and against America's children. *Journal of Juvenile Justice Digest, 17*(12), 6.

National Association of Drug Court Professionals. (1997). *Defining drug courts: The key components, 2. Drug Court Standards Committee.* Washington, DC: National Association of Drug Court Professionals.

National Council of Juvenile and Family Court Judges. (2001). And justice for some. In *Update on minority youth in juvenile justice.* Washington, DC: National Council on Crime and Delinquency, 6.

National Youth Screening Assistance Project. (2001). *Massachusetts Youth Screening Instrument.* University of Massachusetts Medical School. Available from www. umassmed.edu/nysap/maysi2/products.cfm.

Office of the Governor, Criminal Justice Division. (1999a). *Application kit for youth-related, juvenile justice and criminal justice projects.* Austin, TX: State of Texas.

Office of the Governor, Criminal Justice Division. (1999b). *The Criminal Justice Planning Fund, 28, fn. 123.* Austin, TX: State of Texas.

Office of Juvenile Justice and Delinquency Prevention. (1998). *Disproportionate minority confinement, 1997 Update. Juvenile Justice Bulletin.* Washington, DC: U.S. Department of Justice, Office of Justice Programs.

Pagelow, M. (1990). Effects of domestic violence on children and their consequences for custody and visitation agreements. *Mediation Quarterly,* 7(4), 347-363.

Pence, E. (1999). *Duluth domestic abuse intervention project: An overview, 1.* Unpublished document available from www.duluth-model.org.

Pierce-Baker, C. (1998). *Surviving the silence: Black women's stories of rape.* New York: W.W. Norton.

Police Chief's Association of Santa Clara County. (2001). *Domestic violence protocol for law enforcement.* San Jose, CA: Santa Clara County.

Rabin, B. (1995). Violence against mothers equals violence against children: Understanding the connections. *Albany Law Review,* 58, 1109-1117.

Rennison, C., & Wilchans, S. (2001). *Special report, intimate partner violence and age of victim (1993-1999).* Washington, DC: U.S. Department of Justice, Bureau of Justice Statistics.

Rhea, M. H., Chafey, K. H., Dohner, V. A., & Terragno, R. (1996). The silent victims of domestic violence–Who will speak? *Journal of Child and Adolescent Psychiatric Nursing,* 9(3), 7-15.

Ritchie, B. (1998, June). *Defining popular culture interventions.* Paper presented at Institute on Domestic Violence in the African American Community, Minneapolis, MN.

Rodriguez, M., Bauer, H., McLoughlin, E., & Grumbach, K. (1999). Screening and intervention for intimate partner abuse: Practices and attitudes of primary care physicians. *Journal of the American Medical Association,* 282, 468-474.

Santa Clara County Probation Department. (1999). *Domestic violence and family violence protocols manual.* San Jose, CA: Santa Clara County Court.

Shichor, D., & Tibbetts, S. G. (2002). Children as victims and witnesses. In D. Shichor, & S. G. Tibbetts (Eds.), *Victims and victimizations: Essential readings* (pp. 186-204). Prospect Heights, IL: Waveland Press.

Sierra, H. (Executive Producer). (2001, July 26). *CNN Headline News,* 10:50 p.m. Atlanta, GA: Turner Broadcast Systems.

Silverman, J., Raj, A., Mucci, L., & Hathaway, J. (2001). Dating violence against adolescent girls and associated substance use, unhealthy weight control, sexual risk behavior, pregnancy, and suicidality. *Journal of the American Medical Association,* 286(5), 572-579.

Step-Up. (1999). *Step-Up family/domestic violence intervention project, informational packet.* Seattle, WA: King County Attorney's Office.

Travis County Family Violence Task Force. (1999, November). *Domestic violence in juvenile court.* Unpublished report.

Valente, R. (1996). Domestic violence and the law. In R. Valente, & D. Goelman (Eds.), *The impact of domestic violence on your legal practice: A handbook for lawyers* (pp. 1-3). Washington, DC: The American Bar Association Commission on Domestic Violence.

Williams, O. (1994a). Partner abuse treatment programs and cultural competence: The results of a national survey. *Violence and Victims, 9,* 287-295.

Williams, O. (1994b). Group work with African-American men who batter: Toward more ethnically sensitive practice. *Journal of Comparative Family Studies, 25* (1), 91-103.

Youth Issues Committee. (2001, February 26). Youth Issues Committee meeting minutes. Travis County, TX: Author.

Index

South Dakota Cod. Laws. Ann. §§
    22-61-1, 22-16-1.1,
    22-16-15(5), 22-16-20,
    22-16-41, 214
South Dakota Cod. Laws Ann. §
    26-8A-30, 26-8A-31, 253
Spatial pattern assessments
    ecological theory analyses and,
        66-69,77-83
    future perspectives of, 84
    historical perspectives of, 64-69
    incidence explanations and, 65-77
        economic factors, 67-68
        high-risk *vs.* low-risk
            neighborhoods, 66-67
        instability factors, 66-69
        location comparisons, 72-77
        maltreatment type factors, 67-68
        models, 66-69
        overviews of, 65-66
    legal issues of, 65
    overviews of, 63-64
    reference resources for, 84-85
    social action issues of, 65
    studies of, 63-85
        analyses, 77-83
        background and literature
            reviews, 64-69,84-85
        discussions, 83-85
        methods, 69-72
        overviews of, 63-65
        results, 72-77
Spiritual factors
    impact of, 103-105. *See also*
        Religion-related characteristics
    spirituality abuse factors, 91-92
State ex rel. Atkinson v. Wilson, 210
State laws and legislation. *See* Laws
    and legislation
State v. Anonymous, 210
State v. Beale, 210
State v. Brady, 242
State v. Holcomb, 217
State v. Home, 211
State v. Oliver, 210

State v. Sherman, 223-227
Statutory and judicial regulations
    court cases. *See* Court cases
    fetal homicide and, 205-231. *See*
        also Fetal homicide
    laws and legislation. *See* Laws and
        legislation
Step-Up Program (King County,
    Washington), 273-207
Stidam v. Ashmore, 224-227
Strelczyk v. Jett, 224-227
Studies. *See also under individual*
        topics
    of Internet usage, 1-39
    LONGSCAN study, 157-158
    of religion-related characteristics,
        93-110
    of spatial pattern assessments,
        63-85
Summerfield v. Superior Court,
    223-227

Teams (child protection), 138
Teen Dating Violence Project (TDVP),
    297
Tennessee (laws and legislation)
    Tennessee Cod. Ann. §
        25-5-106(c), 224
    Tennessee Cod. Ann. § 39-13-107,
        39-13-214, 215
Terrorism and war, 41-62. *See also*
        War and terrorism
Testimony (closed-circuit television),
    233-271. *See also* Closed-
        circuit television testimony
Texas (laws and legislation)
    Texas Cod. Crim. P. Ann. § 38.071,
        253
    Texas Penal Cod. Ann. § 1.07(26),
        213
Third-party harm, 209-222
Traditional *vs.* multidisciplinary
        medical models, 138
Training and education issues, 153-155

BOOK ORDER FORM!

Order a copy of this book with this form or online at:
http://www.haworthpress.com/store/product.asp?sku=5128

The Victimization of Children
Emerging Issues

_____ in softbound at $34.95 (ISBN: 0-7890-2407-1)
_____ in hardbound at $59.95 (ISBN: 0-7890-2406-3)

COST OF BOOKS _____

POSTAGE & HANDLING _____
US: $4.00 for first book & $1.50
for each additional book
Outside US: $5.00 for first book
& $2.00 for each additional book.

SUBTOTAL _____

In Canada: add 7% GST._____

STATE TAX _____
CA, IL, IN, MN, NY, OH & SD residents
please add appropriate local sales tax.

FINAL TOTAL _____
If paying in Canadian funds, convert
using the current exchange rate,
UNESCO coupons welcome.

❑BILL ME LATER:
Bill-me option is good on US/Canada/
Mexico orders only; not good to jobbers,
wholesalers, or subscription agencies.

❑Signature _____

❑ Payment Enclosed: $ _____

❑ PLEASE CHARGE TO MY CREDIT CARD:

❑Visa ❑MasterCard ❑AmEx ❑Discover
❑Diner's Club ❑Eurocard ❑JCB

Account # _____

Exp Date _____

Signature _____
(Prices in US dollars and subject to change without notice.)

PLEASE PRINT ALL INFORMATION OR ATTACH YOUR BUSINESS CARD

Name	
Address	
City	State/Province	Zip/Postal Code
Country	
Tel	Fax
E-Mail	

May we use your e-mail address for confirmations and other types of information? ❑Yes ❑No We appreciate receiving
your e-mail address. Haworth would like to e-mail special discount offers to you, as a preferred customer.
We will never share, rent, or exchange your e-mail address. We regard such actions as an invasion of your privacy.

Order From Your **Local Bookstore** or Directly From
The Haworth Press, Inc. 10 Alice Street, Binghamton, New York 13904-1580 • USA
Call Our toll-free number (1-800-429-6784) / Outside US/Canada: (607) 722-5857
Fax: 1-800-895-0582 / Outside US/Canada: (607) 771-0012
E-mail your order to us: orders@haworthpress.com

For orders outside US and Canada, you may wish to order through your local
sales representative, distributor, or bookseller.
For information, see http://haworthpress.com/distributors

(Discounts are available for individual orders in US and Canada only, not booksellers/distributors.)

Please photocopy this form for your personal use.
www.HaworthPress.com

BOF04